Fromm

S0-BNX-908

Singapore & Malaysia

5th Edition

by Jennifer Eveland

Here's what the critics say about Frommer's:

"Amazingly easy to use. Very portable, very complete."

—*Booklist*

"Detailed, accurate, and easy-to-read information for all price ranges."
—*Glamour Magazine*

"Hotel information is close to encyclopedic."

—*Des Moines Sunday Register*

"Frommer's Guides have a way of giving you a real feel for a place."
—*Knight Ridder Newspapers*

Wiley Publishing, Inc.

Published by:

Wiley Publishing, Inc.
111 River St.
Hoboken, NJ 07030-5774

ISBN: 978-0-470-10049-3

Editor: Lorraine Festa
Production Editor: M. Faunette Johnston
Cartographer: Andrew Murphy
Photo Editor: Richard Fox
Anniversary Logo Design: Richard Pacifico
Production by Wiley Indianapolis Composition Services

Front cover photo: Chinese New Year in Chinatown, Singapore
Back cover photo: Perhentian Islands, Malaysia

For information on our other products and services or to obtain technical support, please contact our Customer Care Department within the U.S. at 800/762-2974, outside the U.S. at 317/572-3993 or fax 317/572-4002.

Wiley also publishes its books in a variety of electronic formats. Some content that appears in print may not be available in electronic formats.

Manufactured in the United States of America

5   4   3   2   1

Contents

4   Where to Stay in Singapore   67

5   Where to Dine in Singapore   96

6   Singapore Attractions   121

7   Singapore Shopping   165

List of Maps

Acknowledgments

I wish to thank the following people for their continued support: Randolf and his loving family; Debs and Heidi; Marvin and Dionne; Mervyn, Daryl and LeeChin; Robin, Nigel and Nisah; Fadz, Wendy and Mo; and Wai Keet.

—Jennifer Eveland

An Invitation to the Reader

In researching this book, we discovered many wonderful places—hotels, restaurants, shops, and more. We're sure you'll find others. Please tell us about them, so we can share the information with your fellow travelers in upcoming editions. If you were disappointed with a recommendation, we'd love to know that, too. Please write to:

Frommer's Singapore & Malaysia, 5th Edition
Wiley Publishing, Inc. • 111 River St. • Hoboken, NJ 07030-5774

An Additional Note

Please be advised that travel information is subject to change at any time—and this is especially true of prices. We therefore suggest that you write or call ahead for confirmation when making your travel plans. The authors, editors, and publisher cannot be held responsible for the experiences of readers while traveling. Your safety is important to us, however, so we encourage you to stay alert and be aware of your surroundings. Keep a close eye on cameras, purses, and wallets, all favorite targets of thieves and pickpockets.

About the Author

Jennifer Eveland spent part of her childhood in Singapore, has studied in Hong Kong, lived for a spell in Bangkok, and has traveled extensively throughout East and Southeast Asia. In addition to *Frommer's Singapore & Malaysia,* she has authored previous editions of *Frommer's Thailand* and contributes to *Frommer's Southeast Asia.* In 1999 she returned to Singapore to work as a full-time freelance writer. She writes regularly for *The International Herald Tribune,* and contributes travel and lifestyle stories to numerous local and international magazines. She lives in Toa Payoh, one of Singapore's older New Towns, with her husband, a Singaporean musician and producer, their baby son, and their four cats.

Other Great Guides for Your Trip

Frommer's Southeast Asia
Frommer's Thailand
Frommer's Hong Kong
Frommer's China
Frommer's Beijing
Frommer's Shanghai

Frommer's Star Ratings, Icons & Abbreviations

Every hotel, restaurant, and attraction listing in this guide has been ranked for quality, value, service, amenities, and special features using a **star-rating system.** In country, state, and regional guides, we also rate towns and regions to help you narrow down your choices and budget your time accordingly. Hotels and restaurants are rated on a scale of zero (recommended) to three stars (exceptional). Attractions, shopping, nightlife, towns, and regions are rated according to the following scale: zero stars (recommended), one star (highly recommended), two stars (very highly recommended), and three stars (must-see).

In addition to the star-rating system, we also use **eight feature icons** that point you to the great deals, in-the-know advice, and unique experiences that separate travelers from tourists. Throughout the book, look for:

Finds	Special finds—those places only insiders know about
Fun Fact	Fun facts—details that make travelers more informed and their trips more fun
Kids	Best bets for kids and advice for the whole family
Moments	Special moments—those experiences that memories are made of
Overrated	Places or experiences not worth your time or money
Tips	Insider tips—great ways to save time and money
Value	Great values—where to get the best deals
Warning	Warning—traveler's advisories are usually in effect

The following **abbreviations** are used for credit cards:

AE	American Express	DISC	Discover	V	Visa
DC	Diners Club	MC	MasterCard		

Frommers.com

Now that you have this guidebook to help you plan a great trip, visit our website at **www.frommers.com** for additional travel information on more than 3,500 destinations. We update features regularly to give you instant access to the most current trip-planning information available. At Frommers.com, you'll find scoops on the best airfares, lodging rates, and car rental bargains. You can even book your travel online through our reliable travel booking partners. Other popular features include:

- Online updates of our most popular guidebooks
- Vacation sweepstakes and contest giveaways
- Newsletters highlighting the hottest travel trends
- Online travel message boards with featured travel discussions

What's New in Singapore & Malaysia

SINGAPORE

After 2006, Singapore's tourism industry will never be the same again. The government's approval for two casinos marks the end of an era for the squeaky-clean city-state.

The first casino will be built by **Las Vegas Sands,** who is investing S$5 billion (US$3.16 billion/£1.6 billion), to create a casino in Singapore's downtown area, just across the marina from the financial district and downtown convention center. With an eye on the meetings, incentives, conventions, and exhibits (MICE) travel segment, the huge complex will also feature 110,000 sq. m (1,184,040 sq. ft.) of meeting space, two 2,000-seat theaters, three hotel towers, an **ArtScience** museum, luxury retail outlets, dining venues in floating pavilions on the bay, plus innovative public spaces that include a rooftop park with a 360-degree city view, an ice-skating rink, and indoor canals.

The second casino is being developed by **Genting International** and **Star Cruises,** who will invest S$5.2 billion (US$3.3 billion/£1.65 billion) to build an enormous facility on Sentosa Island. Geared toward family and leisure activities, the casino will be supported by spa resort accommodations, restaurants, and bars, plus retail and entertainment outlets. Perhaps the most exciting part of the package will be the addition of **Universal Studios Singapore,** promised to be Asia's largest, with 22 attractions in themed "worlds," including "Journey to Madagascar," and a DreamWorks Digital Animation Studio. Also in the works is the **Quest**

Marine Life Park with the largest single marine tank in the world, and an interactive dolphin habitat. The **Equarius Water Park** will feature water rides and a maritime museum. Three amphitheaters will have international entertainment, including a resident show from the creators of **Cirque du Soleil.**

While the estimated completion date for these projects is 2010, I predict that in super-efficient Singapore, they will be up and running much sooner than that.

In the future also look to **Singapore Airlines** to be the first airline to use the massive Airbus 380 for commercial passenger flights. These double-decker jets have 49% more floor space than Boeing's 747, but incorporate only 35% more seats, allowing room for fun extras like bars, gyms, and duty-free shops. The mammoth plane will be rolled out in 2007 for the "kangaroo route" between Sydney, Singapore, and London.

MALAYSIA

In 2007 Malaysia celebrates **50 years of independence,** and the tourism board has a host of activities for travelers—from music festivals to international sporting events and big nationwide sales—that will showcase the country to the world. August will be the most exciting month, with a weeklong international fireworks competition and a lion dance exhibition leading up to Malaysia's Independence Day celebrations on August 31, with parades, outdoor fairs, concerts, and fireworks. Also in 2007, **The Eye on Malaysia,** a 60m (197-ft.) Ferris wheel with views over Kuala Lumpur, will open in its Lake Gardens location. Visit **www.virtualmalaysia.com** to find out what else in on during your stay.

Malaysia's budget carrier **AirAsia,** which offers some of the cheapest airfares around the country and the region, is teaming up with **Virgin Atlantic** and **EasyJet** to introduce the world's first low-cost long-haul flights. Starting July 2007, the airline is planning to offer trips between Kuala Lumpur and London for as low as half the price you'd pay on a normal carrier. The deal will also give AirAsia's partners access to Kuala Lumpur International Airport (KLIA), creating a nice Asian hub for their operations as well. AirAsia also plans to offer RM100 (US$28/£14) flights to China.

The move will pave the way for Malaysia's KLIA to become a coveted gateway for budget flights from around the world into Southeast Asia and within the Asia Pacific Region.

The Best of Singapore & Malaysia

I could spend a lifetime exploring Singapore. I'm in awe of the cultural mysteries and exotic beauty of the city's old mosques and temples. As I pass the facades of buildings that mark history, I get nostalgic for old tales of colonial romance. Towering overhead, present-day Singapore glistens with the wealth of modern miracles. And when I smell incense, spice, and jasmine swirling in wet tropical breezes, I can close my eyes and know exactly where I am.

The longer I stay in Singapore, the more new curiosities present themselves to me. Singapore thrives on a history that has absorbed a multitude of foreign elements over almost 2 centuries, melding them into a unique modern national identity. Beginning with the landing of Sir Stamford Raffles in 1819, add to the mix the original Malay inhabitants, immigrating waves of Chinese traders and workers, Indian businessmen and laborers, Arab merchants, British colonials, European adventure-seekers, and an assortment of Southeast Asian settlers—this tiny island rose from the ingenuity of those who worked and lived together here. Today, all recognize each group's importance to the heritage of the land, each adding unique contributions to a culture and identity we know as Singaporean.

I'll confess, many travelers complain to me about how westernized Singapore is. For many, a vacation in Asia should be filled with culture shock, unfamiliar traditions, and curious adventures. Today's travel philosophy seems to be that the more underdeveloped and obscure a country is, the more "authentic" the experience will be. But poor Singapore—all those lovely opium-stained coolies and toothless rickshaw pullers are now driving BMWs and exchanging cellular phone numbers. How could anyone possibly find this place so fascinating?

With all its shopping malls, fast-food outlets, imported fashion, and steel skyscrapers, Singapore could look like any other contemporary city you've ever visited—but to peel through the layers is to understand that life here is far more complex. While the outer layers are startlingly Western, just underneath lies a curious area where East blends with West in language, cuisine, attitude, and style. At the core, you'll find a sensibility rooted in the cultural heritage of values, religion, superstition, and memory. In Singapore, nothing is ever as it appears to be.

For me this is where the fascination begins. I detect so many things familiar in this city, only to discover how these imported ideas have been altered to fit the local identity. Like the rows of historic shophouses that line the city's oldest streets—if you look closely you'll see a jumble of colonial architectural mandates, European tastes, Chinese superstitions, and Malay finery. Even the language is a blend: "Singlish," the unofficial local tongue, combines English language with Chinese grammar, common Malay

Southeast Asia

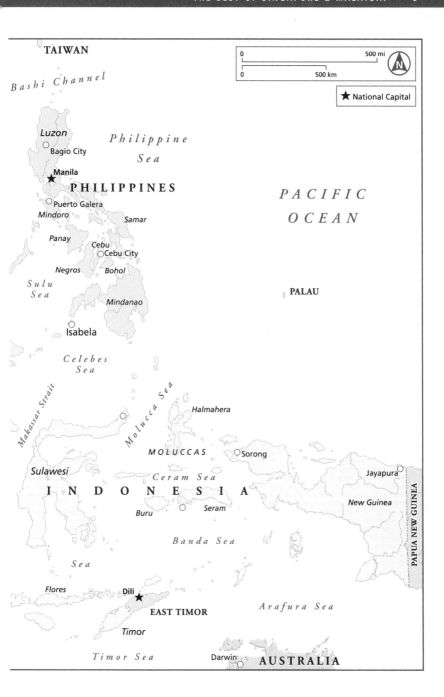

TAIWAN

Bashi Channel

Luzon
○ Bagio City

Philippine

Sea

★ Manila

PHILIPPINES

○ Puerto Galera
Mindoro

Samar

Panay

Cebu
○ Cebu City

Negros *Bohol*

Sulu
Sea

Mindanao

○
Isabela

Celebes
Sea

Makassar Strait

Molucca Sea

Halmahera

MOLUCCAS
○ Sorong

Sulawesi

Ceram Sea

I N D O N E S I A

Buru ○ *Seram*

Banda Sea

Sea

Flores Dili ★

EAST TIMOR

Timor

Timor Sea

Jayapura ○

New Guinea

PAPUA NEW GUINEA

Arafura Sea

Darwin ○ **AUSTRALIA**

PACIFIC
OCEAN

○ **PALAU**

0 _____ 500 mi
0 _____ 500 km

★ National Capital

phrases, and Hokkien slang to form a patois unique to this part of the world. This transformation of cultures has been going on for almost 2 centuries. So, in a sense, Singapore is no different today than it was 100 years ago. And in this I find my "authentic" travel experience.

When the urban jungle gets me crazy, I escape to Malaysia. Even Kuala Lumpur, the capital city, seems relaxed in comparison to Singapore. In fact, many Singapore-ans look to their northern neighbor for the perfect vacation, taking advantage of its pristine national forests and marine parks, relaxing on picture-perfect beaches in sophisticated resorts, taking in culture in its small towns, shopping for inexpensive handicrafts, or eating some of the richest food in Southeast Asia. Malaysia offers some-thing for everyone—history, culture, adventure, romance, mystery, nature, and relax-ation—without the glaring buzz of an overdeveloped tourism industry. It almost makes me overjoyed that few tourists venture here.

My favorite part of Malaysia, however, is the warmth of its people. I have yet to travel in this country without collecting remarkable tales of hospitality, openness, and generosity. I've found the Malaysian people to be genuine in their approach to foreign visitors, another fine byproduct of the underdeveloped tourism industry. For those who want to find a nice little corner of paradise, Malaysia could be your answer.

I've crept down alleys, wandered the streets of cities and towns, combed beaches, and trekked jungles to seek out the most exciting things that Singapore and Malaysia have to offer. In this book I've presented the sights and attractions of these countries with insight into historical, cultural, and modern significance to bring you a complete appreciation of all you are about to experience. I've peeked in every shop door, chat-ting up the local characters inside. I've eaten local food until I can't move. I've stayed out all night. I've done it all and written about it here. I can only hope you will love Singapore and Malaysia as much as I do.

1 Frommer's Favorite Singapore Experiences

Sipping a Singapore Sling at the Long Bar: Ahhhh, the Long Bar, home of the Singapore Sling. I like to come here in the afternoons, before the tourist rush. Shel-tered by long jalousie shutters that close out the tropical sun, the air cooled by lazy *punkahs* (small fans that wave gently back and forth above), you can sit back in old rattan chairs and have your saronged wait-ress serve you sticky alcoholic creations while you toss back a few dainty crab cakes. Life can be so decadent. Okay, so the punkahs are electric, and, come to think of it, the place is air-conditioned (not to mention that it costs a small for-tune), but it's fun to imagine the days when Somerset Maugham, Rudyard Kipling, or Charlie Chaplin would be sit-ting at the bar sipping Slings and spinning

exotic tales of their world travels. Drink up, my friend; it's a lovely high. See p. 185.

Witnessing Bloody Traditions: Saturday nights you can witness the *Kuda Kepang,* which is not your average traditional dance. It features young men on wooden horses who move like warriors, whirling, spinning, and slapping the horses to shake intimidating sounds out of them. Accom-panied by rhythmic and repetitive tradi-tional Malay music, the warriors dance in unison, staging battles with each other until by the end of a long series of dances, the horsemen are in a trance. A pot of burning frankincense is produced, from which they all inhale. After that, all hell breaks loose. The dancers are whipped, fed glass—which they chew and swallow hungrily—walk on glass shards, and shred entire coconuts with their teeth. Although the whipping appears somewhat staged, I assure you the rest is real. It's a traditional dance that's taken very seriously both by the dancers and by the huge and mostly Malay crowds that gather for it. What's more, the next day the dancers don't recall what they did—and they're never injured. The group appears at Malay Village (© **65/6748-4700**). Call ahead to find out what time they'll be performing. See chapter 6.

If you're not able to catch a performance, but still want a little ceremonial gore, check out the calendar of events in chapter 3. During the Thaipusam Festival, men pierce their bodies with skewers, and during the Thimithi Festival, they walk on burning coals. To celebrate the Birthday of the Monkey God, Chinese priests will slice themselves with sharp implements and write chants and prayers with their own blood.

Checking Out the Orchard Road Scene: You can't find better people-watching than on Orchard Road every Saturday afternoon, when it seems like every Singaporean crawls out of the woodwork to join the parade of shoppers, strollers, hipsters, posers, lovers, geeks, and gabbers. Everybody is here, milling around every mall, clustered around every sidewalk bench, checking everybody else out. At the corner of Scotts Road and Orchard, just below the Marriott, there's an alfresco cafe where you'll find local celebrities hanging out to see and be seen. International celebrities and models have been spotted here on occasion, too. In the mix, you're bound to see most every tourist on the island, coming around to see what all the excitement is about.

On Saturdays, school lets out early, so the malls are filled with mobs of bored teenagers kicking around, trying to look cool, and watching the music videos in the front window of the HMV music store in the Heeren. Moms and dads also have half-days at the office, so the strip takes on the feel of an obstacle course as all the parents race around wielding strollers, trying to run errands while they have the chance. Meanwhile, outside in the shady areas, you can see crowds of domestic maids and workers relaxing and catching up on the latest news on their free afternoon.

For some, the scene is a madhouse to be avoided; for others, it's a chance to watch life on a typical Saturday afternoon in downtown Singapore. And it is typical because however huge and delightful the scene is for tourists, it's just part of everyday reality for residents of the Garden City.

2 Frommer's Favorite Malaysia Experiences

Letting the Sea Wash Away All Your Stress: This is paradise. Lying flat, arms outstretched across the surface of the water, I felt the rays of the sun warming my back and the cool ripples of salty sea beneath me. Through the clear water I could see the seabed at the bottom of the bay and all assortment of creatures swimming in and out of corals. My snorkel guide pointed in the shadows to the silhouette of a meter-long shark, too shy to approach.

Back near the beach, I stood in the shallows feeding bread crumbs to the smaller fish. Within minutes I was surrounded by a swarm of brilliant colors—vivid Day-Glo flashes of saltwater fish; thousands of them, dozens of species, swirling around me and plucking bread from my fingertips.

On the beach, my friends and I lazed under the shade of a tree, digging our feet into the soft and powdery sand. One friend climbed a coconut palm and twisted a giant nut off its stem. Using a cleaver from the kitchen, we hacked it open and poured the coconut water over ice in a glass, then picked the sweet flesh from the inside the shell. After a day of this, I was ready to tear up my return ticket.

This kind of paradise is everywhere in Malaysia, and you can find it within an hour's flight from Kuala Lumpur (KL), if you visit Langkawi, Tioman, and Redang, or if you have more time, in Sabah.

Experiencing _Kampung_ Hospitality: _Pakcik_ (uncle) was just slightly older than his ancient Mercedes, but his price was right, so I hired him for the day to drive me around Kota Bharu. Sometime after lunch, during a stop at the kite-maker's house, I spotted a beautiful _gasing,_ a wood-and-steel Malay top. It would be the perfect gift for my brother! I just had to have one.

Well, the kite-maker didn't want to give his up, but Pakcik had a few ideas. After coming up empty at the local shops, he took on my quest with personal conviction. Off we drove through the outskirts of town, the sights becoming increasingly rural. He turned down a dirt road, past grazing water buffaloes lazing near rice paddies. Soon the fields turned to jungle, and a small _kampung_ (village) appeared in the trees. I watched out the window as we passed traditional wooden stilt houses where grannies fanned themselves on the porch watching the children chase chickens in the yard. Beside each house, colorful batik sarongs waved from clotheslines in the breeze.

The path wound to the house of Pakcik's nephew. I was welcomed inside with curiosity, perhaps the first foreigner to visit. They offered me a straw mat, which I used to join the others resting comfortably on the floor. Within minutes, an audience of neighbors gathered around, plucking fruits from the trees in the yard for me. I listened as Pakcik told them of my search for a gasing. That afternoon I was offered every gasing in the village.

My afternoon in Pakcik's kampung is one of my most cherished memories, and a most meaningful experience. As Southeast Asia becomes increasingly affluent and globalized, this way of life becomes steadily endangered. It's a lifestyle that for many urban Malaysians captures the spirit of the good life—simple days when joy was free. And everyone will be proud to show you; all you need is an open heart and a big smile. Malaysian hospitality never ceases to amaze me.

3 The Best Small Towns & Villages

Any Kampung (Tioman Island, Malaysia): Even though Tioman was developed for the tourism industry, you'll never think this place is overdeveloped. The casual and rustic nature of the island's tiny beach villages holds firm, and those who seek escape rarely leave disappointed. See p. 252.

Malacca (Malaysia): As perhaps the oldest trading port in Malaysia, this town hosted a wide array of international traders: Arabs, Portuguese, Dutch, English, Indian, and Chinese, all of whom left their stamp. See p. 226.

Kuching (Sarawak, Malaysia): Renegade adventure-seeker James Brooke thumbed his nose at London's colonial office so that he could claim Sarawak for his own and rule as the region's first White Raja. He built a cozy little capital with quaint tropical-colonial architecture, picturesque back streets, and a pretty riverfront. See p. 269.

4 The Best Beaches

Sentosa Island (Singapore): The three beaches on Sentosa are just about the best you'll find in Singapore, which isn't really known for its beaches. They're lively, with watersports and beach activities plus food and drink. Every so often you'll find an all-night dance party here. See p. 157. However, if you really need pristine seclusion, you'll have to head for Malaysia.

The Four Seasons (Langkawi, Malaysia): Perhaps the most stunning beach in Malaysia, this wide gorgeous stretch of white sand looks out onto crystal-clear, deep-blue waters. Even if you can't afford a room at the resort, I highly recommend a cocktail at their deliciously exotic beachside bar so you can get a chance to enjoy the view. See p. 247.

Kampung Juara (Tioman Island, Malaysia): This beach is what they mean when they say isolated. Be prepared to live like Robinson Crusoe—in tiny huts, many with no electricity at all. But, oh, the beach! Most visitors don't get to this part of the island, so many times you can have it all to yourself. See p. 255.

Cherating (Malaysia): If you're a leatherback turtle, you'll think the best beach in the world is just north of Cherating. Every spring and summer, these giant sea creatures come ashore to lay their eggs, so if you're in town from May to June you might catch a look at the hatchlings. Meanwhile, during the turtles' off season, international windsurfing and water-board enthusiasts gather annually for competitions at this world-famous spot. See p. 255.

5 The Most Exciting Outdoor Adventures

Trekking in Taman Negara (Malaysia): With suitable options for all levels of comfort and desired adventure, peninsular Malaysia's largest national park opens the wonders of primary rainforest and the creatures who dwell in it to everyone. From the canopy walk high atop the forest to night watches for nocturnal life, this adventure is as stunning as it is informative. See p. 223.

Sungei Buloh Wetland Reserve (Singapore): Every year during the winter months, flocks of migrating birds from as far north as Siberia vacation in the warm waters of this unique mangrove swamp park. Easily traversed by a wooden walkway, the park will never disappoint for glimpses of stunning wildlife. See p. 153.

6 The Most Fascinating Temples, Churches & Mosques

Thian Hock Keng (Singapore): One of Singapore's oldest Chinese temples, it is a fascinating testimony to Chinese Buddhism as it combines with traditional Confucian beliefs and natural Taoist principles. Equally fascinating is the modern world that carries on just outside the old temple's doors. See p. 137.

Armenian Church (Singapore): Although not the biggest Christian house of worship in the city, it is perhaps one of the most charming in its architectural simplicity, tropical practicality, and spiritual tranquillity. See p. 124.

Hajjah Fatimah Mosque (Singapore): I love this mosque for its eclectic mix of religious symbols and architectural influences. To me, it represents not just the Singaporean ability to absorb so many different ideas, but also a Muslim appreciation and openness toward many cultures. See p. 142.

Jalan Tokong, Malacca (Malaysia): This street, in the historical heart of the city, supports a Malay mosque, a Chinese temple, and a Hindu temple existing peacefully side by side—the perfect example of how the many foreign religions that came to Southeast Asia shaped its communities and learned to coexist in harmony. See p. 232.

7 The Most Interesting Museums

National Museum of Singapore. Images of Singapore (Sentosa Island, Singapore): After a 3-year restoration that cost S$132.6 million (about US$85 million/£38 million), this historic building has reopened and expanded to more than twice its original size, featuring state-of-the-art multimedia exhibits. They've done a fantastic job. See p. 128.

Asian Civilisations Museum (Singapore): This extremely well-presented museum documents the evolutionary and cultural history of the region's major ethnic groups. A very informative afternoon. See p. 124.

Penang Museum and Art Gallery (Penang, Malaysia): A slick display of Penang's colonial history and multicultural heritage, this place is chock-full of fascinating tidbits about the people, places, and events of this curious island. Plus, it doesn't hurt that the air-conditioning works very well! See p. 242.

State Museums of Malacca (Malaysia): This small city has more museums than any other city in the country, with some unusual displays such as kites and Malaysian literature. See p. 230.

8 The Best Luxury Resorts & Hotels

Raffles Hotel (Singapore): For old-world opulence, Raffles is second to none. It's pure fantasy of the days when tigers still lurked around the perimeters. See p. 72.

Shangri-La Hotel (Singapore): What sets this hotel apart from other city properties is its sprawling grounds. Shang is a meticulously landscaped tropical oasis, with lush garden views from every angle. Three individual wings give you a choice of accommodations styles: urban contemporary, natural resort-style, and Oriental opulence. See p. 84.

Hilton Kuala Lumpur (Kuala Lumpur, Malaysia): The coolest of the cool stay at the new Hilton. Rooms feel like suites, all decorated in slickety-slick contempo style with the latest entertainment and IT built in—even in the bathrooms. See p. 214.

Tanjong Jara Resort (Terengganu, Malaysia): Traditional Malay-style chalets furnished in natural woods and local textiles blend gorgeously with the tropical gardens of this seaside resort. The people here will bend over backward to make sure your stay is perfect. See p. 260.

Four Seasons Langkawi (Langkawi, Malaysia): Raising the bar, this resort is an exotic Moorish paradise on the most gorgeous beach in Malaysia. Rooms and public areas drip with the ambience of the Arabian Nights. Three words: To. Die. For. See p. 247.

9 The Best Hotel Bargains

The SHA Villa (Singapore): This boutique hotel is packed with Southeast Asian charm and has an attentive staff and an ideal location, close to Orchard Road. See p. 93.

Traders Hotel Singapore (Singapore): Value-for-money is the name of the game here. All sorts of promotional packages, self-service launderettes, vending machines, and a checkout lounge are just a few of the offerings that make this the most convenient hotel in the city. See p. 91.

Swiss-Inn (Kuala Lumpur, Malaysia): Location, location, location! Right in the center of Kuala Lumpur's bustling Chinatown, the Swiss-Inn is the perennial favorite for travelers here. A comfortable choice, plus it's so close to everything. See p. 216.

Heeren House (Malacca, Malaysia): This boutique hotel in the heart of the old city is the place to stay in Malacca if you want to really get a feel of the local atmosphere. See p. 229.

Telang Usan Hotel (Kuching, Malaysia): An informal place, Telang Usan is homey and quaint, and within walking distance of many major attractions in Kuching. See p. 272.

10 The Best Local Dining Experiences

Hawker Centers (Singapore and Malaysia): Think of them as shopping malls for food—great food! For local cuisine, who needs a menu with pictures when you can walk around and select anything you want as it's prepared before your eyes? See chapters 5, 10, 11, and 12.

Imperial Herbal (Singapore): In the Chinese tradition of yin and yang, dishes are prepared under the supervision of the house doctor, a traditional healer who will be glad to "prescribe" the perfect cure for whatever ails you. See p. 109.

Chili Crab at UDMC Seafood Centre (Singapore): A true Singaporean favorite, chili crabs will cause every local to rise up in argument over where you can find the best in town. Head out to UDMC to try the juicy crabs cooked in a sweet chili sauce. Prepare to get messy! See p. 118.

Gurney Drive (Penang, Malaysia): Penang is the king of Asian cuisine, from Chinese to Malay to Indian and everything else in between. This large hawker center by the sea is a great introduction to Penang. See p. 241.

11 The Best Markets

Arab Street (Singapore): Even though Singapore is a shopper's paradise, it could still use more places like Arab Street. Small shops selling everything from textiles to handicrafts line the street. Bargaining is welcome. See p. 174.

Central Market (Kuala Terengganu, Malaysia): This huge bustling market turned me into a shopping freak! All of the handicrafts Terengganu is famous for come concentrated in one exciting experience: batik, songket cloth, brassware, basket weaving—the list goes on. See p. 262.

Petaling Street (Kuala Lumpur, Malaysia): This night market gets very, very crowded and crazy with all who come for watches, handbags, computer software, video CDs (which aren't exactly DVDs but can be played on a DVD player), and all manner of blatant disregard for international copyright laws. See p. 221.

12 The Best Shopping Bargains

Batik (Singapore and Malaysia): While most of the batiks you find in Singapore come from Indonesia, most in Malaysia are made at factories that you can often tour. The Indonesian prints usually show traditional motif and colors, while Malaysian designs can be far more modern. Look for batik silk as well. See chapters 7, 10, and 11.

Knockoffs and Pirated Goods (Singapore and Malaysia): Check out how real those watches look! And so cheap! You can find them at any night market. Ever dream of owning a Gucci? Have I got a deal for you! Can I tell you about pirate video CDs and computer software without getting my book banned? Uh, okay, whatever you do, don't buy these items! See chapters 7 and 10.

Silver Filigree Jewelry (Malaysia): This fine silver is worked into detailed filigree jewelry designs to make brooches, necklaces, bracelets, and other fine jewelry.

Pewter (Malaysia): Malaysia is the home of Selangor Pewter, one of the largest manufacturers of pewter in the world, and their many showrooms have all sorts of items to choose from. For locations in Kuala Lumpur, Penang, Malacca, and Johor call the company hot line at © 03/ 422-1000.

13 The Best Nightlife

Singapore, the whole city: Nightlife is becoming increasingly sophisticated in Singapore, where locals have more money for recreation and fun. Take the time to choose the place that suits your personality. Jazz club? Techno disco? Cocktail lounge? Wine bar? Good old pub? The city has it all. See p. 180.

Bangsar (near Kuala Lumpur, Malaysia): Folks in Kuala Lumpur know to go to Bangsar for nighttime excitement. A couple of blocks of concentrated restaurants, cafes, discos, pubs, and wine bars will tickle any fancy. Good people-watching, too. See p. 222.

2

Suggested Itineraries in Singapore & Malaysia

If you've made it all the way to Southeast Asia, you'll likely be on a limited schedule—especially if you've arrived via a long-haul flight from Europe or North America. The good news is, Singapore is easy. It's such a small place that virtually every sight is relatively close. Still, with so many to choose from, it can be tough to whittle down the must-sees. In this chapter I've done that job for you, identifying the best and more important sights and working them into even the shortest stay.

For Malaysia, the options can be overwhelming, and travel time between towns requires a bit of planning, so I've identified the special interests most travelers may have and worked out the best itineraries for each.

1 The Best of Singapore in 1 Day

Perhaps you're only in Singapore overnight en route. Here's how to make the best of it. Since the city is compact, you can take in some sights fairly easily and still make it to the airport for your flight out. If your time is very limited, I recommend you bypass the museums and head straight for the streets, where you'll find a "living museum" of sorts, with local people, food, shops, and places of worship, plus a couple of interesting cultural displays. Do yourself a favor and stop first at a **Singapore Tourism Board (STB) Visitors' Centre** to pick up copies of their walking tour pamphlets, one for each of Singapore's ethnic neighborhoods. The brochures identify points of interest and bits of local color as you walk along neighborhood streets. They're very well done. I recommend you start in Kampong Gelam, Singapore's historical home base for Malay heritage (Malays were, after all, the original inhabitants). Chinatown makes an excellent afternoon of strolling, and in the evening, the night safari in Singapore Zoological Gardens is always a good time. *Start: Taxi to Arab Street.*

❶ Arab Street

This short street is lined with shops that sell Malaysian and Indonesian batik cloth and home decor items, baskets, carved wood, objets d'art, and other gifts. Most places will be open by 10am, but if it's a Sunday they'll be closed; in that case, head straight to the Sultan Mosque instead. See p. 174.

❷ Sultan Mosque ⭐

Just off Arab Street, you can't miss the towering onion dome of this mosque. The most historic in Singapore, its grounds are open so feel free to explore within its walls, including the ablutions area, where worshipers wash up before prayers according to Muslim tradition, and a small grave site with unmarked stones. Inside the front entrance they can provide robes if you're wearing shorts or a sleeveless top. Come before the noontime prayers, especially on Fridays; otherwise you may be asked to wait until they're finished. Non-Muslims are not permitted inside the main prayer hall. See p. 144.

❸ Malay Heritage Centre

Just a 2-minute stroll from the mosque, the Malay Heritage Centre is inside the restored palace of the original sultanate. The staff here is really nice, and can also chat about the local Malay culture from their personal experiences. See p. 142.

Take a taxi from Arab Street to the Chinatown Heritage Centre.

❹ Chinatown Heritage Centre ★★

Say goodbye to Malay culture and hello to Chinese *and* a welcome respite from the midday heat (it's air-conditioned!). The streets surrounding the center are packed with souvenir shops with tons of curious finds, plus some beautiful art and antiques galleries, so be sure to wander around a bit. See p. 135.

❺ Yue Hwa ★★

This Chinese emporium is practically a museum of Chinese handicrafts, filled with floor after floor of fabulous shopping. Excellent buys here include ready-made silk clothing, embroidered handbags, carved jade, pottery, and cloisonné. Unusual buys include musical instruments, men's coolie outfits, and plenty of strange Chinese interpretations of Western goods. See p. 174.

Take a taxi from Yue Hwa to Thian Hock Keng Temple.

❻ Thian Hock Keng Temple ★★★

If you see any one Chinese temple in Singapore, this is it. One of the earliest built, it is a meaningful tribute to the Taoist gods and goddesses that have guided the Chinese community here. Try to get here before 5pm, so you have time for relaxed exploration. See p. 137.

❼ Night Safari ★★★

If you come from temperate climes, this is a rare chance to see nocturnal animals. This is the one place where all Singaporeans bring their foreign visitors, and I have yet to see anyone walk away unimpressed. Also, an easy dinner can be had from local- and fast-food stalls at the park entrance. See p. 152.

2 The Best of Singapore in 2 Days

On your second day, continue to explore life at ground level with a morning meander through Little India, the heart of Singapore's Indian community. After lunch escape the afternoon heat at the Asian Civilisations Museum, then finish your day with a Singapore Sling at Raffles Hotel. *Start: Taxi to Serangoon Road or MRT to Little India station.*

❶ Serangoon Road

A long strip where the locals come to buy spices (check out the old grinding mill on Cuff Rd. just off Serangoon), flowers (see the sellers making jasmine garlands by the roadside), Bollywood DVDs (you can hear the music blaring out into the street), saris (you can have one made for yourself), and all kinds of ceremonial items, many of which make excellent gifts. This is one of the few old neighborhoods in Singapore that hasn't been "Disney-fied" by the government. If you love chaos, come on Sundays, when most workers have their day off. This place is packed like Calcutta!

❷ Sri Veerama Kaliamman ★★

Midway down Serangoon Road you'll find this brightly colored temple humming with devotees all times of the day. Take off your shoes to explore the dioramas inside. If you get here early enough, you can watch as the statues inside are bathed. The water, considered blessed,

The Best of Singapore: Day 1 & Day 2

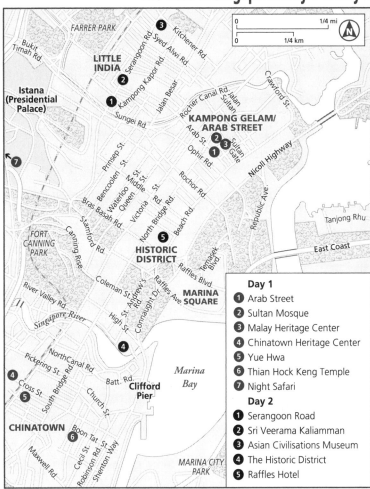

FARRER PARK

Bukit Timah Rd.

LITTLE INDIA

Istana (Presidential Palace)

Kitchener Rd.
Syed Alwi Rd.
Serangoon Rd.
Kampong Kapor Rd.
Jalan Besar
Sungei Rd.
Rocher Canal Rd.
Jalan Sultan
Crawford St.

KAMPONG GELAM/ ARAB STREET

Arab St.
Ophir Rd.
Sultan Gate
Nicoll Highway
Republic Ave.
Tanjong Rhu

Prinsep St.
Bencoolen St.
St.
Middle St.
St.
Waterloo St.
Queen St.
Bras Basah Rd.
Victoria St.
North Bridge Rd.
Beach Rd.
Rochor Rd.

Stamford Rd.

FORT CANNING PARK

Canning Rise

River Valley Rd.

Coleman St.
St. Andrew's Rd.
Raffles Ave.

HISTORIC DISTRICT

Raffles Blvd.
Temasek Blvd.
East Coast

MARINA SQUARE

Singapore River

High St.
Connaught Dr.

NorthCanal Rd.
Pickering St.
Cross St.
South Bridge Rd.
Batt. Rd.
Church St.

Clifford Pier

Marina Bay

CHINATOWN

Boon Tat St.
Maxwell Rd.
Cecil St.
Robinson Rd.
Shenton Way

MARINA CITY PARK

0 ——— 1/4 mi
0 ——— 1/4 km

Day 1
1. Arab Street
2. Sultan Mosque
3. Malay Heritage Center
4. Chinatown Heritage Center
5. Yue Hwa
6. Thian Hock Keng Temple
7. Night Safari

Day 2
1. Serangoon Road
2. Sri Veerama Kaliamman
3. Asian Civilisations Museum
4. The Historic District
5. Raffles Hotel

runs off a small spout behind the left side of the main altar. See p. 141.

3 Mustapha's 👌👌

Farther along Serangoon Road, Mustapha's is a crazy Indian emporium. While many of the goods are pretty standard, look for all the neat India imports. Explore the basement sari fabric department, one of the largest in Singapore. I love the groceries section with row after row of boxed curry mixes—great to take back home! Or check out Mustapha's three floors of the most elaborate gold jewelry you've ever seen. See p. 175.

Take a taxi from Mustafa's to the Asian Civilisations Museum.

4 Asian Civilisations Museum 👌👌👌

This is my favorite museum, for its well-planned displays and handsome presentations of the many cultures that influenced

Singapore's heritage. Don't leave without checking out the gift shop, which features regional handicrafts of exceptional quality. They take special care to support crafting communities. See p. 124.

❺ The Historic District

From ACM, take a walk through the downtown civic center, where you'll pass the Old Parliament House, The Padang, the Supreme Court, City Hall, and St. Andrew's Cathedral. The stroll takes only about a half-hour, a bit more if you linger at any of the sights. See p. 124.

❻ The Singapore Sling

Walk past Raffles City Shopping Centre and you'll find Raffles Hotel. Take your time to wander through her public spaces (visitors are not allowed in residents' corridors). There's upscale shopping, pretty courtyards, and lots of dining options. Head for the Long Bar where you can sip a sweet Singapore Sling at the place where the drink was invented. To be honest, this isn't the actual bar, the current Long Bar is a replica built into Raffles' new wing. But after a couple of these powerful concoctions, you won't care. See p. 185.

3 The Best of Singapore in 3 Days

According to the Singapore Tourism Board the average visitor stays 3.5 days. If this describes you, there's still plenty of good stuff to see and do before you depart. An early-morning visit to the Singapore Botanic Gardens is especially recommended for joggers and photographers. Once the sun has burned away the dew, head for the newly renovated National Museum of Singapore to cool off (notice I always recommend the air-conditioned attractions during the hottest time of the day). A late-afternoon visit to the Jurong BirdPark rounds out a relaxing day of sights. ***Start: Orchard MRT then bus no. 7, 105, 106, or 174 from Orchard Blvd.***

❶ Singapore Botanic Gardens ★★

There's no reason to stop your workout routine just because you're traveling. Start your jog—or walk—early (it opens at 5am!) to beat the heat and so you won't feel rushed through the beautiful displays of tropical plants, shady trees, vivid blooms, and delicate bonsai, and don't forget to visit the National Orchid Garden (open at 8:30am) while you're there. See p. 149.

❷ National Museum of Singapore ★★★

Recently redone, there's nothing musty about this history lesson. An interactive,

multimedia, IMAX-ed good time, it's also highly recommended for children—after all, the goal of the National Heritage Board was to make history accessible to everyone. They did a great job. See p. 128.

❸ Jurong BirdPark ★

As long as you're in the Tropics, check out the birds in this beautifully executed park. Feeding activities, educational tours, and shows keep it lively. See p. 149.

4 The Best of Malaysia

Most visitors to Malaysia will arrive at Kuala Lumpur's (KL's) international airport, spend a day in the capital, then run around the country trying to see as much as they can in a short span of time. While it's natural to want to maximize your vacation time,

The Best of Singapore: Day 3

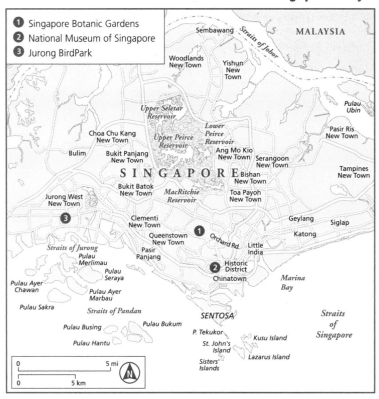

1 Singapore Botanic Gardens
2 National Museum of Singapore
3 Jurong BirdPark

I am of the philosophy that to try to pack too much into your holiday will actually detract from your overall travel experience. I've advised countless people on their trips and have been horrified to see some of the itineraries put together by well-meaning but ill-informed travel agents in the West. All are absolutely exhausting, some physically impossible. I recommend that you see no more than three destinations in 1 week, preferably only two. That way you have time not just to see the sights, but to stop and feel the rhythm of local life—to eat the food, smell the smells, speak with the people.

The itineraries I've suggested are all based on 1-week stays in Malaysia. Each itinerary differs depending on your point of interest: Do you like historical sights and museums? Do you want to appreciate nature and explore the great outdoors? Or do you just want to relax on the best beaches, scuba, or snorkel?

A major consideration when planning your trip is the heat! Especially if you're not used to it, the heat and humidity can sap the energy from you. By the time you've finished lunch, you'll barely have the stamina to keep up with the rest of your planned activities. Combined with jet lag, you'll be asleep before dinner. Not a swell time. Keep daily itineraries simple, and make time for afternoon coffee or tea!

Also, when flying between cities, budget your time like this: One flight will take about a half-day. So if you're flying from Penang to KL, either set aside a whole morning or a whole afternoon for the flight. That will include airport transfers and whatnot. Along the same lines, all domestic flights either originate or end up in KL. What this means is, if you're flying from Penang to, say, Kota Kinabalu, you'll fly from Penang to KL in the morning, have lunch in the airport, then spend the afternoon flying from KL to Kota Kinabalu. It will take a whole day.

5 Malaysia for History Buffs & Culture Vultures

This route brings you to Peninsular Malaysia's most historically significant destinations: Kuala Lumpur, Penang, and Malacca. You'll learn about the earliest trading ports and colonial history, and have time to shop and savor local treats.

Days ❶ & ❷: Arrive in Kuala Lumpur

After arriving in Malaysia's capital city, allow yourself a full day to recover and just spend your time wandering through the city's streets. Start at **Merdeka Square,** the focal point of colonial KL. Just behind the Moorish Sultan Abdul Samad Building, in the streets surrounding the Jame Mosque, you'll find KL's Little India of sorts. Continue your walk to the **Central Market** ✵, where nearby coffee shops can provide a place to rest. After exploring stall after stall of Malaysian handicrafts at the Central Market, if you still have time and energy, cross the street to **Chinatown,** where you'll find more shopping, a street bazaar, and the **Sri Mahamariaman Hindu Temple.** See p. 219.

Day ❸: Malacca ✵✵

Take an early-morning bus to Malacca and spend the day exploring the town's historic heart. The most important things to see here are the **Stadthuys** ✵ (p. 231), the history museum, located in the hard-to-miss red colonial building, the **Cultural Museum** ✵ (p. 231), in a replica of a Malay-style palace, and the **Baba Nyonya Heritage Museum** ✵ (p. 230), located inside an old millionaire's mansion. From the Baba Nyonya Museum, head to **Jonker Walk** to wander through temples and antiques shops. See p. 232.

Day ❹: Penang

Take an early-morning bus back to KL, then board a flight to Penang. Allow 1 day for the journey. Check into your resort at **Batu Feringgi** so that when you arrive, you can unwind with a cocktail as you watch the setting sun from the beach. See p. 238.

Day ❺: Georgetown ✵✵✵

Here's what I have to say about Georgetown: Don't plan your time too closely. Start off at the **Penang Museum and Art Gallery** ✵✵ (p. 242), where you'll get a brilliant overview of the island's history and cultures, then just spend your time walking through the streets. Attractions are all situated within walking distance, but don't rush: Take time to peek in the shop doors and snack on the local treats you'll find along the way. Just make sure you're at the **Cheong Fatt Tze Mansion** ✵✵✵ (p. 238), in time for the 11am or 3pm tour—consider it a must! Afterward, mosey over to the **E&O Hotel** ✵✵ (p. 238) for either lunch or high tea in the old colonial dame. See p. 240.

Day ❻: Penang Hill

The funicular train up the side of Penang Hill was built in 1923 to take British colonials up to the cooler climate of the hill, where they built lovely country homes and gardens. Today the train still

The Best of Malaysia

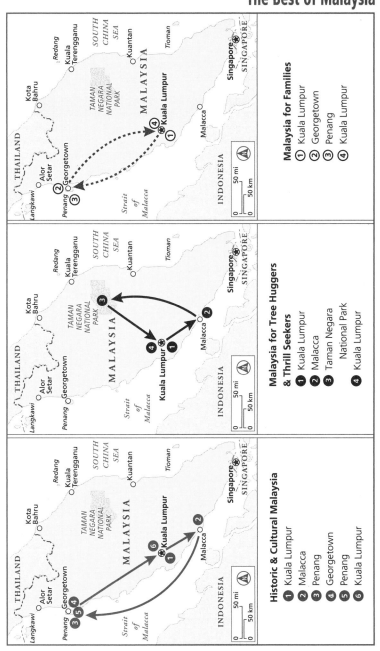

Malaysia for Families
① Kuala Lumpur
② Georgetown
③ Penang
④ Kuala Lumpur

Malaysia for Tree Huggers & Thrill Seekers
① Kuala Lumpur
② Malacca
③ Taman Negara National Park
④ Kuala Lumpur

Historic & Cultural Malaysia
① Kuala Lumpur
② Malacca
③ Penang
④ Georgetown
⑤ Penang
⑥ Kuala Lumpur

operates as a commuter service to the communities in this part of the island. Get there before 9am to beat the long queue. At the top of the hill you'll find restaurants, temples, and trails, one of which will lead you down to the botanical gardens. See p. 243.

Days ❼ & ❽: Back to KL

Hop a flight back to KL to prepare for your return home. If you have time, you can stock up on gifts at **KL Craft Complex** (p. 222)—you'll find something for everyone on your list, in all price ranges, at this handicrafts showroom.

6 Malaysia for Tree-Huggers & Thrill Seekers

This route gives you some choices, depending on your particular interests. Peninsular Malaysia's Taman Negara preserve is hopping distance from KL, so if you want to mix history and nature, it's very easy to combine an overnight trip to Malacca with a 3-night package to the park—I have included this itinerary below. If you want to delve deeper into rainforest habitats, fly to Kota Kinabalu and sign up for a tour of the area's national parks; specialty trips take you into wildlife preserves or trekking up Mt. Kinabalu. If it's indigenous cultures you'd like to visit, fly out to Sarawak, spend a day exploring Kuching, then join a boat trip into the interior to visit longhouse communities. The diverse range of forests in Sabah and Sarawak offer all kinds of adventures, from nature walks to animal sanctuaries to cave exploring or white-water rafting.

Remember, if you go the outdoor adventure route, be sure to check monsoon seasons with your adventure tour coordinator. You don't want the rains to wash out your trek or the dry season to take the thrill out of your white-water rapids. Also, for dive tours you'll have to allow extra time between flights and dives for your body to acclimate to the change in altitudes.

Days ❶–❸: Kuala Lumpur & Malacca

Follow the itinerary in "Malaysia for History Buffs & Culture Vultures," above, for Days 1, 2, and 3.

Days ❹–❼: Taman Negara National Park ✦✦✦

Take an early-morning bus back from Malacca to KL, then board an afternoon bus to Malaysia's premier, and most accessible, national park. Hop a boat upstream to the resort and check in for a good night's rest. Taman Negara can be done very nicely in a full-board package. You'll have the chance to jungle trek, traverse a canopy walk, view wildlife from observation stations, go on a night trek, river raft and fish, and meet Orang Asli communities. See p. 223.

Days ❼ & ❽: Back to KL

See Days 7 and 8 in "Malaysia for History Buffs & Culture Vultures," above.

7 Malaysia for Families

Malaysia is a terrific destination for families. It's safe, friendly, and free of some of the seedier trappings of tourism that can be seen in other parts of Asia. For this itinerary I've included an equal mix of beach and culture—sightseeing in the mornings and fun in the afternoons—at a pace that allows for maximum flexibility.

Days ❶ & ❷: Arrive in Kuala Lumpur

After arriving in Malaysia's capital city, allow yourself a full day to recover and just spend your time wandering through the city's streets. Start in **Chinatown** on Petaling Street (p. 221), where you'll find a street bazaar and the **Sri Mahamariaman Hindu Temple** (p. 221), then cut through the bustling Central Market to **Merdeka Square** (p. 220), the focal point of colonial KL. From the Jame Mosque, hop on the train to Jalan Imbi. Next to the station you'll find **Berjaya Times Square** (p. 221), KL's largest shopping mall, filled with tons of food and shopping, not to mention **Cosmo's World Theme Park** ★★★ (p. 219), the world's largest indoor amusement park.

Day ❸: Penang

Take an early-morning flight to Penang. Check into the **Holiday Inn Resort Penang** (p. 239) at Batu Feringgi, where they have special kids' suites. Have a ball at the beach! Don't forget to book watersports activities for the following days.

Day ❹: Georgetown ★★★

Spend your morning in Georgetown. Hit the **Penang Museum and Art Gallery** ★★ (p. 242) at 9am when it opens. Afterward, head over to the **Cheong Fatt Tze Mansion** ★★★ (p. 238) for the 11am tour. Afterwards, wander free through the streets before heading back to your resort for an afternoon of relaxation at the beach. See p. 234.

Day ❺: Penang Hill

The funicular train up the side of Penang Hill was built in 1923 to take British colonials up to the cooler climate of the hill, where they built lovely country homes and gardens. Today the train still operates as a commuter service to the communities in this part of the island. At the top you'll find restaurants, temples, and trails, one of which will lead you down to the botanical gardens. The trek lasts only an hour or two, so if your children aren't too young it should be a nice little adventure. Carry water and snacks! See p. 243.

Days ❻ & ❼: Back to KL

See Days 7 and 8 in "Malaysia for History Buffs & Culture Vultures," above.

8 The Best of Singapore & Malaysia in 1 Week

It is possible to see the best of Singapore and Malaysia in a short amount of time if you plan well. Two days in Singapore is just enough to see the major sights. I've suggested Penang and Langkawi in Malaysia because Penang has the best historical sights and Langkawi has the best beach resorts, so you can get in a little culture, plus downtime. However, as you plan your trip be advised that flights from Singapore can also take you directly to Borneo as well as other areas in peninsular Malaysia, so you can substitute other destinations that suit your interests.

Days ❶ & ❷: Arrive in Singapore

After arriving in Singapore, allow yourself time to recover and just spend your time wandering through the city's streets. My suggested itinerary for "The Best of Singapore in 1 Day," earlier in this chapter, is a good place to start. You will explore **Arab Street** and **Chinatown** with stops inside cultural exhibits to escape the weather.

Day ❸: Singapore

For your second day, "The Best of Singapore in 2 Days," earlier in this chapter, will steer you through **Little India** and to the lovely **Asian Civilisations Museum.**

Day ❹: Penang

Take an early-morning flight to Penang. After checking into your hotel, visit the **Penang Museum and Art Gallery** ★★ (p. 242), where you'll get a brilliant overview of the island's history and cultures. See p. 233.

Singapore & Malaysia in 1 Week

1 Singapore
2 Penang
3 Georgetown
4 Langkawi
5 Kuala Lumpur

Day 5: Georgetown ⭑⭑⭑
Follow my itinerary for Day 5 in "Malaysia for History Buffs & Culture Vultures," above.

Day 6: Langkawi ⭑⭑
Hop the early-morning ferry to Langkawi and arrive in time for lunch and a little R & R at your resort. Book scuba, snorkel, or watersports activities for the next day if you haven't done so already. See p. 244.

Day 7: Langkawi
Spend a day unwinding in tropical island paradise. No sense going home without some good downtime. I suggest after soaking in sun and sea all day, book yourself a late-afternoon/early-evening spa visit for the icing on the relaxation cake. See p. 244.

Days 8 & 9: Back to KL
See Days 7 and 8 in "Malaysia for History Buffs & Culture Vultures," above.

3

Planning Your Trip
to Singapore

The seasoned traveler typically has as many stories of travel nightmares as he does of glorious experiences—your luggage gets sent to Timbuktu, your hotel reservations get mixed up, and your taxi driver takes you to Lord-knows-where. The good news about traveling to Singapore? This place works. A seamless communications infrastructure means that you can plan your own trip, without a middleman travel agent, and still have everything go as smoothly as if you were on an organized coach tour. Reliable phone lines, fax technology, and Internet presence make advance planning a breeze. Of course, it helps that so many Singaporeans speak English. Additionally, the Singapore Tourism Board (STB) is a wealthy and well-oiled machine that has anticipated the needs of travelers.

The STB is perhaps one of the most visible government agencies in Singapore, and it's impossible for any tourist to get out of the country without encountering at least one of its many publications or postings or coming face-to-face with one of its innumerable representatives. If you have access to one of its offices before your trip, it's a great source of information. (More information on STB is listed under "Visitor Information," later in this chapter.)

In this chapter, I'll run through the nuts and bolts of travel to Singapore, letting you in on everything from how much your money will buy to the best time of year to travel, what to wear, how to get here, and how to find your way around.

1 The Regions in Brief

On a world map, Singapore is nothing more than a speck nestled in the heart of Southeast Asia, at the tip of the Malaysian peninsula. In the north, it's linked to Malaysia by a causeway over the Strait of Johor, which is its only physical connection to any other body of land. The country is made up of one main island, Singapore, and around 60 smaller ones, some of which—like Sentosa, Pulau Ubin, Kusu, and St. John's Island—are popular retreats. The main island is shaped like a flat, horizontal diamond, measuring in at just over 42km (25 miles)

from east to west and almost 23km (14 miles) north to south. With a total land area of only 585 sq. km (351 sq. miles), Singapore is almost shockingly tiny.

Singapore's geographical position, sitting approximately 137km (82 miles) north of the Equator, means that its climate features uniform temperatures, plentiful rainfall, and high humidity.

Singapore is a city-state, which basically means the city *is* the country. The urban center starts at the Singapore River at the southern point of the island. Within the urban center are neighborhoods that are handy for visitors to become familiar with: the Historic District, Chinatown, Orchard Road, Kampong Gelam, and Little India.

Beyond the central urban area you'll find older suburban neighborhoods such as Katong, Geylang, or Holland Village, neighborhoods that feature prewar homes with charming architectural details. Travel farther and you'll find New Towns, for example Ang Mo Kio or Toa Payoh, which are clusters of government-subsidized housing that have sprung up around the island, supported by their own shopping malls, schools, and clinics, many of them connected by the subway system.

THE CITY: URBAN SINGAPORE

The urban center of Singapore spans quite far from edge to edge, so walking from one end to the other, say from Kampong Gelam to Chinatown, will be too much for a relaxed walk. But within each neighborhood, the best way to explore is by foot, wandering along picturesque streets, in and out of shops and museums.

The main focal point of the city is the Singapore River, which on a map is located at the southern point of the island, flowing west to east into a marina. It's along the banks of this river that Sir Stamford Raffles landed and built his settlement for the East India Trading Company. As trade prospered, the banks of the river were expanded to handle commerce, behind which neighborhoods and administrative offices took root. In 1822, Raffles developed a Town Plan which allocated neighborhoods to each of the races who'd come in droves to find work and begin lives. The lines drawn then remain today, shaping the major ethnic enclaves held within the city limits.

CHINATOWN

On the south bank of the river, go-downs, or warehouses, lined the waterside. Behind, offices and residences sprang up

for the Chinese community of merchants and "coolie" laborers who worked the river- and sea-trade. Raffles named this section Chinatown, a name that stands today.

TANJONG PAGAR

Neighboring Chinatown to the southwest is Tanjong Pagar, a small district where wealthy Chinese and Eurasians built plantations and manors. With the development of the steamship, Keppel Harbour, a deep natural harbor just off the shore of Tanjong Pagar was built up to receive the larger vessels. Tanjong Pagar quickly developed into a commercial and residential area filled with workers who flocked there to support the industry.

In the early days both Chinatown and Tanjong Pagar were amazing sights of city activity. Row houses lined the streets with shops on the bottom floors and homes on the second and third. Chinese coolie laborers commonly lived 16 to a room, and the area flourished with gambling casinos, clubs, and opium dens for them to spend their spare time and money. Indians also thronged to the area to work on the docks, a small reminder that although races had their own areas, they were never exclusive communities.

As recently as the 1970s, a walk down the streets in this area was an adventure: The shops housed Chinese craftsmen and artists. On the streets, hawkers peddled food and other merchandise. Calligrapher scribes set up shop on sidewalks to write letters for a fee. Housewives would bustle, running their daily errands. Overhead, laundry hung from bamboo poles.

Today, both of these districts are sleepy in comparison. New Towns offering affordable housing have siphoned residents off to the suburbs, and though the government has renovated many of the old shophouses in an attempt to preserve history, they're now tenanted by law offices and architectural, public relations,

Singapore

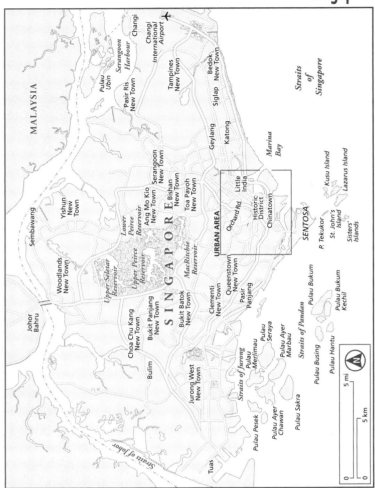

and advertising firms. About the only time you'll see this place hustle any more is during weekday lunchtime when all the professionals dash out for a bite.

HISTORIC DISTRICT

The north bank was originally reserved for colonial administrative buildings and is today commonly referred to as the Historic District. The center point was the Padang, the field on which the Europeans would play sports and hold outdoor ceremonies. Around the field, the Parliament Building, Supreme Court, City Hall, and other municipal buildings sprang up in grand style. Government Hill, the present-day Fort Canning Hill, was home of the governors. The Esplanade along the waterfront was a center for European social activities and music gatherings,

Urban Singapore Neighborhoods

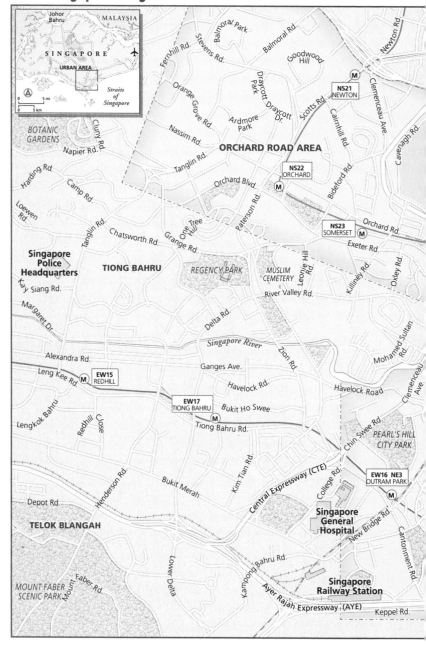

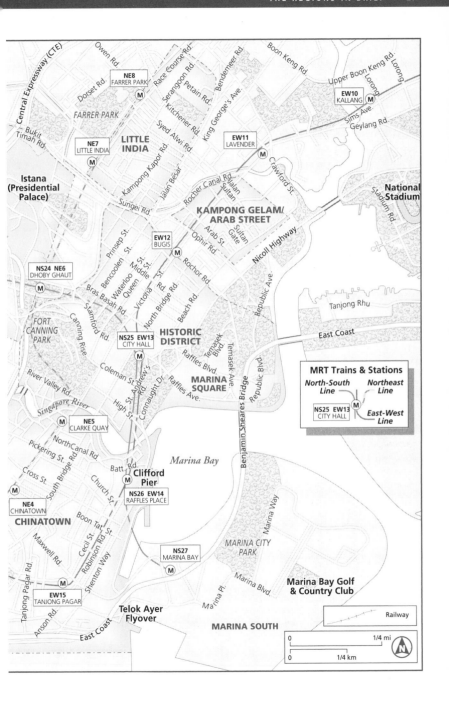

when colonials would don their finest western styles and walk the park under parasols or cruise in horse-drawn carriages. These days the Historic District is still the center of most of the government's operations and home to numerous high-rise hotels and shopping malls. The area on the bank of the river is celebrated as Raffles' landing site.

ORCHARD ROAD

To the northwest of the Historic District, in the area along Orchard and Tanglin roads, a residential area was created for Europeans and Eurasians. Homes and plantations were eventually replaced by apartment buildings and shops, and in the early 1970s luxury hotels ushered tourism into the area in full force. In the 1980s, huge shopping malls were erected along the sides of Orchard Road, turning the Orchard-scape into the shopping hub it continues to be. The Tanglin area is home to most of the foreign embassies in Singapore.

LITTLE INDIA

The natural landscape of Little India made it a natural location for an Indian settlement. Indians were the original cattle hands and traders in Singapore, and this area's natural grasses and springs provided their cattle with food and water while bamboo groves supplied necessary lumber for their pens. Later, with the establishment of brick kilns, Indian construction laborers flocked to the area to find work. Today many elements of Indian culture persist, although Indians make up a small percentage of the current population. Shops, restaurants, and temples still serve the community, and on Sundays Little India is a true mob scene, when all the workers have their day off and come to the streets here to socialize and relax.

KAMPONG GELAM

Kampong Gelam, neighboring Little India, was given to Sultan Hussein and his family as part of his agreement to turn Singapore over to Raffles. Here he built his *Istana* (palace) and the Sultan Mosque, and the area subsequently filled with Malay and Arab Muslims who imported a distinct Islamic flavor to the neighborhood. The area is still a focal point of Muslim society in Singapore thanks to Sultan Mosque, and the Istana has been opened as a new exhibit celebrating Malay culture. Arab Street is a regular draw for both tourists and locals who come to find deals on fabrics and local and regional crafts.

SHENTON WAY: DOWNTOWN

Two areas of the city center are relatively new, having been built atop huge parcels of reclaimed land. Where the eastern edges of Chinatown and Tanjong Pagar once touched the water's edge, land reclamation created the present-day downtown business district that is named after its central thoroughfare, Shenton Way. This Wall Street–like district is home to the magnificent skyscrapers that grace Singapore's skyline and to the banks and businesses that have made the place an international financial capital. During weekday business hours, Shenton Way is packed with scurrying businesspeople—after-hours and on weekends it's nothing more than a quiet forest of concrete, metal, and glass.

MARINA BAY

The other area is Marina Bay, on the opposite side of the Marina, just east of the historic district. Suntec City, Southeast Asia's largest convention and exhibition center, is located here and has become the linchpin of a thriving hotel, shopping mall, and amusement zone.

SUBURBAN SINGAPORE

With rapid urbanization in the 20th century, plantations and farms turned into suburban residential areas, many with their own ethnic roots.

KATONG

To the east of the city is Katong, a famous residential district inhabited primarily by Peranakan (Straits Chinese) and Eurasian families. Its streets were, and still are, lined with Peranakan-style terrace houses, a residential variation of the shophouse found in commercial districts. The Peranakans and Eurasians were tolerant groups, a result of interracial marriages and multicultural family life, who created a close-knit community that's carried over to the present day. Main streets are still lined with Peranakan restaurants as well as many Catholic churches and schools that served the Eurasians.

GEYLANG

As public transportation opened up the eastern sections of the island, neighborhoods extended farther out. Geylang, the neighborhood just beyond Katong, was and still is primarily a Malay district. Joo Chiat and Geylang roads were once lined with antiques shops and restaurants where halal foods, in accordance with Islamic laws, were served. Today, a lot of the shophouses are being renovated, but it's still a good area to find housewares, fabrics, and modern furniture shops. At night, parts of Geylang are notorious for partially regulated prostitution.

CHANGI VILLAGE

Also to the east is Changi Village, at the far eastern tip of the island. It was built as the residential section of a British military post, but the Brits are gone now and Changi is pretty quiet with not much to see other than a large hawker center with some great seafood and a public beach from which you can see Singapore's northern islands, Malaysia, and Indonesia. The one notable aspect of the place is that it's where you pick up ferries to Pulau Ubin.

Kampong Life

When the stress of modern society gets them down, many Singaporeans look back with longing to the days when life was simple, before the government housing schemes shifted everyone out of their kampongs.

Kampongs, Malay for villages (and spelled *kampung* in Malaysia), were, once upon a time, home to most of Singapore's population. Chinese, Malays, and Indians lived side by side in small clusters of houses that were built from wood and *attap* thatch and raised on stilts. Built along the shores of the island and close to jungles, the houses and buildings were nestled against backdrops of idyllic greenery surrounded by banana and coconut groves and marshes. Homes had land for chicken coops and kitchen gardens, and backyards in which children could play. The kampongs had central wells, provision shops, and sometimes temples and mosques. Despite their poverty, the kampong villages represented community.

The 1950s and 1960s were the heyday of kampong life. Later the houses were improved with corrugated metal, concrete, and linoleum, all of which rusted and rotted over time, making the kampongs look more like slums than the homey villages they once were. Inside, modernization brought government-mandated running water, plumbing, and even electrical appliances like TVs, refrigerators, and telephones. Still, all in all, life was hardly opulent.

TIONG BAHRU

To the west is an old neighborhood, Tiong Bahru. Its original inhabitants were Chinese from the Chinatown and Tanjong Pagar district and the neighborhood remains largely Chinese today. In the 1960s the government replaced small homes and makeshift housing with high-rise public apartment housing. The younger generations have since moved on to bigger housing in the New Towns leaving the place mostly populated by the elderly.

HOLLAND VILLAGE

Located to the west of the city, Holland Village is another famous neighborhood that's become a tourist attraction in its own right. Its nucleus of shops carries merchandise catering to the wants and needs of westerners, many of whom reside in the vicinity. Despite western customers, there aren't necessarily western goods here, but rather the kind of rattan furnishings, baskets, pottery, and other regional gifts and housewares that add Asian touches to otherwise western-style homes.

THE NEW TOWNS

In the 1960s to deal with the growing Singapore populations the government created a scheme to build residential areas along an imaginary circle around the center of the island. These New Towns consist of blocks of high-rise public apartments around which shops, markets, schools, and clinics settled to support the residents. Villages, farms, and orchards were leveled, swamps were drained, and local streams turned into concrete

channels to make way for towns such as Bedok, Tampines, Pasir Ris, Toa Payoh, Bishan, Ang Mo Kio, Yishun, Woodlands, and Clementi. One trip on the subway and all these names become familiar as the Mass Rapid Transit (MRT) system was brought into the scheme to provide affordable transportation to all the towns.

Since 1960 almost one million government-subsidized apartments have been built, allowing over 80% of Singapore's population to own their own homes. But however appealing this housing scheme sounded at first, residents in New Towns have their complaints. The apartments have become extremely expensive, and long waiting lists are filled with couples who want to buy their first homes and families who need to upgrade to larger digs. Beyond questions of expense, though, there's the fact that the New Towns are singularly characterless, with high-rises looming overhead and compartmentalized living creating an urban anonymity among the many inhabitants.

Today this entire way of life is just a memory. Every last kampong has been razed, the inhabitants relocated by the government to public housing estates. Many former kampong inhabitants have had a difficult time adjusting to life in concrete high-rises with no front porch or backyard and neighbors who are too busy to remember their names. Despite the truth that kampong life reflected poverty and struggle its memory remains a link to older days that, however irrelevant to the modern world, still warm the hearts of many Singaporeans.

2 Visitor Information

The long arm of the **Singapore Tourism Board (STB)** reaches many overseas audiences through its branch offices, which will gladly provide brochures and booklets to help you plan your trip, and through its website, at **www.visitsingapore.com**.

After you arrive in Singapore, several visitor centers are staffed to assist, beginning with information desks at the Arrival Halls in Terminals 1 and 2 at Changi Airport, open daily from 6am to

Destination Singapore: Pre-Departure Checklist

- Visitors from the U.S., Canada, the U.K, Australia, and New Zealand can obtain a visa upon arrival, provided they carry a passport valid for at least 6 months from date of entry. Singapore does not require any vaccinations to enter the country, unless you've been traveling in Africa or South America within 6 days of arrival, in which case you'll need a certificate that shows you've been vaccinated against yellow fever.
- It is advised to book your hotel and travel arrangements prior to arrival, especially if you are traveling *anywhere in Asia* from mid-December through to the end of the Chinese Lunar New Year, which is super-peak season. Because Chinese holidays follow the lunar calendar, they fall on different dates each year. In 2007 Chinese New Year began on February 18. In 2008 it will start on February 7, and in 2009 on January 26.
- Did you make sure your favorite attraction is open? Many children's activities are open only on weekends, public holidays, and during school holidays (which in Singapore fall between mid-May and the end of June, and again from mid-Nov through the end of Dec). If you're traveling from mid-December through to the end of the Chinese Lunar New Year, please be advised that many mom-and-pop businesses, shops, and eateries close for anywhere between 3 days and 2 weeks. Larger stores and main attractions will remain open, sometimes for shorter hours.
- If you purchased traveler's checks, have you recorded the check numbers and stored the documentation separately from the checks?
- Do you have a safe, accessible place to store money?
- Did you bring adequate supplies of any prescription drugs you are taking? Local pharmacies will not dispense drugs with foreign prescriptions.
- Do you have your credit card PIN?
- If you have an e-ticket, do you have your printed confirmation slip?
- Did you leave a copy of your itinerary with someone at home?
- Do you have a photocopy of the identification page of your passport?
- Do you have the address and phone number of your country's embassy with you? See page 63 for details.

2am. Other visitor centers are located in the city as follows: at the junction of Orchard and Cairnhill roads (cater-cornered from the Meritus Mandarin Hotel), open daily from 9:30am to 10:30pm; and on Level 1 at the Liang Court Shopping Centre, 177 River Valley Rd. (near Clarke Quay), open daily from 10:30am to 9:30pm.

STB operates a 24-hour information hot line that is toll-free within Singapore at **1800-736-2000.** Generally STB has up-to-date information, but if you need accurate information about travel timetables, I recommend you call airlines, ferry services, bus companies, or train stations directly.

3 Entry Requirements & Customs

ENTRY REQUIREMENTS
PASSPORTS

For information on how to get a passport, go to "Passports" in the "Fast Facts: Singapore" section, later in this chapter—the websites listed provide downloadable passport applications as well as the current fees for processing passport applications. For an up-to-date, country-by-country listing of passport requirements around the world, go to the "Foreign Entry Requirement" Web page of the U.S. State Department at **http://travel.state.gov**.

VISAS

To enter Singapore, you must have a passport valid for at least 6 months from your date of entry. Visitors from the United States, Canada, Australia, New Zealand, and the United Kingdom are not required to obtain a visa prior to arrival. A Social Visit Pass (with combined social and business status) good for up to 30 days (up to 90 days for U.S. visitors) will be awarded upon entry for travelers arriving by plane, or for 14 days if your trip is by ship or overland from Malaysia or Indonesia. Immigration officers are not required to grant you the maximum amount of days allotted, but rather have discretion to grant you as many days as they feel you need. Children traveling with parents from countries that qualify for a Social Visit Pass upon arrival can obtain entry with their own passport (provided it's valid for at least 6 months). Infants can enter on their parents' passports.

MEDICAL REQUIREMENTS

For information on medical requirements and recommendations, see "Health & Safety," p. 44.

CUSTOMS
WHAT YOU CAN BRING INTO SINGAPORE

There's no restriction on the amount of currency you can bring into Singapore.

For those over 18 years of age who have arrived from countries other than Malaysia and have spent more than 48 hours outside Singapore, allowable duty-free concessions are 1 liter of spirits; 1 liter of wine; and 1 liter of either port, sherry, or beer, all of which must be intended for personal consumption only. There are no duty-free concessions on cigarettes or other tobacco items. If you exceed the duty-free limitations, you can bring your excess items in upon payment of goods and services tax (GST) and Customs duty.

PROHIBITED ITEMS

It is important to note that Singapore has some very unique prohibitions on the import of certain items. While pretty much every country in the world, including Singapore, prohibits travelers from bringing items like plutonium, explosives, and firearms through Customs—the same goes with agricultural products such as live plants and animals, controlled substances, and poisons—Singapore adds to the list any type of printed or recorded pornography; pirated movies, music, or software; and toy or decorative guns, knives, or swords. A detailed rundown of prohibited items can be found on the Net at the Ministry of Home Affairs home page www.mha.gov.sg.

SINGAPORE'S DRUG POLICY

With all of the publicity surrounding the issue, Singapore's strict drug policy shouldn't need recapitulation, but here it is: Importing, selling, or using illegal narcotics is absolutely forbidden. Punishments are severe, up to and including the death penalty (automatic for morphine quantities exceeding 30 grams, heroin exceeding 15 grams, cocaine 30 grams, marijuana 500 grams, hashish 200 grams, opium 1.2 kilograms, or methamphetamines 250 grams). If you're carrying smaller sums (anything above: morphine 3 grams, heroin 2 grams, cocaine 3 grams, marijuana 15 grams, hashish 10 grams, opium 100 grams, or methamphetamines 25 grams) you'll still be considered to have intent to traffic and may face the death penalty if you can't prove otherwise. If you're crazy enough to try to bring these things into the country and you are caught, no measure of appeal to your home consulate will grant you any special attention.

WHAT YOU CAN TAKE HOME FROM SINGAPORE
U.S. Citizens
Returning **U.S. citizens** who have been away for at least 48 hours are allowed to bring back, once every 30 days, $800 worth of merchandise duty-free. You'll be charged a flat rate of duty on the next $1,000 worth of purchases. Any dollar amount beyond that is dutiable at whatever rates apply. On mailed gifts, the duty-free limit is $200. Be sure to have your receipts or purchases handy to expedite the declaration process. *Note:* If you owe duty, you are required to pay on your arrival in the U.S., either by cash, personal check, government or traveler's check, money order, or in some locations, a Visa or MasterCard.

To avoid having to pay duty on foreign-made personal items you owned before you left on your trip, bring along a bill of sale, insurance policy, jeweler's appraisal, or receipts of purchase. Or you can register items that can be readily identified by a permanently affixed serial number or marking—think laptop computers, cameras, and CD players—with Customs before you leave. Take the items to the nearest Customs office or register them with Customs at the airport from which you're departing. You'll receive, at no cost, a Certificate of Registration, which allows duty-free entry for the life of the item.

With some exceptions, you cannot bring fresh fruits and vegetables into the United States. For specifics on what you can bring back and the corresponding fees, download the invaluable free pamphlet *Know Before You Go* online at **www.cbp.gov**. (Click on "Travel," and then click on "Know Before You Go.") Or contact the **U.S. Customs & Border Protection (CBP),** 1300 Pennsylvania Ave., NW, Washington, DC 20229 (© **877/287-8667**), and request the pamphlet.

Canadian Citizens
For a clear summary of Canadian rules, write for the booklet *I Declare,* issued by the **Canada Border Services Agency** (© **800/461-9999** in Canada, or 204/983-3500; **www.cbsa-asfc.gc.ca**). Canada allows its citizens a C$750 exemption, and you're allowed to bring back duty-free one carton of cigarettes, one can of tobacco, 40 imperial ounces of liquor, and 50 cigars. In addition, you're allowed to mail gifts to Canada valued at less than C$60 a day, provided they're unsolicited and don't contain alcohol or tobacco (write on the package "Unsolicited gift, under $60 value"). All valuables should be declared on the Y-38 form before departure from Canada, including serial numbers of valuables you already own, such as expensive foreign cameras. *Note:* The C$750 exemption can only be used once a year and only after an absence of 7 days.

U.K. Citizens
U.K. citizens returning from a non-E.U. country have a Customs allowance of 200 cigarettes; 50 cigars; 250 grams of smoking tobacco; 2 liters of still table wine; 1 liter of spirits or strong liqueurs (over 22% volume); 2 liters of fortified wine, sparkling wine, or other liqueurs; 60cc (ml) perfume; 250cc (ml) of toilet water; and £145 worth of all other goods, including gifts and souvenirs. People under 17 cannot have the tobacco or

alcohol allowance. For information, contact **HM Customs & Excise** at (℃ **0845/ 010-9000** (from outside the U.K., 020/ 8929-0152), or consult their website at **www.hmce.gov.uk**.

Australian Citizens

The duty-free allowance in **Australia** is A$400 or, for those under 18, A$200. Personal property mailed back from Singapore should be marked "Australian goods returned" to avoid payment of duty. Upon returning to Australia, citizens can bring in 250 cigarettes or 250 grams of loose tobacco and 1,125mL of alcohol. If you're returning with valuable goods you already own, such as foreign-made cameras, you should file form B263. A helpful brochure available from Australian consulates or Customs offices is *Know Before You Go*. For more information, call the **Australian Customs Service** at (℃ **1300/363-263,** or log on to **www.customs.gov.au**.

New Zealand Citizens

The duty-free allowance for **New Zealand** is NZ$700. Citizens over 17 can bring in 200 cigarettes, 50 cigars, or 250 grams of tobacco (or a mixture of all three if their combined weight doesn't exceed 250 grams); plus 4.5 liters of wine and beer, or 1.125 liters of liquor. New Zealand currency does not carry import or export restrictions. Fill out a certificate of export, listing the valuables you are taking out of the country; that way, you can bring them back without paying duty. Most questions are answered in a free pamphlet available at New Zealand consulates and Customs offices: *New Zealand Customs Guide for Travellers, Notice no. 4.* For more information, contact **New Zealand Customs,** The Customhouse, 17–21 Whitmore St., Box 2218, Wellington (℃ **04/473-6099** or 0800/428-786; **www.customs.govt.nz**).

4 Money

Compared to its Southeast Asian neighbors Singapore is considered expensive; however, visitors from the West will find their money still goes quite far. *The Economist* came up with a clever way to compare the standard of living from country to country. The Big Mac Index is a surprisingly credible way to consider the value of the exact same item as it differs from place to place around the globe. For example, according to the March 2006 Big Mac Index, the average price of a Big Mac in Singapore was S$3.60. Convert that into U.S. dollars, and it's US$1.55 for a Big Mac—is that how much you're paying for your burger at home? How about the U.K. at £1.20 per burger? Or Australia at A$3?

CURRENCY FOR SINGAPORE

The local currency unit is the **Singapore dollar.** It's commonly referred to as the "Sing dollar," and retail prices are often marked as S$ (a designation I've used throughout this book). Notes are issued in denominations of S$2, S$5, S$10, S$50, S$100, S$500, and S$1,000. S$1 bills exist but are rare. Notes vary in size and color from denomination to denomination. Coins are issued in denominations of S1¢, S5¢, S10¢, S20¢, S50¢, and the fat, gold-colored S$1. Singapore has an interchangeability agreement with Brunei Darussalam, so don't be alarmed if you receive Brunei currency with your change, as it's legal tender.

At the time of this writing, exchange rates on the Singapore dollar were as follows: US$1 = S$1.54, C$1 = S$1.35, £1 = S$3.5, A$1 = S$1.21, NZ$1 = S$1.06. The exchange rate used throughout this book is US$1 = S$1.60, which is about the average exchange rate during the year

What Things Cost in Singapore	S$	US$	UK£
Taxi from the airport to city center	22.00	14.08	7.26
MRT from Orchard to Chinese Garden stations	1.40	0.90	0.46
Local telephone call (3 min.)	0.10	0.06	0.03
Double room at an expensive hotel	350.00	224.00	115.50
Double room at a moderate hotel	250.00	160.00	82.50
Double room at an inexpensive hotel	120.00	76.80	39.60
Dinner for one at an expensive restaurant	60.00	38.40	19.80
Dinner for one at a moderate restaurant	25.00	16.00	8.25
Dinner for one at an inexpensive restaurant	5.00	3.20	1.65
Glass of beer	9.00	5.76	2.97
Coca-Cola	1.10	0.70	0.36
Cup of coffee at common coffee shop	0.70	0.45	0.23
Cup of coffee at Starbucks, Coffee Club, and so on	2.80	1.79	0.92
Roll of 36-exposure color film	4.50	2.88	1.49
Admission to the Asian Civilisations Museum	8.00	5.12	2.64
Movie ticket	9.00	5.76	2.97

2006. Before you begin budgeting your trip, I suggest you obtain the latest conversions so you don't suffer any last-minute surprises. A neat and easy customizable currency conversion program can be found on the Internet through **www.xe.com**.

It's not an absolute necessity to buy Singapore dollars before your trip, because you can find ATMs that accept cards from the Cirrus and Plus networks at the Arrival Halls of Changi Terminals 1 and 2 as you exit the baggage claim area. If you do need currency changed, a few banks operate money-changing booths, plus an American Express Foreign Exchange office at Changi Terminal 2 (*© 65/6543-0671*) is open from noon to midnight daily.

In town it's best to exchange currency or traveler's checks at a local authorized money changer, found in most shopping malls throughout the city. They'll give you the best rate. You'll lose money with the high rates at banks, hotels, and shops.

ATMs

The easiest and best way to get cash away from home is from an ATM (automated teller machine), sometimes referred to as a "cash machine," or a "cashpoint." The **Cirrus** (*© 800/424-7787*; www.mastercard.com) and **PLUS** (*© 800/843-7587*; www.visa.com) networks span the globe; look at the back of your bank card to see which network you're on, then call or check online for ATM locations at your destination. Be sure you know your personal identification number (PIN) and daily withdrawal limit before you depart. *Note:* Remember that many banks impose a fee every time you use a card at another bank's ATM, and that fee can be higher for international transactions (up to $5 or more) than for domestic ones (where they're rarely more than $2). In addition, the bank from which you withdraw cash may charge its own fee. For international withdrawal fees, ask your bank.

Singapore Dollar Conversion Chart

S$	US$	UK£	euro€
0.10	0.06	0.03	0.04
0.20	0.13	0.07	0.09
0.50	0.32	0.1	0.20
1.00	0.64	0.33	0.49
2.00	1.28	0.60	0.98
5.00	3.20	1.65	2.45
10.00	6.40	3.30	4.90
20.00	12.80	6.60	9.80
50.00	32.00	16.50	24.50
100.00	64.00	33.00	49.00
500.00	320.00	165.00	245.00
1,000.00	640.00	330.00	490.00

CREDIT CARDS

Credit cards are another safe way to carry money. They also provide a convenient record of all your expenses, and they generally offer relatively good exchange rates. You can withdraw cash advances from your credit cards at banks or ATMs, provided you know your PIN. Keep in mind that you'll pay interest from the moment of your withdrawal, even if you pay your monthly bills on time. Also, note that many banks now assess a 1% to 3% "transaction fee" on **all** charges you incur abroad (whether you're using the local currency or your native currency). In Singapore, American Express, Visa, MasterCard, Diners Club, and JCB (Japan Credit Bureau) are accepted at virtually all major hotels, restaurants, nightclubs, and shopping centers. Even taxis accept payment by credit card. Smaller food and retail merchants generally don't accept plastic, and be advised, if you are trying to negotiate a discount with a vendor, you will always get a better price with good old-fashioned cash. Some retailers will insist on adding a credit card "service charge" to your bill. While it is true that the credit card companies charge the retailers a small fee each time a customer uses a card, it is a cost the retailers are supposed to bear themselves. If anyone tries to foist this charge onto you, sadly your only recourse is to report him to your credit card company.

TRAVELER'S CHECKS

You can buy traveler's checks at most banks. They are offered in denominations of $20, $50, $100, $500, and sometimes $1,000. Generally, you'll pay a service charge ranging from 1% to 4%.

The most popular traveler's checks are offered by **American Express** (✆ **800/ 807-6233,** or 800/221-7282 for card holders—this number accepts collect calls, offers service in several foreign languages, and exempts Amex gold and platinum cardholders from the 1% fee); **Visa** (✆ **800/732-1322**)—AAA members can obtain Visa checks for a $9.95 fee (for checks up to $1,500) at most AAA offices or by calling ✆ **866/339-3378;** and **MasterCard** (✆ **800/223-9920**).

American Express, Thomas Cook, Visa, and **MasterCard** offer **foreign currency traveler's checks,** which are useful if you're traveling to one country, or to the euro zone; they're accepted at locations where dollar checks may not be.

If you carry traveler's checks, keep a record of their serial numbers separate from your checks in the event that they are stolen or lost. You'll get a refund faster if you know the numbers.

5 When to Go

A steady supply of business travelers keep occupancy rates high year-round in Singapore, however, some hotels report that business travel gets sluggish during the months of July and August, when they target the leisure market more aggressively. This is probably your best time to negotiate a favorable rate. Peak season for travel falls between December and June, with "super-peak" beginning in mid-December and lasting through the Chinese Lunar New Year, which falls in January or February, depending on the moon's cycle. During this season, Asian travel routes are booked solid and hotels are maxed out. Favorable deals are rare, because most of Asia takes annual leave at this time.

The Chinese Lunar New Year presents problems and opportunities for travelers. On the one hand, it's the biggest holiday for the Chinese, who make up the majority of Singaporeans, so you'll get a chance to see fun street markets, festive decorations, curious traditions, and the popular Chingay Parade. On the other hand, in the weeks leading up to the holiday, prices for everyday items are grossly inflated—don't shop before Chinese New Year!—and Chinatown turns into a swarming sea of panic-stricken last-minute shoppers. Then on the first day of the holiday, virtually everything Chinese closes—eateries, shops, businesses. Forget about it! Most reopen on the third day of the holiday, but many choose to stay closed for the full 2 weeks, the traditional amount of time for Chinese to observe this holiday. Not to fear! If you're in Singapore for the holiday, your hotel will still be serving meals, and you can always trek down to Little India or Kampong Gelam for some tasty Indian or Malay eats.

As for weather, because Singapore is 137km (82 miles) north of the Equator, you can pretty much guarantee that it's hot. In terms of seasonal variations, you've got some months that are not as warm as others, but for the most part, they're all still hot.

What does vary greatly is rainfall. Singapore lies between two monsoon winds. The Northeast Monsoon arrives the beginning of November and stays until mid-March, when temperatures are slightly cooler, relatively speaking, than other times of the year. The heaviest rainfall occurs between November and January, with daily showers that sometimes last for long periods of time; at other times, it comes down in short, heavy gusts and goes quickly away. Wind speeds are rarely anything more than light. The Southwest Monsoon falls between June and September. Temperatures are much higher and, interestingly, it's during this time of year that Singapore gets the *least* rain (with the very least reported in July).

By and large, year-round temperatures remain uniform, with a daily average of 81°F (27°C), afternoon temperatures reaching as high as 87°F (31°C), and an average sunrise temperature as low as 75°F (24°C). Relative humidity often exceeds 90% at night and in the early morning. Even on a "dry" afternoon, don't expect it to drop much below 60%. (The daily average is 84% relative humidity.)

HOLIDAYS

In recent years Singapore has also been building up the Chingay Parade, a colorful procession of floats, marching bands, acrobats and dancers, martial artists, and stilt-walkers who perform in a parade

Ringing in the New Year, Chinese-style

Chinese New Year, a 15-day celebration of the new year according to the lunar calendar, is the most important festival of the Chinese culture and a huge occasion in Singapore. It was originally called *Chun Kie*, or Spring Festival, to celebrate the passing of winter and spring's promise of a fertile and prosperous growing season. In modern times, it's still seen as a chance to put the past behind and start afresh, with new hopes for prosperity, health, and luck. During the celebration, homes and businesses display large red banners with the characters *Gong Xi Fa Cai*, which mean "Wishing you great prosperity." You'll also witness lion dances outside businesses to attract good luck, staged by troupes of young men who don the traditional lion costume and perform an age-old dance to accompanying drum and cymbal clashes.

Outside private homes, the Chinese hang the character *fu*, which means luck. The *fu* is usually hung upside down because in Chinese the words for "luck upside down" sound similar to the words "luck arrives." Red, the most auspicious color according to the Chinese, is predominant in banners and is the color of *hong bao*, packets of money given to children and single young adults by parents and married friends. Oranges and tangerines are given as gifts, symbolizing gold and luck both in their colors and according to Chinese puns. Also important are noisy firecrackers, which are believed to ward off evil spirits and serve (through their noise) as a sign of life. Unfortunately, firecrackers are banned in Singapore, so you won't find much of that going on.

New Year's Day, the first day of celebration, can fall anywhere between mid-January and end of February. In preparation for New Year's Day, the Chinese pay off old debts, because debt is believed to lead to bad luck in the coming year if not taken care of, and clean their homes, sweeping the floors in a symbolic clearing away of old misfortunes. All cleaning is done before

through the downtown area. Contact the STB to find out which day they will host the parade during your visit. There are 11 official public holidays: New Year's Day (Jan 1), Chinese New Year or Lunar New Year (Feb 18, 19, and 20 observed, 2007; Feb 7 and 8, 2008), Good Friday (Apr 6, 2007; Mar 21, 2008), Labour Day (May 1), Vesak Day (May 31, 2007; May 19, 2008), National Day (Aug 9), Hari Raya Puasa (Oct 13, 2007; Oct 2, 2008), Deepavali (Nov 8, 2007; Oct 27, 2008), Hari Raya Haji (Dec 20, 2007; Dec 9, 2008), and Christmas Day (Dec 25). On these days, expect government offices, banks, and some shops to be closed.

CALENDAR OF PUBLIC HOLIDAYS & EVENTS
January/February

New Year's Day. The first day of the calendar year is celebrated in Singapore by all races and religions. New Year's Eve in Singapore is always cause for parties and celebrations similar to those in the West. Look for special events and parties at restaurants and nightclubs, but don't expect to find a taxi when you need one! January 1.

Lunar New Year or Chinese New Year. If you want to catch the biggest event in the Chinese calendar and

New Year's Day because to sweep on this day would be to clear away good luck. Most go so far as to hide the broom. New Year's Eve is the night of the Reunion Dinner, where family members put on bright new clothes (red colors are best), get together, and invite the spirits of deceased ancestors to gather for a meal. The central dish of the feast is the *yu sheng*, a raw fish salad. Once it's placed on the table, everyone gathers around the *yu sheng*, digs in with their chopsticks, and tosses the salad high—the higher you toss the better your luck.

If you are visiting Singapore around Chinese New Year, there are a few things to note. Shopping leading up to the holiday is insane. The streets of Chinatown are a mob scene, with people chasing last-minute holiday goodies. Crowds are thick and queues are long. Prices are also inflated for things like haircuts, clothing, traditional foods, and decorations—not a good time to come looking for bargains.

On Chinese New Year's Eve, most businesses let their staff off early to prepare for the Reunion Dinner—this is when crowds are thickest. However, expect Singapore to be a ghost town on the first and second days of the new year, when almost all local businesses, including restaurants, are closed tight. Although folks spend the first and second days visiting friends and family, the third is considered unlucky for socializing, so most return to work. Still, many mom-and-pop businesses use this time to take annual leave and will close for a full 15 days. If you find yourself in Singapore during this time, don't panic. Hotel restaurants are always open, and, if worse comes to worst, there's always the ethnic Indian and Malay enclaves at Little India and Kampong Gelam for good food and shopping!

pretty much the biggest in Singapore, come during the Chinese New Year celebrations, which include parades and festivals. In 2008 it begins on February 7.

Thaipusam Festival. If you're lucky enough to be in Singapore during this event, you're in for a bizarre cultural treat. This annual festival is celebrated by Hindus to give thanks to Lord Subramaniam, the child god who represents virtue, youth, beauty, and valor. During Thaipusam, male Hindus who have made prayers to Subramaniam for special wishes must carry *kavadis* in gratitude. These huge steel racks are decorated with flowers and fruits and are held onto the men's bodies by skewers and hooks that pierce the skin. Carrying the *kavadis*, the devotees parade from Sri Perumal Temple in Little India to the Sri Thandayuthapani Temple (called the Tank Rd. temple), where family members remove the heavy structures. For an additional spectacle, they will pierce their tongues and cheeks with skewers and hang fruits from hooks in their flesh. The devotees have all undergone strict diet and prayer before the festival, and it is reported that, afterward, no scars remain. Late January/early February.

March/April

Good Friday. Churches and cathedrals hold special services on this Christian holiday to remember the crucifixion of Christ. St. Joseph's on Victoria Street holds an annual candlelight procession. Late March/early April.

Qing Ming (All Souls' Day). Qing Ming, or All Souls' Day, was originally a celebration of spring. On this day, Chinese families have picnics at ancestral graves, cleaning the graves and pulling weeds, lighting red candles, burning joss sticks and "Hell Money" (paper money whose smoke rises to the afterworld to be used by the ancestors), and bringing rice, wine, and flowers for the deceased in a show of ancestral piety. Early April.

The Singapore International Film Festival. This event showcases critically acclaimed works, including international films and Singaporean short productions. It's become a renowned showcase for Asian films, which constitute 40% of those featured. The festival includes competitions, workshops, and tributes to filmmakers. Schedule and ticketing information can be obtained from its website at www.filmfest.org.sg. April.

May

Vesak Day. Buddhist shrines and temples are adorned with banners, lights, and flowers; and worshipers gather to pray and chant in observance of the birth, enlightenment, and death of the Buddha, which all occurred on this day. Good places to watch the festivities, unless you're afraid of crowds, are the Temple of a Thousand Lights in Little India or Thian Hock Keng Temple in Chinatown. On this day, Buddhists will refrain from eating meat, donate food to the poor, and set animals (especially birds) free to show kindness and generosity. It falls on the full moon of the fifth month of the lunar calendar—which means somewhere around mid-May.

Singapore Arts Festival. During this month-long festival, premier local, regional, and international music and dance performances are staged in a number of venues. The cultural performances, some modern and some traditional, are always excellent and are highly recommended. Check out www.singaporeartsfest.com. Late May to mid-June.

June

Singapore World Invitational Dragon Boat Races. The annual dragon boat races are held to remember the fate of Qu Yuan, a patriot and poet during the Warring States period in Chinese history (475–221 B.C.), who threw himself into a river to end his suffering at watching his state fall into ruin under the hands of corrupt leadership. The people searched for him in boats shaped like dragons, beating gongs and throwing rice dumplings into the water to distract the River Dragon. Today, the dragon boat races are an international event, with rowing teams from 20 countries coming together to compete. Drums are still beaten, and rice dumplings are still a traditional favorite. Contact the STB for information. Late June/early July.

July

The Singapore Food Festival. Local chefs compete for honors in this month-long exhibition of international culinary delights. It's a good time to be eating in Singapore, as restaurants feature the brand-new creations they have entered in the events. Contact the STB for details. July.

The Great Singapore Sale. This is a month-long promotion to increase retail sales, and most shops will advertise huge savings for the entire month.

It's well publicized with red banners all over Orchard Road. July.

Maulidin Nabi. Muslims celebrate the birth of the Prophet Mohammed on this day. Sultan Mosque is the center of the action for Muslims who come to chant in praise. July 17.

August

National Day. On August 9, 1965, Singapore separated from the Federation of Malaysia, becoming an independent republic. Patriotism is celebrated with a big parade held in the National Stadium with live performances, music, and fireworks. Tickets are available only through lottery, so few short-term visitors ever get the chance to see it live. August 9.

Festival of the Hungry Ghosts. The Chinese believe that once a year the gates of purgatory are opened and all the souls inside are let loose to wander among the living. To appease these restless spirits and prevent evil from falling upon themselves, the Chinese burn joss, Hell money, and paper replicas of luxury items, the latter two meant to appear in the afterworld for greedy ghosts to use. The main celebration is on the 15th day of the 7th month of the lunar calendar and is celebrated with huge feasts. At markets, altars offer mountains of goodies for hungry ghosts as well. Chinese operas are performed throughout the month to entertain the spirits and make them more docile. Nowadays, with Chinese Opera becoming a dying art, a lot of the street performances are karaoke acts. Mid-August/mid-September.

September

The Mooncake and Lantern Festivals. Traditionally called the Mid-Autumn Festival, it was celebrated to give thanks for a plentiful harvest. The origins date from the Sung Dynasty (A.D. 970–1279) when Chinese officials would exchange round mirrors as gifts

to represent the moon and symbolize good health and success. Today, the holiday is celebrated by eating moon cakes, which are sort of like little round hockey pucks filled with lotus seeds or red bean paste and a salted duck egg yolk. Children light colorful plastic or paper lanterns shaped like fish, birds, butterflies, and, more recently, cartoon characters. There's an annual lantern display and competition out at the Chinese Garden, with acrobatic performances, lion dances, and night bazaars. Late September/early October.

Birthday of the Monkey God. In the Chinese temples ceremonies are performed by mediums who pierce their faces and tongues and write prayers with the blood. In the temple courtyards you can see Chinese operas and puppet shows. The Tan Si Chong Su Temple on Magazine Road, upriver from Boat Quay, is a good bet for seeing the ceremonies. Contact the STB for information. Late September/early October.

October/November

Hari Raya Puasa. Hari Raya Puasa marks the end of Ramadan, the Muslim month of fasting during daylight hours. During Ramadan, food stalls line up around the Sultan Mosque in Kampong Gelam, ready to sell tasty Malay goodies at sundown. It's a 3-day celebration (though only the first day is a public holiday) of thanksgiving dinners, and non-Muslims are often invited to these feasts, as the holiday symbolizes an openness of heart and mind and a renewed sense of community. During the course of the 3 evenings, Geylang—especially the areas surrounding Malay Village—is decorated with lights and banners and the whole area is open for a giant *pasar malam,* or night market. In 2007, Hari Raya Puasa falls on October 13, and in 2008 it falls on October 2.

Pilgrimage to Kusu Island. During this month-long period, plan your trips to Kusu Island wisely, as the place becomes a mob scene. Throughout the month (the lunar month, that is), Chinese travel to this small island to visit the temple there and pray for another year of health and wealth. See chapter 6 for more information on Kusu. October/November.

Festival of the Nine-Emperor God. During this celebration, held over the first 9 days of the ninth month of the lunar calendar (to the Chinese, the double nines are particularly auspicious), temples are packed with worshipers, hawkers sell religious items outside, and Chinese operas are performed for the Nine-Emperor God, a composite of nine former emperors who control the prosperity and health of worshipers. At the height of the festival, priests write prayers with their own blood. On the ninth day, the festival closes as the Nine-Emperor God's spirit, contained in an urn, is sent to sea on a small decorated boat. Contact the STB for information. Late October.

Navarathiri Festival. During this 9-day festival, Hindus make offerings to the wives of Shiva, Vishnu, and Brahma. The center point in the evenings is Chettiar's Temple (at 15 Tank Rd.), where dances and musical performances are staged. Performances begin around 7:30pm. Contact the STB for information. Late October/early November.

Deepavali. Hindus and Sikhs celebrate Deepavali as the first day of their calendar. The new year is ushered in with new clothing, social feasts, and gatherings. It's a beautiful holiday, with Hindu temples aglow from the tiny earthen candles placed in crevices up the sides of the buildings. Hindus believe that the souls of the deceased come to earth during this time, and the candles help to light their way back to heaven. During the celebration, Serangoon Road in Little India is a crazy display of colored lights and decorative arches. In 2007 this holiday falls on November 8, and on October 27 in 2008.

Thimithi Festival. Thimithi begins at the Sri Perumal Temple in Little India and makes its way in parade fashion to the Sri Mariamman Temple in Chinatown. Outside the temple, a bed of hot coals is prepared and a priest will lead the way, walking first over the coals, to be followed one at a time by devotees. Crowds gather to watch the spectacle, which begins around 5pm. Make sure you're early so you can find a good spot. Contact the STB for information. Late October/early November.

Christmas Light-Up. Orchard Road is brilliant in bright and colorful streams of Christmas lights and garlands. All of the hotels and shopping malls participate, dressed in the usual Christmas regalia of nativity scenes and Santa Clauses. Most years, the decorations started coming up by mid-October. Puh-leeze!

December

Hari Raya Haji. One of the five pillars of Islam involves making a pilgrimage to Mecca at least once in a lifetime, and Hari Raya Haji is celebrated the day after pilgrims make this annual voyage to fulfill their spiritual promise. Muslims who have made the journey adopt the title of Haji (for men) and Hajjah (for women). After morning prayers, sheep and goats are sacrificed and their meat is distributed to poor families. In 2007, this holiday falls on December 20. In 2008 it falls on December 9.

Christmas Day. On this day, Christian Singaporeans celebrate the birth of Christ. December 25.

6 Travel Insurance

The cost of travel insurance varies widely, depending on the cost and length of your trip, your age and health, and the type of trip you're taking, but expect to pay between 5% and 8% of the vacation itself. You can get estimates from various providers through **InsureMyTrip.com**. Enter your trip cost and dates, your age, and other information, for prices from more than a dozen companies.

TRIP-CANCELLATION INSURANCE

Trip-cancellation insurance will help retrieve your money if you have to back out of a trip or depart early, or if your travel supplier goes bankrupt. Permissible reasons for trip cancellation can range from sickness to natural disasters to the State Department declaring a destination unsafe for travel.

For more information, contact one of the following recommended insurers: **Access America** (© 866/807-3982; www.accessamerica.com); **Travel Guard International** (© 800/826-4919; www.travelguard.com); **Travel Insured International** (© 800/243-3174; www.travelinsured.com); and **Travelex Insurance Services** (© 888/457-4602; www.travelexinsurance.com).

MEDICAL INSURANCE

For travel overseas, most U.S. health plans (including Medicare and Medicaid) do not provide coverage, and the ones that do often require you to pay for services upfront and reimburse you only after you return home. As a safety net, you may want to buy travel medical insurance, particularly if you're traveling to a remote or high-risk area where emergency evacuation might be necessary. If you require additional medical insurance, try **MEDEX Assistance** (© 410/453-6300; www.medexassist.com) or **Travel Assistance International** (© 800/821-2828; www.travelassistance.com; for general information on services, call the company's Worldwide Assistance Services, Inc. at © 800/777-8710).

LOST-LUGGAGE INSURANCE

On flights within the U.S., checked baggage is covered up to $2,500 per ticketed passenger. On international flights (including U.S. portions of international trips), baggage coverage is limited to approximately $9.07 per pound, up to approximately $635 per checked bag. If you plan to check items more valuable than what's covered by the standard liability, see if your homeowner's policy covers

Travel in the Age of Bankruptcy

Airlines go bankrupt, so protect yourself by **buying your tickets with a credit card.** The Fair Credit Billing Act guarantees that you can get your money back from the credit card company if a travel supplier goes under (and if you request the refund within 60 days of the bankruptcy). **Travel insurance** can also help, but make sure it covers against "carrier default" for your specific travel provider. And be aware that if a U.S. airline goes bust mid-trip, a 2001 federal law requires other carriers to take you to your destination (albeit on a space-available basis) for a fee of no more than $25, provided you rebook within 60 days of the cancellation.

your valuables, get baggage insurance as part of your comprehensive travel-insurance package, or buy Travel Guard's "BagTrak" product.

If your luggage is lost, immediately file a lost-luggage claim at the airport, detailing the luggage contents. Most airlines require that you report delayed, damaged, or lost baggage within 4 hours of arrival. The airlines are required to deliver luggage, once found, directly to your house or destination free of charge.

7 Health & Safety

STAYING HEALTHY

As some intrepid travelers are so fond of accusing Singapore of being overly "squeaky-clean," *sane* travelers who don't want to spend their holiday infirm can rest assured that they are safe from most of the tropical world's nastiest scourges in sanitary Singapore. Food is clean virtually everywhere, tap water is potable, restaurants and food vendors are regulated by the government, and many other airborne, bug-borne, and bite-borne whathave-yous have been eradicated.

Singapore doesn't require that you have any vaccinations to enter the country but recommends immunization against diphtheria, tetanus, hepatitis A and B, and typhoid for anyone traveling to Southeast Asia in general. If you're particularly worried, follow their advice; if not, don't worry about it.

On February 25, 2003, Singapore reported its first case of Severe Acute Respiratory Syndrome, more commonly known as **SARS.** What exploded into an epidemic effecting almost 8,500 people worldwide was quickly brought under control in the island state due to immediate and effective actions taken by the Ministries of Health and Education and the media, combined with the tireless vigilance of Singaporeans themselves. After 3 months of battle, SARS had claimed the lives of 33 people in Singapore but had mobilized the entire country to take daily precautions against the spread of the disease in an effort that was highly lauded by the World Health Organization (WHO). The respiratory infection is passed on through droplets when an infected person sneezes or coughs, however, most SARS infections are transmitted only through very close contact. Today, casual travelers face no threats of contracting this disease in Singapore.

Also in the news, cases of **Asian bird flu,** or Avian influenza, have been reported all over Asia Pacific, with countries culling over 100 million poultry to contain outbreaks. Avian influenza is an acute viral infection affecting birds and poultry. Cross-infection to humans is rare; however, it does happen among people who have come in contact with sick or dead birds. To protect the country, Singapore keeps a close watch on its poultry farms and has developed safe channels for the import of all poultry products to make sure infected meats and eggs don't cross its borders.

Although you have no risk of contracting malaria in Singapore (the country's been declared malaria-free for decades by the World Health Organization), there is a similar deadly virus, **dengue fever,** that's carried by mosquitoes and for which there is no immunization. A problem in the Tropics around the world, dengue fever is controlled in Singapore with an aggressive campaign to prevent the responsible mosquitoes from breeding. Still, each year cases of infection are reported, almost all of them occurring in suburban neighborhoods and rural areas. Symptoms of dengue fever include sudden fever and tiny red spotty rashes on the body. If you suspect you've contracted dengue, seek medical attention immediately (see the listing of hospitals under "Fast Facts: Singapore," later in this chapter). If left untreated, this disease can cause internal hemorrhaging and even death. Your best protection is to wear insect repellent that contains DEET, especially if you're heading out to the zoo, bird park, or any of the gardens or nature preserves, especially during the daytime.

It seems inevitable for travelers from the West to suffer some sort of Montezuma's revenge or Delhi-belly when they visit the Tropics. If you suffer a bout of **diarrhea,** it could be from many causes: weakness from jet lag, adjustments to the climate, new foods, spices, or an increase in physical activity. Always carry Immodium, or a comparable antidiarrheal, but most importantly, don't forget to drink plenty of water to avoid dehydration. If symptoms include painful cramps, fever, or rash, seek medical attention immediately, otherwise it'll probably just clear up by itself.

Singapore's climate guarantees heat and humidity year-round; you should remember to take precautions. Give yourself plenty of time to relax and regroup on arrival to adjust your body to the new climate (and to the new time, if there is a time difference for you). Also, drink plenty of water. Avoid overexposure to the sun. The tropical sun will burn you like thin toast in no time at all. You may also feel more lethargic than usual. This is typical in the heat, so take things easy and you'll be fine. Be careful of the air-conditioning, though. It's nice and cooling, but if you're prone to catching a chill, or find yourself moving in and out of air-conditioned buildings a lot, you can wind up with a horrible summer cold.

GENERAL AVAILABILITY OF HEALTHCARE

If you require medical assistance for general health or emergencies, the best thing to do is contact your hotel's front desk or concierge, who have doctors on call and emergency numbers at close hand. You can be assured that Singapore's healthcare system, facilities, and professionals are of excellent quality, with ambulance and paramedic care standing by via emergency hot lines.

WHAT TO DO IF YOU GET SICK AWAY FROM HOME

If you require hospitalization, the centrally located **Mount Elizabeth Hospital** is near Orchard Road at 3 Mount Elizabeth (© **65/6737-2666,** for accidents and emergencies call 65/6731-2218). You can also try **Singapore General Hospital,** Outram Road (© **65/6222-3322,**

Avoiding "Economy-Class Syndrome"

Deep vein thrombosis, or as it's know in the world of flying, "economy-class syndrome," is a blood clot that develops in a deep vein. It's a potentially deadly condition that can be caused by sitting in cramped conditions—such as an airplane cabin—for too long. During a flight (especially a long-haul flight), get up, walk around, and stretch your legs every 60 to 90 minutes to keep your blood flowing. Other preventative measures include frequent flexing of the legs while sitting, drinking lots of water, and avoiding alcohol and sleeping pills. If you have a history of deep vein thrombosis, heart disease, or another condition that puts you at high risk, some experts recommend wearing compression stockings or taking anticoagulants when you fly; always ask your physician about the best course for you. Symptoms of deep vein thrombosis include leg pain or swelling, or even shortness of breath.

Healthy Travels to You

The following government websites offer up-to-date health-related travel advice.

- **U.S.:** www.cdc.gov/travel
- **Canada:** www.hc-sc.gc.ca/index_e.html
- **U.K.:** www.dh.gov.uk/PolicyAndGuidance/HealthAdviceForTravellers/fs/en
- **Australia:** www.dfat.gov.au/travel

for accidents and emergencies call 65/ 6321-4311).

Any foreign consulate can provide a list of area doctors who speak English. If you get sick, consider asking your hotel concierge to recommend a local doctor—even his or her own. You can also try the emergency room at a local hospital. Many hospitals also have walk-in clinics for emergency cases that are not life-threatening; you may not get immediate attention, but you won't pay the high price of an emergency room visit. We list **hospitals** and **emergency numbers** under "Fast Facts: Singapore," p. 62.

If you suffer from a chronic illness, consult your doctor before your departure. Pack **prescription medications** in your carry-on luggage, and carry them in their original containers, with pharmacy labels—otherwise they won't make it through airport security. Carry the generic name of prescription medicines, in case a local pharmacist is unfamiliar with the brand name.

For travel abroad, you may have to pay all medical costs upfront and be reimbursed later. See "Medical Insurance," under "Travel Insurance," above.

STAYING SAFE

Singapore is a safe place by any standards. There's very little violent crime, even late at night. If you stay out, there's little worry about making it home safe. If your children are missing, they probably aren't kidnapped, but are being consoled by a friendly passerby while you search for them. This may sound naive, but Asians are culturally a very family-oriented people, and most would never dream of harming a child.

In recent years, some pickpocketing has been reported. Hotel safe-deposit boxes are the best way to secure valuables, and traveler's checks solve theft problems in a jiff.

Before you go always check the U.S. State department website to see if any warnings have been issued in this region: **http://travel.state.gov/travel/cis_pa_tw/ tw/tw_1764.html**.

8 Specialized Travel Resources

TRAVELERS WITH DISABILITIES

Most disabilities shouldn't stop anyone from traveling. There are more options and resources out there than ever before.

There's a free guide called *The Access Singapore Physically Disabled Person's Guide to Accessible Places,* put together by the Singapore Council of Social Services, with charts to rate accessibility features of hotels, airports, places of interest, shops, and public buildings. It's published on the Net at **www.dpa.org.sg/DPA/access/ contents.htm**.

Most hotels have accessible rooms, and some cab companies offer special van services. I've found most of the newer buildings are constructed with access ramps for wheelchairs, but older buildings are very problematic, especially the shophouses, with narrow sidewalks and many uneven steps.

Many travel agencies offer customized tours and itineraries for travelers with disabilities. Among them are **Flying Wheels Travel** (© 507/451-5005; www.flyingwheelstravel.com); **Access-Able Travel Source** (© 303/232-2979; www.access-able.com); and **Accessible Journeys** (© 800/846-4537 or 610/521-0339; www.disabilitytravel.com). **Avis Rent a Car** has an "Avis Access" program that offers such services as a dedicated 24-hour toll-free number (© 888/879-4273) for customers with special travel needs; special car features such as swivel seats, spinner knobs, and hand controls; and accessible bus service.

Organizations that offer assistance to disabled travelers include **MossRehab** (www.mossresourcenet.org); the **American Foundation for the Blind (AFB;** © 800/232-5463; www.afb.org); and **SATH** (Society for Accessible Travel & Hospitality; © 212/447-7284; www.sath.org). **AirAmbulanceCard.com** is now partnered with SATH and allows you to preselect top-notch hospitals in case of an emergency.

The community website **iCan** (www.icanonline.net/channels/travel) has destination guides and several regular columns on accessible travel. Also check out the quarterly magazine *Emerging Horizons* (www.emerginghorizons.com), and *Open World* magazine, published by SATH.

GAY & LESBIAN TRAVELERS

The conservative Singaporean government doesn't recognize or support alternative lifestyles; however, gay and lesbian culture is alive and well in Singapore. What you'll find is that older gays and lesbians are more conservative and therefore less open to discussion, while the younger generations have very few qualms about describing the local scene and their personal experiences in Singapore.

There are tons of websites on the Internet for gays and lesbians in Singapore. Start at www.utopia-asia.com, an extremely comprehensive "insider" collection of current events, meeting places, travel tips, topical Web discussions, and links to resources.

The International Gay and Lesbian Travel Association (IGLTA; © 800/448-8550 or 954/776-2626; www.iglta.org) is the trade association for the gay and lesbian travel industry, and offers an online directory of gay- and lesbian-friendly travel businesses; go to their website and click on "Members."

Many agencies offer tours and travel itineraries specifically for gay and lesbian travelers. Among them are **Above and Beyond Tours** (© 800/397-2681; www.abovebeyondtours.com); **Now, Voyager** (© 800/255-6951; www.nowvoyager.com); and **Olivia Cruises & Resorts** (© 800/631-6277; www.olivia.com).

Gay.com Travel (© 800/929-2268 or 415/644-8044; www.gay.com/travel or www.outandabout.com), is an excellent online successor to the popular *Out & About* print magazine. It provides regularly updated information about gay-owned, gay-oriented, and gay-friendly lodging, dining, sightseeing, nightlife, and shopping establishments in every important destination worldwide.

The following travel guides are available at many bookstores, or you can order them from any online bookseller: *Frommer's Gay & Lesbian Europe* (www.frommers.com), an excellent travel resource to the top European cities and resorts; *Spartacus International Gay Guide* (Bruno Gmünder Verlag; www.spartacusworld.com/gayguide) and *Odysseus: The International Gay Travel Planner* (Odysseus Enterprises Ltd.); and the *Damron* guides (www.damron.com), with separate, annual books for gay men and lesbians.

SENIOR TRAVEL

It's a good idea to mention the fact that you're a senior when you first make your travel reservations, because almost all major airlines offer discounts for seniors. In Singapore you'll find very few hotels that offer such discounts; however, virtually every attraction with an entrance fee offers a special discounted rate, and some tour companies will quote you a better rate as well.

Upon request, the STB can also help plan your trip, and can offer its own advice for senior travelers. Regarding this service, here's my advice: If you work out your itinerary with the help of STB, make sure you're firm about time constraints. Many of the tours and daily itineraries are rushed, with little time for a rest here and there. A common complaint is exhaustion by the end of just 1 day. In the heat, this is not only uncomfortable, but dangerous as well.

Members of **AARP** (formerly known as the American Association of Retired Persons), 601 E St. NW, Washington, DC 20049 (© **888/687-2277**; www.aarp. org), get discounts on hotels, airfares, and car rentals. AARP offers members a wide range of benefits, including *AARP: The Magazine* and a monthly newsletter. Anyone over 50 can join.

Many reliable agencies and organizations target the 50-plus market. **Elderhostel** (© **877/426-8056**; www.elder hostel.org) arranges study programs for those aged 55 and over. **ElderTreks** (© **800/741-7956**; www.eldertreks.com) offers small-group tours to off-the-beaten-path or adventure-travel locations, restricted to travelers 50 and older. **INTRAV** (© **800/456-8100**; www.intrav. com) is a high-end tour operator that caters to the mature, discerning traveler (not specifically seniors), with trips around the world that include guided safaris, polar expeditions, private-jet adventures, and small-boat cruises down jungle rivers.

Recommended publications offering travel resources and discounts for seniors include: the quarterly magazine *Travel 50 & Beyond* (www.travel50andbeyond. com); *Travel Unlimited: Uncommon Adventures for the Mature Traveler* (Avalon); *101 Tips for Mature Travelers,* available from Grand Circle Travel (© **800/221-2610** or 617/350-7500; www.gct.com); and *Unbelievably Good Deals and Great Adventures That You Absolutely Can't Get Unless You're Over 50* (McGraw-Hill), by Joann Rattner Heilman.

FAMILY TRAVEL

Because of their focus on business travelers, hotels in Singapore are not especially geared toward children. You can get extra beds in hotel rooms (this can cost anywhere from S$15–S$50/US$9.60–US$32/£4.95–£17), and most hotels will arrange a babysitter for you on request, though most ask for at least 24 hours notice. While almost all hotels have pools to keep the kiddies cool and happy, only two, the YMCA International House and Metro YMCA, have lifeguards on duty, and only one, Shangri-La's Rasa Sentosa Resort, has activity programs specifically for children. See chapter 4 for more information on these hotels.

Children have their own special rates of admission for just about every attraction and museum. The cutoff age for children is usually 12 years of age, but if your kids are older, be sure to ask if the attraction has a student rate for teens. If the kids get edgy during all the "boring" historical and cultural aspects of your trip, the best places to take them are the Singapore Zoo and Night Safari, the Singapore Science Centre, Underwater World on Sentosa, and Escape Theme Park and Wild Wild Wet, all of which are covered in chapter 6. I can almost guarantee that your teen(s) (and you) will have a great time at any of these attractions.

9 Planning Your Trip Online

SURFING FOR AIRFARE

The most popular online travel agencies are **Travelocity** (**www.travelocity.com**, or www.travelocity.co.uk); **Expedia** (**www. expedia.com**, www.expedia.co.uk, or www. expedia.ca); and **Orbitz** (**www.orbitz. com**).

In addition, most airlines now offer online-only fares that even their phone agents know nothing about. For the websites of airlines that fly to and from your destination, go to "Getting There," p. 51.

Other helpful websites for booking airline tickets online include:

- www.biddingfortravel.com
- www.cheapflights.com
- www.hotwire.com
- www.kayak.com
- www.lastminutetravel.com
- www.opodo.co.uk
- www.priceline.com
- www.sidestep.com
- www.site59.com
- www.smartertravel.com

SURFING FOR HOTELS

In addition to **Travelocity, Expedia, Orbitz, Priceline,** and **Hotwire** (see above), the following websites will help you with booking hotel rooms online:

- www.hotels.com
- www.quickbook.com
- www.travelaxe.net
- www.travelweb.com
- www.tripadvisor.com

It's a good idea to **get a confirmation number** and **make a printout** of any online booking transaction.

TRAVEL BLOGS & TRAVELOGUES

Some general travel blogs include:

- www.gridskipper.com
- www.salon.com/wanderlust
- www.travelblog.com
- www.travelblog.org
- www.worldhum.com
- www.writtenroad.com

Frommers.com: The Complete Travel Resource

For an excellent travel-planning resource, we highly recommend **Frommers. com** (www.frommers.com), voted Best Travel Site by *PC Magazine*. We're a little biased, of course, but we guarantee that you'll find the travel tips, reviews, monthly vacation giveaways, bookstore, and online-booking capabilities to be thoroughly indispensable. Special features include our popular **Destinations** section, where you can access expert travel tips, hotel and dining recommendations, and advice on the sights to see in more than 3,500 destinations around the globe; the **Frommers.com Newsletter,** with the latest deals, travel trends, and money-saving secrets; and our **Travel Talk** area featuring **Message Boards,** where Frommer's readers post queries and share advice, and where our authors sometimes show up to answer questions. Once you finish your research, the **Book a Trip** area can lead you to Frommer's preferred online partners' websites, where you can book your vacation at affordable prices.

10 The 21st-Century Traveler

INTERNET ACCESS AWAY FROM HOME

Travelers have any number of ways to check their e-mail and access the Internet on the road. Of course, using your own laptop—or even a PDA (personal digital assistant) or electronic organizer with a modem—gives you the most flexibility. But even if you don't have a computer, you can still access your e-mail and even your office computer from cybercafes.

WITHOUT YOUR OWN COMPUTER

To find cybercafes in your destination check **www.cybercaptive.com** and **www.cybercafe.com**.

Aside from formal cybercafes, most **backpacker guesthouses** have Internet access. Avoid **hotel business centers** unless you're willing to pay exorbitant rates.

Most major airports now have **Internet kiosks** scattered throughout their gates. These give you basic Web access for a per-minute fee that's usually higher than cybercafe prices.

WITH YOUR OWN COMPUTER

In December 2006, the Infocomm Development Authority of Singapore (IDA) began a campaign of Wi-Fi (wireless fidelity) Internet access island-wide free of charge to Singaporeans and international visitors. It offers the service at about 250 locations, including cafes and restaurants, commercial buildings and libraries, some hotels and tourist attractions, plus shopping centers in an effort to push Singapore to new, competitive, info-com heights. Log on to www.ida.gov.sg to find out how to register and to find out which locations are included in the service.

In addition, more and more hotels, cafes, and retailers are signing on as Wi-Fi "hotspots." To locate other hotspots that provide **free wireless networks** in cities around the world, go to **www.personaltelco.net/index.cgi/WirelessCommunities**.

For dial-up access, virtually all business-class hotels in Singapore have in-room dataports with high-speed Internet access for laptop modems. In addition, major Internet Service Providers (ISPs) have **local access numbers** around the world, allowing you to go online by placing a local call. The **iPass** network also has dial-up numbers around the world. You'll have to sign up with an iPass provider, who will then tell you how to set up your computer for your destination(s). For a list of iPass providers, go to www.ipass.com and click on "Individuals Buy Now." One solid provider is **i2roam** (www.i2roam.com; ✆ **866/811-6209** or 920/235-0475).

While your laptop can adjust to the local 220-volt currency, you may need a plug adaptor. These and phone cords can be obtained from most hotel business centers or concierges, free of charge.

CELLPHONE USE

The three letters that define much of the world's wireless capabilities are GSM (Global System for Mobiles), a big, seamless network that makes for easy cross-border cellphone use throughout Europe and dozens of other countries worldwide. In the U.S., T-Mobile, AT&T Wireless, and Cingular use this quasi-universal system; in Canada, Microcell and some Rogers customers are GSM, and all Europeans and most Australians use GSM. If your cellphone is on a GSM system, and you have a world-capable multiband phone such as many Sony Ericsson, Motorola, or Samsung models, you can make and receive calls across civilized areas around much of the globe. Just call your wireless operator and ask for "international roaming" to be activated on your

Online Traveler's Toolbox

Veteran travelers usually carry some essential items to make their trips easier. Following is a selection of online tools to bookmark and use.

- **Cybercafes.com** (www.cybercafes.com) or **Net Café Guide** (www.netcafe guide.com/mapindex.htm). Locate Internet cafes at hundreds of locations around the globe. Catch up on your e-mail and log onto the web for a few dollars per hour.

- **Foreign Languages for Travelers** (www.travlang.com). Learn basic terms in more than 70 languages and click on any underlined phrase to hear what it sounds like. *Note:* Free audio software and speakers are required.

- **Intellicast** (www.intellicast.com) and **Weather.com** (www.weather.com). Check weather forecasts for all 50 states and for cities around the world.

- **Mapquest** (www.mapquest.com). This best of the mapping sites lets you choose a specific address or destination, and in seconds, it will return a map and detailed directions.

- **Universal Currency Converter** (www.xe.net/currency). See what your dollar or pound is worth in more than 100 other countries.

- **U.S. State Department Travel Warnings** (www.travel.state.gov). Read reports on places where health concerns or unrest might threaten U.S. travelers. It also lists the locations of U.S. embassies around the world.

- Check out **Visa ATM Locator** (www.visa.com) for locations of Plus ATMs worldwide, or **MasterCard ATM Locator** (www.mastercard.com) for locations of Cirrus ATMs worldwide.

account. Unfortunately, per-minute charges can be high—usually $1 to $1.50 in western Europe and up to $5 in places like Russia and Indonesia.

In Singapore, SingTel (http://home. singtel.com) has special offers for visitors, with options to either subscribe for monthly fees that range from S$20 (US$13/£6.60) to S$197 (US$126/£65), depending on your usage package, or to buy a prepaid SIM card that just deducts value as you use it. You can use these services with your own cellular phone, or you can purchase a new phone here cheaply, with simple handsets going for under S$100 (US$64/£33). An interesting note: A local calls his cellular phone his *handphone.*

11 Getting There

BY PLANE

If you're hunting for the best airfare, there are a few things you can do. First, plan your trip for the low-volume season, which runs from September 1 to November 30. Between January 1 and May 31, you'll pay the highest fares. Plan your travel on weekdays only, and, if you can, plan to stay for at least a full week. Book your reservations in advance—waiting until the last minute can mean you'll pay sky-high rates. Also, if you have access to the Internet, there are a number of great sites that'll search out decent fares for you.

In my experience, the best deals are offered through Asian carriers. Compare fares at Japan Airlines (www.jal.co.jp), Korean Air (www.koreanair.com), Cathay Pacific Airways (www.cathaypacific.com), Malaysia Airlines (www.malaysiaairlines. com), and Thai Airways International (www.thaiair.com). Otherwise, I've listed information for a few major airlines below.

Singapore's national carrier, **Singapore Airlines** (© **800/742-3333** in the U.S. and Canada, © 0870/608-8886 in the U.K., © 131011 in Australia, © 0800/ 808-909 in New Zealand, or © 65/6223-8888 in Singapore; www.singaporeair. com), is arguably one of the finest airlines in the world, with reliable service that is second to none. It's the most luxurious way to fly to Singapore, but the most expensive as well. They connect major cities in North America, Europe, Australia, and New Zealand to Singapore with daily flights.

From North America, **United Airlines** (© **800/241-6522** in the U.S. or 65/ 6873-3533 in Singapore; www.ual.com) and **Northwest Airlines** (© **800/447-4747** in the U.S. or 65/6336-3371 in Singapore; www.nwa.com) link all major destinations in the U.S. with Singapore.

From the U.K. and Australia, **British Airways** and **Qantas** collaborate to provide flights to Asia Pacific from major cities in the U.K. and Australia. (British Airways: © **0870/850-9850** in the U.K., © 1300/767-177 in Australia, or © 65/ 6589-7000 in Singapore; www.british airways.com. Qantas: © **0845/774-7767** in the U.K., © 131313 in Australia, or © 65/6589-7000 in Singapore; www. qantas.com.)

From New Zealand, **Air New Zealand** (© **0800/737-000** in New Zealand or © 65/6535-8266 in Singapore; www. airnewzealand.co.nz) has daily flights from Auckland and Christchurch.

GETTING INTO TOWN FROM THE AIRPORT

Most visitors to Singapore will land at Changi International Airport, which is located toward the far eastern corner of the island. Compared to other international airports, Changi is a dream come true, providing clean and very efficient space and facilities. Expect to find intransit accommodations, restaurants, duty-free shops, money-changers, ATMs, car-rental desks, accommodations assistance, and tourist information all marked in English with clear signs. When you arrive, keep your eyes peeled for the many Singapore Tourism Board brochures that are so handily displayed throughout the terminal.

The city is easily accessible by public transportation. A taxi trip to the city center will cost around S$22 to S$25 (US$14–US$16/£7.25–£8.25), which is the metered fare plus an airport surcharge, usually S$3 to S$5 (US$1.90–US$3.20/£1–£1.65) depending on the time of pickup. It takes around 20 minutes to reach the city; double it if you're traveling during weekday rush hours. You'll traverse the wide Airport Boulevard to the Pan-Island Expressway (PIE) or the East Coast Parkway (ECP), past public housing estates and other residential neighborhoods in the eastern part of the island, over causeways, and into the city center.

If you've got a lot of people and luggage, **CityCab** offers a six-seater maxicab to anywhere in the city for a flat rate of S$35 (US$22/£12). You can inquire at the taxi queue or call © **65/6542-8297.**

There's an **airport shuttle,** a six-seater maxicab that traverses between the airport, all major hotels, plus stops at Orchard Road, Chinatown, and Bugis Junction. A booking counter at both terminals is open daily from 6am to 2am. When you book your trip into town, you can also make an advanced reservation for your departure. Pay S$7 (US$4.50/ £2.30) for adults or S$5 (US$3.20/ £1.65) for children directly to the driver, but try not to pay with bills that are $50

(Tips) Getting Through the Airport

- Arrive at the airport 1 hour before a domestic flight and 2 hours before an international flight; if you show up late, tell an airline employee and he or she will probably whisk you to the front of the line.
- Beat the ticket-counter lines by using airport electronic kiosks or even online check-in from your home computer, from where you can print out boarding passes in advance. Curbside check-in is also a good way to avoid lines.
- Bring a current, government-issued photo ID such as a driver's license or passport. Children under 18 do not need government-issued photo IDs for flights within the U.S., but they do for international flights to most countries.
- Speed up security by removing your jacket and shoes before you're screened. In addition, remove metal objects such as big belt buckles. If you've got metallic body parts, a note from your doctor can prevent a long chat with the security screeners.
- Use a TSA-approved lock for your checked luggage. Look for Travel Sentry certified locks at luggage or travel shops and Brookstone stores (or online at www.brookstone.com).

or larger. Call the counter at © **65/6542-8297.**

The **MRT,** Singapore's subway system (see map, inside back cover), now operates to the airport, linking you with the city and areas beyond. STB will tell you the trip takes 30 minutes, but really, give yourself at least an hour, because you'll need time to wait for the train to arrive, then you'll have to transfer trains at Tanah Merah station, and if you're arriving in Terminal 1, you'll need to hop on yet another train—a shuttle between terminals. After you get to your station in town, you'll still have to find your way, with your luggage, to your hotel. Personally, I think it's a pain in the neck, but hey, it only costs S$1.40 (US90¢/45p) to get to City Hall station. Trains operate roughly from 6am to midnight daily.

A couple of **buses** run from the airport into the city as well. SBS bus no. 36 is the best, saving time by hopping on East Coast Parkway before making stops

through the Historic District and along Orchard Road. Pick up the bus in the basement of either terminal. The trip will take over an hour, and you'll need to get exact change before you board. A trip to town will be roughly S$1.40 (US90¢/45p).

For arrival and departure information, you can call **Changi International Airport** at © **65/6542-4422.**

FLYING FOR LESS: TIPS FOR GETTING THE BEST AIRFARE

- Passengers who can book their ticket either **long in advance or at the last minute,** or who **fly midweek** or **at less-trafficked hours** may pay a fraction of the full fare. If your schedule is flexible, say so, and ask if you can secure a cheaper fare by changing your flight plans.
- Search **the Internet** for cheap fares (see "Planning Your Trip Online," earlier in this chapter).

- Keep an eye on local newspapers for **promotional specials** or **fare wars,** when airlines lower prices on their most popular routes. You rarely see fare wars offered for peak travel times, but if you can travel in the off-months, you may snag a bargain.

- Try to book a ticket **in its country of origin.** If you're planning a one-way flight from Johannesburg to Bombay, a South Africa–based travel agent will probably have the lowest fares. For multi-leg trips, book in the country of the first leg; for example, book New York–London–Amsterdam–Rome–New York in the U.S. The best agency I've found for terrific deals on flights throughout Asia and Southeast Asia is **Misa Travel,** Blk. 531A Upper Cross St., #03-106, © **65/6538-0318;** www.airfares.com.sg.) They've got great deals, so check their website regularly.

- **Consolidators,** also known as bucket shops, are great sources for international tickets, although they usually can't beat Internet fares within North America. Start by looking in Sunday newspaper travel sections; U.S. travelers should focus on the *New York Times, Los Angeles Times,* and *Miami Herald.* U.K. travelers should search in the *Independent, The Guardian,* or *The Observer.* For less-developed destinations, small travel agents who cater to immigrant communities in large cities often have the best deals. *Beware:* Bucket shop tickets are usually nonrefundable or rigged with stiff cancellation penalties, often as high as 50% to 75% of the ticket price, and some put you on charter airlines, which may leave at inconvenient times and experience delays. Several reliable consolidators are worldwide and available online. **STA Travel** has been the world's lead consolidator for students since purchasing Council Travel, but their fares are competitive for travelers of all ages. **ELTExpress** (**Flights.com;** © **800/TRAV-800;** www.eltexpress.com) has excellent fares worldwide, particularly to Europe. They also have "local" websites in 12 countries. **FlyCheap** (© **800/FLY-CHEAP;** www.1800flycheap.com), owned by package-holiday megalith MyTravel, has especially good fares to sunny destinations. **Air Tickets Direct** (© **800/778-3447;** www.air ticketsdirect.com) is based in Montreal and leverages the currently weak Canadian dollar for low fares; they also book trips to places that U.S. travel agents won't touch, such as Cuba.

- Join **frequent-flier clubs.** Frequent-flier membership doesn't cost a cent, but it does entitle you to better seats, faster response to phone inquiries, and prompter service if your luggage is stolen or your flight is canceled or delayed, or if you want to change your seat. And you don't have to fly to earn points; **frequent-flier credit cards** can earn you thousands of miles for doing your everyday shopping. With more than 70 mileage awards programs on the market, consumers have never had more options. Investigate the program details of your favorite airlines before you sink points into any one. Consider which airlines have hubs in the airport nearest you, and, of those carriers, which have the most advantageous alliances, given your most common routes. To play the frequent-flier game to your best advantage, consult Randy Petersen's **Inside Flyer** (www.inside flyer.com). Petersen and friends review all the programs in detail and post regular updates on changes in policies and trends.

LONG-HAUL FLIGHTS: HOW TO STAY COMFORTABLE

- Your choice of airline and airplane will definitely affect your leg room. Find more details about U.S. airlines at **www.seatguru.com**. For international airlines, the research firm Skytrax has posted a list of average seat pitches at **www.airlinequality.com**.

- Emergency exit seats and bulkhead seats typically have the most legroom. Emergency exit seats are usually left unassigned until the day of a flight (to ensure that someone able-bodied fills the seats); it's worth getting to the ticket counter early to snag one of these spots for a long flight. Many passengers find that bulkhead seating (the row facing the wall at the front of the cabin) offers more legroom, but keep in mind that bulkheads are where airlines often put baby bassinets, so you may be sitting next to an infant.

- To have two seats for yourself in a three-seat row, try for an aisle seat in a center section toward the back of coach. If you're traveling with a companion, book an aisle and a window seat. Middle seats are usually booked last, so chances are good you'll end up with three seats to yourselves.

- Ask about entertainment options. Many airlines offer seatback video systems where you get to choose your movies or play video games—but only on some of their planes. (Boeing 777s are your best bet.)

- To sleep, avoid the last row of any section or the row in front of an emergency exit, as these seats are the least likely to recline. Avoid seats near highly trafficked toilet areas. Avoid seats in the back of many jets—these can be narrower than those in the rest of coach. You also may want to reserve a window seat so you can rest your head and avoid being bumped in the aisle.

- Get up, walk around, and stretch every 60 to 90 minutes to keep your blood flowing. See the box "Avoiding 'Economy-Class Syndrome,'" under "Health & Safety," p. 45.

- Drink water before, during, and after your flight to combat the lack of humidity in airplane cabins. Avoid alcohol, which will dehydrate you.

- If you're flying with kids, don't forget to carry on toys, books, pacifiers, and chewing gum to help them relieve ear pressure buildup during ascent and descent.

BY TRAIN

While most visitors to Singapore will arrive by air, some will come via train from Malaysia. The Keretapi Tanah Melayu (KTM) operates a rail system that connects Singapore all the way up the Malay peninsula, with stops in Kuala Lumpur, Penang, and even connections to service in Thailand to Bangkok. Train passengers will stop for immigration at the checkpoint at Woodlands, just across the strait from Malaysia, but will not alight until they reach the **Singapore Railway Station** on Keppel Road (⟁ 65/ 6222-5165), not far from Singapore's Shenton Way downtown financial district. Taxis to most major hotels will cost under S$10 (US$6.40/£3.30).

For train information from Kuala Lumpur call the **Sentral Railway Stesen** at ⟁ 03/2267-1200. In Bangkok call the **Hua Lamphong Railway Station** at ⟁ 622/223-7010.

BY BUS

Buses from Malaysia will drop off passengers at any number of points around the city, depending on the bus operator—there is no proper inbound bus station. For bus service from major Malaysian cities, refer to bus listings in each section. Operators will be able to tell you where you will be dropped off.

12 Packages for the Independent Traveler

Package tours are simply a way to buy the airfare, accommodations, and other elements of your trip (such as car rentals, airport transfers, and sometimes even activities) at the same time and often at discounted prices.

One good source of package deals is the airlines themselves. Most major airlines offer air/land packages, including **American Airlines Vacations** (© 800/321-2121; www.aavacations.com), **Delta Vacations** (© 800/221-6666; www.deltavacations.com), **Continental Airlines Vacations** (© 800/301-3800; www.covacations.com), and **United Vacations** (© 888/854-3899; www.unitedvacations.com). Several big **online travel agencies**—Expedia, Travelocity, Orbitz, Site59, and Lastminute.com—also do a brisk business in packages.

Because Singapore is compact and efficient and most people speak English, few travelers feel the need for a travel operator to hold their hand during their stay. Still, package tour operators can get you the best deals on travel and hotel stays. One company I recommend is **Absolute Asia** (15 Watts St., 5th Floor, New York, NY 10013; © **800/736-8187;** fax 212/627-4090; www.absoluteasia.com) with packages that give you plenty of free time to explore on your own and innovative itineraries that combine Singapore with one or more if its Southeast Asian neighbors. **Asia Transpacific Journeys** (2995 Center Green Court, Boulder, CO 80301; © **800/642-2742;** fax 303/443-7078; www.southeastasia.com) is another great operator, specializing in customized tours with particular attention to cultural and ecological sensitivity.

Travel packages are also listed in the travel section of your local Sunday newspaper. Or check ads in the national travel magazines such as *Arthur Frommer's Budget Travel Magazine, Travel + Leisure, National Geographic Traveler,* and *Condé Nast Traveler.*

(*Tips* **Ask Before You Go**

Before you invest in a package deal or an escorted tour:

- Always ask about the **cancellation policy.** Can you get your money back? Is there a deposit required?
- Ask about the **accommodations choices and prices** for each. Then look up the hotels' reviews in a Frommer's guide and check their rates online for your specific dates of travel. Also find out what types of rooms are offered.
- Request a complete **schedule.** (Escorted tours only.)
- Ask about the **size** and demographics of the group. (Escorted tours only.)
- Discuss what is included in the **price** (transportation, meals, tips, airport transfers, and so on). (Escorted tours only.)
- Finally, look for **hidden expenses.** Ask whether airport departure fees and taxes, for example, are included in the total cost—they rarely are.

13 Getting Around Singapore

The many inexpensive mass transit options make getting around Singapore pretty easy. Of course, taxis always simplify the ground transportation dilemma. They're also very affordable and, by and large, drivers are helpful and honest if not downright personable. The **Mass Rapid Transit (MRT) subway service** has lines that cover the main areas of the city and out to the farther parts of the island. Buses present more of a challenge because there are so many routes snaking all over the island, but they're a great way to see the country while getting where you want to go.

Of course, if you're just strolling around the urban limits, many of the sights within the various neighborhoods are within walking distance, but walking between the different neighborhoods can be a hike, especially in the heat. The STB Visitors' Centres carry a variety of free city maps and walking tour maps of individual neighborhoods to help you find your way around.

Stored-value EZ-Link fare cards can be used on both the subway and buses, and can be purchased at TransitLink offices in MRT stations. These save you the bother of trying to dig up exact change for bus meters. The card does carry a S$5 (US$3.20/£1.65) deposit—for a S$15 (US$9.60/£4.95) initial investment, you'll get S$10 (US$6.40/£3.30) worth of travel credit.

When you pick up your EZ-Link card, I recommend purchasing the latest edition of the *TransitLink Guide* for about S$3.90 (US$2.50/£1.30) at the TransitLink office where you buy your card. This tiny book details both MRT and bus routes with maps of each MRT station surroundings, and it indicates connections between buses and MRT stations. It also tells you fares for each trip.

BY TAXI

Taxis are by far the most convenient way to get around Singapore. Fares are cheap, cars are clean, and drivers speak English. Taxi queues can be found at every hotel, shopping mall, and public building; otherwise you can flag one down from the side of the road. Most destinations in the main parts of the island can be reached fairly inexpensively, while trips to the outlying attractions can cost from S$10 to S$15 (US$6.40–US$9.60/£3.30–£4.95) one-way. That said, I caution against becoming too dependent on them. During the morning and evening rush you can wait a maddeningly long time in the queue, and sometimes if you're at a destination outside the main city area, they're few and far between. If it's raining, you might as well stay put; you'll never get a cab.

If you do find yourself stranded, there are a few things you can do. If you're at an attraction or a restaurant, you can ask the cashier or help desk to call a taxi company and book a cab for you. If you're near a phone, you can make your own booking: **CityCab** (© **65/6552-2222**), **Comfort** (© **65/6552-1111**), and **TIBS** (© **65/6555-8888**). There's an extra charge for the booking: for CityCab it's S$3 (US$1.90/£1), Comfort S$3.20 (US$2.05/£1.05) and TIBS S$2.80 (US$1.80/90p).

Taxis charge the metered fare, which is S$2.50 (US$1.60/80p) for the first kilometer (⁹⁄₁₀ mile) and S10¢ (US5¢/3p) for each additional 175 to 210m (575–690 ft.) or 25 seconds of waiting. Extra fares are levied on top of the metered fare depending on where you're going and when you go. At times, figuring your fare seems more like a riddle. Here's a summary:

Trips during peak hours: Between the hours of 7 and 9:30am Monday to

Friday, and 5 and 8pm Monday to Saturday, trips will carry an additional S$2 (US$1.30/66p) peak-period surcharge. If you're traveling within the Central Business District (CBD), you also pay an additional S$1 (US60¢/30p) surcharge. (To accurately outline the boundaries of the CBD, I'd need to fill a couple of encyclopedic volumes, so for this purpose, let's just say it's basically Orchard Rd., the Historic District, Chinatown, and Shenton Way.)

Additional charges rack up each time you travel through an Electronic Road Pricing (ERP) scheme underpass. On the Central Expressway (CTE), Pan-Island Expressway (PIE), and selected thoroughfares in the CBD, charges from S30¢ to S$1.10 (US20¢–US$1/10p–35p) are calculated by an electronic box on the driver's dashboard. The driver will add this amount to your fare.

And for special torture, here are some more charges: From midnight to 6am, add 50% to your fare. From 6pm on the eve of a public holiday to midnight the following day, you pay an additional S$1 (US60¢/35p). From Changi Airport add S$5 (US$3.20/£1.65) if you're traveling Fridays, Saturdays, or Sundays between 5pm and midnight. Other times, it's S$3 (US$1.90/£1). And for credit card payments (yes, they take plastic!) add 10%.

BY MASS RAPID TRANSIT (MRT)

The MRT is Singapore's subway system. It's cool, clean, safe, and reliable, providing service around the central parts of the city, extending into the suburbs around the island. There are stops along Orchard Road into the Historic District, to Chinatown and Little India—chances are there will be a stop close to your hotel (see the map on the inside back cover for specifics).

Fares range from S80¢ to S$1.80 (US50¢–US$1.20/25p–60p), depending on which stations you travel between. System charts are prominently displayed in all MRT stations to help you find your appropriate fare, which you pay with an EZ-Link fare card. Single-fare cards can be purchased at vending machines inside MRT stations. See above for information on stored-fare cards for multiple trips. (**One caution:** A fare card cannot be used by two people for the same trip; each must have his own.)

MRT operating hours vary between lines and stops, with the earliest train beginning service daily at 5:15am and the last train ending at 12:47am. For more information, call the **TransitLink Hot Line** at ✆ **1800-767-4333** (daily 24 hr.).

BY BUS

Singapore's bus system comprises an extensive web of routes that reach virtually everywhere on the island. It can be intimidating for newcomers, but after you get your feet wet, you'll feel right at home. Start off by purchasing an EZ-Link stored value card, so you can pay for your trips, and TransitLink Guide, so you can find your way around (see above for more details). All buses have a gray machine with a sensor pad close to the driver. Tap your EZ-Link card when you board and alight, and the fare will be automatically deducted. It'll be anywhere between S80¢ and S$1.80 (US50¢– US$1.20/25p–60p). If you're paying cash, be sure to have exact change; place the coins in the red box by the driver and announce your fare to him. He'll issue a ticket, which will pop out of a slot on one of the TransitLink machines behind him.

For more information, contact either of the two operating bus lines during standard business hours: **Singapore Bus Service (SBS;** ✆ **1800-287-2727)** or **the Trans-Island Bus Service (TIBS;** ✆ **1800-482-5433)**.

BY TROLLEY

You have a couple of trolley options; both services are offered for the convenience of travelers, making stops at most major tourist destinations. The **Singapore Explorer** (© **65/6339-6833**) shuttles down Orchard Road, through the Historic District, over the Singapore River, and down to Marina Square. For S$9 (US$5.80/£2.95) adults and S$7 (US$4.50/£2.30) children, you can enjoy unlimited rides for 1 day. Buy your tickets either from your hotel's front desk or directly from the driver.

Singapore Airlines hosts the **SIA Hop-on bus.** Plying between Suntec City, the Historic District, the Singapore River, Chinatown, Orchard Road and the Singapore Botanic Gardens, Little India, and Sentosa, the Hop-on comes every 30 minutes between the hours of 9am and 7:30pm. Unlimited rides for 1 day cost S$12 (US$7.70/£3.95) adults and S$6 (US$3.80/£2) children. If you flew Singapore Airlines to get here, you only have to pay S$3 (US$1.90/£1) if you flash your boarding pass. Buy your tickets from your hotel's front desk, from a Singapore Airlines office, or from the bus drivers. For info, call **SH Tours** © **65/6374-9923.**

BY RENTAL CAR

Visitors to Singapore rarely rent cars for sightseeing. Why? Because they cost a bomb. At Avis, the lowest priced compact car rents for S$260 per day; about US$153/£86. Compare that to the rental of the same compact car out of the Avis office at New York's JFK airport—a steal at US$76/£39 per day! Same thing for the U.K., where rental of a compact car from Heathrow would set you back only US$75/£39.

Bottom line is it's just not worth it. Local transportation is excellent and affordable, you don't have to worry about adjusting to local driving rules and habits, plus you don't have to worry about where to park. Still, if you must, contact **Avis** at Changi Airport, Arrival Hall, Terminal 2 (© **65/6542-8855;** daily 7am–11pm).

14 Tips on Accommodations

SAVING ON YOUR HOTEL ROOM

Singapore hotels overlook the leisure market for the more lucrative corporate-travel one, which means that most hotels offer services and facilities aimed at busy working executives—club room facilities, business centers, fitness centers, rooms with big desks and Internet access—all at a cost. Most leisure travelers will be out and about, seeing the sights, and will never use most of the facilities a hotel has to offer. If this sounds like you, I'd recommend staying in a small but cheap boutique hotel rather than a big-name international chain hotel. However, if a luxury room is a big part of your ideal vacation, then Singapore has plenty of options to pamper you—for a price.

The **rack rate** is the maximum rate that a hotel charges for a room. Hardly anybody pays this price, however, except in high season or on holidays. To lower the cost of your room:

- **Ask about special rates or other discounts.** You may qualify for corporate, student, military, senior, frequent flyer, trade union, or other discounts.
- **Dial direct.** When booking a room in a chain hotel, you'll often get a better deal by calling the individual hotel's reservation desk rather than the chain's main number.
- **Book online.** Many hotels offer Internet-only discounts, or supply rooms to Priceline, Hotwire, or Expedia at rates much lower than the ones you can get through the hotel itself.
- **Remember the law of supply and demand.** Resort hotels are most crowded and therefore most expensive

---

Tips **Dial E for Easy**

For quick directions on how to call Singapore, see the "Telephones" listing in the "Fast Facts: Singapore" section at the end of this chapter.

---

on weekends, so discounts are usually available for midweek stays. Business hotels in downtown locations are busiest during the week, so you can expect big discounts over the weekend. Many hotels have high-season and low-season prices, and booking even 1 day after high season ends can mean big discounts.

- **Look into group or long-stay discounts.** If you come as part of a large group, you should be able to negotiate a bargain rate. Likewise, if you're planning a long stay (at least 5 days), you might qualify for a discount. As a general rule, expect 1 night free after a 7-night stay.
- **Avoid excess charges and hidden costs.** When you book a room, ask whether the hotel charges for parking. Use your own cellphone, pay phones, or prepaid phone cards instead of dialing direct from hotel phones, which usually have exorbitant rates. And don't be tempted by the room's minibar offerings. Finally, ask about local taxes and service charges, which can increase the cost of a room by 15% or more.
- **Consider enrolling in hotel "frequent-stay" programs,** which are upping the ante lately to win the loyalty of repeat customers. Frequent guests can now accumulate points or credits to earn free hotel nights, airline miles, in-room amenities, merchandise, tickets to concerts and events, discounts on sporting facilities—and even credit toward stock in the participating hotel, in the case of the Jameson Inn hotel group. Perks are awarded not only by many chain

hotels and motels (Hilton HHonors, Marriott Rewards, Wyndham By-Request, to name a few), but individual inns and B&Bs. Many chain hotels partner with other hotel chains, car-rental firms, airlines, and credit card companies to give consumers additional incentive to do repeat business.

- **Consider a serviced apartment.** If you are planning to stay for a long time, check out the Ascott (www. the-ascott.com) or Frasiers (www. frasiershospitality.com) for apartments that have facilities and services similar to a hotel.

LANDING THE BEST ROOM

Somebody has to get the best room in the house. It might as well be you. You can start by joining the hotel's frequent-guest program, which may make you eligible for upgrades. A hotel-branded credit card usually gives its owner "silver" or "gold" status in frequent-guest programs for free. Always ask about a corner room. They're often larger and quieter, with more windows and light, and they often cost the same as standard rooms. When you make your reservation, ask if the hotel is renovating; if it is, request a room away from the construction. Ask about nonsmoking rooms, rooms with views, rooms with twin, queen- or king-size beds. If you're a light sleeper, request a quiet room away from vending machines, elevators, restaurants, bars, and discos. Ask for a room that has been most recently renovated or redecorated.

If you aren't happy with your room when you arrive, ask for another one. Most lodgings will be willing to accommodate you.

15 Recommended Books

If you're having trouble finding books about Singapore in bookstores where you live, I suggest you wait until you arrive, then browse local shelves, where you'll find tons of books about the country, its history, culture, arts, food, and local fiction. For interesting and informative reads that you can find (or order) through your neighborhood bookstore, here's a good place to start:

From Third World to First: The Singapore Story: 1965–2000 by Lee Kuan Yew (HarperCollins) details the history and policies behind Singapore's remarkable economic success written by the man who was at the helm.

The Singapore Story: Memoirs of Lee Kuan Yew by Lee Kuan Yew (Prentice Hall). An intimate account of Minister Mentor Lee's personal journey, this book will give insight into one of the world's most talked-about leaders.

Crossroads: A Popular History of Malaysia & Singapore by Jim Baker (Times Books International). A readable history of Singapore and Malaysia from a longtime resident and expert.

The Singapore Grip by J. G Farrell (Knopf). A highly enjoyable work of historical fiction written by a Booker Prize winner takes you back to Singapore on the brink of World War II to examine the last days of the British Empire.

West from Singapore by Louis L'Amour (Bantam). Few knew that Mr. L'Amour was a Merchant Marine in Southeast Asia. In this novel he creates his brand of fascinating American West storytelling, only this tale takes place in the waters around pre–World War II Singapore.

16 Etiquette & Customs

While in Singapore, try to use only your right hand in social interaction. Why? Because in Indian and Muslim society, the left hand is used only for bathroom chores. Not only should you eat with your right hand and give and receive all gifts with your right hand, but you should make sure all gestures, especially pointing (and especially in temples and mosques), are made with your right hand. By the way, you should also try to point with your knuckle rather than your finger, to be more polite.

The other important etiquette tip is to remember to remove your shoes before entering places of worship (except for churches and synagogues) and all private residences.

In cosmopolitan Singapore, most people will shake hands in greeting, but it's good to remember that Muslim women are not allowed to touch men to whom they are not related by blood or marriage.

Unless they initiate a handshake, a simple smile and nod is fine.

Also, it's common for Singaporeans to exchange business cards. Always receive cards with two hands and always treat the card with respect—don't stash it in your pocket without paying attention to it. The business card is an extension of a person's identity and status.

If you're touring around during the day, shorts and a T-shirt are fine; however, if you plan to enter a temple or mosque, you will be required to cover your legs and upper arms. I usually carry a sarong in my bag to tie around my waist in a pinch. I also recommend slip-on shoes, so you can take them on and off easily when entering places of religious worship. If you're dining in a restaurant or attending an event or business function, the local dress code is "smart casual," meaning slacks and pressed shirt for men and either slacks or skirt with a top for women, or a dress. For most business meetings a suit and tie is still necessary, but you needn't wear your jacket everywhere. For women, business suits are also expected.

If you would like to give a gift to a Singaporean, my advice is to consult your hotel concierge for appropriate gift recommendations. For example, avoid giving sweets or foods to Muslim friends, unless you are certain the gift is *halal*.

For the Chinese, it's more tricky. Gifts should never be knives, clocks, or handkerchiefs, and don't send anybody white flowers. (The sharp blades of knives symbolize the severing of a friendship; in Cantonese, the word for clock sounds the same as the word for funeral; handkerchiefs bring to mind tears and sadness; and white

is the color of funeral mourning—you get the drift.)

The main rules regarding table manners revolve around the use of chopsticks. Don't stick them upright in any dish, don't gesture with them, and don't suck on them. Dropped chopsticks are also considered bad luck. Southern Indian food can be eaten by hand, but make sure you wash your hands first and always use your right hand.

For more information, check out *The Global Etiquette Guide to Asia,* by Dean Foster (Wiley Publishing, Inc.); *Kiss, Bow or Shake Hands: How to Do Business in 60 Countries,* by Terri Morrison (Adams Media); and *Culture Shock! Singapore* by Joann Craig (Graphic Arts Center Publishing Co.)

FAST FACTS: **Singapore**

American Express The American Express office is located at 300 Beach Rd., #18-01 The Concourse (① 65/6880-1333). It's open Monday to Friday 9am to 5pm and Saturday 9am to 1pm. There's a more convenient kiosk that handles traveler's checks and simple card transactions (including emergency check guarantee) on Orchard Road just outside the Marriott Hotel at Tangs (① 65/6735-2069). It's open daily from 9am to 9pm. An additional foreign exchange office is open at Changi Airport Terminal 2 (① 65/6546-5456). It's open from noon to midnight daily. See the "Money" section earlier in this chapter for more on member privileges.

ATM Networks See "Money," p. 34.

Business Hours Shopping centers are open Monday through Saturday from 10am to 9pm and stay open until 10pm on some public holidays. Banks are open from 9:30am to 3pm Monday through Friday and from 9 to 11am on Saturday. Restaurants open at lunchtime from around 11am to 2:30pm, and for dinner they reopen at around 6pm and take the last order sometime around 10pm. Government offices are open from 9am to 5pm Monday through Friday and from 9am to 1pm on Saturdays. Post offices conduct business from 8:30am to 5pm on weekdays and from 8:30am to 1pm on Saturday.

Cashpoints See "Money," p. 34.

Climate See "When to Go," p. 37.

Currency See "Money," p. 34.

Drugstores Guardian Pharmacies fills prescriptions with name-brand drugs (from a licensed physician within Singapore) and carries a large selection of toiletries. Convenient locations include #B1-05 Centrepoint Shopping Centre (© 65/6737-4835), Changi International Airport Terminal 2 (© 65/6545-4233), #02-139 Marina Sq. (© 65/6333-9565), and #B1-04 Raffles Place MRT Station (© 65/6535-2762).

Electricity Standard electrical current is 220 volts AC (50 cycles). Local electrical outlets are made for plugs with three square prongs. Consult your concierge to see if your hotel has converters and plug adapters in-house for you to use. If you are using sensitive equipment, do not trust cheap voltage transformers. Nowadays, a lot of electrical equipment—including portable radios and laptop computers—comes with built-in converters, so you can follow the manufacturer's directions for changing them over. FYI, videocassettes taped on different voltage currents are recorded on machines with different record and playback cycles. Prerecorded videotapes are not interchangeable between currents unless you have special equipment that can play either kind.

Embassies & Consulates Contacts for major embassies in Singapore are as follows: U.S. Embassy, 27 Napier Rd. (© **65/6476-9100**); Canadian Embassy, 80 Anson Rd. (© **65/6325-3240**); U.K. Embassy, Tanglin Road (© **65/6473-9333**); Australian Embassy, 391A Orchard Rd., Ngee Ann City Tower A, #15–06 (© **65/6836-4100**).

Emergencies For **police** dial © **999**. For **medical** or **fire** emergencies call © **995**.

Holidays See the "Calendar of Public Holidays & Events," p. 38.

Hospitals If you require hospitalization, the centrally located Mount Elizabeth Hospital is near Orchard Road at 3 Mount Elizabeth (© **65/6737-2666**); for accidents and emergencies call (© **65/6731-2218**). You can also try Singapore General Hospital, Outram Road (© **65/6222-3322**); for accidents and emergencies call (© **65/6321-4311**).

Information See "Visitor Information," p. 30.

Internet Access Internet cafes are becoming common throughout the city, with usage costs about S$5 (US$3.20/£1.65) per hour (keep in mind, if you use the Internet in your hotel's business center, you'll pay a much higher price). Almost every shopping mall has one, especially along Orchard Road, and there are cybercafes in both terminals at Changi Airport. In the Historic District, there are a few in Stamford House, just across from City Hall MRT Station. Check out Chills Café, #01–07 Stamford House, 39 Stamford Rd. (© 65/6883-1016; open 9am–midnight daily).

Language Singapore's four official languages are Malay, Chinese (Mandarin dialect), Tamil, and English. Malay is the national language while English is the language for government operations, law, and major financial transactions. Most Singaporeans are at least bilingual, with many speaking one or more dialects of Chinese, English, and some Malay.

Liquor Laws The legal age for alcohol purchase and consumption is 18 years—clubs rarely check foreigners. Bars and pubs will usually open in the afternoon and stay open until 1am on weeknights or until 2am on Fridays and Saturdays. Nightclubs and discos will open about 8pm and will stay open until 2am on weekdays or 3am on Fridays and Saturdays. Unless you come from New York,

London, or Tokyo, alcohol can be very expensive here in comparison because of heavy "sin taxes."

Lost & Found Be sure to tell all of your credit card companies the minute you discover your wallet has been lost or stolen and file a report at the nearest police precinct. Your credit card company or insurer may require a police report number or record of the loss. Most credit card companies have an emergency toll-free number to call if your card is lost or stolen; they may be able to wire you a cash advance immediately or deliver an emergency credit card in a day or two.

To report lost or stolen credit cards within Singapore, use the following toll-free hot lines: American Express (© 800/737-8188); MasterCard (© 800/110-0113); VISA (© 800/110-0344).

If you need emergency cash over the weekend when all banks and American Express offices are closed, you can have money wired to you via Western Union at most SingPost branches.

Mail Most hotels have mail services at the front counter. Singapore Post has centrally located offices at #04-15 Ngee Ann City/Takashimaya Shopping Centre (© 65/6738-6899); Chinatown Point, 133 New Bridge Rd. #02-42/43/44 (© 65/6538-7899); Change Alley, 16 Collyer Quay #02-02 Hitachi Tower (© 65/6538-6899); and 231 Bain St. #01-03 Bras Basah Complex (© 65/6339-8899). Plus there are five branches at Changi International Airport.

The going rate for international airmail letters to North America and Europe is S$1 (US64¢/35p) for 20 grams plus S35¢ (US22¢/10p) for each additional 10 grams. For international airmail service to Australia and New Zealand, the rate is S70¢ (US45¢/£2.30) for 20 grams plus S30¢ (US19¢/10p) for each additional 10 grams. Postcards and aerograms to all destinations are S50¢ (US32¢/15p).

Your hotel will accept mail sent for you at its address.

Maps The STB Visitors' Centres carry a variety of free city maps and walking tour maps of individual neighborhoods to help you find your way around.

Newspapers & Magazines Local English newspapers available are the *International Herald Tribune, The Business Times, The Straits Times, Today,* and *USA Today International.* Following an article criticizing the Singapore government, the Asian *Wall Street Journal* was banned from wide distribution in Singapore. Most of the major hotels carry it, though, so ask around and you can find one. *I-S Magazine* is a good resource for nightlife happenings. The STB Visitors' Centres carry a few free publications for travelers including *Where Singapore, This Week Singapore,* and *Singapore Business Visitor.* Major bookstores and magazine shops sell a wide variety of international magazines.

Passports Allow plenty of time before your trip to apply for a passport; processing normally takes 3 weeks but can take longer during busy periods (especially spring). And keep in mind that if you need a passport in a hurry, you'll pay a higher processing fee.

For Residents of Australia: You can pick up an application from your local post office or any branch of Passports Australia, but you must schedule an interview at the passport office to present your application materials. Call the **Australian Passport Information Service** at © 131-232, or visit the government website at www.passports.gov.au.

For Residents of Canada: Passport applications are available at travel agencies throughout Canada or from the central **Passport Office,** Department of Foreign Affairs and International Trade, Ottawa, ON K1A 0G3 (© **800/567-6868;** www.ppt.gc.ca).

For Residents of Ireland: You can apply for a 10-year passport at the **Passport Office,** Setanta Centre, Molesworth Street, Dublin 2 (© **01/671-1633;** www.irl gov.ie/iveagh). Those under age 18 and over 65 must apply for a 3-year passport. You can also apply at 1A South Mall, Cork (© **021/272-525**) or at most main post offices.

For Residents of New Zealand: You can pick up a passport application at any New Zealand Passports Office or download it from their website. Contact the **Passports Office** at © **0800/225-050** in New Zealand or 04/474-8100, or log on to www.passports.govt.nz.

For Residents of the United Kingdom: To pick up an application for a standard 10-year passport (5-year passport for children under 16), visit your nearest passport office, major post office, or travel agency or contact the **United Kingdom Passport Service** at © **0870/521-0410** or search its website at www.ukpa. gov.uk.

For Residents of the United States: Whether you're applying in person or by mail, you can download passport applications from the U.S. State Department website at **http://travel.state.gov**. To find your regional passport office, either check the U.S. State Department website or call the **National Passport Information Center** toll-free number (© **877/487-2778**) for automated information.

Police Given the strict reputation of law enforcement in Singapore, you can bet the officers here don't have the greatest sense of humor. If you find yourself being questioned about anything, big or small, be dead serious and most respectful. For emergencies, call © **999**. If you need to call the police headquarters, dial © **800/255-0000**.

If you are arrested, you have the right to legal council, but only when the police decide you can exercise that right. Bottom line: Don't get arrested.

Safety See "Health & Safety," earlier in this chapter.

Smoking It's against the law to smoke in public buses, elevators, theaters, cinemas, air-conditioned restaurants, shopping centers, government offices, and taxi queues.

Taxes Many hotels and restaurants will advertise rates followed by "+++." The first + is the goods and services tax (GST), which is levied at 5% of the purchase. The second + is 1% cess (a 1% tax levied by the STB on all tourism-related activities). The third is a 10% gratuity. See section 1, "Singapore Shopping: The Ground Rules" in chapter 7 for information on the GST Tourist Refund Scheme, which lets you recover the GST for purchases of goods over S$300 (US$192/£99) in value.

Telephones Public telephones can be found in booths on the street or back near the toilets in shopping malls, public buildings, or hotel lobbies. Because most Singaporeans now carry mobile phones, public phones aren't always properly maintained. Local calls cost S10¢ (US5¢/3p) for 3 minutes at coin- and card-operated phones. International calls can be made only from public phones designated specifically for this purpose. International public phones will accept either a stored-value phonecard or a credit card. Phonecards for local and international calls can be purchased at Singapore Post branches, 7-Eleven convenience stores, or money changers—make sure you specify local or international phonecard when you make your purchase.

To call Singapore: If you're calling Singapore from the United States:

1. Dial the international access code: 011
2. Dial the country code: 65
3. Then dial the 8-digit number. So the whole number you'd dial would be 011-65-0000-0000.

To make international calls: To make international calls from Singapore, first dial 001 and then the country code (U.S. or Canada 1, U.K. 44, Ireland 353, Australia 61, New Zealand 64). Next you dial the area code and number. For example, if you wanted to call the British Embassy in Washington, D.C., you would dial ℰ 001-1-202/588-7800.

For directory assistance: Dial ℰ **100** if you're looking for a number inside Singapore and dial ℰ **104** for numbers to all other countries.

For operator assistance: If you need operator assistance in making a call, dial ℰ **104** if you're trying to make an international call and ℰ **100** if you want to call a number in Singapore.

Toll-free numbers: Numbers beginning with 1800 within Singapore are toll-free, but calling a 1-800 number in the States from Singapore is not toll-free. In fact, it costs the same as an overseas call.

Time Zone   Singapore Standard Time is 8 hours ahead of Greenwich Mean Time (GMT). International time differences will change during daylight saving or summer time. Basic time differences are: New York –13, Los Angeles –16, Montreal –13, Vancouver –16, London –8, Brisbane +3, Darwin +1, Melbourne +2, Sydney +3, and Auckland +4. For the current time in Singapore, call ℰ 1711.

Tipping   Tipping is discouraged at hotels, bars, and in taxis, so the general rule is not to tip. A gratuity is automatically added into guest checks, and there's no need to slip anyone an extra buck for carrying bags or such. It's not expected.

Toilets   Clean public toilets can be found in all shopping malls, hotels, and public buildings. Smaller restaurants may not be up on their cleanliness, and beware of the "squatty potty," the Asian-style squat toilet, which you see in the more "local" places. Carry plenty of tissues with you, as they often run out.

Useful Phone Numbers

U.S. Dept. of State Travel Advisory: ℰ **202/647-5225** (manned 24 hr.)
U.S. Passport Agency: ℰ **202/647-0518**
Singapore Tourism Board: ℰ **65/1800-736-2000**
U.S. Centers for Disease Control International Traveler's Hot Line: ℰ **404/332-4559**

Water   Tap water in Singapore passes World Health Organization standards and is potable.

4

Where to Stay in Singapore

Competition is fierce among hotels in the Garden City, driven by a steady stream of business and convention travelers, many of whom stay at international hotel chains such as Hyatt, Hilton, Sheraton, and Marriott (all represented here). These companies invest millions in a never-ending cycle of renovations, constantly upgrading their super-royal-regal executive facilities, all in an attempt to lure suits and CEOs and—eventually, it is hoped—land lucrative corporate accounts.

Sadly, this means that good-quality budget accommodations are not a high priority on the island. Between the business community's demand for luxury on the one hand and the inflated Singaporean real estate market on the other, room prices tend to be high. What this means for leisure travelers is that you may end up paying for a business center you'll never use or a 24-hour stress-reliever masseuse you'll never call—and all this without the benefit of a corporate discount rate.

Don't fret, though: I'm here to tell you that there's a range of accommodations out there—you just have to know where to look. In this chapter, I'll help you pick the right accommodations for you, based on your vacation goals and your budget, so you can make the most of your stay.

CHOOSING YOUR NEIGHBORHOOD

In considering where you'll stay, think about what you'll be doing in Singapore—that way, you can choose a hotel that's close to the particular action that suits you. (On the other hand, because Singapore is a small place and public transportation is excellent, really nothing's ever too far away.)

Orchard Road has the largest cluster of hotels in the city and is right in the heart of Singaporean shopping mania—the malls and wide sidewalks where locals and tourists stroll to see and be seen. The **Historic District** has hotels that are near museums and sights, while those in **Marina Bay** center more around the business professionals who come to Singapore for Suntec City, the giant convention and exhibition center located there. **Chinatown** and **Tanjong Pagar** have some lovely boutique hotels in quaint back streets, and **Shenton Way** has a couple of high-rise places for the convenience of people doing business in the downtown business district. Many hotels have free morning and evening shuttle buses to Orchard Road, Suntec City, and Shenton Way. I've also listed two hotels on **Sentosa,** an island to the south that's a popular day or weekend trip for many Singaporeans and might be a good choice for families or honeymooners. (It's connected to Singapore by a causeway, cable cars, and a light-rail system.)

CHOOSING YOUR HOME AWAY FROM HOME

What appeals to you? A big, flashy, internationalist palace or a small, homier place? Hyatt, Sheraton, Hilton, and InterContinental are just a few of the international

Urban Singapore Accommodations

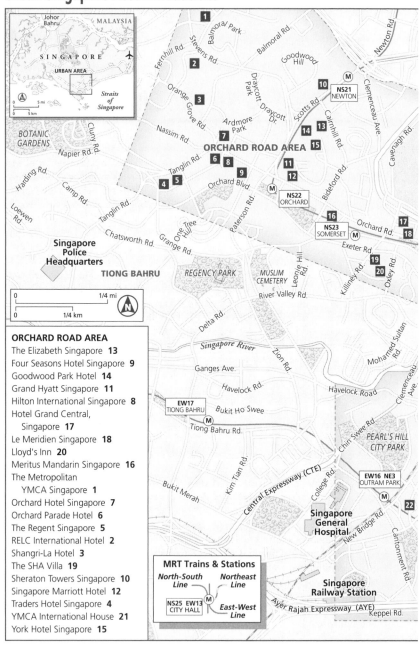

ORCHARD ROAD AREA

The Elizabeth Singapore **13**
Four Seasons Hotel Singapore **9**
Goodwood Park Hotel **14**
Grand Hyatt Singapore **11**
Hilton International Singapore **8**
Hotel Grand Central,
   Singapore **17**
Le Meridien Singapore **18**
Lloyd's Inn **20**
Meritus Mandarin Singapore **16**
The Metropolitan
   YMCA Singapore **1**
Orchard Hotel Singapore **7**
Orchard Parade Hotel **6**
The Regent Singapore **5**
RELC International Hotel **2**
Shangri-La Hotel **3**
The SHA Villa **19**
Sheraton Towers Singapore **10**
Singapore Marriott Hotel **12**
Traders Hotel Singapore **4**
YMCA International House **21**
York Hotel Singapore **15**

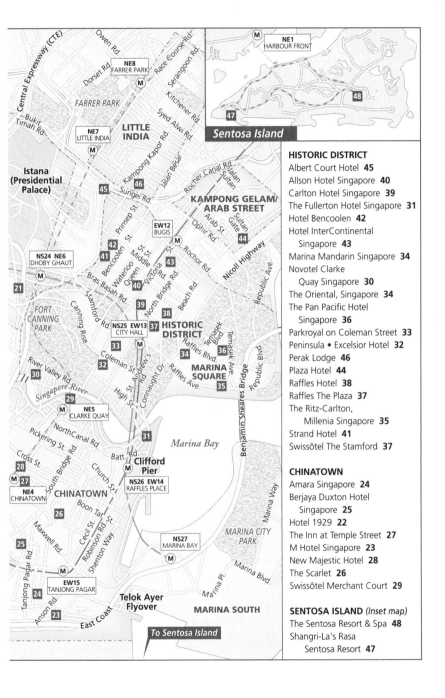

HISTORIC DISTRICT
Albert Court Hotel **45**
Allson Hotel Singapore **40**
Carlton Hotel Singapore **39**
The Fullerton Hotel Singapore **31**
Hotel Bencoolen **42**
Hotel InterContinental
   Singapore **43**
Marina Mandarin Singapore **34**
Novotel Clarke
   Quay Singapore **30**
The Oriental, Singapore **34**
The Pan Pacific Hotel
   Singapore **36**
Parkroyal on Coleman Street **33**
Peninsula • Excelsior Hotel **32**
Perak Lodge **46**
Plaza Hotel **44**
Raffles Hotel **38**
Raffles The Plaza **37**
The Ritz-Carlton,
   Millenia Singapore **35**
Strand Hotel **41**
Swissôtel The Stamford **37**

CHINATOWN
Amara Singapore **24**
Berjaya Duxton Hotel
   Singapore **25**
Hotel 1929 **22**
The Inn at Temple Street **27**
M Hotel Singapore **23**
New Majestic Hotel **28**
The Scarlet **26**
Swissôtel Merchant Court **29**

SENTOSA ISLAND (Inset map)
The Sentosa Resort & Spa **48**
Shangri-La's Rasa
   Sentosa Resort **47**

chain hotels you will find in Singapore. For the most part, these city hotels are non-descript towers—though Swissôtel The Stamford has the distinction of being the tallest hotel in Southeast Asia, with 71 floors. A few exceptions stand out. The Shangri-La, operating a highly reputable luxury hotel chain in Asia, has a property near Orchard Road with gorgeous landscaped grounds and pool area, making it truly a resort inside the city. Meanwhile, Shangri-La's Rasa Sentosa Resort and the Sentosa Resort & Spa on Sentosa Island are out-of-the-way, but have a real "get-away-from-it-all" ambience. In addition, a few hotels offer charming accommodations in historical premises. The most notable is Raffles, a Southeast Asian classic, and the Fullerton Hotel Singapore, converted from the old general post office building. But you need not pay a fortune for quaint digs. Budget places like Albert Court Hotel and the SHA Villa offer budget rooms with old-world charm in great locations.

A newer trend is the boutique hotel. Conceived as part of the Urban Restoration Authority's renewal plans, rows of old shophouses and historic buildings in ethnic areas like Chinatown and Tanjong Pagar have been restored and transformed into small, lovely hotels. Places like the Scarlet Hotel and the Inn at Temple Street are beautiful examples of local flavor turned into quaint accommodations. Although these places can put you closer to the heart of Singapore, they do have their drawbacks—for one, both the hotels and their rooms are small, and due to building codes and a lack of space, they're unable to provide facilities like swimming pools, Jacuzzis, or fitness centers.

Although budget hotels have very limited facilities and simpler interior style, you can always expect a clean room. What's more, service can sometimes be more personal in smaller hotels, where front desk staff has fewer faces to recognize and is accustomed to helping guests with the sorts of things a business center or concierge would handle in a larger hotel. Par for the course, many of the guests in these places are backpackers, and mostly Western backpackers at that. However, you will see some regional folks staying in these places. **Note:** The budget accommodations listed here are places decent enough for any standards. While cheaper digs are available, the rooms can be dreary and depressing, musty and old, or downright sleazy.

Unless you choose one of the extreme budget hotels, there are some standard features you can expect to find everywhere. Although no hotels offer a courtesy car or limousine, many have courtesy shuttles to popular parts of town. Security key cards are catching on, and while in-room safes are standard, many are shifting to safes that incorporate a plug so you can charge electronics gadgets while they're locked away. You'll also see in-house movies and many times CNN, ESPN, and HBO on your TV. Voice mail is gaining popularity, and fax services can always be provided upon request. You'll find most places have adequate fitness center facilities, almost all of which offer a range of massage treatments—hotels generally do not offer in-room massage treatments. Pools tend to be on the small side, and Jacuzzis are often placed in men's and women's locker rooms, making it impossible for couples to use them together. Although tour desks can be found in some lobbies, car-rental desks are non-existent.

Many of the finest restaurants in Singapore are located in hotels, either operated by the hotel directly or just inhabiting rented space. Some hotels can have up to five or six restaurants, each serving a different cuisine. Generally, you can expect these restaurants to be more expensive than places located outside hotels. In each hotel review, the distinguished restaurants have been noted; these restaurants are also fully reviewed in chapter 5.

> **Tips** **Making Hotel Reservations Online**
>
> The website **www.asiarooms.com** offers the best rates I've seen for Internet bookings, particularly for hotels in the Very Expensive and Expensive categories; however they don't have deals for every hotel property. It's worth it to browse and compare.

RATES

Let's talk money. Singapore's hotel industry experienced a record year in 2006, with September witnessing a record high average room rate of S$190 (US$122/£63), the highest it's been since before the 1997 East Asian economic crisis. In fact, in updating this guidebook, I've been shocked at some of the jumps in rack rates—some have increased up to S$200 (US$128/£66) per night. In general, rack rates for double rooms range from as low as S$100 (US$64/£33) at the Strand on Bencoolen (a famous backpacker's strip) to as high as S$1,000 (US$640/£330) a night at the exclusive Raffles Hotel. Rack rates for average rooms are usually in the S$350 (US$226/£116) range, but keep in mind that although all prices listed in this book are the going rates, they rarely represent what you'll actually pay. In fact, you should never have to pay the advertised rate in a Singapore hotel, as many offer promotional rates, often up to 50% less than the official rack rate. When you call for your reservation, always ask what special deals they are running and how you can get the lowest price for your room. Hotels that have just completed renovations offer discounts, and most have special weekend or long-term stay programs. Also be sure to inquire about free add-ons. Complimentary breakfast and other services can have added value that makes a difference in the end.

For the purposes of this guide, I've divided hotels into the categories very expensive, S$450 (US$288/£149) and up; expensive, S$350 to S$450 (US$224–US$288/£116–£149); moderate, S$150 to S$350 (US$96–US$224/£50–£224); and inexpensive, under S$150 (US$96/£50).

TAXES & SERVICE CHARGES

All rates listed are in Singapore dollars, with U.S. dollar and British pound equivalents provided as well (remember to check the exchange rate when you're planning, though, because the rate may fluctuate). Most rates do not include the so-called "+++" taxes and charges: the 10% service charge, 5% goods and services tax (GST), and 1% *cess* (a tax levied by the Singapore Tourism Board [STB] on all tourism-related activities). Keep these in mind when figuring your budget. Some budget hotels will quote discount rates inclusive of all taxes.

THE BUSY SEASON

Busy season? It's all busy season in Singapore, with month-by-month occupancy rates holding steady over 80%. Visitors are well advised to book rooms well in advance, and check with the Singapore Tourism Board to make sure there are no huge conventions in town during your dates. That said, probably the worst time to find a last-minute room or to negotiate a favorable rate will be between Christmas and the Chinese New Year, when folks travel on vacation and to see their families.

MAKING RESERVATIONS ON THE GROUND

If you are not able to make a reservation before your trip, a reservation service is available at Changi International Airport. The Singapore Hotel Association operates desks in both Terminals 1 and 2, with reservation services based upon room availability for many hotels. The desks are open daily from 7:30am to 11:30pm.

1 The Historic District

VERY EXPENSIVE

The Fullerton Hotel Singapore 🏨🏨　Standing guard at the mouth of the Singapore River, The Fullerton's historic edifice holds ground against a backdrop of the city's modern skyline. Originally built in 1928, this squat administrative building at the mouth of the Singapore River once housed the General Post Office. Today it is flanked by the urban skyline, and its classical facade, with Doric columns and tall porticos, looks more mundane than opulent. But designers have done a superb job, restoring Italian marble floors, coffered ceilings, and cornices inside. The courtyard lobby is grand, with skylights above and Courtyard guest room windows lining the inner face of the building. Rooms have been cleverly arranged to fit the original structure, featuring vaulted ceilings and tall windows. Although the architectural style is antique, the rooms are anything but. They feature large writing desks, deluxe stationery kits, flatscreen TVs, PlayStations, and electronic safes big enough to hold your laptop. Big bathrooms have separate bath and shower stalls, mini-StairMasters, and stylish Philippe Starck fixtures. The attentive service here is second to none.

1 Fullerton Sq., Singapore 049178. (✆ 800/44-UTELL in the U.S. and Canada, 800/221-176 in Australia, 800/933-123 in New Zealand, or 65/6733-8388. Fax 65/6735-8388. www.fullertonhotel.com. 400 units. S$670 (US$429/£221) double; from S$900 (US$576/£297) suite. AE, DC, MC, V. 5-min. walk to Raffles Place MRT. **Amenities:** 3 restaurants; bar and lobby lounge; outdoor infinity pool w/view of the Singapore River; fitness center w/Jacuzzi, sauna, and steam; spa w/massage and beauty treatments; concierge; limousine service; business center; shopping arcade; salon; 24-hr. room service; babysitting; same-day laundry service; dry cleaning; nonsmoking rooms; executive-level rooms. *In room:* A/C, TV w/satellite programming and in-house movie, dataport w/direct Internet access, minibar, coffee/tea-making facilities, hair dryer, iron, safe.

Raffles Hotel 🏨🏨　Legendary since its establishment in 1887 and named after Singapore's first British colonial administrator, Sir Stamford Raffles, this posh hotel is one of the most recognizable names in Southeast Asian hospitality. Originally it was a bungalow, but by the 1920s and 1930s it had expanded to become a mecca for celebrities like Charlie Chaplin and Douglas Fairbanks, writers like Somerset Maugham and Noël Coward, and various and sundry kings, sultans, and politicians (the famous Long Bar, where the Singapore Sling was invented, is located here). Always at the center of Singapore's colonial high life, the Raffles hosted balls, tea dances, and jazz functions, and during World War II was the last rallying point for the British in the face of Japanese occupation and the first place for refugee prisoners of war released from concentration camps. In 1987, the hotel was declared a landmark and restored to its early-20th-century splendor, with grand arches, 4.2m (14-ft.) molded ceilings with spinning fans, tiled teak and marble floors, Oriental carpets, and period furnishings. Outside, the facade of the main building was similarly restored, complete with the elegant cast-iron portico and the verandas that encircle the upper stories.

Because it is a national landmark, thousands of people pass through the open lobby each day, so the hotel maintains a private inner lobby marked off for "residents" only.

Historic District Accommodations

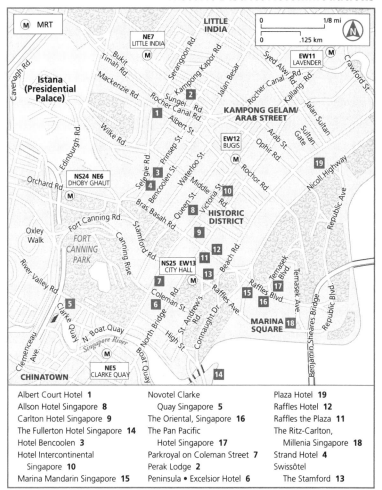

MRT

Albert Court Hotel **1**	Novotel Clarke Quay Singapore **5**	Plaza Hotel **19**
Allson Hotel Singapore **8**	The Oriental, Singapore **16**	Raffles Hotel **12**
Carlton Hotel Singapore **9**	The Pan Pacific Hotel Singapore **17**	Raffles the Plaza **11**
The Fullerton Hotel Singapore **14**	Parkroyal on Coleman Street **7**	The Ritz-Carlton, Millenia Singapore **18**
Hotel Bencoolen **3**	Perak Lodge **2**	Strand Hotel **4**
Hotel Intercontinental Singapore **10**	Peninsula • Excelsior Hotel **6**	Swissôtel The Stamford **13**
Marina Mandarin Singapore **15**		

Nothing feels better than walking along the dark teak floors of the verandas, past little rattan-furnished relaxation areas overlooking the green tropical courtyards. Each suite entrance is like a private apartment door: Enter past the small living and dining area dressed in Oriental carpets and reproduction furniture, then pass through louvered doors into the bedroom with its four-poster bed and period armoire, ceiling fan twirling high above. Raffles is the only hotel in Singapore where you can play out the colonial traveler fantasy, and it can be a lot of fun. Other unique features include a hotel museum, popular theater playhouse, and an excellent culinary academy.

1 Beach Rd., Singapore 189673. ℂ **800/232-1886** in the U.S. and Canada, or 65/6337-1886. Fax 65/6339-7650. www.raffleshotel.com. 103 suites. From S$1,000 (US$640/£330) suite. AE, DC, MC, V. Next to City Hall MRT. **Amenities:** 8 restaurants; 2 bars and a billiard room; small outdoor pool; fitness center w/Jacuzzi, sauna, steam, and spa; concierge; limousine service; business center; shopping arcade; salon; 24-hr. room service; babysitting; same-day

laundry service; dry cleaning; personal butler service. *In room:* A/C, TV w/satellite programming and in-room VCR, fax, dataport w/direct Internet access, minibar, coffee/tea-making facilities, hair dryer, safe.

Raffles The Plaza ✦✦✦   This has to be the best location in the city. Above an MRT hub and next to one of the largest shopping centers in Singapore, you won't find any inconveniences here. The lobby is peaceful with soft lighting and music, a lovely escape from the crazy mall and hot streets. Perhaps the best reason to stay is the Amrita spa and fitness center; Singapore's largest spa, it features a huge state-of-the-art gym with exercise and relaxation classes, a pool, hot and cold plunge pools, steam and sauna, and endless treatment rooms with Asian and European treatments for beauty and rejuvenation. Standard rooms are large and comfortable. Premier deluxe rooms are stunningly contemporary, with cushy bedding, big desk spaces, Bose Wave systems, and incredible bathrooms—crisp white tiles, glistening glass countertops, polished chrome fixtures, and a shower that simulates rainfall.

2 Stamford Rd., Singapore 178882. © **65/6339-7777.** Fax 65/6337-1554. http://singapore-plaza.raffles.com. 769 units. S$520 (US$333/£172) double; suites from S$1,600 (US$1,024/£528). AE, DC, MC, V. City Hall MRT. **Amenities:** 10 restaurants; martini bar, lobby lounge, and a live jazz venue; outdoor pool; spa w/gym, Jacuzzi, sauna, steam, and massage; concierge; limousine service; business center; shopping arcade adjacent; 24-hr. room service; babysitting; same-day laundry service; dry cleaning; nonsmoking rooms; executive-level rooms. *In room:* A/C, TV w/satellite programming and in-house movie, minibar, coffee/tea-making facilities, hair dryer, safe.

The Ritz-Carlton, Millenia Singapore ✦✦✦   The ultimate in luxury hotels, The Ritz-Carlton blazes trails with sophisticated ultramodern design, sumptuous comfort, and stimulating art. Grand public spaces, lighted by futuristic window designs and splashed with artworks from the likes of Frank Stella, Dale Chihuly, David Hockney, and Andy Warhol, are a welcome change from international chain hotel design cliché. In comparison, guest rooms display a great deal of warmth and hominess. All rooms have spectacular views of either Kallang Bay or the more majestic Marina Bay. Even the bathrooms have views, as the huge tubs are placed under octagonal picture windows so you can gaze as you bathe. Oh, the decadence! Guest rooms here are about 25% larger than most five-star rooms elsewhere, providing ample space for big two-poster beds and full walk-in closets.

7 Raffles Ave., Singapore 039799. © **800/241-3333** in the U.S. and Canada, 800/241-33333 in Australia, 800/241-33333 in New Zealand, 800/234-000 in the U.K., or 65/6337-8888. Fax 65/6338-0001. www.ritzcarlton.com. 610 units. S$560 (US$358/£185) double; from S$820 (US$525/£271) suite. AE, DC, MC, V. 10-min. walk to City Hall MRT. **Amenities:** 3 restaurants; lobby lounge; outdoor pool and Jacuzzi; outdoor, lighted tennis court; fitness center w/sauna, steam, and massage; concierge; limousine service; business center; shopping mall adjacent; 24-hr. room service; babysitting; same-day laundry service; dry cleaning; nonsmoking rooms; executive-level rooms. *In room:* A/C, TV w/satellite programming and in-house movie, dataport w/direct Internet access, minibar, coffee/tea-making facilities, hair dryer, iron, safe.

EXPENSIVE

Carlton Hotel Singapore ✦✦   This Carlton property comprises two buildings, the 26-story Main Wing and the newer (2002), 19-story Annex Wing next door. Leisure travelers will be most interested in the lower-priced superior and deluxe rooms in the Main Wing. While rooms in both categories are the same size and have all been smartly redone in contemporary neutral tones, deluxe rooms have broadband Internet access in-room, a flatscreen TV, plus marble bathroom decor (superiors are humble ceramic tile). The Annex houses premier deluxe rooms, which, for a premium, feature larger bathrooms with separate bath and shower stall, an in-room safe to fit your laptop, and access to a coin-operated launderette. All public spaces have been upgraded as well, including the lobby entrance, alfresco coffee shop, and a tiny wine and cigar room. The location, in the center of the historic district, is terrific. Ask for a room with a view of the city.

76 Bras Basah Rd., Singapore 189558. ℂ 65/6338-8333. Fax 65/6339-6866. www.carltonhotel.sg. 627 units. S$370 (US$237/£122) double; from S$500 (US$320/£165) suite. AE, DC, MC, V. 5-min. walk to City Hall MRT. **Amenities:** 2 restaurants; lobby lounge; outdoor pool; fitness center w/sauna, steam, and massage; concierge; tour desk; car-rental desk; limousine service; shuttle service; business center; 24-hr. room service; babysitting; same-day laundry service; dry cleaning; nonsmoking rooms; executive-level rooms. In room: A/C, TV w/satellite programming and in-house movie, minibar, coffee/tea-making facilities.

Hotel InterContinental Singapore ⭐

The government let InterContinental build a hotel in this spot with one ironclad stipulation: The hotel chain had to retain the original shophouses on the block and incorporate them into the hotel design. No preservation, no hotel. Reinforcing the foundation, Hotel InterContinental built up from there, giving touches of old architectural style to the lobby, lounge, and other public areas on the bottom floors while imbuing it with the feel of a modern hotel. Features like beamed ceilings and wooden staircases are warmly accentuated with Chinese and European antique reproductions, Oriental carpets, and local artworks. The second and third floors have "Shophouse Rooms" styled with such Peranakan trappings as carved hardwood furnishings and floral linens, and with homey touches like potted plants and carpets over wooden floors. These rooms are very unique, presenting a surprising element of local flair that you don't often find in large chain hotels. Guest rooms on higher levels are large, with formal European styling and large luxurious bathrooms.

80 Middle Rd., Singapore 188966 (near Bugis Junction). ℂ 800/327-0200 in the U.S. and Canada, 800/221-335 in Australia, 800/442-215 in New Zealand, 800/0289-387 in the U.K., or 65/6338-7600. Fax 65/6338-7366. www.intercontinental. com. 406 units. S$440 (US$282/£145) double; from S$500 (US$320/£165) suite. AE, DC, MC, V. Bugis MRT. **Amenities:** 3 restaurants; bar and lobby lounge; outdoor pool; fitness center w/Jacuzzi, sauna, and massage; concierge; limousine service; business center; shopping mall adjacent; 24-hr. room service; babysitting; same-day laundry service; dry cleaning; executive-level rooms. In room: A/C, TV w/satellite programming and in-house movie, minibar, coffee/tea-making facilities, hair dryer, safe.

Marina Mandarin Singapore ⭐⭐

A few hotels in the Marina Bay area are built around the atrium concept, and of them, this one is the loveliest, having just come out of an enormous renovation to all guest rooms and public spaces. The atrium lobby opens up to ceiling skylights 21 stories above, guest corridor balconies fringed with vines line the sides, and in the center hangs a glistening metal mobile sculpture in red and gold. One of the most surprising details is the melodic chirping of caged songbirds, which fills the open space every morning. In the evening, live classical music from the lobby bar drifts upward. The guest rooms are equally impressive: large and cool, with built-in desk spaces and entertainment consoles, plus balconies standard for each room. Try to get the Marina view for that famous Shenton Way skyline towering above the bay. All bathrooms have double sinks, a separate shower and tub, and a bidet. Unique Venus Rooms, for women travelers, include potpourri, bath oils, custom pillows, and hair curlers. One plus, the Marina Square Shopping Center, adjacent to the lobby, adds scores of shops, services, restaurants, and entertainment options.

6 Raffles Blvd., Marina Square, Singapore 039594. ℂ 65/6845-1000. Fax 65/6845-1001. www.marina-mandarin. com.sg. 575 units. S$450 (US$288/£149) double; from S$700 (US$448/£231) suite. AE, DC, MC, V. 10-min. walk to City Hall MRT. **Amenities:** 3 restaurants; English pub and lobby lounge; outdoor pool; outdoor, lighted tennis courts; squash courts; 24-hour fitness center, spa w/Jacuzzi, sauna, steam, and massage; concierge; limousine service; 24-hour business center; shopping mall adjacent; salon; 24-hr. room service; babysitting; same-day laundry service; dry

cleaning; nonsmoking rooms; executive-level rooms. *In room:* A/C, TV w/satellite programming and in-house movie, minibar, coffee/tea-making facilities, hair dryer, safe.

Novotel Clarke Quay Singapore ⽊   Novotel took over the old Hotel New Otani, and reopened in late 2005 after a complete renovation. The hotel towers over the Singapore River just next to Clarke Quay (a popular spot for nightlife, dining, and shopping) and is a stroll away from the Historic District. At night, you have access to nearby Boat Quay bars and restaurants to one side and to the unique clubs of Mohamed Sultan Road on the other. All rooms have small balconies with good views of the river, the financial district, Fort Canning Park, or Chinatown, and the standard rooms have large bathrooms like those you typically see in more deluxe accommodations. Guest room decor is contemporary in shades of brown and tan, with small desks next to floor-to-ceiling picture windows with ergonomically designed chairs. The main lobby is an elevator ride up from the ground level. A small adjacent shopping mall has groceries in the basement and a few handy shops.

177A River Valley Rd., Singapore 179031. ⓒ **800/515-5679** in the U.S. and Canada, or 65/6338-3333. Fax 65/6339-2854. www.novotel.com. 398 units. S$450 (US$288/£149) double; from S$630 (US$403/£208) suite. AE, DC, MC, V. 5-min. walk to Clarke Quay MRT. **Amenities:** 3 restaurants; lobby lounge; outdoor pool; fitness center; Jacuzzi; concierge; tour desk; limousine service; shuttle service; business center; shopping mall adjacent; 24-hr. room service; babysitting; same-day laundry service; dry cleaning; executive-level rooms. *In room:* A/C, TV w/satellite programming, minibar, coffee/tea-making facilities, safe.

The Oriental, Singapore ⽊⽊⽊   Another atrium-concept hotel similar to neighboring properties Marina Mandarin and the Pan Pacific, The Oriental is one notch above the others. Public spaces are quiet, with subdued lighting, the lobby adorned with polished black marble, leather seating, and Asian decorative arts and accents. A recent renovation has introduced a sophisticated contemporary Asian look to rooms, with plush carpeting and shimmering throw silk pillows and bed runners. Pay more for rooms with a view of the city's skyline through each room's floor-to-ceiling windows—it's worth it. Also worth it, the Oriental Spa drips with a studied sense of Asian serenity, through quiet spaces graced with Chinese antiques and a spa menu that focuses on Asian beauty and relaxation techniques. The staff is always available but never in your face. The Oriental also benefits from the adjacent Marina Square Shopping Center, which adds scores of shops, services, restaurants, and entertainment options.

5 Raffles Ave., Marina Square, Singapore 039797. ⓒ **800/526-6566** in the U.S. and Canada, 800/123-693 in Australia, 800/2828-3838 in New Zealand or the U.K., or 65/6338-0066. Fax 65/6339-9537. www.mandarinoriental.com/singapore. 524 units. S$450 (US$288/£149) double; from S$780 (US$499/£257) suite. AE, DC, MC, V. 10-min. walk to City Hall MRT. **Amenities:** 4 restaurants; bar and lobby lounge; outdoor pool; fitness center; spa w/Jacuzzi, sauna, and steam; concierge; limousine service; business center; salon; 24-hr. room service; babysitting; same-day laundry service; dry cleaning; nonsmoking rooms; executive-level rooms. *In room:* A/C, TV w/satellite programming and in-house movie, minibar, coffee/tea-making facilities, hair dryer, safe.

The Pan Pacific Hotel Singapore ⽊⽊   Few know this, but Pan Pacific is Singapore's largest hotel, with over 780 rooms. But a recent face-lift has given the hotel a new look, and due to a clever atrium layout, you'd never know you were in a building so huge. Competing with Marina Mandarin and the Oriental to grab a slice of the Suntec City Convention Center and business travel pie, Pan Pac avoids the Asian flavor for something a bit more colorful—a lobby with a checkerboard inlay reception counter, vibrant carpeting, and a lobby lounge with walls of lights that change colors. Guest rooms are large, with wood paneling in geometric panels, Asian-inspired fabrics, and large oval desktops with Herman Miller chairs. Hands down, Pan Pac has Singapore's best business center—a full floor designated to private offices, with full secretarial services, every piece of office equipment you'd need, plus meeting rooms and even snacks and cocktail lounges. The hotel's many restaurants are some of the top choices in Singapore. The rooftop pool has a huge open sun deck area and a spa and fitness center with pool view.

7 Raffles Blvd., Marina Square, Singapore 039595 (near Suntec City). © 800/327-8585 in the U.S. and Canada, 800/525-900 in Australia, 800/969-496 in the U.K., or 65/6336-8111. Fax 65/6339-1861. www.singapore.panpacific.com. 784 units. S$480 (US$307/£158) double; from S$510 (US$326/£168) suite. AE, DC, MC, V. 10-min. walk to City Hall MRT. **Amenities:** 6 restaurants; lobby lounge; outdoor pool; 2 outdoor, lighted tennis courts; fitness center w/Jacuzzi, sauna, steam, massage, and spa treatments; concierge; limousine service; shuttle service; business center; shopping arcade adjacent; 24-hr. room service; babysitting; same-day laundry service; dry cleaning; nonsmoking rooms; executive-level rooms. *In room:* A/C, TV w/satellite programming and in-house movie, dataport w/direct Internet access, minibar, coffee/tea-making facilities, hair dryer, safe.

Parkroyal on Coleman Street ⊛   Formerly the Grand Plaza Parkroyal, this property was built on top of (and incorporating) 2 blocks of prewar shophouses, and you can see hints of shophouse detail throughout the lobby, which is otherwise like any other hotel's. The old alleyway that ran between the shophouse blocks has been transformed into a courtyard where dinner is served alfresco. The hotel is located at the corner of Coleman and Hill streets, close to the Armenian Church, the Asian Civilisations Museum, and Fort Canning Park—plus a shuttle to Orchard Road. Guest rooms are of smaller size than average, have decent closet space, and sport sharp Italian contemporary furniture in natural tones, with homey touches like snuggly comforters on all the beds. Overall, this property does not stand out from the crowd, except for the St. Gregory Marine Spa, a popular and discrete full-service facility. I also like the pool area for its landscaping.

10 Coleman St., Singapore 179809. © 65/6336-3456. Fax 65/6339-9311. http://coleman.singapore.parkroyalhotels. com. 326 units. S$370 (US$237/£122) double; from S$500 (US$320/£165) suite. AE, DC, MC, V. 5-min. walk to City Hall MRT. **Amenities:** 3 restaurants; lobby lounge; outdoor pool w/view of Armenian Church across the street; fitness center; spa w/Jacuzzi, sauna, steam, and massage; concierge; shuttle service; business center; 24-hr. room service; babysitting; same-day laundry service; dry cleaning; executive-level rooms. *In room:* A/C, TV w/satellite programming, minibar, coffee/tea-making facilities, safe.

Swissôtel The Stamford ⊛ *(Value)*   You'd think a room in the tallest hotel in Southeast Asia would cost a bundle, but this gem is reasonably priced. Besides, with an amazing location, right on top of a subway hub and a huge shopping complex, walking distance from many sights and attractions, the Swissôtel is a great value for the money. On a clear day you can see over urban Singapore's downtown financial district, so make sure you request a room with a view. However, guest rooms, while larger than the city's average, feel bland and barren, in boring neutral tones with few decorator touches. In some spots, furnishings and carpets can use a face-lift—while a good bargain, this hotel is desperate for a re-haul to keep up with its neighbors.

2 Stamford Rd., Singapore 178882. © 800/637-9477 in the U.S. and Canada, 800/121-043 in Australia, or 65/6338-8585. Fax 65/6338-2862. www.swissotel-thestamford.com. 1,200 units. S$480 (US$307/£158) double; S$1,300 (US$832/£429) suite. AE, DC, MC, V. City Hall MRT. **Amenities:** 10 restaurants; martini bar, lobby lounge, and a live jazz venue; outdoor pool; spa w/gym, Jacuzzi, sauna, steam, and massage; concierge; limousine service; business center; shopping arcade adjacent; 24-hr. room service; babysitting; same-day laundry service; dry cleaning; nonsmoking rooms; executive-level rooms. *In room:* A/C, TV w/satellite programming and in-house movie, minibar, coffee/tea-making facilities, hair dryer, safe.

MODERATE

Albert Court Hotel ⊗ *(Value)*   This hotel was first conceived as part of the Urban Renewal Authority's master plan to revitalize this block, which involved the restoration of two rows of prewar shophouses. The eight-story boutique hotel that emerged has all the Western comforts but has retained the charm of its shophouse roots. Decorators placed local Peranakan touches everywhere from the carved teak furnishings in traditional floral design to the antique china cups used for tea service in the rooms. (Guaranteed: The sight of these cups brings misty-eyed nostalgia to the hearts of Singaporeans.) Guest room details like the teak molding, bathroom tiles in bright Peranakan colors, and old-time brass electrical switches give this place true local charm and distinction. A recent refurbishment gives an added freshness to the rooms. Albert Court offers new courtyard rooms in the renovated houses that front the hotel's courtyard; these rooms contain all the local touches that make this hotel stand out from the rest. This hotel is especially attractive if you wish to spend a lot of time shopping and eating in Little India, which is just across the street.

180 Albert St., Singapore 189971. ℂ **65/6339-3939.** Fax 65/6339-3252. www.albertcourt.com.sg. 136 units. S$180 (US$115/£59) double; S$350 (US$224/£116) suite. AE, DC, MC, V. 5-min. walk to either Bugis or Little India MRT. **Amenities:** 3 restaurants; small lobby lounge; tour desk; limited room service; babysitting; same-day laundry service; dry cleaning. *In room:* A/C, TV w/satellite programming, minibar, coffee/tea-making facilities, hair dryer, safe.

Allson Hotel Singapore ⊗ *(Value)*   Allson continues to be a strong tourist class hotel in the city's historic district. In 2003 the facade got a complete face-lift, adding a soundproofing layer to keep out traffic noise from busy Victoria Street below. Guest rooms have fresh carpeting, paint, and drapes, and new bed coverings and upholstery. Carved rosewood furniture—headboards, side tables, and armchairs in quaint Ming-style carvings are an elegant touch for such a moderately priced accommodations. Even the heavy doors leading into the rooms are carved rosewood. Bathrooms have been recently retiled with spotless grout. The small pool area and even smaller gym have received some maintenance touch ups. With a good location and modest prices, Allson is a great choice for value-conscious leisure travelers.

101 Victoria St., Singapore 188018. ℂ **65/6336-0811.** Fax 65/6339-7019. www.allsonhotels.com. 450 units. S$260 (US$166/£86) double; from S$450 (US$288/£149) suite. AE, DC, MC, V. 5-min. walk from Bugis Junction MRT. **Amenities:** 3 restaurants; lounge; small outdoor pool; fitness center w/Jacuzzi, sauna, steam, and massage; tour desk; business center; salon; 24-hr. room service; babysitting; same-day laundry service; dry cleaning; nonsmoking rooms; executive-level rooms. *In room:* A/C, TV w/satellite programming and in-house movie, minibar, coffee/tea-making facilities, safe.

Peninsula • Excelsior Hotel ⊗⊗ *(Value)*   Recently, two of Singapore's busiest tourist-class hotels merged, combining their lobby and facilities into one giant value-for-money property. The location is excellent, in the Historic District within walking distance to Chinatown and Boat Quay. It's a popular pick for groups, but don't let the busloads of tourists steer you away. There are some great deals to be had here, especially if you request the guest rooms in the Peninsula tower. These are large and colorful, with big picture windows, some of which have stunning views of the city, the Singapore River, and the marina. Surprisingly, these rooms are priced the same as rooms in the Excelsior tower, which are smaller and, frankly, look like they haven't seen a decor update since the far-out 1970s.

5 Coleman St., Singapore 179805. ℂ **65/6337-2200.** Fax 65/6336-3847. www.ytchotels.com.sg. 600 units. S$170 (US$109/£56) double; from S$550 (US$352/£192) suite. AE, DC, MC, V. 5-min. walk to City Hall MRT. **Amenities:** Restaurant; bar and lobby lounge; 2 outdoor pools; fitness center w/Jacuzzi; concierge; tour desk; business center;

shopping mall adjacent; 24-hr. room service; babysitting; same-day laundry service; dry cleaning. *In room:* A/C, TV, minibar, coffee/tea-making facilities, hair dryer, safe.

Plaza Hotel   Situated just across from the Arab Street and Kampong Gelam areas, you're a little off the beaten track at the Plaza Hotel—you'll need to take buses or taxis just about everywhere—but the trade-off is that if you stick around you can take advantage of the attractive recreation and relaxation facilities, which include a half-size Olympic pool with a diving board (a rarity in Singapore), a lovely sun deck decorated in a lazy-days Balinese-style tropical motif, and a Bali-themed poolside cafe, cooled by ceiling fans. Two gyms to the side have plenty of space and new equipment, but the most exquisite facility of all is the exotic Bali-inspired spa. Other hotel facilities include outdoor and indoor Jacuzzis, a sauna, and a steam room. Guest rooms are midsize and quite nondescript but good value, especially if you can negotiate a good rate.

7500A Beach Rd., Singapore 199591. ✆ **65/6298-0011.** Fax 65/6296-3600. www.plazapacifichotels.com. 350 units. S$330 (US$211/£109) double; from S$600 (US$384/£198) suite. AE, DC, MC, V. 20-min. walk to Bugis MRT. **Amenities:** 2 restaurants; lounge; outdoor pool; fitness center; spa w/Jacuzzi, sauna, steam, and massage; concierge; tour desk; limousine service; business center; 24-hr. room service; babysitting; same-day laundry service; dry cleaning; executive-level rooms. *In room:* A/C, TV w/satellite programming and in-house movie, dataport w/direct Internet access, minibar, coffee/tea-making facilities, hair dryer, safe.

INEXPENSIVE

Hotel Bencoolen   Bencoolen is the signature backpacker hotel on a block that's best known for budget accommodations. A tiny lobby has a reception desk, bellhop, and one computer for Internet access. Upstairs, the rooms are equally small, with barely room to move around a queen-size bed, only a narrow closet for clothes, and a tiny TV hanging from the ceiling. King-size rooms have space for a small desk, while family rooms have one queen and one slightly oversize single bed. For an extra S$25 (US$16/£7) per day you can have wireless Internet access throughout the hotel. Despite the size, all rooms have been redone within the past 5 years—major repairs have been made, walls have been repainted, and soft furnishings added, so that now colors and furnishings seem coordinated. Small bathrooms are newly tiled as well but are already beginning to show some age. The hotel has a rooftop restaurant.

47 Bencoolen St., Singapore 189626. ✆ **65/6336-0822.** Fax 65/6336-2250. www.hotelbencoolen.com. 74 units. S$148 double (US$95/£49); S$178 (US$114/£59) family. MC, V. 10-min. walk to City Hall or Dhoby Ghaut MRT. **Amenities:** Restaurant; sauna; same-day laundry service; nonsmoking rooms. *In room:* A/C, TV, coffee/tea-making facilities.

Perak Lodge ✦   Set in a cozy corner on the edge of Little India, this place is popular with backpackers; the lobby is a nice place to read the paper or chat with other travelers from around the world. Located on a quaint alley in a row of restored prewar shophouses, the lodge feels very homey, with a friendly family-run ambience. The lobby cafe has only simple wooden tables and chairs, serving breakfast and snacks to house guests only. Upstairs, guest room corridors can be a bit noisy from footsteps on the wooden floors, but otherwise the place is quite smart. Small tidy rooms have spotless en-suite bathrooms with shower stalls. Simple furniture provides closet, desk, and bedside storage. Some local textiles add a bit of charm. Good management and a congenial travel-friendly atmosphere make this a top pick for budget-conscious travelers.

12 Perak Rd., Singapore 208133. ✆ **65/6299-7733.** Fax 65/6392-0919. www.peraklodge.com. 34 units. S$98 (US$63/£32) double; S$138 (US$88/£46) triple, including breakfast. AE, DC, MC, V. 5-min. walk to Bugis or Little India MRT. **Amenities:** Cafe; tour desk; business center; laundry service; dry cleaning. *In room:* A/C, TV.

Strand Hotel ⊛   The Strand is by far one of the best of the backpacker places in Singapore. The lobby doesn't look or feel like a budget hotel, with marble floors, a smart bellhop, and a long reception desk. There's also an inviting cafe to one side, plus a small gift shop. Guest rooms are the largest I've seen in a budget hotel in Singapore, in fact larger than a lot of more expensive rooms as well. They're pretty funky, too, with bright-colored painted walls to offset very simple wooden furnishings. Whatever you do, don't go for the "special room," with the bathtub/shower separated from the main room by only a thin glass wall. Anybody for a free show?

25 Bencoolen St., Singapore 189619. ✆ **65/6338-1866**. Fax 65/6338-1330. 130 units. S$100 (US$64/£33) double; S$120 (US$77/£40) 3-person sharing. AE, DC, MC, V. 10-min. walk to City Hall or Dhoby Ghaut MRT. **Amenities:** Restaurant; 24-hr. room service; same-day laundry service. In room: A/C, TV.

2 Chinatown
VERY EXPENSIVE

The Scarlet   A truly novel approach to accommodations, The Scarlet is a groovy little boutique hotel dripping with the sensuality of an old-time bordello. From the moment you enter, your every sense is tickled, from the sound of a trickling fountain to the glistening polished black marble floors, soft red velvet furnishings, and cool soundtrack from the leather-clad lobby lounge. The location, in a group of restored shophouses, means rooms are small; in fact, I don't even recommend the postage stamp–size guest rooms (which are actually quite moderately priced) unless you're Lilliputian. The only real way to experience the Scarlet is to splurge for one of the suites, charmingly outfitted in all assortment of luxury fabrics—glittering, plush, velvety, silky, fluffy, textiles, draped and dangled with tassels, custom furnishings in black, gold or silver lacquer, and with names like Swank, Passion, Lavish, Splendour, and Opulent. Perfect if you love over-the-top glam. A tiny rooftop Jacuzzi and fitness center are the only leisure facilities available.

33 Erskine Rd., Singapore 069333. ✆ **65/6511-3333**. Fax 65/6511-3303. www.thescarlethotel.com. 84 units. S$220 (US$141/£73) double; from S$550 (US$352/£182) suite. AE, DC, MC, V. 5-min. walk to Chinatown or Tanjong Pagar MRT Far from MRT. **Amenities:** 2 restaurants; lounge; outdoor Jacuzzi; fitness center; concierge; same-day laundry service; dry cleaning; executive-level rooms. In room: A/C, TV w/satellite programming, dataport w/direct Internet access, minibar, coffee/tea-making facilities, safe.

EXPENSIVE

Amara Singapore   Amara, located in the Shenton Way financial district, attracts primarily business travelers, so if your vacation includes a little business too, this hotel puts you closer to the action. If you're simply in town for a vacation, though, Amara probably isn't your best choice. The top eight floors of this hotel are reserved for the corporate set—not only do they have better views, but modern decor and services attractive to business visitors as well. Rooms on the Leisure Floors have an unappealing combination of green and white painted furniture and very little to offer in terms of views.

165 Tanjong Pagar Rd., Singapore 088539. ✆ **65/6879-2555**. Fax 65/6224-3910. www.amarahotels.com. 338 units. S$380 (US$243/£125) double; from S$700 (US$448/£231) suite. AE, DC, MC, V. 5-min. walk to Tanjong Pagar MRT. **Amenities:** 2 restaurants; lounge; outdoor pool; outdoor, lighted tennis courts; fitness center w/Jacuzzi, jogging track, sauna, steam, and massage; concierge; limousine service; business center; shopping arcade; salon; 24-hr. room service; babysitting; same-day laundry service; dry cleaning and self-service laundry; nonsmoking rooms; executive-level rooms. In room: A/C, TV w/satellite programming and in-house movie, dataport w/direct Internet access, minibar, coffee/tea-making facilities, hair dryer, safe.

Chinatown Accommodations

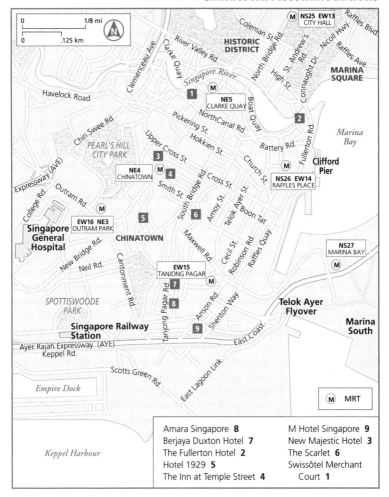

Amara Singapore **8**
Berjaya Duxton Hotel **7**
The Fullerton Hotel **2**
Hotel 1929 **5**
The Inn at Temple Street **4**

M Hotel Singapore **9**
New Majestic Hotel **3**
The Scarlet **6**
Swissôtel Merchant
Court **1**

M Hotel Singapore ★★   If you absolutely must stay in the Shenton Way downtown business district, then M Hotel is your best bet. Cornering the international business travel market, everything here is designed to make life easier for those with places to go and people to see. Rooms feature large, comfortable workspaces in clutter-free tones (blond wood furnishings, bone upholstery, tan carpeting), with some splashes of darker textiles for variety. Broadband Internet access and laptop safes make for extra convenience. The 11th floor is reserved for unwinding, with pool, spa, and fitness center all in sanitary contemporary white with glass-and-chrome accents everywhere. Operated by local firm Haatch, the spa has an excellent menu and reputation for quality. M Hotel's restaurants are packed for power lunches, so book in advance.

81 Anson Rd., Singapore 079908. ✆ **866/866-8086** in the U.S. and Canada, 800/147-803 in Australia, 800/782-542 in New Zealand, 800/8686-8086 in the U.K., or 65/6224-1133. Fax 65/6222-0749. www.millenniumhotels.com. **413**

units. S$300 (US$192/£99) double; S$700 (US$448/£231) suite. AE, DC, MC, V. 10-min. walk to Tanjong Pagar MRT. **Amenities:** 3 restaurants; bar; outdoor pool w/2 Jacuzzis; fitness center w/rock climbing wall; spa; business center; 24-hr. room service; babysitting; same-day laundry service; dry cleaning; executive-level rooms. *In room:* A/C, TV w/satellite programming, minibar, coffee/tea-making facilities, hair dryer, safe.

Swissôtel Merchant Court ✦   Merchant Court's convenient location and facilities make it very popular with leisure travelers. Situated on the Singapore River, the hotel has easy access not only to Chinatown and the Historic District, but also to Clarke Quay and Boat Quay, with their multitude of dining and nightlife options. In 2003 it became even more convenient when the new MRT stop opened just outside its doors. While this hotel's guest rooms aren't the biggest or most plush in the city, I never feel claustrophobic due to the large windows, uncluttered decor, and cooling atmosphere. Try to get a room with a view of the river or landscaped pool area. Convenience is provided by a self-service launderette, drink and snack vending machines on each floor, and a small fridge, so you can buy your own provisions. The hotel touts itself as a city hotel with a resort feel, with a small but nicely landscaped pool area (with a view of the river).

20 Merchant Rd., Singapore 058281. ✆ **800/637-9477** in the U.S. and Canada, 800/121-043 in Australia, 800/637-94771 in the U.K., or 65/6337-2288. Fax 65/6334-0606. www.swissotel-merchantcourt.com. 476 units. S$400 (US$256/£132) double; from S$850 (US$544/£281) suite. AE, DC, MC, V. Clarke Quay MRT. **Amenities:** Restaurant; bar; outdoor pool; fitness center and spa w/Jacuzzi, sauna, steam, massage and beauty treatments; 24-hr. room service; babysitting; same-day laundry service; dry cleaning; nonsmoking rooms; executive-level rooms. *In room:* A/C, TV w/satellite programming and in-house movie, dataport w/direct Internet access, coffee/tea-making facilities, hair dryer, safe.

MODERATE

Berjaya Duxton Hotel Singapore   Formerly the Duxton, this was one of the first accommodations in Singapore to experiment with the boutique hotel concept, transforming its shophouse structure into a small hotel and doing it with an elegance that earned it great international acclaim. From the outside, the place has old-world charm equal to any lamplit European cobblestone street, but step inside and there are very few details to remind you that you are in a quaint old shophouse—or in the historic Chinese district, for that matter. It's done entirely in turn-of-the-20th-century styling that includes reproduction Chippendale furniture, hand-painted wallpapers, and pen-and-ink Audubon-style drawings. Unfortunately, in recent years the hotel has dropped in service quality and the place has grown frayed around the edges. Its recent takeover by the Malaysian four-star hotel chain Berjaya holds little promise: the company has no plans to undertake any refurbishments, which this place really needs. Each room is different (to fit the structure of the building), and some can be quite small with limited views. Garden suites feature a lovely little courtyard. Building regulations do not allow for a pool and space does not allow for a fitness center.

83 Duxton Rd., Singapore 089540. ✆ **65/6227-7678.** Fax 65/6227-1232. www.berjayaresorts.com. 50 units. S$220 (US$141/£73) double; S$400 (US$256/£132) suite. AE, DC, MC, V. 5-min. walk to Tanjong Pagar MRT. **Amenities:** Restaurant; lobby bar; shuttle service; limited room service; babysitting; same-day laundry service; dry cleaning. *In room:* A/C, TV w/satellite programming and in-house movie, minibar, coffee/tea-making facilities, hair dryer, safe.

The Inn at Temple Street ✦✦   They've done a lovely job with this boutique hotel. In the heart of Chinatown's tourism hustle and bustle, step into the small lobby to be greeted by pretty antiques and tasteful Chinese trappings. To the side of the lobby, a charming cafe serves Western and local meals three times a day. The front desk handles everything from business center services to arranging laundry, tours, and postal services, but never seems frazzled. Rooms are quite modern for this type of hotel, with keycard locks, in-room safe, minibar, and room service. Decor is atmospheric as well, with local touches of carved woods and rich fabrics. I like the black-and-white-tiled bathrooms. This place is a welcome addition to Singapore's smattering of affordable accommodations.

36 Temple St., Singapore 058581. ☎ **65/6221-5333.** Fax 65/6225-5391. www.theinn.com.sg. 42 units. S$228 (US$146/£75) double; S$328 (US$210/£108) family. AE, DC, MC, V. 5-min. walk to Chinatown MRT. **Amenities:** Restaurant; lounge; limited room service; same-day laundry service; dry cleaning. In room: A/C, TV, minibar, coffee/tea-making facilities, in-room safe.

New Majestic Hotel ✦✦   A Chinatown landmark, the old 1928 Art Deco Majestic building is now a swank hotel, and Singapore's hottest spot for culture vultures. The concept—each guest room is individually designed by an emerging Singaporean artist. With wood floors, mosaic tiled bathrooms with claw-foot cast iron tubs, lots of glass, and contemporary fittings, these small rooms come alive with murals and artworks that say a little something about Singapore and the local arts scene. Themed rooms include garden rooms with wooden decks and outside tubs, hanging bed rooms, loft bed rooms, a mirror room, and an aquarium room. The devil is in the details: Top-of-the-line bedding, toiletries by Kiehl's, Bose systems, and Wi-Fi throughout add real value. The lobby is special as well, in stark white, with polished terrazzo floors, a spiral staircase and the owner's collection of vintage design-icon chairs. The rooftop lap pool is small, in contrasting black-and-white tiles, and the hotel's Chinese restaurant is as chic and quirky as the rest of the place.

31–37 Bukit Pasoh Rd., Singapore 089845. ☎ **65/6511-4700.** Fax 65/6227-3301. www.newmajestichotel.com. 30 units. S$280 (US$179/£92) double; from S$600 (US$384/£198) suite. AE, MC, V. 5-min. walk to Chinatown MRT. **Amenities:** Restaurant; outdoor pool; fitness center; concierge; same-day laundry service; dry cleaning. In room: A/C, TV w/satellite programming, minibar, coffee/tea-making facilities, hair dryer, safe.

INEXPENSIVE

Hotel 1929 ✦ (Finds)   Opened by the same people behind the New Majestic Hotel, this tiny boutique hotel shares the same love for vintage chairs as its more upmarket sister property. Located in a row of restored prewar shophouses in a former red-light district of Chinatown (with some elements remaining . . .), this building has no space for big guest rooms. In fact sizes and shapes can be a bit awkward at times, and the cheapest rooms have no windows, but what they lack in size they make up for in interior style, bright colors, and humor. The hotel doesn't have much in the way of guest facilities—a rooftop Jacuzzi and wooden sun deck about cover it—but if you're in town to shop and sightsee, then this is a good way to save some money but still enjoy a little style.

50 Keong Saik Rd., Singapore 089154. ☎ **65/6347-1929.** fax 65/6327-1929. S$140 (US$90/£46) double, from S$280(US$181/£92) suite. AE, DC, MC, V. 10-min. walk to Chinatown MRT. **Amenities:** Restaurant; Jacuzzi; laundry service. In room: A/C, TV, minibar, coffee/tea-making facilities, hair dryer, safe.

3 Orchard Road Area

VERY EXPENSIVE

Four Seasons Hotel Singapore ✦✦✦   Many upmarket hotels strive to convince you that staying with them is like visiting a wealthy friend. Four Seasons delivers this promise. The guest rooms are very spacious and inviting, and even the standard rooms have creature comforts you'd expect from a suite, such as complimentary fruit, terry bathrobes and slippers, CD and video disk players, and an extensive complimentary video disk and CD library from which the concierge is just waiting to deliver selections to your room. Each room has two-line speakerphones with voice mail and an additional dataport. The Italian marble bathrooms have double vanities, deep tubs, bidets, Neutrogena amenities, and surround speakers for the TV and stereo. Did I mention remote-control drapes? Everything here is comfort and elegance done to perfection (in fact, the beds here are so comfortable that they've sold almost 100 through the gift shop). In the waiting area off the lobby you can sink into soft sofas and appreciate the antiques and artwork selected from the owner's private collection. The fitness center has a state-of-the-art gymnasium with TV monitors, videos, tape players and CD and video disk players, a virtual-reality bike, aerobics, sauna, steam rooms, massage, facials, body wraps and aromatherapy treatments, and a staff of fitness professionals. Two indoor, air-conditioned tennis courts and two outdoor courts are staffed with a resident professional tennis coach to provide instruction or play a game. There are two pools: a 20m (66-ft.) lap pool and a rooftop sun deck pool, both with adjacent Jacuzzis. Consider a standard room here before a suite in a less expensive hotel. You won't regret it.

190 Orchard Blvd., Singapore 248646. (©) **800/332-3442** in the U.S., 800/268-6282 in Canada, or 65/6734-1110. Fax 65/6733-0682. www.fourseasons.com. 254 units. S$550 (US$352/£182) double; from S$720 (US$461/£238) suite. AE, DC, MC, V. 10-min. walk to Orchard MRT. **Amenities:** 2 restaurants; bar; 2 outdoor pools w/adjacent Jacuzzis; 2 outdoor, lighted tennis courts and 2 indoor air-conditioned tennis courts; Singapore's best equipped fitness center; spa w/sauna, steam, massage, and full menu of beauty and relaxation treatments; billiards room; concierge; limousine service; business center; 24-hr. room service; babysitting; same-day laundry service; dry cleaning; nonsmoking rooms; executive-level rooms. *In room:* A/C, TV w/satellite programming and in-room laserdisc player w/complimentary disks available, minibar, coffee/tea-making facilities, hair dryer, safe.

Shangri-La Hotel ⭐⭐⭐   The Shangri-La is a lovely place, with strolling gardens and an outdoor pool paradise that are great diversions from the hustle and bustle all around. Maybe that's why visiting VIPs like George Bush (both of them), Benazir Bhutto, and Nelson Mandela have all stayed here.

The hotel has three wings: The Tower Wing is the oldest, housing the lobby and most of the guest rooms, which were completely redone. Instead of the usual square-block hotel rooms of typical city hotels, Shang's added unusual angles and curves, sophisticated contemporary furnishings, and a refreshing wall of glass blocks that welcomes natural light into the giant bathroom and dressing area. Balconies were melded into the rooms to become reading nooks. The Garden Wing surrounds an open-air atrium with cascading waterfall and exotic plants. Rooms here are more resortlike, with natural textured wall coverings, tweed carpeting, and woven bedspreads. These larger-size rooms also have bougainvillea-laden balconies overlooking the tropical landscaped pool area. The exclusive Valley Wing has a private entrance and very spacious rooms (I'd say the largest rooms in Singapore), linked to the main tower by a sky bridge that looks out over the hotel's 6 hectares (15 acres) of landscaped lawns, fruit trees, and flowers. These rooms, with large bathrooms and dressing areas, reopened after a massive-scale renovation. The new decor reflects the exclusivity of the facility, an Oriental sanctuary. These rooms come with personalized butler service, personalized stationery, access to complimentary airport limousine service, and a champagne bar in the lobby.

22 Orange Grove Rd., Singapore 258350. (©) **800/942-5050** in the U.S., 866/344-5050 in Canada, 800/222-448 in Australia, 800/442-179 in New Zealand, or 65/6737-3644. Fax 65/6737-3257. www.shangri-la.com. 750 units. S$640 (US$410/£211) Tower double; S$740 (US$474/£244) Garden double; S$875 (US$560/£289) Valley double; from S$1,000 (US$640/£330) suite. AE, DC, MC, V. 10-min. walk to Orchard MRT. **Amenities:** 5 restaurants; lobby lounge;

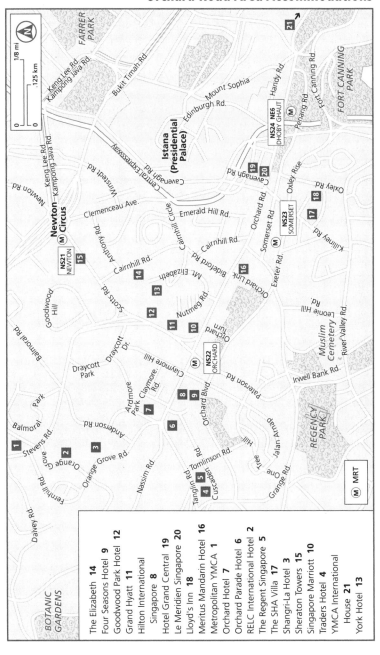

The Elizabeth **14**
Four Seasons Hotel **9**
Goodwood Park Hotel **12**
Grand Hyatt **11**
Hilton International
  Singapore **8**
Hotel Grand Central **19**
Le Meridien Singapore **20**
Lloyd's Inn **18**
Meritus Mandarin Hotel **16**
Metropolitan YMCA **1**
Orchard Hotel **7**
Orchard Parade Hotel **6**
RELC International Hotel **2**
The Regent Singapore **5**
The SHA Villa **17**
Shangri-La Hotel **3**
Sheraton Towers **15**
Singapore Marriott **10**
Traders Hotel **4**
YMCA International
  House **21**
York Hotel **13**

resort-style outdoor landscaped pool; 3-hole pitch and putt course; 4 outdoor, lighted tennis courts; fitness center w/glass walls looking out into gardens; Jacuzzi; sauna; steam; massage; concierge; limousine service; business center; shopping arcade; salon; 24-hr. room service; babysitting; same-day laundry service; dry cleaning; nonsmoking rooms; executive-level rooms. *In room:* A/C, TV w/satellite programming and in-house movie, minibar, coffee/tea-making facilities, hair dryer, iron, safe.

Sheraton Towers Singapore *★★*   One of the first things you see when you walk into the lobby of the Sheraton Towers is the service awards the place has won; check in, and you'll begin to see why they won them. With the deluxe (standard) room they'll give you a suit pressing on arrival, daily newspaper delivery, shoeshine service, and complimentary movies. These refurbished rooms are handsome with textured walls, plush carpeting, and a bed luxuriously fitted with down pillows and dreamy 100% Egyptian cotton bedding. Upgrade to a Tower room and you get a personal butler, complimentary nightly cocktails and morning breakfast, free laundry, free local calls, your own pants press, and free use of the personal trainer in the fitness center. The cabana rooms, off the pool area, have all the services of the Tower Wing in a very private resort room. The 23 one-of-a-kind suite rooms each feature a different theme. Chinese regency, French, Italian, jungle, you name it—very unique, with handpicked furnishings. Although Sheraton is a luxe choice, you can find better deals, price-wise.

39 Scotts Rd., Singapore 228230. ✆ **800/325-3535** in the U.S. and Canada, 800/073-535 in Australia, 800/325-35353 in New Zealand, 800/353535 in the U.K., or 65/6737-6888. Fax 65/6737-1072. www.sheraton.com. 413 units. S$520 (US$333/£172) double; from S$1,200 (US$768/£396) suite. AE, DC, MC, V. 5-min. walk to Newton MRT. **Amenities:** 3 restaurants; lobby lounge; outdoor landscaped pool; fitness center w/sauna and massage; concierge; limousine service; 24-hr. business center; 24-hr. room service; babysitting; same-day laundry service; dry cleaning; nonsmoking rooms; executive-level rooms. *In room:* A/C, TV w/satellite programming and in-house movie, dataport w/direct Internet access, minibar, coffee/tea-making facilities, hair dryer, safe.

Singapore Marriott Hotel *★★*   You can't get a better location than this—at the corner of Orchard and Scotts roads. Marriott's green-roofed pagoda tower is a well-recognized landmark on Orchard Road, but guest rooms inside tend to be smaller than average to fit in the octagonal structure. Luckily the recent refurbishing scheme added lively colors to brighten the spaces with natural greens and floral fabrics. The palatial lobby has been overtaken by the Marriott Cafe, with weekend buffets that are so popular with the locals that there's a long queue. Outside, the Crossroads Café, spilling out onto the sidewalk, is a favorite of international and Singaporean celebrities who like to be seen. Service in this hotel is very personable and professional.

Marriott, which took over management of this property in 1995, caters to the business traveler, so the rooms on the club floors get most of the hotel's attention. The club lounge, for instance, has a great view and there's not a tacky detail in the comfortable seating and dining areas.

320 Orchard Rd., Singapore 238865. ✆ **800/228-9290** in the U.S. and Canada, 800/251-259 in Australia, 800/22-12-22 in the U.K., or 65/6735-5800. Fax 65/6735-9800. www.singaporemarriott.com. 373 units. S$500 (US$320/£165) double; from S$800 (US$512/£264) suite. AE, DC, MC, V. Orchard MRT. **Amenities:** 4 restaurants; lobby lounge; bar w/live jazz, and dance club w/live pop bands; outdoor pool w/Jacuzzi; outdoor basketball court; fitness center w/Jacuzzi, sauna, steam, and massage; concierge; limousine service; 24-hr. business center; shopping arcade; 24-hr. room service; babysitting; same-day laundry service; dry cleaning; nonsmoking rooms; executive-level rooms. *In room:* A/C, TV w/satellite programming and in-house movie, dataport w/direct Internet access, minibar, coffee/tea-making facilities, hair dryer, iron, safe.

EXPENSIVE
Goodwood Park Hotel *★*   This national landmark, built in 1900, resembles a castle along the Rhine—having served originally as the Teutonia Club, a social club for

The Best of Singapore's Spas

In the mid-'90s, spas began making a splash in the Singapore hotel scene. By the millennium, every luxury hotel was planning either a full-blown spa facility or at least an offering spa services to its residents. At the same time, day spas sprouted up in shopping centers; and despite the economic downturn, these businesses have stayed afloat. Now, the Singapore Tourism Board is positioning Singapore as an urban spa hub in Southeast Asia, luring visitors from the region and beyond with luxurious facilities that go above and beyond the call of relaxation and hedonistic pampering. Here are the best among the many:

Singapore's most celebrated spa, **Amrita** (Raffles The Plaza, Level 6, 2 Stamford Rd.; ✆ **65/6336-4477**; and Swissôtel Merchant Court, Level 2, 20 Merchant Rd.; ✆ **65/6239-1780**; www.amritaspas.com), is operated by Raffles International and has proven so wildly successful that the hotel chain has opened Amritas in Germany, Switzerland, and beyond. This flagship spa at Raffles The Plaza is the largest spa in Singapore, with Southeast Asian–inspired interiors and treatments—over 1,000 to choose from.

Amrita is convenient if you want to stay in the city center; however, if you want more of a retreat spa experience **Spa Botanica** (2 Bukit Manis Rd., The Sentosa; ✆ **65/6371-1318**; www.spabotanica.com) is a gorgeous pick. Located at the Sentosa, a scenic resort dripping with laid-back, yet elegant, tropical Southeast Asian decor. Spa Botanica has 6,000 sq. m (64,584 sq. ft.) of designated spa space, with pools, mud baths, and treatment pavilions nestled in lush gardens. Treatments center around natural recipes for beauty and relaxation, including spice and floral treatments.

the early German community. During World War II, high-ranking Japanese military used it as a residence, and later it served as a British war-crimes court before being converted into a hotel. Since then the hotel has expanded from 60 rooms to 235 and has hosted a long list of international celebrities and dignitaries.

For the money, there are more luxurious facilities, but although most hotels have bigger and better business and fitness centers (Goodwood has the smallest fitness center), only Raffles Hotel can rival Goodwood Park's historical significance. The poolside suites off the Mayfair Pool are fabulous in slate tiles and polished wood, offering direct access to the small Mayfair Pool with its lush Balinese-style landscaping. There are also suites off the main pool, which is much larger but offers little privacy from the lobby and surrounding restaurants. The original building has large and airy guest rooms in a classic European decor, but beware of the showers, which have hand-held shower heads that clip to the wall, making it difficult to aim and impossible to keep the water from splashing out all over the bathroom floor. Newer rooms in the main wing are renovated in stark contemporary style. The extremely attentive staff always serves with a smile.

22 Scotts Rd., Singapore 228221. ✆ **800/772-3890** in the U.S., 800/665-5919 in Canada, 800/89-95-20 in the U.K., or 65/6737-7411. Fax 65/6732-8558. www.goodwoodparkhotel.com.sg. 235 units. S$425 (US$272/£140) double;

from S$525 (US$336/£173) suite. AE, DC, MC, V. 5-min. walk to Orchard MRT. **Amenities:** 6 restaurants; bar and lobby lounge; 2 outdoor pools; tiny fitness center; spa; concierge; limousine service; business center; 24-hr. room service; babysitting; same-day laundry service; dry cleaning. *In room:* A/C, TV w/satellite programming and in-house movie, minibar, coffee/tea-making facilities, hair dryer, safe.

Grand Hyatt Singapore 🏨🏨   Despite its fantastic location, this hotel was doing pretty poorly until they had a feng shui master come in and evaluate it for redecorating. According to the Chinese monk, because the lobby entrance was a wall of flat glass doors that ran parallel to the long reception desk in front, all the hotel's wealth was flowing from the desk right out the doors and into the street. To correct the problem, the doors are now set at right angles to each other, a fountain was built in the rear, and the reception was moved around a corner to the right of the lobby. Since then, the hotel has enjoyed some of the highest occupancy rates in town. Feng shui or not, the new decor is modern, sleek, and sophisticated, an elegant combination of polished black marble and deep wood. Terrace Wing guest rooms invite with plush duvet and golden colors, plus unique glass-enclosed alcoves looking over the hotel gardens. Bathrooms are large, with lots of marble counter space. If you've booked through a travel agent, these are the rooms you'll get. If you make your booking on your own, they'll more likely put you in a Grand Wing room. These are really suites with separate living areas, small walk-in closets, and separate work area. They're very deluxe since a 2003 refurbishment that freshened up the decor. The pool and fitness center are amazing. Located in the center of this city hotel, a four-story waterfall provides the perfect soundscape to match a lush jungle garden hugging the free-form pool and state-of-the-art gym.

Important note: Grand Hyatt no longer publishes a rack rate; rather, it selects the "best rate" for the dates of your stay. Below, the rates reflect the average best rates for January 2007.

10 Scotts Rd., Singapore 228211. ✆ **800/223-1234** in the U.S. and Canada, or 65/6738-1234. Fax 65/6732-1696. www.singapore.grand.hyatt.com. 685 units. S$380 (US$243/£125) double; from S$720 (US$461/£238) suite. AE, DC, MC, V. Near Orchard MRT. **Amenities:** 3 restaurants; lobby lounge; live music bar; landscaped outdoor pool; 2 outdoor, lighted tennis courts; squash court and badminton court; excellent fitness center w/Jacuzzi, sauna, steam, massage, and spa treatments; concierge; limousine service; business center; 24-hr. room service; babysitting; same-day laundry service; dry cleaning; executive-level rooms. *In room:* A/C, TV w/satellite programming and in-house movie, dataport w/direct Internet access, minibar, coffee/tea-making facilities, hair dryer, iron, safe.

Orchard Hotel Singapore 🏨   The Orchard Hotel, with its wonderful attached shopping mall, provides accommodations for leisure and business travelers in two wings. The main lobby, in Mediterranean flair, has a giant central clock with wrought iron detail and seating beneath. Between the lobby lounge to the left and coffee shop to the right, the place always feels energized. Lower-priced rooms in the older Orchard Wing were renovated in 2005, and are contemporary with touches of Asian style, such as the glass headboards etched in Oriental design. Though small, guest rooms have state-of-the-art fixtures like adjustable bedside reading lamps and huge flatscreen TVs. A round window peers into the bathroom, which shines in white marble and chrome. The Claymore Wing houses deluxe rooms in comfortable contemporary style, with large glass desktops, rosewood bed stands, and fabrics and carpeting in neutral tones. The staff is friendly and always greets you with a smile.

442 Orchard Rd., Singapore 238879. ✆ **800/637-7200** in the U.S. and Canada, 800/655-147 in Australia, 800/442-519 in New Zealand, 800/25-28-40 in the U.K., or 65/6734-7766. Fax 65/6733-5482. www.orchardhotel.com.sg. 672 units. S$385 (US$246/£127) double; S$900 (US$576/£297) suite. AE, DC, MC, V. 5-min. walk to Orchard MRT. **Amenities:**

2 restaurants; lobby lounge; outdoor pool; fitness center w/sauna; concierge; tour desk; business center; shopping mall adjacent; salon; 24-hr. room service; babysitting; same-day laundry service; dry cleaning; nonsmoking rooms; executive-level rooms. *In room:* A/C, TV w/satellite programming, minibar, coffee/tea-making facilities, safe.

The Regent Singapore ☆   The Regent is tucked between Cuscaden and Tanglin roads, at the northern end of Orchard Road—you'll have to hike about 10 minutes to get to the center of things. But check out the lobby in this place! It's a huge, three-level atrium affair with windows on three sides, a skylight, fountains, plenty of small private meeting nooks, and raised walkways straight out of *The Jetsons.* The guest rooms have high ceilings and are decorated with Chinese motifs in refurbished fabrics, but the bathrooms are smaller than at most other comparable hotels. You have to request coffee/tea-making facilities in your room; otherwise the service is free in the tea lounge, which also serves a high tea the old-fashioned way, with silver tray service.

1 Cuscaden Rd., Singapore 249715. ✆ **800/545-4000** in the U.S. and Canada, 800/022-800 in Australia, 800/440-800 in New Zealand, 800/917-8795 in the U.K., or 65/6733-8888. Fax 65/6732-8838. www.regenthotels.com. 441 units. S$425 (US$272/£140) double; from S$525 (US$336/£173) suite. AE, DC, MC, V. 15-min. walk to Orchard MRT. **Amenities:** 2 restaurants; very cool bar; lobby tea lounge; outdoor pool; fitness center w/steam and massage; concierge; limousine service; business center; 24-hr. room service; babysitting; same-day laundry service; dry cleaning; nonsmoking rooms; executive-level rooms. *In room:* A/C, TV w/satellite programming and in-house movie, dataport w/direct Internet access, minibar, hair dryer, safe.

MODERATE

The Elizabeth Singapore   This small, quaint hotel has cozy rooms and the most friendly and accommodating staff around. Done in dark, cool European styling throughout, this modern hotel's most dramatic feature is the lobby area's fantastic cascading waterfalls, which drop over a vertical tropical rock-and-plant garden nestled behind three-story-high glass panels. The Elizabeth has seen some recent refurbishment to freshen the rooms. Newer touches include wall coverings, floral bedspreads, and drapes. The burl-wood furnishings are handsome. Recreation facilities are few and small compared to similar properties. Business center services are provided by the front office staff. There is a small but imaginative gift shop specializing in feng shui items. Attractive rates make this hotel an excellent bargain.

24 Mount Elizabeth, Singapore 228518. ✆ **65/6738-1188.** Fax 65/6732-3866. www.theelizabeth.com. 256 units. S$280 (US$179/£92) double; S$600 (US$384/£198) suite. AE, DC, MC, V. 10-min. walk to Orchard MRT. **Amenities:** Restaurant; lobby lounge; small outdoor pool; tiny fitness center w/sauna; concierge; tour desk; 24-hr. room service; babysitting; same-day laundry service; dry cleaning. *In room:* A/C, TV w/satellite programming, minibar, coffee/tea-making facilities, hair dryer, safe.

Hilton International Singapore   If you count the luxury cars that drive up to the valet at the Hilton, you'd think this is a good address to have while staying in Singapore. Well, to be honest this Hilton doesn't measure up with some of their other properties worldwide and definitely can't compete with other hotels in this price category in Singapore. The most famous feature of the Hilton is its glamorous shopping arcade, where you can find your Donna Karan, Louis Vuitton, Gucci—all the greats. Ask the concierge for a pager, and they'll page you for important calls while you window-shop or try some of the 45 fragrant vodkas at the lobby bar. With all this, the guest rooms should be pretty sumptuous, no? Well, no. The rooms are simpler than you'd expect, with nothing flashy or overdone. Floor-to-ceiling windows are in each, and although views in the front of the hotel are of Orchard Road and the Thai Embassy property, views in the back are not so hot. In this day and age when business-class hotels are wrestling to outdo each other, Hilton has a lot of catching up to do.

Important note: Hilton no longer publishes a rack rate; rather, it selects the "best rate" for the dates of your stay. Below, the rates reflect the average best rates for January 2007.

581 Orchard Rd., Singapore 238883. (©) **800/445-8667** in the U.S., or 65/6737-2233. Fax 65/6732-2917. www.singapore. hilton.com. 423 units. S$300 (US$192/£99) double; from S$660 (US$422/£218) suite. AE, DC, MC, V. Near Orchard MRT. **Amenities:** 2 restaurants; lobby lounge; outdoor pool; fitness center w/sauna and steam; concierge; limousine service; business center; shopping arcade; salon; 24-hr. room service; babysitting; same-day laundry service; dry cleaning; nonsmoking rooms; executive-level rooms. *In room:* A/C, TV w/satellite programming and in-house movie, minibar, coffee/tea-making facilities, hair dryer, safe.

Le Meridien Singapore

Atrium lobbies are popular in Singapore, and I think Le Meridien's is the original and one of the brightest. Long, straight corridors look out into the huge, open, skylighted space and below to the colorful lobby lounge decorated with plants and fresh flowers. Just at the southern tip of Orchard Road, Le Meridien offers good access to shopping activities, plus the attractions of the nearby Historic District. Standard rooms are light and fresh with simple European decor and subtle Chinese accents. Voice mail and extra dataports for laptop usage make for convenience, and some rooms have balconies. Bathrooms are state-of-the-art. The Jade and Opal suites are the best spaces, but the executive club facilities are not as attractive as other hotels in this category.

100 Orchard Rd., Singapore 238840. (©) **800/543-4300** in the U.S. and Canada, 800/622240 in Australia, 800/454-040 in New Zealand, 800/404040 in the U.K., or 65/6733-8855. Fax 65/6732-7886. www.lemeridien.com. 407 units. S$350 (US$224/£116) double; from S$470 (US$301/£155) suite. AE, DC, MC, V. 10-min. walk to Dhoby Ghaut or Somerset MRT. **Amenities:** 2 restaurants; lobby lounge; outdoor pool; fitness center w/sauna; concierge; limousine service; business center; shopping arcade; salon; 24-hr. room service; babysitting; same-day laundry service; dry cleaning; executive-level rooms. *In room:* A/C, TV w/satellite programming and in-house movie, minibar, coffee/tea-making facilities, hair dryer, safe.

Meritus Mandarin Singapore ✦

Smack in the center of Orchard Road is the Mandarin Hotel, a two-tower complex with Singapore's most famous revolving restaurant topping it off like a little hat. The 39-story Main Tower opened in 1973, and with the opening of the South Wing 10 years later the number of rooms expanded to 1,200. True to its name, the hotel reflects a Chinese aesthetic, beginning in the lobby with the huge marble mural of the "87 Taoist Immortals" and the carved wood chairs lining the walls. The South Wing is predominantly for leisure travelers, who have access to the tower through a side entrance. These guest rooms are the same size as those in the Main Tower but feel slightly smaller, most likely because of the dark wood modular units that fill up major wall space with imposing TV and minibar cabinets and a built-in seating area. Mandarin refurbished the carpets, drapes, and linens in this wing in 2003, which really freshened up these rooms from previous dull colors. While rooms in this wing are priced for greater value, be warned that this is where they put all the tour groups. Be prepared for large groups milling around the public spaces during peak tourist seasons.

333 Orchard Rd., Singapore 238867. (©) **65/6737-4411**. Fax 65/6732-2361. www.asiatravel.com/singapore/mandarin. 1,200 units. S$240 (US$154/£79) double; from S$840 (US$538/£277) suite. AE, DC, MC, V. Near Orchard MRT. **Amenities:** 4 restaurants; revolving observation lounge and lobby lounge; outdoor pool; fitness center w/Jacuzzi, sauna, steam, and massage; concierge; tour desk; limousine service; business center; shopping arcade; salon; 24-hr. room service; babysitting; same-day laundry service; dry cleaning; nonsmoking rooms; executive-level rooms. *In room:* A/C, TV w/satellite programming and in-house movie, minibar, coffee/tea-making facilities, safe.

Orchard Parade Hotel ⭐⭐ (Value) (Kids)   This fine hotel, after a S$40-million (US$26-million/£13-million), 2-year renovation, sports a new swimming pool, guest rooms, lobby, driveway, front entrance, and food and beverage outlets, decorated in a Mediterranean theme integrating marble mosaics, plaster walls, beamed ceilings, and wrought-iron railings. The midsize pool on the sixth-floor roof features colorful tiles and draping arbors, a motif carried over through the new fitness center. Rooms also feature Mediterranean style in terra-cotta wall sconces, wrought-iron table legs, and shades of teal and aqua. If it's important to you, you need to specify a room with a view here. For good value, the Family Studio fits a king-size bed and two twins with separate family room and dining area and plenty of space for just S$100 (US$64/£33) extra. Just outside, a long terrace along Orchard Road hosts many restaurant choices, the most popular of which, Modestos, serves good pasta and pizzas at affordable prices.

1 Tanglin Rd., Singapore 247905. (C) **65/6737-1133.** Fax 65/6733-0242. www.orchardparade.com.sg. 387 units. S$300 (US$192/£99) double; S$550 (US$352/£182) family studio; from S$450 (US$290/£149) suite. AE, DC, MC, V. Orchard MRT. **Amenities:** 5 restaurants; lobby lounge; outdoor pool; fitness center; concierge; tour desk; business center; salon; 24-hr. room service; babysitting; same-day laundry service; dry cleaning; executive-level rooms. *In room:* A/C, TV w/satellite programming, minibar, coffee/tea-making facilities, hair dryer.

Traders Hotel Singapore ⭐⭐   A fantastic bargain for leisure travelers in Singapore, Traders advertises itself as a "value-for-money" hotel. A spinoff of Shangri-La (see earlier), this hotel anticipates the special needs of travelers and tries on all levels to accommodate them. Rooms have an empty fridge that can be stocked from the supermarket next door (show your room card key at nearby Tanglin Mall for discounts from many of the shops); there are spanking-clean self-service launderette facilities with ironing boards on six floors; and there are vending machines and ice machines (a rarity in Asian hotels). They even provide a hospitality lounge for guests to use after checkout, with seating areas, work spaces with dataports, card phones, safe-deposit boxes, vending machines, and a shower. Guest rooms are smaller than average but feature child-size sofa beds and large drawers for storage. The large, landscaped pool area has a great poolside alfresco cafe, **Ah Hoi's Kitchen** (p. 116), serving up tasty local dishes at reasonable prices. Be sure to ask about promotion rates when you book your room. If you're planning to stay longer than 2 weeks, they have a long-stay program that offers discount meals, laundry and business center services, and half-price launderette tokens.

One caveat: The distance from MRT service and Orchard Road makes you dependent on taxi service. However, I like Trader's option to cross-sign (at no extra charge) with its two sister properties, the Shangri-La Hotel, which is only a 5-minute taxi ride away, and the Shangri-La's Rasa Sentosa Resort on Sentosa Island, giving you access to their awesome pools, spas, and fitness centers plus the latter's beachfront access.

1A Cuscaden Rd., Singapore 249716. (C) **800/942-5050** in the U.S. and Canada, 800/222-448 in Australia, 0800/442-179 in New Zealand, or 65/6738-2222. Fax 65/6831-4314. www.shangri-la.com. 547 units. S$260 (US$166/£86) double; from S$585 (US$374/£193) suite. AE, DC, MC, V. 15-min. walk to Orchard MRT. **Amenities:** 2 restaurants; bar and lobby lounge; outdoor pool; fitness center w/Jacuzzi, sauna, steam, and massage; spa; concierge; limousine service; shuttle service; business center; salon; 24-hr. room service; babysitting; same-day laundry service; dry cleaning; self-service launderette; executive-level rooms. *In room:* A/C, TV w/satellite programming, dataport w/direct Internet access, minibar, coffee/tea-making facilities, hair dryer, iron, safe.

York Hotel Singapore ⭐   This small tourist-class hotel has some of the most consistently professional and courteous staff I've encountered. A short walk from Orchard,

York is convenient though far enough removed to provide a relaxing atmosphere. Guest rooms reflect a sharp contemporary style in light woods, natural tones, and simple lines. Combined with an already spacious room, the result is an airy, cooling effect. Bathrooms throughout are downright huge. Cabana rooms look out to a pool and sun deck decorated with giant palms. Despite surrounding buildings, it doesn't feel claustrophobic, as do some of the more centrally situated hotels. There's a Jacuzzi, but the business center is tiny as is the fitness center. The rates here have gone up a bit, so make sure you ask for promotional discounts.

21 Mount Elizabeth, Singapore 228516. (C) **800/223-5652** in the U.S. and Canada, 800/553-549 in Australia, 800/447-555 in New Zealand, 800/89-88-52 in the U.K., or 65/6737-0511. Fax 65/6732-1217. www.yorkhotel.com.sg. 406 units. S$190 (US$122/£63) double; from S$340 (US$218/£112) suite. AE, DC, MC, V. 10-min. walk to Orchard MRT. **Amenities:** Restaurant; lobby lounge; outdoor pool; fitness center; Jacuzzi; tour desk; business center; 24-hr. room service; babysitting; same-day laundry service; dry cleaning. *In room:* A/C, TV w/satellite programming, minibar, coffee/tea-making facilities.

INEXPENSIVE

Hotel Grand Central, Singapore   Most of the hotels in this price category are at least a 10-minute walk outside the main drag, but Hotel Grand Central is right on it, with an exclusive Orchard Road address. The hotel always runs at high occupancy, its lobby a hustle and bustle of mostly regional vacation travelers who, truth to tell, seem to have worn dull the front counter staff's service edge. The building was originally eight floors, but renovations added an extra floor to the top, which houses executive-club rooms. The corridors are on the dreary side, and the guest rooms and bathrooms are a little run-down. Windows are positioned high, so there's not much in the way of views—although rooms in the center of the building offer views of rooms on the opposite side, if that's your idea of fun. To the side of the rooftop pool is a special corner reserved for dead hotel houseplants.

22 Cavenagh Rd./Orchard Rd., Singapore 229617. (C) **65/6737-9944.** Fax 65/6733-3175. www.grandcentral.com.sg. 390 units. S$158 (US$101/£52) double; S$298 (US$191/£182) suite. AE, DC, MC, V. 10-min. walk to Somerset or Dhoby Ghaut MRT. **Amenities:** Restaurant; lounge; outdoor pool; fitness center w/Jacuzzi and steam; tour desk; business center; shopping arcade; salon; same-day laundry service; dry cleaning. *In room:* A/C, TV w/in-house movie, minibar, coffee/tea-making facilities.

Lloyd's Inn   Lloyd's is a budget motel in every sense. It's a two-story building on a relatively quiet, low-traffic street. The corridors are open-air and the rooms are small, with a definite budget feeling, though all have air-conditioning and phones. Rooms are midsize with windows and en-suite bathrooms. They seem to be doing a better job with upkeep than they have in the past. The published rates include the "+++" taxes (see "Taxes & Service Charges," earlier in this chapter); there's no discount offered for long-term stays; you must pay for your room when you check in; and if you use a credit card, it'll cost you an extra 2%. No pool, no fitness center, no nothing—you got your room, that's what you got. Front counter staff is very nice.

2 Lloyd Rd., Singapore 239091. (C) **65/6737-7309.** Fax 65/6737-7847. www.lloydinn.com. 34 units. S$75–S$85 (US$48–US$54/£25–£28) double. MC, V. 10-min. walk to Somerset MRT. **Amenities:** Same-day laundry service plus self-service launderette. *In room:* A/C, TV, minibar, coffee/tea-making facilities.

The Metropolitan YMCA Singapore   This place is a little out-of-the-way in terms of walking distance to anywhere, and the rooms are showing their age, but they're clean and efficient. *One caution here:* The least expensive rooms have no windows; for sunlight, you'll have to pay a little extra. Nine family rooms are outfitted with either three twin beds or a double and a twin. The family rooms are the same size

as the other rooms, but the bathrooms are bigger and there's a lot more closet space. There is a fitness center and a trainer. The pool is a nice size, as is the kiddie pool, and there's a lifeguard on duty from 9am to 9pm daily. No dorm rooms are available, but concierge, dry cleaning, laundry, and secretarial services are. Plus, there's a self-service launderette, a coffee shop, a tour desk, and a shuttle service to Orchard Road.

60 Stevens Rd., Singapore 257854. © **65/6839-8333**. Fax 65/6235-5528. www.mymca.org.sg. 91 units. S$75 (US$48/£25) double; S$140 (US$90/£46) family; S$150 (US$96/£50) suite. AE, DC, MC, V. Far from MRT. **Amenities:** Restaurant; outdoor pool; fitness center; concierge; tour desk; babysitting; business center; same-day laundry service; dry cleaning; nonsmoking rooms. *In room:* A/C, TV, minibar, coffee/tea-making facilities.

RELC International Hotel *&& Value*   RELC offers real value-for-money in terms of location (a 10-min. walk to Orchard Rd.) and an excellent facility. I found the service and convenience here superior to some hotels in the higher-priced categories. RELC has four types of rooms—superior twin, executive twin, Hollywood queen, and alcove suite—but no matter what the size, none of the rooms ever feel cluttered, close, or cramped. All rooms have balconies, TVs with two movie channels, and a fridge with free juice boxes and snacks. Bathrooms are large, with full-length tubs and hair dryers standard. If you're interested in the higher-priced rooms, I'd choose the Hollywood queen over the alcove suite—its decor is better and it can sleep a family very comfortably.

30 Orange Grove Rd., Singapore 258352. © **65/6885-7888**. Fax 65/6733-9976. www.relc.org.sg. 128 units. S$129 (US$83/£43) double; from S$175 (US$112/£58) suite. AE, DC, MC, V. 15-min. walk to Orchard MRT. **Amenities:** Restaurant; tour desk; same-day laundry service plus self-service launderette; nonsmoking rooms. *In room:* A/C, TV w/in-house movie, dataport w/direct Internet access, minibar, fridge, coffeemaker (in some rooms), hair dryer.

The SHA Villa *&& Finds*   SHA Villa is an interesting pick. Formerly the Regalis Court, this charming colonial-style mansion has been restored beautifully and outfitted with Peranakan-inspired touches. Everything here will make you feel as if you're staying in a quaint guesthouse rather than a hotel, from the open-air lobby (under the *porte-cochere*) and corridors to the guest rooms, which have comforting touches like teakwood furnishings, textile wall hangings, Oriental throws over wooden floors, and bamboo blinds to keep out the sun. What makes this place truly unique is its management. SHA stands for Singapore Hotel Association—this property serves as a training ground for hospitality service staff, from bellhops to chefs. Everyone is eager to please because, well, they're being graded. Centrally located just a 10-minute walk from Orchard Road and with an excellent Western restaurant, you can't go wrong here.

64 Lloyd Rd., Singapore 239113. © **65/6734-7117**. Fax 65/6736-1651. www.sha.org.sg. 40 units. S$180 (US$115/£59) double. AE, DC, MC, V. 10-min. walk from Somerset MRT. **Amenities:** Restaurant; car-rental desk; babysitting; same-day laundry service; nonsmoking rooms. *In room:* A/C, TV, dataport w/direct Internet access, coffee/tea-making facilities, safe.

YMCA International House *Kids*   Of the two YMCA's in Singapore, this one has the better location. At the lower end of Orchard Road, it's only a short walk to the Dhoby Ghaut MRT station, making it very convenient for getting around by mass transit. The guest rooms have been renovated and have private bathrooms that are better than I've seen at some much pricier hotels. All rooms have air-conditioning, a telephone (with free local calls), color television, and a stock-it-yourself refrigerator, but be warned, all standard double-occupancy rooms are twin beds only. The dormitories are small, dark, and quiet, with two bunk beds per room. Across the hall are men's and women's locker rooms for showering. Most of the public areas have no air-conditioning, including the old fitness facility, billiards center, and squash courts—so be warned: They can become unbearably hot. The rooftop pool is nothing to write home about, but a full-time lifeguard is on duty. There's a coffee shop in the lobby. The hotel staff is amazingly friendly.

1 Orchard Rd., Singapore 238824. ℂ **65/6336-6000.** Fax 65/6337-3140. www.ymcaih.com.sg. 111 units. S$105 (US$67/£35) double; S$135 (US$86/£45) family room; S$145 (US$93/£48) superior room. AE, DC, MC, V. 5-min. walk to Dhoby Ghaut MRT. **Amenities:** 2 restaurants; outdoor pool; small gym; game room; tour desk; babysitting; same-day laundry service, Internet center. *In room:* A/C, TV, fridge.

4 Sentosa Island

There are only two hotel properties on Sentosa Island, the Shangri-La's Rasa Sentosa, located right on the water and designed for families and fun, and the Sentosa Resort & Spa, located on a cliff above the water, closer to golfing and designed for secluded, romantic getaways.

The Sentosa Resort & Spa ★★   Designed with romance in mind, the Sentosa Resort & Spa's small resort-style buildings, fashioned after the famous resorts of Phuket, Thailand, are connected with covered walkways encircling lily ponds and courtyard gardens. Here, the designers have done a great job combining clean modern lines with tropical touches to produce a sophisticated getaway with relaxing charm. Lazy terraces and cozy alcoves tucked all over the grounds invite guests to unwind in privacy—perfect for intimate candlelight dinners that can be requested anywhere you like. The centerpiece is the new spa, built into a garden setting—it is opulent and relaxing.

The standard guest rooms in the five-story hotel building are small but stunning, featuring camphor burl-wood doors and accents, Thai silk screens in natural browns and greens, and deep tubs and separate showers in the bathrooms, surrounded by thick celadon green tiling and sleek black granite details. Ask for views of the golf course, which are prettier than the views of the hotel courtyards and buildings. Butlers wait round-the-clock to serve you—a standard feature for all rooms.

2 Bukit Manis Rd., Sentosa, Singapore 099891. ℂ **65/6275-0331.** Fax 65/6275-0228. www.thesentosa.com. 214 units. S$380 (US$243/£125) double; from S$550 (US$352/£182) suite; S$1,500 (US$960/£495) villa. AE, DC, MC, V. See "Sentosa Island," in chapter 6, for public transportation. **Amenities:** 2 restaurants; lounge; gorgeous midnight blue-tiled outdoor pool w/views of the harbor; golf at nearby facilities; 2 outdoor, lighted tennis courts w/coach; 2 squash courts; fitness center w/20m lap pool, Jacuzzi, and sauna; brand-new luxury spa w/private pool, mud baths, steam, Jacuzzis, exercise and relaxation classes, salon, beauty treatments, and massage; concierge; tour desk; limousine service; shuttle service; 24-hr. room service; babysitting; same-day laundry service; dry cleaning. *In room:* A/C, TV w/satellite programming and in-house movie, dataport w/direct Internet access, minibar, coffee/tea-making facilities, hair dryer, safe.

Shangri-La's Rasa Sentosa Resort *Kids*   Set on an immaculate white-sand beach fringed with coconut palms, Shangri-La's Rasa Sentosa Resort is Singapore's only true beachfront hotel. It's frequented by Singaporeans looking to get away from it all, but as a visitor to Singapore you may find it isolated from the city's attractions. Still, you can always take advantage of the resort's complimentary shuttle service for trips to the action, only to return to the serenity of the resort at the end of a busy day.

Great outdoor activities make the Rasa Sentosa particularly attractive. The resort's extensive recreational facilities, including a sea-sports center, offer windsurfing, sailing, and paddle skiing. Other facilities include a large outdoor free-form swimming pool, a jogging track, aqua bike rentals, an outdoor Jacuzzi, and a fully equipped spa with gym, sauna, body and facial treatments, hydromassage, and massage therapies. The hotel also organizes nature walks, cycling tours, rock-wall climbing, and beach volleyball. For children, there is a separate pool with water slides (no lifeguard, though), a playground, a nursery, and a video arcade.

As for the rooms, the decision between whether to take the hill-view room or the slightly more expensive sea-facing room is a no-brainer: The view of the sea is exceptional, and if you don't go for it, you'll be missing out on glorious mornings, throwing back the curtains, and taking in the view from the balcony.

101 Siloso Rd., Sentosa, Singapore 098970. ℂ 800/942-5050 in the U.S. and Canada, 800/222-448 in Australia, 800/442-179 in New Zealand, or 65/6275-0900. Fax 65/6275-1055. www.shangri-la.com. 459 units. S$375 (US$240/£124) double; from S$870 (US$557/£287) suites. AE, DC, MC, V. See "Sentosa Island," in chapter 6, for public transportation. **Amenities:** 3 restaurants; poolside bar and lobby lounge; outdoor lagoon-style pool w/children's pool and Jacuzzi; golf at nearby facilities; fitness center; spa w/sauna, steam, and massage; children's center; game room; shuttle service; business center; 24-hr. room service; babysitting; same-day laundry service; dry cleaning; executive-level rooms. *In room:* A/C, TV w/satellite programming and in-house movie, dataport w/direct Internet access, minibar, coffee/tea-making facilities, hair dryer, iron, safe.

5

Where to Dine in Singapore

Singapore claims an estimated 2,000-plus eating establishments, so you'll never go hungry. But to simply say, "If you like food you'll love Singapore!" doesn't do justice to the modern concept of eating in this city. Here you'll find a huge selection of local, regional, and international cuisine, served in settings that range from bustling hawker centers to grand and glamorous palaces of gastronomy. The food is authentic and many times the dining experience is entertainment in its own right. Various ethnic restaurants, with their traditional decor and serving styles, hold their own special sense of theater for foreigners; but Singaporeans don't stop there, dreaming up new concepts in cuisine and ambience to add fresh dimensions to the fine art of dining.

In this chapter, I'll begin by providing an overview of the main types of traditional cuisine to help you decide, and also list those signature dishes that each style has contributed to the "local cuisine," dishes that have crossed cultures to become time-honored favorites—the Singaporean equivalent to bangers and mash or burgers and fries. These suggestions are especially helpful when navigating the endless choices at **hawker centers** (large

groupings of informal open-air food stalls).

The restaurants reviewed here offer a crosscut of cuisine and price ranges and were selected for superb quality or authenticity of dishes. Some were selected for the sheer experience, whether it's a stunning view or just plain old fun. Beyond this list, you're sure to discover favorites of your own without having to look too far.

A good place to start is right in your hotel. Many of Singapore's best restaurants are in its hotels, whether they're run by the hotel itself or operated by outfits just renting the space. Hotels generally offer a wide variety of cuisine, and coffee shops almost always have Western selections. Shopping malls have everything from food courts with local fast food to mid-priced and upmarket establishments. Western fast-food outlets are always easy to find—McDonald's burgers or Starbucks coffee—but if you want something a little more local, you'll find coffee shops (called *kopitiam*) and small home-cookin' mom-and-pop joints down every back street. Then there are hawker centers and food courts, where, under one roof, the meal choices go on and on.

1 One Little Island, Lots & Lots of Choices

CHINESE CUISINE

The large Chinese population in Singapore makes this obviously the most common type of food you'll find, and by right, any good description of Singaporean food should begin with the most prevalent Chinese regional styles. Many Chinese restaurants in the West are lumped into one category—Chinese—with only mild acknowledgment of

Sichuan and dim sum. But China's a big place, and its size is reflected in its many different tastes, ingredients, and preparation styles.

A lot of hawker-center fare is inspired by regional Chinese home cooking. Local favorites like carrot cake (white radishes that are steamed and pounded until soft, then fried in egg, garlic, and chili), Hokkien *bak ku teh* (boiled pork ribs in an herbal soup), Teochew *kway teow* (stir-fried rice noodles with egg, prawns, and fish), and the number-one favorite for foreigners, Hainanese *chicken rice* (poached sliced chicken breast served over rice cooked in chicken stock). See section 9, "Hawker Centers," later in this chapter for more on the hawker food scene.

Fusion cuisine has been hitting the market hard as globalization takes control of Singaporean palates. Also called "East meets West" or "New Asia," this cuisine combines Eastern and Western ingredients and cooking styles for a whole new eating experience. Some of it works, some of it doesn't, but true gourmet connoisseurs consider it all a culinary atrocity.

CANTONESE CUISINE   Cantonese-style food is what you usually find in the West: Your stir-fries, wontons, and sweet-and-sour sauces all come from this southern region. Cantonese cooks emphasize freshness of ingredients, and typical preparation involves quick stir-frying in light oil or steaming for tender meats and crisp, flavorful vegetables. These are topped with light sauces that are sometimes sweet. Cantonese-style food also includes roasted meats like suckling pig and the red-roasted pork that's ever present in western Chinese dishes. Compared to northern styles of Chinese cuisine, Cantonese food can be bland, especially when sauces and broths are over-thickened and slimy. Singaporean palates demand the standard dish of chili condiment at the table, which sometimes helps the flavor. One hearty Cantonese dish that has made it to local cuisine fame is **clay pot rice,** which is rice cooked with chicken, Chinese sausage, and mushrooms, prepared in—you guessed it—a clay pot.

The Cantonese are also responsible for *dim sum* (or *tim sum,* as you'll sometimes see it written around Singapore). Meaning "little hearts," dim sum is a variety of deep-fried or steamed buns, spring rolls, dumplings, meatballs, spareribs, and a host of other bite-size treats. It's a favorite in Singapore, especially for lunch. At a dim sum buffet, dishes are offered from table to table and you simply point to what appeals. Food is served in small portions, sometimes still in the steamer. Take only one item on your plate at a time and stack the empty plates as you finish each one. Traditionally, you'd be charged by the plate, but sometimes you can find great all-you-can-eat buffets for a good price.

BEIJING CUISINE   Beijing cuisine, its rich garlic and bean-paste flavoring betraying just a touch of chili, comes to us from the north of China. Heavier sauces allow for greater selections of beef and mutton, rarely found on southern Chinese menus. The most famous Beijing-style dish is **Beijing duck** (also known as Peking duck). The crispy skin is pulled away and cut into pieces, which you then wrap in thin pancakes with spring onion and a touch of sweet plum sauce. The meat is served later in a dish that's equally scrumptious.

SHANGHAINESE CUISINE   Shanghainese cuisine is similar to its Beijing counterpart but tends to be more oily. Because of Shanghai's proximity to the sea, Shanghainese recipes also include more fish. The exotic **drunken prawns** and the popular **drunken chicken** are both from this regional style, as is the mysterious **bird's nest soup,** made from swift's nests.

SICHUAN CUISINE   Sichuan cuisine, second only to Cantonese in the West, also relies on the rich flavors of garlic, sesame oil, and bean paste, but is heavier on the chilies than Shanghainese cuisine—*much* heavier on the chilies. Sugar is also sometimes added to create tangy sauces. Some dishes can really pack a punch, but there are many Sichuan dishes that are not spicy. Popular are **chicken with dried chilies** and **hot-and-sour soup.** Another regional variation, **Hunan cuisine,** is also renowned for its fiery spice and can be distinguished from Sichuan-style by its darker sauces.

TEOCHEW CUISINE   Teochew cuisine uses fish as its main ingredient and is also known for its light soups. Many dishes are steamed, and in fact **steamboat,** which is a popular poolside menu item in hotels, gets its origins from this style. For steamboat, boiling broth is brought to the table, and you dunk pieces of fish, meat, and vegetables into it, a la fondue. Other Teochew contributions to local cuisine are the **Teochew fish ball,** a springy ball made from pounded fish served in a noodle soup, and the traditional Singaporean breakfast dish *congee* (or *moi*), which is rice porridge served with fried fish, salted vegetables, and sometimes boiled egg. Also, if you see **braised goose** on the menu, you're definitely in a Teochew restaurant.

HOKKIEN CUISINE   Although the Hokkiens are the most prevalent dialect group in Singapore, their style of cuisine rarely makes it to restaurant tables, basically because it's simple and homey. Two dishes that have made it as local cuisine favorites, however, are the **oyster omelet,** flavored with garlic and soy, and ***Hokkien mee,*** thick wheat noodles with seafood, meat, and vegetables in a heavy sauce.

MALAY CUISINE

Malay cuisine combines Indonesian and Thai flavors, blending ginger, turmeric, chilies, lemon grass, and dried shrimp paste to make unique curries. Heavy on coconut milk and peanuts, Malay food can at times be on the sweet side. The most popular Malay curries are ***rendang,*** a dry, dark, and heavy coconut-based curry served over meat; ***sambal,*** a red and spicy chili sauce; and ***sambal belacan,*** a condiment of fresh chilies, dried shrimp paste, and lime juice.

The ultimate Malay dish in Singapore is ***satay,*** sweet barbecued meat kabobs dipped in chili peanut sauce. Most Malay food is served as ***Nasi padang***—a big pile of rice surrounded by meat, egg, vegetable, tofu, and condiments smothered in tasty, spicy gravy.

PERANAKAN CUISINE

Peranakan cuisine came out of the Straits-born Chinese community and combines such mainland Chinese ingredients as noodles and oyster sauces with local Malay flavors of coconut milk and peanuts. ***Laksa lemak*** is a great example of the combination, mixing Chinese rice flour noodles into a soup of Malay-style spicy coconut cream with chunks of seafood. Another favorite, ***popiah,*** is the Peranakan version of a spring roll, combining sweet turnip, chopped egg, chili sauce, and prawns in a delicate wrap. ***Otak-otak*** is very unique. It's toasted mashed fish with coconut milk and chili, wrapped in a banana leaf and grilled over flames.

INDIAN CUISINE

SOUTHERN INDIAN CUISINE   Southern Indian food is a super-hot blend of spices in a coconut milk base. Rice is the staple, along with thin breads such as *prata* and *dosai,* which are good for curling into shovels to scoop up drippy curries. Vegetarian dishes are abundant, a result of Hindu-mandated vegetarianism, and use lots of chickpeas and lentils in curry and chili gravies. *Vindaloo,* meat or poultry in a tangy and spicy sauce, is also well known.

Banana leaf restaurants, surely the most interesting way to experience southern Indian food in Singapore, serve up meals on banana leaves cut like place mats. It's very informal. Spoons and forks are provided, but if you want to act local and use your hands, remember to use your right hand only (see "Etiquette & Customs," in chapter 3), and don't forget to wash up before and after at the tap.

One tip for eating very spicy foods is to mix a larger proportion of rice to gravy. Don't drink in between bites, but eat through the burn. Your brow may sweat but your mouth will build a tolerance as you eat, and the flavors will come through more fully.

NORTHERN INDIAN CUISINE   Northern Indian food combines yogurts and creams with a milder, more delicate blend of herbs and chilies than is found in its southern neighbor. It's served most often with breads like fluffy nans and flat chapatis. Marinated meats like chicken or fish, cooked in the tandoor clay oven, are always the highlight of a northern Indian meal.

Northern Indian restaurants are more upmarket and expensive than the southern ones, but although they offer more of the comforts associated with dining out, the southern banana leaf experience is more of an adventure.

Some Singaporean variations on Indian cuisine are *mee goreng,* fried noodles with chili and curry gravy, and **fish head curry,** a giant fish head simmered in a broth of coconut curry, chilies, and fragrant seasonings.

Muslim influences on Indian food have produced *roti prata,* a humble late-night snack of fried bread served with chickpea gravy, and *murtabak,* a fried prata filled with minced meat, onion, and egg. Between the Muslims' dietary laws *(halal)* forbidding pork and the Hindus' regard for the sacred cow, Indian food is the one cuisine that can be eaten by every kind of Singaporean.

SEAFOOD

One cannot describe Singaporean food without mentioning the abundance of fresh seafood. But most important is the uniquely Singaporean **chili crab,** chopped and smothered in a thick tangy chili sauce. **Pepper crabs** and **black pepper crayfish** are also a thrill. Instead of chili sauce, these shellfish are served in a thick black-pepper-and-soy sauce.

FRUITS

A walk through a wet market at any time of year will show you just what wonders the Tropics can produce. Varieties of banana, fresh coconut, papaya, mango, and pineapple are just a few of the fresh and juicy fruits available year-round; in addition, Southeast Asia has an amazing selection of exotic and almost unimaginable fruits. From the light and juicy star fruit to the red and hairy rambutan, they are all worthy of a try, either whole or juiced.

Dare to try it if you will, the fruit to sample—the veritable king of fruits—is the *durian,* a large, green, spiky fruit that, when cut open, smells worse than old tennis shoes. The "best" ones are in season every June, when Singaporeans go wild over them. In case you're curious, the fruit has a creamy texture and tastes lightly sweet and deeply musky.

One interesting note on fruits: The Chinese believe that foods contain either yin or yang qualities with corresponding "heaty" and "cooling" effects. According to Traditional Chinese Medicine (TCM) practitioners, fried and oily foods are heaty, producing

Eating Enclaves

If you're looking for someplace to dine but want to browse around a bit, a few neighborhoods around Singapore host clusters of smaller, and many times quite excellent, restaurants and lounges creating mini-scenes here and there. For example, **CHIJMES,** a charming colonial orphanage located within the Historic District, provides a home for some excellent restaurants ranging from Cantonese to Mediterranean. In this chapter, I've reviewed Lei Garden, but if you stroll about, you might be tempted by one of the other eateries here.

Boat Quay and **Clarke Quay,** located along the Singapore River, provide boatloads of options. I've reviewed Our Village at Boat Quay, but this is just one of many.

If you want to get away from the tourist traffic, try **Club Street** in China-town, a short hilly lane lined with restored shophouses that became a chic after-work place for the nearby ad agencies, graphic designers, and law firms that make their offices in this neighborhood. Stroll past the many quaint bistros that serve everything from Italian to Vietnamese and you're sure to find something.

Holland Village, located outside the city to the northwest, is the center of Singapore's expatriate community, so you'll find restaurants, bars, and cafes that cater to Western residents living around this neighborhood. Start at the row of restaurants along **Chip Bee Gardens,** and if you still haven't found something (I'd be surprised) then cross Holland Road to Lorong Liput and Lorong Mambong. In this chapter I've reviewed Original Sin, which is an excellent place to start in this neighborhood.

heat in the body, and therefore should be kept to a minimum in the Tropics, and the same is true for some fruits. Whereas watermelon, star fruit, and oranges are cooling, mangoes, litchi, and especially durians are heaty. Taking too many heaty foods is believed to result in a fever, body aches, and sore throat, for which the best remedy is to take Chinese tea.

2 Tips on Dining

In many foreign destinations, the exotic cuisine isn't the only thing that keeps you guessing. Here, I give you the ground rules on Singapore dining.

HOURS   Most restaurants are open for lunch as early as 11am but close around 2:30pm or 3pm to give them a chance to set up for dinner, which begins around 6pm. Where closing times are listed, that is the time when the last order is taken. If you need to eat at odd hours, food centers serve all day and some hawker centers are open all night—see the section "Hawker Centers," later in this chapter.

TIPPING   Don't. Restaurants always add a gratuity to the bill. Sometimes I just leave the small change, but it's not expected.

RESERVATIONS   Some restaurants, especially the more fashionable or upscale ones, may require that reservations be made up to a couple of days in advance. Reservations are always recommended for Saturday and Sunday lunch and dinner, as eating is a favorite national pastime and a lot of families take meals out for weekend quality time.

ATTIRE   Because Singapore is so hot, "smart casual" (a local term, meaning a shirt and slacks for men and a dress or skirt/slacks and blouse for women) is always a safe bet in moderate to expensive restaurants. For the very expensive restaurants, "smart elegant" is required, which in Singapore means jacket and tie for men and a dressier outfit for women. For the cheap places, come as you are, as long as you're decent.

ORDERING WINE WITH DINNER   Singaporeans have become more wine savvy in recent years and have begun importing estate-bottled wines from California, Australia, New Zealand, Peru, South Africa, France, and Germany. However, these bottles are heavily taxed. A bottle of wine with dinner starts at around S$50 (US$29/£17) and a single glass runs between S$10 (US$5.90/£3.30) and S$25 (US$15/£8.25), depending on the wine and the restaurant. Chinese restaurants usually don't charge corkage fees for bringing your own.

ORGANIZATION OF RESTAURANT LISTINGS   I've organized the restaurants in this chapter in a few different ways. First, I've grouped them in a simple list by style of cuisine, so if you decide you want a nice Peranakan dinner, for instance, you can scope out your choices all together before referring to the individual restaurant reviews. Second, I've arranged the reviews into four basic neighborhoods: the Historic District, Chinatown, Little India, and the Orchard Road area. Within these divisions, I've arranged them by price. Keep in mind that the divisions by neighborhood are almost as arbitrary as they were when Stamford Raffles created them in 1822. Everything in the city is relatively close and easily accessible, so don't think you should plan your meals by the neighborhood your hotel sits in when a short taxi ride will take you where you really want to go.

Also, it has become the trend if you've got a terrific restaurant that people love, to open branches in other locations. Some may believe this dilutes the unique appeal of a special restaurant, but in Singapore, generally I find that good restaurateurs retain the consistent quality of food and service for all their outlets. You'll notice many restaurants in the sections that follow have branches in other parts of the city, which I have also listed.

Tips How to Handle Your Asian Meal

You'll notice that not all Asians use chopsticks. The Chinese, Japanese, Koreans, and Vietnamese use them, while the Thais, Malays, and Indians do not (except for some noodle dishes). How can you tell who uses what? If your rice is served in a bowl, use chopsticks. If it's served on a flat plate, use a combination fork and spoon (the spoon is the actual eating utensil, the fork used only to push the food around).

Southern Indians and Malays also eat with their hands. If you choose to try this traditional style of eating, make sure to wash your hands before and after your meal, and only use your right hand for the task.

Urban Singapore Dining

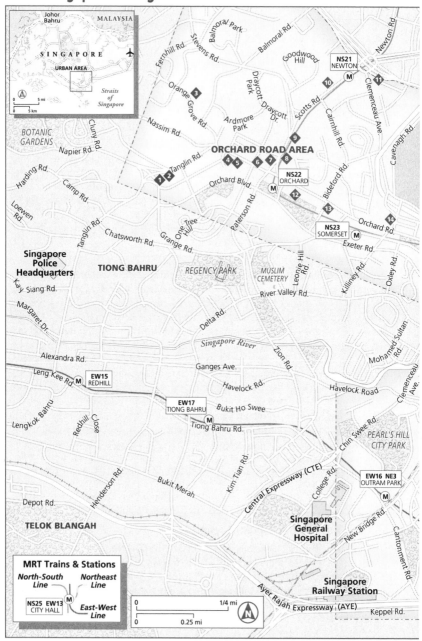

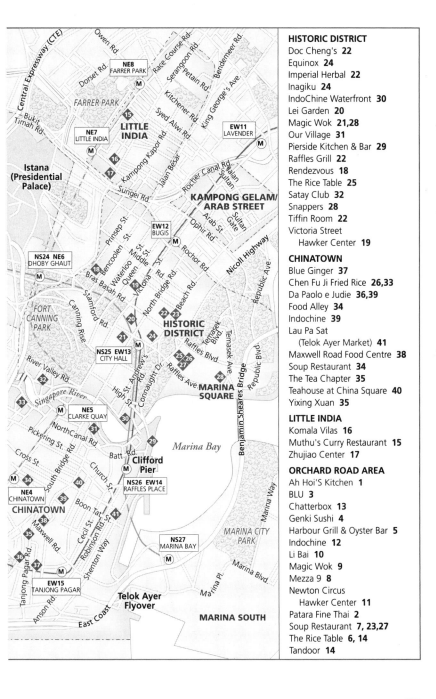

HISTORIC DISTRICT
Doc Cheng's **22**
Equinox **24**
Imperial Herbal **22**
Inagiku **24**
IndoChine Waterfront **30**
Lei Garden **20**
Magic Wok **21,28**
Our Village **31**
Pierside Kitchen & Bar **29**
Raffles Grill **22**
Rendezvous **18**
The Rice Table **25**
Satay Club **32**
Snappers **28**
Tiffin Room **22**
Victoria Street
  Hawker Center **19**

CHINATOWN
Blue Ginger **37**
Chen Fu Ji Fried Rice **26,33**
Da Paolo e Judie **36,39**
Food Alley **34**
Indochine **39**
Lau Pa Sat
  (Telok Ayer Market) **41**
Maxwell Road Food Centre **38**
Soup Restaurant **34**
The Tea Chapter **35**
Teahouse at China Square **40**
Yixing Xuan **35**

LITTLE INDIA
Komala Vilas **16**
Muthu's Curry Restaurant **15**
Zhujiao Center **17**

ORCHARD ROAD AREA
Ah Hoi'S Kitchen **1**
BLU **3**
Chatterbox **13**
Genki Sushi **4**
Harbour Grill & Oyster Bar **5**
Indochine **12**
Li Bai **10**
Magic Wok **9**
Mezza 9 **8**
Newton Circus
  Hawker Center **11**
Patara Fine Thai **2**
Soup Restaurant **7, 23,27**
The Rice Table **6, 14**
Tandoor **14**

One from Column A, One from Column B . . .

Western cuisine serves each diner a plate with a complete meal for one. Not so with the Asians, where, even in the finest restaurants, Chinese, Indian, and every other kind of Asian fare is served "family style." To fully appreciate the experience, order a meat dish, a seafood dish, and a vegetable dish to share between two or three people. With your rice bowl in front of you, take only small servings of each dish at a time. For a larger party add on a soup dish, plus other meat, seafood, and veggie selections for a variety of tastes to go round.

I've selected the restaurants listed here because they have some of the best food and most memorable atmospheres, but there are hundreds of other restaurants serving any kind of food in a variety of price ranges. Many magazines on dining in Singapore are available at newsstands and can help you find other favorite restaurants.

LUNCH COSTS   Lunch at a hawker center can be as cheap as S$3.50 (US$2.20/ £1.15), truly a bargain. Many places have set-price buffet lunches, but these can be as high as S$45 (US$29/£15). Indian restaurants are great deals for inexpensive buffet lunches, which can be found as reasonably as S$10 (US$6.40/£3.30) per person for all you can eat.

DINNER COSTS   In this chapter, prices for Western restaurants list the range for standard entrees and prices for Asian restaurants list the range for small dishes intended for two people to share. As a guideline, here are the relative costs for dinner in each category of restaurant, without wine, beer, cocktails, or coffee, and ordered either a la carte or from a set-price menu:

- **Very Expensive ($$$$):** Expect to pay as much as S$145 (US$93/£48) per person. Continental and Japanese cuisines will be the priciest, but a full-course Cantonese dinner, especially if you throw in shark's fin, can be well over S$150 (US$96/£50) per person.
- **Expensive ($$$):** Expect dinner to run between S$50 (US$32/£17) and S$80 (US$51/£26) per person.
- **Moderate ($$):** At a moderate restaurant, dinner for one can be as low as S$25 (US$16/£17) and as high as S$50 (US$32/£17).
- **Inexpensive ($):** Some inexpensive dinners can be under S$5 (US$3.20/£1.65) at hawker stalls and up to around S$15 (US$9.60/£4.95) for one if you eat at local restaurants. Fortunately, Singapore is not only a haven for cultural gastronomic diversity, but it's also possible to eat exotic foods here to your heart's content, all while maintaining a shoestring budget.

3 Restaurants by Cuisine

ASIAN

Equinox ★ (Historic District, $$$, p. 106)

CHINESE

Imperial Herbal ★★ (Historic District, $$, p. 109)

Lei Garden ★★ (Historic District, $$$, p. 108)

Li Bai ★★★ (Orchard Road, $$$, p. 113)

Soup Restaurant ★ (Chinatown, $, p. 112)

4 Historic District

VERY EXPENSIVE

Inagiku ✿✿ JAPANESE   At Inagiku, you'll have excellent Japanese food that gets top marks for ingredients, preparation, and presentation. In delicately lighted and subtle decor, you can enjoy house favorites like sashimi, tempura, and teppanyaki—with separate dining areas for tempura and a sushi bar. The *tokusen sashimi morikimi* is masterful in its presentation: an assortment of raw fish—including salmon, prawns, and clams—is laid out in an ice-filled shell inside of which nestles the skeleton of a whole fish. It's odd and delightful at the same time. I recommend the tempura *mori-awase,* a combination of seafood and vegetables that's very lightly deep-fried. Also highly recommended are the teppanyaki prawns. In addition to sake, there is also a good selection of wines.

Raffles The Plaza, Level 3, 80 Bras Basah Rd. ⓒ **65/6431-6156.** Reservations recommended. Set lunch S$40–S$100 (US$26–US$64/£13–£33); set dinner S$180–S$220 (US$115–US$141/£60–£73). AE, MC, V. Daily noon–2:30pm and 6:30–10:30pm.

Raffles Grill ✿✿✿ FRENCH   Dining in the grande dame of Singapore achieves a level of sophistication unmatched by any other five-star restaurant. The architectural charm and historic significance of the old hotel will transform dinner into a cultural event, but don't just come here for the ambience; the food is outstanding as well. An ever-changing menu means that any dishes I recommend here might not be around by the time you make it, but I assure you, anything you order will still be divine. The degustation menu, seven courses at S$180 (US$115/£59), is the best way to explore their finest dishes if you have trouble choosing from an a la carte menu that features pigeon, lamb, suckling pig, veal, and a carving trolley of amazing cuts of beef prepared to perfection. The 400-label wine list (going back to 1890 vintages) could be a history lesson, and if you'd like you can request the cellar master to select a wine to match each course. The fabulously attentive service from the waitstaff will make you feel like you own the place. Formal dress is required.

Raffles Hotel, 1 Beach Rd. ⓒ **65/6331-1612.** Reservations required. Main courses S$65–S$79 (US$42–US$51/£21–£26). AE, DC, MC, V. Mon–Fri noon–2pm and 7–10pm; Sat 7–10pm.

EXPENSIVE

Doc Cheng's ✿✿ FUSION   If you're growing tired of your travel partner, I recommend Doc Cheng's. The witty menu tells the story of Doc Cheng, a mythological colonial figure who was a sought-after physician, local celebrity, and notorious drunk. His concept of "restorative foods" is therefore rather decadent, on the menu you'll find fabulous "fusion" dishes that are more flavorful than medicinal. Guest chefs make the menu ever changing—the latest and greatest, a trio of beef cuts prepared in three different styles (Western, Indian, and Chinese) on the same plate, or the unique and mouthwatering Sichuan rack of lamb. The house wine is a Riesling (sweet wines are more popular with Singaporeans) from Raffles's own vineyard. Two dining areas allow you to dine alfresco under the veranda or in cool air-conditioning inside.

1 Beach Rd., Raffles Hotel Arcade #02–20, Level 2. ⓒ **65/6331-1612.** Reservations required. Main courses S$32–S$41 (US$21–US$26/£11–£14). AE, DC, MC, V. Mon–Fri noon–1:30pm and 7–9:30pm; Sat–Sun 7–9:30pm.

Equinox ✿ CONTINENTAL/ASIAN   What a view! From the top of the tallest hotel in Southeast Asia, you can see out past the marina to Malaysia and Indonesia—and the

Historic District Dining

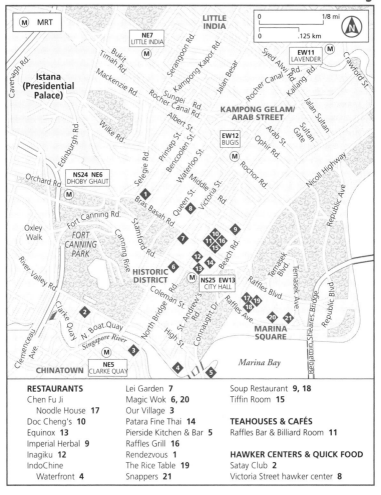

RESTAURANTS
Chen Fu Ji
    Noodle House **17**
Doc Cheng's **10**
Equinox **13**
Imperial Herbal **9**
Inagiku **12**
IndoChine
    Waterfront **4**

Lei Garden **7**
Magic Wok **6, 20**
Our Village **3**
Patara Fine Thai **14**
Pierside Kitchen & Bar **5**
Raffles Grill **16**
Rendezvous **1**
The Rice Table **19**
Snappers **21**

Soup Restaurant **9, 18**
Tiffin Room **15**

TEAHOUSES & CAFÉS
Raffles Bar & Billiard Room **11**

HAWKER CENTERS & QUICK FOOD
Satay Club **2**
Victoria Street hawker center **8**

restaurant's three-tier design and floor-to-ceiling windows mean every table has a view. It's decorated in contemporary style with nice Chinese accents. Lunch is an extensive display of seafood served in a host of international recipes, with chefs searing scallops to order. Dinner is a la carte, with a menu that's divided between Eastern and Western cuisine, plus some dishes that combine Eastern and Western ingredients and cooking styles such as *yuzu* (Japanese citrus fruit) marinated cod with braised enoki and *tasoi* (Japanese spinach) and grilled beef tenderloin with foie gras. For dessert, order the Equinox Temptation sampler plate.

Raffles City, 2 Stamford Rd., Level 70. © **65/6837-3322.** Reservations required. Daily buffet lunch S$56 (US$36/£18); dinner main courses S$24–S$48 (US$15–US$31/£7.90–£16). AE, DC, MC, V. Mon–Sat noon–2:30pm and 6:30–11pm; Sun 11am–2:30pm and 7–11pm.

IndoChine Waterfront 🐠🐠🐠 VIETNAMESE/LAO/CAMBODIAN/FRENCH
IndoChine Waterfront shares the stately Empress Place Building with the Asian Civilisations Museum, enhancing the sophistication of its chic Oriental decor. The views over the water make for true romance. The menu combines the best dishes from the Indochinese region, many with hints of the French cuisine that was added into regional palates during colonial days. Their two most popular dishes are the house specialty beef stew ragout and the pepper beef with sweet-and-sour sauce. More traditional Vietnamese favorites, like spring rolls and prawns grilled on sugar cane, are fresh starters. After dinner, don't miss the Vietnamese coffee; it's mindblowingly delicious. IndoChine has two sister restaurants, one in a quaint Chinatown shophouse (49B Club St.; ℂ **65/6323-0503**) and another in Wisma Atria on Orchard Road #01–18/23 (ℂ **65/6238-3470**).

1 Empress Place, Asian Civilisations Museum. ℂ **65/6339-1720.** Reservations required. Small dishes S$20–S$38 (US$13–US$24/£6.60–£13). AE, DC, MC, V. Sun–Thurs noon–2:30pm and 6:30–11pm; Fri–Sat noon–2:30pm and 6:30pm–midnight.

Lei Garden 🐠🐠 CHINESE/CANTONESE   Lei Garden lives up to a great reputation for the highest quality Cantonese cuisine in one of the most elegant settings, nestled within the unique ambience of CHIJMES just outside its towering picture windows. Highly recommended dishes are the "Buddha jumps over the wall," a very popular Chinese soup made from abalone, fish maw (stomach), shark's fin, and Chinese ham. It's generally served only on special occasions. To make the beggar's chicken, they take a whole stuffed chicken and wrap and bake it in a lotus leaf covered in yam, which makes the chicken moist with a delicate flavor you won't forget. For either of these dishes, you must place your order at least 24 hours in advance when you make your reservation. Also try the barbecued Beijing duck, which is exquisite. Dim sum here is excellent. A small selection of French and Chinese wines is available.

30 Victoria St., CHIJMES #01–24. ℂ **65/6339-3822.** Reservations required. Small dishes S$18–S$58 (US$12–US$37/ £5.95–£19). AE, DC, MC, V. Daily 11:30am–2:30pm and 6–10:30pm.

Snappers 🐠🐠 SEAFOOD   With a view of the Ritz-Carlton's lovely pool and gardens, this restaurant is hardly your typical poolside snack bar. Snappers invents mouthwatering recipes for new ways to enjoy fresh seafood—the menu is ever-changing. The grilled halibut with artichoke is served with potato confit, rocket salad, and marinated octopus. If the a la carte menu doesn't have what you're looking for, you can have your choice of live seafood prepared to your specs. A couple of meat dishes include grilled black angus beef tenderloin with petit *farçis,* spring onion, and dried tomato vinaigrette. This is one of the city's top choices for delicious dining with a terrific wine list and impeccable service. You won't be disappointed.

The Ritz-Carlton Millenia Singapore, Level 1, 7 Raffles Ave. ℂ **65/6434-5288.** Reservations required. Live seafood is priced by weight, the average dish S$65 (US$38/£21). Main courses S$40–S$148 (US$26–US$95/£13–£49). AE, DC, MC, V. Sun–Thurs noon–2pm and 6:30–10pm; Sat–Sun noon–2pm and 6:30–10:30pm.

Tiffin Room 🐠 NORTHERN INDIAN   Tiffin curry came from India and is named after the three-tiered containers that Indian workers would use to carry their lunch. The tiffin box idea was stolen by the British colonists, who changed around the recipes a bit so they weren't as spicy. The cuisine that evolved is pretty much what you'll find served at Raffles's Tiffin Room, where a buffet spread lets you select from a variety of curries, chutneys, rice, and Indian breads. The restaurant is just inside the lobby entrance of Raffles Hotel and carries the trademark Raffles elegance throughout its decor. Very British Raj.

Raffles Hotel, 1 Beach Rd. (©) 65/6331-1612. Reservations recommended. All meals served buffet-style. Breakfast S$42 (US$27/£14); lunch S$43 (US$28/£14); high tea S$37 (US$24/£12); dinner S$46 (US$29/£15). AE, DC, MC, V. Daily 7–10:30am, noon–2:30pm, 3:30–5:30pm (high tea), and 7–10:30pm.

MODERATE

Imperial Herbal 🍴🍴 CHINESE HERBAL People come again and again for the healing powers of the food served here, enriched with herbs and other secret ingredients prescribed by a resident Chinese herbalist. Upon entering, you'll be ushered to the herb counter. The herbalist, who is also trained in Western medicine, will ask for the symptoms of what ails you and take your pulse. While you sit and order (from an extensive menu of meats, seafood, and vegetable dishes that are delicious in their own right), he'll prepare a packet of ingredients and ship them off to the kitchen, where they'll be added to the food in preparation. Surprisingly, dishes turn out tasty, without the anticipated medicinal aftertaste.

The herbalist is in-house every day but Sunday. It's always good to call ahead, though, as he's the main attraction. When you leave, present him with a small *ang pau*—a gift of cash in a red envelope—maybe S$5 (US$3.20/£1.65) or S$7 (US$4.50/£2.30). Red envelopes are available in any card or gift shop.

Metropole Hotel, 3rd Floor, 41 Seah St. (near Raffles Hotel). (©) 65/6337-0491. Reservations recommended for lunch, necessary for dinner. Small dishes S$12–S$25 (US$7.70–US$16/£3.95–£8.25). AE, DC, MC, V. Daily 11:30am–2:30pm and 6:30–10:30pm.

Pierside Kitchen & Bar 🍴 SEAFOOD A light and healthy menu centers on seafood prepared with fresh flavors in a wide variety of international recipes, like the house specialty cumin-spiced crab cakes with marinated cucumber and chili or grilled hazelnut-crusted king prawns in lobster and lemon-grass sauce. Raw oysters are served with a tangy lime and chili sauce which is out of this world. The place itself is airy, sparsely decorated with light wood and white walls. Nothing can compete with the view, really—the panoramic view of the Esplanade Theatres and the marina is lovely. After sundown, the alfresco dining area cools off with breezes from the water and the stars make for some romantic dining. Relax, enjoy the scenery, and order dessert from their gorgeous selection of chocoholic sugar-coma treats.

Unit 01–01, One Fullerton, 1 Fullerton Rd. (©) 65/6438-0400. Reservations recommended. Main courses S$21–S$55 (US$13–US$35/£6.95–£18). AE, DC, MC, V. Mon–Thurs 11:30am–2:30pm and 7–10:30pm; Fri–Sat 7–11pm.

INEXPENSIVE

Magic Wok 🍴Value THAI Here's an excellent value-for-money restaurant in town. The decor doesn't do much, it's usually crowded, and staff don't pamper, but food is reliably good and cheap. Thai favorites include a spicy tom yam seafood soup that doesn't skimp on the seafood, a mild green curry with chicken, and sweet pineapple rice. If you come too late, the yummy fried chicken chunks wrapped in pandan leaf will be sold out. If you're adventurous, the fried baby squid look like cute, tiny octopi and are crunchy and sweet. During busy times, you'll have to queue, but it moves fast. Other outlets are located at #04–22/24 Far East Plaza on Scotts Road (© **65/6738-3708**) and #02–05 Marina Liesureplex (© **65/6837-0826**).

#01–20 Capitol Building, Stamford Rd. (©) 65/6338-1882. Reservations not accepted. Small dishes S$4–S$18 (US$2.60–US$12/£1.30–£5.95). MC, V. Daily 11am–10pm.

Our Village ⍟ NORTHERN INDIAN   With its antique white walls stuccoed in delicate and exotic patterns and glistening with tiny silver mirrors, you'll feel like you're in an Indian fairyland here. Even the ceiling twinkles with silver stars, and hanging lanterns provide a subtle glow for the heavenly atmosphere—it's a perfect setting for a delicate dinner. Every dish here is made fresh from hand-selected imported ingredients, some of them coming from secret sources. In fact, the staff is so protective of its recipes, you'd almost think their secret ingredient was opium—and you'll be floating so high after tasting the food that it might as well be. There are vegetarian selections as well as meats (no beef or pork) prepared in luscious gravies or in the tandoor oven. The dishes are light and healthy, with all natural ingredients and not too much salt.

46 Boat Quay (take elevator to 5th floor). ✆ **65/6538-3058.** Reservations recommended on weekends. Small dishes S$9–S$20 (US$5.80–US$13/£2.95–£6.60). AE, MC, V. Mon–Fri 11:30am–1:30pm and 6–10:30pm; Sat–Sun 6–10:30pm.

Rendezvous MALAY/INDONESIAN   I was sad when, after a few months away from Singapore, I couldn't find Rendezvous at its previous location in Raffles City Shopping Center, only to learn it had shifted to a nicer space at the new (coincidentally named?) Rendezvous Hotel. Line up to select from a large number of Malay dishes, cafeteria-style, like sambal squid in a spicy sauce of chili and shrimp paste, and beef *rendang,* in a dark spicy curry gravy. The waitstaff will bring your order to your table. The coffee shop setting is as far from glamorous as the last Rendezvous, but on the wall black-and-white photos trace the restaurant's history back to its opening in the early '50s. It's a great place to experiment with a new cuisine.

#02–02 Hotel Rendezvous, 9 Bras Basah Rd. ✆ **65/6339-7508.** Reservations not necessary. Meat dishes sold per piece S$3–S$5 (US$1.90–US$3.20/£1–£1.65). AE, DC, MC, V. Daily 11am–9pm. Closed on public holidays.

5 Chinatown

MODERATE

Da Paolo e Judie ⍟⍟⍟ ITALIAN   Beautiful ambience is created in this shophouse restaurant remodeled in contemporary elegance, with alfresco dining and a wine bar. At the time of writing this restaurant was closed for renovations, so expect it to be reopened and ultra swank by the time you arrive. The Italian fare features fresh seafood in classic and modern recipes, with main courses prepared to perfection. No doubt the entire city will be excited to sample the new menu in the new digs, so make your reservations early. For the quality of food and service, the prices can't be beat. The owners have other branches that are equally satisfying: **Da Paolo il Ristorante** (80 Club St., also in Chinatown; ✆ **65/6224-7081**), **Da Paolo il Giardino** (501 Bukit Timah Rd., #01–05 Cluny Court, beside the Singapore Botanic Gardens; ✆ **65/6463-9628**) and **Da Paolo la Terrazza** (44 Jalan Merah Saga, #01–56, at Chip Bee Gardens in Holland Village; ✆ **65/6476-1332**).

81 Neil Rd. ✆ **65/6225-8306.** Reservations highly recommended for dinner. Main courses S$24–S$34 (US$15–US$22/£7.90–£11). AE, DC, MC, V. Mon–Sat 11:30am–2:30pm and 6:30–10:30pm.

INEXPENSIVE

Blue Ginger ⍟ PERANAKAN   The standard belief is that Peranakan cooking is reserved for home-cooked meals, and therefore restaurants are not as plentiful—and where they do exist, are very informal. Not so at Blue Ginger, where traditional and modern mix beautifully in a style so fitting for Singapore. Snuggled in a shophouse, the decor combines clean and neat lines of contemporary styling with paintings by

Chinatown Dining

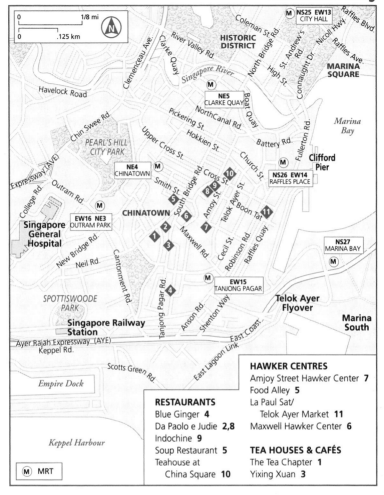

RESTAURANTS
Blue Ginger **4**
Da Paolo e Judie **2,8**
Indochine **9**
Soup Restaurant **5**
Teahouse at
    China Square **10**

HAWKER CENTRES
Amjoy Street Hawker Center **7**
Food Alley **5**
La Paul Sat/
    Telok Ayer Market **11**
Maxwell Hawker Center **6**

TEA HOUSES & CAFÉS
The Tea Chapter **1**
Yixing Xuan **3**

Ⓜ MRT

local artists and touches of Peranakan flair like carved wooden screens. The cuisine is Peranakan from traditional recipes, making for some very authentic food—definitely something you can't get back home. A good appetizer is the *kueh pie tee:* bite-size "top hats" filled with turnip, egg, and prawn with sweet chili sauce. A wonderful entree is the *ayam panggang* "Blue Ginger," really tender grilled, boneless, chicken thigh and drumstick with a mild coconut-milk sauce. One of the most popular dishes is the *ayam buah keluak* (my favorite), a traditional chicken dish made with a hard black Indonesian nut with sweetmeat inside. The favorite dessert here is *durian chendol,* red beans and *pandan* jelly in coconut milk with *durian* purée. Served with shaved ice on top, it smells strong.

97 Tanjong Pagar Rd. Ⓒ **65/6222-3928**. Reservations recommended. Small dishes S$6.50–S$23 (US$4.20–US$15/ £2.15–£7.60). AE, DC, MC, V. Daily 11:30am–2:30pm and 6–10pm.

Chen Fu Ji Fried Rice SINGAPOREAN   With bright fluorescent lighting, the fast-food ambience is nothing to write home about, but after you try the fried rice here, you'll never be able to eat it anywhere else again, ever. These people take loving care of each fluffy grain, frying the egg evenly throughout. The other ingredients are added abundantly, and there's no hint of oil. On the top is a crown of shredded crabmeat. If you've never been an aficionado, you'll be one now. Other dishes are served here to accompany the fried rice, and their soups are also very good. There is an additional branch, the **Chen Fu Ji Noodle House,** at Suntec City Mall, 3 Temasek Blvd. #03–020 Sky Garden (✆ **65/6334-2966**).

#02–31 Riverside Point, 30 Merchant Rd. ✆ 65/6533-0166. Reservations not accepted. Small dishes S$10–S$20 (US$6.40–US$13/£3.30–£6.60). No credit cards. Daily noon–2:30pm and 6–9:45pm.

Soup Restaurant ✪ CHINESE   Tasty, traditional, exotic, and affordable. This simple eatery specializes in Samsui ginger chicken, moist, fragrant steamed chicken dipped in ginger sauce and wrapped in lettuce. It is unique and delicious. The menu is limited, but simple dishes like stews of meats simmered in herbs served in "beggars' bowls" or baked in clay pots are as authentic as they come. The quaint coffee-shop decor is also a treat. If you're game to try something new, I highly recommended this place. More locations: 39 Seah St., across from Raffles Hotel (✆ **65/6333-9388**); #B1–44 Paragon, 290 Orchard Rd. (✆ **65/6333-6228**); DFS Scottswalk, 25 Scotts Rd. #02–01 (✆ **65/6333-8033**); and #B1–59 Suntec City Mall (✆ **65/6333-9886**).

25 Smith St. ✆ 65/6222-9923. Reservations accepted. Small dishes S$6–S$24 (US$3.80–US$15/£2–£7.90). AE, DC, MC, V. Daily noon–2:30pm; Mon–Fri 6–10pm; Sat–Sun 5:30–10pm.

Teahouse at China Square CHINESE/CANTONESE   For those who dare, the Teahouse is a terrific place for dim sum served in traditional style. The coffee-shop atmosphere is as loud and chaotic as you'd imagine a Chinese eatery should be, but the dim sum is served in the authentic style, by waitstaff who push carts around to each table. If you ask, they will tell you what is inside each dumpling and bun and identify each meat treat. Baskets of goodies are slammed on the table as soon as you can wink, so make sure you get only what you order. But the dishes are mouthwatering. My tip: Arrive at the very beginning of meal time so you can get waitress's attention and spend less time shouting over the munching hoard.

China Square Food Centre Level 3, 51 Telok Ayer St. ✆ 65/6533-0660. Reservations recommended. Small dishes S$2.20–S$6 (US$1.40–US$3.80/75p–£2). AE, DC, MC, V. Daily 11am–10:30pm.

6 Little India

INEXPENSIVE

Komala Vilas ✪ SOUTHERN INDIAN   Komala Vilas is famous with Singaporeans of every race. Don't expect the height of ambience—it's pure fast food, local-style—but to sit here during a packed and noisy lunch hour is to see all walks of life come through the doors. Komala serves vegetarian dishes in southern Indian style, so there's nothing fancy about the food; it's just plain good. Order the *dosai,* a huge, thin pancake used to scoop up luscious and hearty gravies and curries. Even for carnivores, it's very satisfying. What's more, it's cheap: two samosas, *dosai,* and an assortment of stew-style gravies *(dhal)* for two are only S$8 (US$4.70/£2.65) with tea. For a quick fast-food meal, this place is second to none.

76–78 Serangoon Rd. ✆ 65/6293-6980. Reservations not accepted. Dosai S$2 (US$1.30/65p); lunch for two S$8 (US$5.10/£2.65). No credit cards. Daily 11:30am–3pm and 6:30–10:30pm.

Muthu's Curry Restaurant SOUTHERN INDIAN   Muthu's is a local institution that is synonymous with one local delicacy, fish head curry, a giant fish head floating in a huge portion of delicious curry soup, its eye staring and teeth grinning. The cheek meat is the best part of the fish, but to be truly polite, let your friend eat the eye. The list of accompanying dishes is long and includes crab *masala,* chicken *biryani,* and mutton curry, with fish cutlet and fried chicken sold by the piece. We're not talking the height of dining elegance here, but Muthu's really has come a long way since its simple coffee shop opening, with its recent shift to newer, larger digs, with matching tables and chairs! I miss the old grotty ambience, but still it's a good place to try this dish. Go either at the start or toward the end of mealtime, so you don't get lost in the rush and can find staff with more time to help you. They've recently opened another branch in town at 3 Temasek Blvd., #B1–056, Suntec City Mall (✆ **65/6835-7707**).

138 Race Course Rd. ✆ **65/6293-2389.** Reservations not accepted. Small dishes S$3.50–S$6.50 (US$2.20–US$4.20/£1.15–£215); fish head curry from S$18 (US$12/£5.95). AE, DC, MC, V. Daily 10am–10pm.

7 Orchard Road Area

EXPENSIVE

BLU ✪✪✪ CONTEMPORARY   Commanding an awe-inspiring view of Orchard Road from its 24th-floor perch, BLU represents the best in stylish dining. A perfect spot for a get-together or a little quiet self-indulgence, the restaurant is decorated with modern glass sculptures by Danny Lane, Philippe Starck table lamps, fiber optics on the glass bar and floor, and Wedgwood table settings. With new Michelin-starred chef de cuisine Robin Zavou onboard, expect mind-blowing signature dishes such as pan-fried foie gras with vanilla apples and black truffle, scallops with cauliflower mousse and spiced carrot sauce, filet of beef with onion ice-cream, as well as ginger parfait with green tea and peppermint jelly. The wine list is extensive with over 200 sparkling, white, red, and dessert wines, including rare and vintage wines. Jazz performances are Monday through Thursday 8:30 to 11:15pm and Friday and Saturday from 9pm to 12:30am.

Shangri-La Hotel, 22 Orange Grove Rd., 24th Floor. ✆ **65/6213-4598.** Reservations recommended. Main courses S$40–S$60 (US$26–US$38/£13–£20). AE, DC, MC, V. Daily 7–10:30pm.

Harbour Grill & Oyster Bar ✪✪✪ CONTINENTAL   Grilled seafood and U.S. prime rib are perfectly prepared and served with attentive style in this award-winning restaurant. The Continental cuisine is lighter than most, with recipes that focus on the natural freshness of their ingredients rather than on creams and fat. Caesar salad is made at your table so you can request your preferred blend of ingredients, and the oyster bar serves juicy fresh oysters from around the world. For the main course, the prime rib is the best and most requested entree, but the rack of lamb is another option worth considering—it melts in your mouth. Guest chefs from international culinary capitals are flown in for monthly specials. The place is small and cozy, with nautical-inspired murals and a finishing kitchen in the dining room.

Hilton Singapore, Level 3, 581 Orchard Rd. ✆ **65/6730-3393.** Reservations recommended. Main courses S$42–S$50 (US$27–US$32/£14–£17). AE, DC, MC, V. Mon–Fri noon–2pm; Mon–Sat 7–10pm.

Li Bai ✪✪✪ CHINESE/CANTONESE   Chinese restaurants are typically unimaginative in the decor department—slapping up a landscape brush painting or two here and there is sometimes about as far as they go. Not at Li Bai, which is very sleekly decorated in contemporary black and red lacquer, with comfortable black leather seating. Creative chefs and guest chefs turn out a constantly evolving menu, refining specialties, and jade-and-silver chopsticks and white bone china add opulent touches to their flawless meals. Shark's fin soup and abalone creations are a requirement for any self-respecting Cantonese restaurant, and although Li Bai's preparation of these delicacies is tops, I recommend you bypass them—too much hype and expense. Go for the chef's special creations, which are always imaginative. Or try the duck smoked with jasmine tea leaves, a succulent dish, as is the barbecued meats assortment. The crab fried rice is fabulous, with generous chunks of fresh meat, and the beef in mushroom and garlic brown sauce is some of the most tender meat you'll ever feast upon. The wine list is international, with many vintages to choose from.

Sheraton Towers, Lower Lobby Level, 39 Scotts Rd. ✆ **65/6839-5623**. Reservations required. Small dishes S$16–S$48 (US$10–US$31/£5.30–£16) and up. AE, DC, MC, V. Daily 11:30am–2:30pm and 6:30–10:30pm.

Mezza9 ✿✿ FUSION   This is your best bet if your party can't agree on what to eat because Mezza9 offers an extensive menu that includes Chinese steamed treats, Japanese, Thai, deli selections, Italian, fresh seafood, and Continental grilled specialties. Start with big and juicy raw oysters on the half-shell. If you want to consider more raw seafood, the combination sashimi platter is also very fresh. Grilled meats include various cuts of beef, rack of lamb, and chicken dishes with a host of delicious sides to choose from. The enormous 450-seat restaurant has a warm atmosphere, with glowing wood and contemporary Zen accents, but service can be harried. Before you head in for dinner, grab a martini in their très chic martini bar.

Grand Hyatt, 10 Scotts Rd. ✆ **65/6416-7189**. Reservations recommended. Main courses S$25–S$45 (US$16–US$29/£8.25–£15). AE, DC, MC, V. Daily noon–3pm and 6–11:30pm.

MODERATE

Chatterbox SINGAPOREAN   If you'd like to try the local favorites but don't want to deal with hawker food, then Chatterbox is the place for you. Their Hainanese chicken rice is highly acclaimed, though the famous chef behind the recipe left this past year. Other dishes—like *nasi lemak, laksa,* and carrot cake—are as close to the street as you can get. For a quick and tasty snack, order *tahu goreng,* deep-fried tofu in peanut chili sauce. This is also a good place to experiment with some of those really weird local drinks. *Chin chow* is the dark brown grass jelly drink; *chendol* is green jelly, red beans, palm sugar, and coconut milk; and *bandung* is pink rose syrup milk with jelly. For dessert, order the ever-favorite sago pudding, made from the hearts of the sago palm. This informal and lively coffee shop dishes out room service for the Mandarin Hotel and is open 24 hours a day.

Mandarin Hotel, 333 Orchard Rd. ✆ **65/6737-4411**. Reservations recommended for lunch and dinner. Main courses S$15–S$39 (US$9.60–US$25/£4.95–£13). AE, DC, MC, V. Daily 24 hr.

Patara Fine Thai THAI   Patara may say fine dining in its name, but the food here is home cooking: not too haute, not too traditional. Seafood and vegetables are the stars here. Deep-fried *garoupa* (grouper) is served in a sweet sauce with chili that can be added sparingly upon request. Curries are popular, too. The roast duck curry in red curry paste with tomatoes, rambutans, and pineapple is juicy and hot. For something really different, Patara's own invention, the Thai taco, isn't exactly traditional but is good, filled with chicken, shrimp, and sprouts. Their green curry, one of my favorites, is perhaps the best in town. Their Thai-style iced tea (which isn't on the menu, so

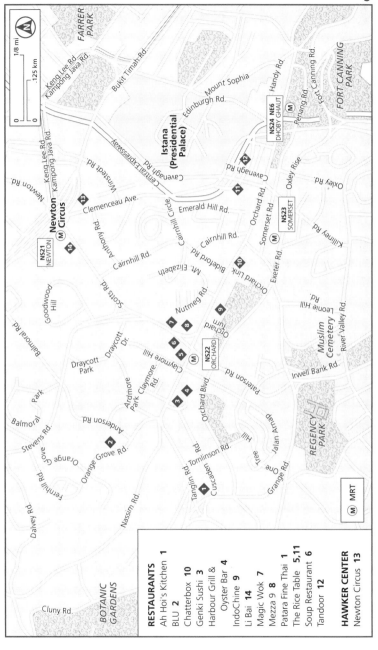

RESTAURANTS
Ah Hoi's Kitchen **1**
BLU **2**
Chatterbox **10**
Genki Sushi **3**
Harbour Grill &
  Oyster Bar **4**
IndoChine **9**
Li Bai **14**
Magic Wok **7**
Mezza 9 **8**
Patara Fine Thai **1**
The Rice Table **5,11**
Soup Restaurant **6**
Tandoor **12**

HAWKER CENTER
Newton Circus **13**

you'll have to ask for it) is fragrant and flowery. A small selection of wines is also available. Patara has another outlet at Swissôtel The Stamford, Level 3, Stamford Road (© 65/6339-1488).

#03–14 Tanglin Mall, 163 Tanglin Rd. © 65/6737-0818. Reservations recommended for lunch, required for dinner. Small dishes S$12–S$49 (US$7.70–US$31/£3.95–£16). AE, DC, MC, V. Daily noon–2:30pm and 6–10:30pm.

Tandoor ★★ NORTHERN INDIAN   Live music takes center stage in this small restaurant, adorned with carpets, artwork, and wood floors and furnishings. Entrees prepared in their tandoor oven come out flavorful and not as salty as most tandoori dishes. The tandoori lobster is rich, but the chef's specialty is crab *lababdar:* crabmeat, onions, and tomato sautéed in a coconut gravy. Fresh cottage cheese is made in-house for fresh and light *saag panir,* a favorite here. Chefs keep a close eye on the spices to ensure the spice enhances the flavor rather than drowning it out—more times than not, customers ask them to add more spices. A final course of creamy *masala* tea perks you up and aids digestion.

Holiday Inn Parkview, 11 Cavenagh Rd. © 65/6730-0153. Reservations recommended. Small dishes S$20–S$40 (US$13–US$26/£6.60–£13). AE, DC, MC, V. Daily noon–2:30pm and 7–10:30pm.

INEXPENSIVE

Ah Hoi's Kitchen SINGAPOREAN   I like Ah Hoi's for its casual charm and its selection of authentic local cuisine. The menu is extensive, specializing in local favorites like fried black pepper *kuay teow* (noodles), *sambal kang kong* (a spinach-like vegetable fried with chili), and fabulous grilled seafood. The alfresco poolside pavilion location gives it a real "vacation in the Tropics" sort of relaxed feel—think of a hawker center without the dingy florescent bulbs, greasy tables, and sludgy floor. Also good here is the chili crab—if you can't make it out to the seafood places on the east coast of the island, it's the best alternative for tasting this local treat. Make sure you order the fresh lime juice. It's very cooling.

Traders Hotel, 1A Cuscaden Rd., 4th level. © 65/6831-4373. Reservations recommended. Small dishes S$12–S$24 (US$7.70–US$15/£3.95–£7.90). AE, DC, MC, V. Daily 11:30am–2:30pm and 6:30–10:30pm.

Genki Sushi *Value* JAPANESE   I ducked into Genki Sushi for lunch. I sat at the counter, where a tiny conveyor belt snaked along in front of me carrying colored plates full of glistening sushi, rolls, sashimi, and other treats. Just pick and eat—and pay per plate. So the goofy Japanese guy next to me got chatty. We discussed the conveyor-belt sushi bar concept and how much we both loved it, then he poked some buttons on his electronic translator and showed me the screen. "This name in Japan." The translator spelled *revolution.* Makes sense, the "revolution" sushi bar, but now I'll never shake the image of Che Guevara sitting there plucking sushi off the belt.

#01–16 Forum The Shopping Mall, Orchard Rd. © 65/6734-2513. Reservations not accepted. Revolving plates S$1.90–S$6.50 (US$1.20–US$4.20/65p–£2.15). AE, DC, MC, V. Sun–Thurs 11:30am–9pm; Fri–Sat 11:30am–10pm.

The Rice Table ★ MALAY/INDONESIAN/DUTCH   Indonesian Dutch *rijsttafel,* meaning "rice table," is a service of many small dishes (up to almost 20) with rice. Traditionally, each dish would be brought to diners by beautiful ladies in pompous style. Here, busy waitstaff brings all the dishes out and places them in front of you—feast on favorite Indo-Malay wonders like beef *rendang,* chicken *satay, otak otak,* and *sotong assam* (squid) for a very reasonable price. It's an enormous amount of food and everything is terrific. Pay extra for your drinks and desserts. There's an additional outlet at

Cuppage Terrace at 43–45 Cuppage Rd. (℃ **65/6735-9117**) and a new one at Suntec City Mall, #03–028 Sky Garden (℃ **65/6333-0248**).

International Bldg., 360 Orchard Rd., #02–09/10. ℃ **65/6835-3783**. Reservations not necessary. Lunch set S$15 (US$9.80/£5.05); dinner set S$23 (US$15/£7.65). AE, DC, MC, V. Tues–Sun noon–2:45pm and 6–9:45pm.

8 Restaurants a Little Farther Out

Many travelers will choose to eat in town for convenience, and although there's plenty of great dining in the more central areas, there are some other really fantastic dining finds if you're willing to hop in a cab for 10 or 15 minutes. These places are worth the trip—for a chance to dine along the water at UDMC or go for superior seafood at Long Beach Seafood Restaurant. And don't worry about finding your way back: Most places always have cabs milling about. If not, restaurant staff will always help you call a taxi.

EXPENSIVE

Halia ✿ CONTINENTAL/FUSION   Most notable for its location within the Singapore Botanic Gardens, you really need to come to Halia for a daytime meal, either a weekend breakfast buffet, relaxing lunch, or weekday high tea, if you want to enjoy the lush greenery of the surroundings. Cuisine is contemporary fare, with ginger permeating quite a few of the recipes—*halia* being "ginger" in Malay. The specialty of the house is the chunks of seafood stewed in Asian flavors of chili and lemon grass served over a bed of *papardelle* pasta. To get there, ask the taxi driver to take you along Tyersall Avenue and look for the HALIA signboard at the Tyersall Gate near the Ginger Garden.

1 Cluny Rd., in the Singapore Botanic Gardens, Tyersall Gate. ℃ **65/6476-6711**. Reservations recommended. Main courses S$26–S$43 (US$17–US$28/£8.60–£14); breakfast buffet S$18 (US$12/£5.95). AE, DC, MC, V. Daily noon–3pm and 6:30–11pm; breakfast Sat–Sun 8–10:45am; high tea Mon–Sat 3–5:30pm.

MODERATE

Long Beach Seafood Restaurant SEAFOOD   They really pack 'em in at this place. Tables are crammed together in what resembles a big indoor pavilion, complete with festive lights and the sounds of mighty feasting. This is one of the best places for fresh seafood of all kinds: fish like *garoupa* (grouper), sea bass, marble goby, and kingfish, and other creatures of the sea from prawns to crayfish. The chili crab here is good, but the house specialty is really the pepper crab, chopped and deliciously smothered in a thick concoction of black pepper and soy. Huge chunks of crayfish are also tasty in the black pepper sauce and can be served in variations like barbecue, sambal, steamed with garlic, or in a bean sauce. Don't forget to order buns so you can sop up the sauce. You can also get vegetable, chicken, beef, or venison dishes to complement, or choose from their menu selection of local favorites.

1018 East Coast Pkwy. ℃ **65/6445-8833**. Reservations recommended. Seafood is sold by weight according to seasonal prices. Most nonseafood dishes S$9–S$16 (US$5.80–US$10/£2.95–£5.30). AE, DC, MC, V. Daily 11am–3pm; Sun–Fri 5pm–12:15am; Sat 5pm–1:15am.

Original Sin ✿ MEDITERRANEAN/VEGETARIAN   This cozy place is a perennial favorite with Singapore's expatriate population. Located in Holland Village, Singapore's expatriate enclave, the restaurant is close to shopping, pubs, and numerous other dining choices that cater to this international group. This particular restaurant is a favorite, with generous portions of favorites like baba ghanouj, *tzatziki,* and hummus served with olives, feta, and pita bread. And although the menu features standard

Mediterranean fare like moussaka and risotto dishes, people always seem to go for the pizzas, which are loaded with interesting Middle Eastern toppings. The owners also run two other properties of equal quality and popularity in Chip Bee Gardens, Italian restaurants **Michelangelo's,** Block 44, Jalan Merah Saga #01–60 (© **65/6475-9069**) and **Sistina,** Block 44, Jalan Merah Saga #01–58 (© **65/6476-7782**). All of these restaurants have a casual, congenial bistro-style atmosphere inside and sidewalk dining outside.

Block 43 Jalan Merah Saga, #01–62, Chip Bee Gardens, Holland Village. © **65/6475-5605.** Reservations recommended. Main courses S$24–S$28 (US$15–US$18/£7.90–£9.25). AE, DC, MC, V. Tues–Sun 11:30am–2:30pm and 6–10:30pm; Mon 6–10:30pm.

True Blue Cuisine ✺✺ PERANAKAN Katong, the central neighborhood of the Peranakan, or Straits Chinese, community, is also famous for excellent local cuisine. True Blue, housed in a restored prewar shophouse in this historic neighborhood, shares a block with other Peranakan heritage sites, like Rumah Bebe, a shop for Peranakan fashions (see chapter 7). Inside, the restaurant is decorated with cultural trappings that will make Singaporeans nostalgic and foreigners feel as if they've been welcomed into a private home. Home-cooked from family recipes (the owner's mother runs the kitchen), luscious favorites such as *ayam buah keluak,* which is a dish of chicken- and mincemeat-stuffed nuts in a sourish curry, is some if the best I've tasted. The friendly staff will help you navigate other classics on the menu, like *otak-otak,* pounded fish and chili grilled in banana leaves, and beef *rendang,* beef stewed in a thick, mildly spicy coconut gravy. Tell your taxi driver to take you to East Coast Road at the junction with Joo Chiat Road. You can follow the shop numbers a short walk until you find the place. Taxis back to town are plentiful.

117 East Coast Rd., 2nd Floor. © **65/6440-0449.** Reservations required. Small dishes S$12–S$24 (US$7.70–US$15/ £3.95–£7.90). AE, DC, MC, V. Daily noon–2:30pm and 6–9:30pm.

UDMC Seafood Centre ✺✺ SEAFOOD Eight seafood restaurants are lined side by side in 2 blocks, their fronts open to the view of the sea outside. UDMC is a fantastic way to eat seafood Singapore-style, in the open air, in restaurants that are more like grand stalls than anything else. Eat the famous local chili crab and pepper crab here, along with all sorts of squid, fish, and scallop dishes. Noodle dishes are also available, as are vegetable dishes and other meats. But the seafood is the thing to come for. Of the eight restaurants, there's no saying which is the best, as everyone seems to have his own opinions about this one or that one (I like Jumbo at the far eastern end of the row; call © **65/6442-3435** for reservations, which are recommended for weekends). Have a nice stroll along the walkway and gaze out to the water while you decide which one to go for.

Block 1202 East Coast Pkwy. No phone. Seafood dishes are charged by weight, with dishes starting from around S$12 (US$7.70/£3.95). AE, DC, MC, V. Daily 5pm–midnight.

INEXPENSIVE

Samy's Curry Restaurant ✺ SOUTHERN INDIAN There are many places in Singapore to get good southern Indian banana leaf (see description under "One Little Island, Lots & Lots of Choices," earlier in this chapter), but none quite so unique as Samy's out on Dempsey Road. Because it's part of the Singapore Civil Service Clubhouse, at lunchtime nonmembers must pay S50¢ (US30¢/15p) to get in the door. Not that there's much of a door, because Samy's is situated in a huge, high-ceilinged, open-air hall, with shutters thrown back and fans whirring above. Wash your hands at the back and have a seat, and soon someone will slap a banana leaf place mat in front of you. A blob of white rice will be placed in the center, and then buckets of vegetables, chicken, mutton, fish, prawn, and you-name-it will be brought out, swimming in the richest and spiciest curries to ever pass your lips. Take a peek in each bucket, shake your head yes when you see one you like, and a scoop will be dumped on your banana leaf. Eat with your right hand or with a fork and spoon. When you're done, wipe the sweat from your brow, fold the banana leaf away from you, and place your tableware on top. Samy's serves no alcohol, but the fresh lime juice is nice and cooling.

Block 25 Dempsey Rd., Civil Service Club. ℭ **65/6472-2080.** Reservations not accepted. Sold by the scoop or piece, S80¢–S$3 (US50¢–US$1.90/25p–£1). V. Daily 11am–3pm and 6–10pm. No alcohol served.

9 Hawker Centers

Hawker centers—large groupings of informal open-air food stalls—were Singapore's answer to fast and cheap food in the days before McDonald's and are still the best way to sample every kind of Singaporean cuisine. The traditional hawker center is an outdoor venue, usually under cover with fans whirring above, and individual stalls each specializing in different dishes. In between rows of cooking stalls, tables and stools offer open seating for diners.

Each center has an array of food offerings, with most dishes costing between S$3.50 and S$5 (US$2.20–US$3.20/£1.15–£1.65). You'll find traditional dishes like *char kway teow,* flat rice noodles fried with seafood; **fishball noodle soup,** with balls made from pounded fish and rice flour; **claypot chicken rice,** chicken and mushrooms baked with rice and fragrant soy sauce; *bak kut teh,* pork ribs stewed with Chinese herbs; **Hainanese chicken rice,** soft chicken over rice prepared in rich chicken stock; *laksa,* seafood and rice noodles in a spicy coconut chili soup; *popiah,* turnip, egg, pork, prawn, and sweet chili sauce wrapped in a thin skin; *rojak,* fried dough, tofu, cucumber, pineapple, and whatever the chef has handy, mixed with a sauce made from peanuts and fermented shrimp paste; plus many, many more Chinese, Malay, and Indian specialties. You'll also find hot and cold drink stalls and usually a stall selling fresh fruits and fruit juices.

If you want to become a real Singapore Foodie, buy a copy of *Makansutra* by K. F. Seetoh (Makansutra Publishing) at any bookstore. Seetoh's the local guru of hawker foods and has sniffed out the tastiest, most authentic local delicacies you can imagine.

Within the city limits, most traditional-style hawker centers have been closed down, but you can still find a few. Singapore's two most famous, or notorious, hawker centers are **Newton Circus Hawker Center** and the **Satay Club.** Newton, a 24-hour center near the Newton MRT stop, is a tour-bus darling; beware of gouging, especially when ordering seafood dishes, which are sold by the kilo. The Satay Club, at Clarke Quay, is a touristy version of a Singaporean institution. The original Satay Club was a simple gathering of stalls by the water where Esplanade–Theatres on the Bay is now located. This reincarnation of the Satay Club is certainly not as authentic, in atmosphere or in food quality, but generally hawkers here tend to be an honest lot.

For local-style hawker centers, in Chinatown you can find stalls at the **Maxwell Road Food Centre** at the corner of Maxwell and South Bridge roads or you can try **Lau Pa Sat** at the corner of Raffles Way and Boon Tat Street. A new food attraction, a row of stalls along Smith Street called **Food Alley** was conceived by the STB. Rumor has it, these guys are having a hard time making a living selling local food to the very touristy crowd that passes down this street in the evenings. In the Historic District, try the **small center next to Allson Hotel** on Victoria Street, or Makansutra, next to the Esplanade–Theatres on the Bay. In Little India, **Zhujiao Centre** features more Indian and Muslim hawker fare, as opposed to the mainstay Chinese cuisine at most places.

When you eat at a hawker center, the first thing to do is claim a seat at a table (local trick: If you put a tissue packet down on the table in front of your seat, people will understand it's reserved). Remember the number on your table so that when you order from each stall, you can let them know where you're seated. They will deliver your food to the table, and you must pay upon delivery. Change will be provided. When you are finished, there's no need to clear your dishes; it will be taken care of for you.

The modern version of the hawker center is the **food court.** Similar to hawker centers, food courts are air-conditioned spaces inside shopping malls and public buildings. They also have individual stalls offering a variety of foods and tables with free seating. Generally, food courts offer a more "fast-food," less authentic version of local cuisine, but you also get greater variety—many food courts have a stall that sells Western burgers and fish and chips, and stalls with Japanese *udon* or Korean barbecue. Food courts also differ in that they're self-service. When you approach the stall, you take a tray, pay when you order, then carry the food yourself to your own table, similar to cafeteria-style. When you finish, you are not expected to clear your tray.

Food courts are everywhere within the city, most of them operated by popular chains like **Food Junction, Kopitiam,** and **Banquet.** You'll find them in shopping malls and public buildings, most likely on the top floor or in the basement. Your hotel's concierge will be able to point you to the nearest food court, no problem.

10 Cafe Society

In Singapore, traditions such as British high tea and the Chinese tea ceremony live side by side with a growing coffee culture. These popular hangouts are all over the city. Here are a few places to try.

BRITISH HIGH TEA

Two fabulous places to take high tea in style are at **Raffles Bar & Billiard Room** at Raffles Hotel, 1 Beach Rd. (✆ **65/6331-1746**), and **Equinox** at Swissôtel The Stamford, 2 Stamford Rd. (✆ **65/6431-6156**). Both places are lovely, if pricey. The buffet will cost anywhere from S$35 to S$45 (US$22–US$29/£12–£15). High tea is served in the afternoons from 3 until 5 or 5:30pm.

CHINESE TEA

There are a few places in Chinatown where tea is still as important today as it has always been in Chinese culture. **The Tea Chapter,** 11A Neil Rd. (✆ **65/6226-1175**), and **Yixing Xuan,** 30–32 Tanjong Pagar Rd. (✆ **65/6224-6961**), offer tranquil respites from the day and cultural insight into Chinese tea appreciation.

CAFES

Western-style coffee joints have been popping up left and right all over the island, so coffee-addicted travelers can rest assured that in the morning their favorite blends are brewing close by—as long as you don't mind spending up to S$4 (US$2.60/£1.30) for a cup of brew. **Starbucks,** the **Coffee Bean & Tea Leaf,** the **Coffee Club, Spinelli,** and many more international chain cafes have outlets in just about every shopping mall in the city.

THE TRAVELOCITY GUARANTEE

...THAT SAYS EVERYTHING YOU BOOK WILL BE RIGHT, OR WE'LL WORK WITH OUR TRAVEL PARTNERS TO MAKE IT RIGHT, RIGHT AWAY.

*To drive home the point,
we're going to use the word "right" in every single sentence.*

Let's get right to it. Right to the meat! Only Travelocity guarantees everything about your booking will be right, or we'll work with our travel partners to make it right, right away. Right on!

Here's a picture taken smack dab right in the middle of Antigua, where the Guarantee also covers you.

The Guarantee covers all but one of the items pictured to the right.

For example, what if the ocean view you booked actually looks out at a downright ugly parking lot? You'd be right to call – we're there for you. And no one in their right mind would be pleased to learn the rental car place has closed and left them stranded. Call Travelocity and we'll help get you back on the right track.

Now, you may be thinking, "Yeah, right, I'm so sure." That's OK; you have the right to remain skeptical. That is until we mention help is always right around the corner. Call us right off the bat, knowing our customer service reps are there for you 24/7. Righting wrongs. Left and right.

Now if you're guessing there are some things we can't control, like the weather, well you're right. But we can help you with most things – to get all the details in righting,* visit travelocity.com/guarantee.

*Sorry, spelling things right is one of the few things not covered under the Guarantee.

I'd give my right arm for a guarantee like this, although I'm glad I don't have to.

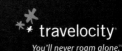

travelocity

You'll never roam alone.℠

6

Singapore Attractions

Of Singapore's many sights and attractions, I enjoy the historical and cultural sights the most. The city's many old buildings and well-presented museum displays bring history to life. Chinese and Hindu temples and Muslim mosques welcome curious observers to discover their culture as they play out their daily activities, and the country's natural parks make the great outdoors easily accessible from even the most urban neighborhood. That's the best benefit of traveling in Singapore: Most attractions are situated within the heart of the city, and those that lie outside the urban center still can be easily reached.

Singapore also has a multitude of planned attractions for visitors and locals alike. Theme parks devoted to cultural heritage, sporting fun, and even kitsch amusement pop up all over the place. In this chapter, I've outlined the many attractions here and provided historical and cultural information to help you appreciate each sight in its local context. To help you plan your activities, I've put stars next to those attractions I've enjoyed the most—either for significance, excellent planning, or just plain curiosity.

I've divided this chapter into the main sections of the urban center—the Historic District, Chinatown, Little India, Kampong Gelam, and Orchard Road, where you'll find the more historical sights of the city—and those outside the city, to the west, north, and east, where

you'll find large areas dedicated to nature reserves, a zoo, other wildlife attractions, theme parks, and sprawling temple complexes, all easily accessible by public transportation or a cab ride. As a kicker, I'll take you to Sentosa (a small island to the south with amusements, historical exhibits, nature displays, and outdoor activities for families) and to some of the smaller outlying islands and will fill you in on sports and recreation options.

When you're traveling to attractions outside the urban area, I recommend keeping this book handy—taxis are not always easy to find, so you may need to refer to the guide to call for a pick up or use the bus and MRT system, route numbers for which I've included with listings of most noncentral attractions.

A note: Many of the sights to see in Singapore are not of the "pay your fee and see the show" variety, but rather historic buildings, monuments, and places of religious worship. Monuments and statues tell the stories of events and heroes important to Singapore in both the past and the present. The places of worship listed in this chapter are open to the public and free of entrance charge. Expect temples to be open from sunup to sundown. Visiting hours are not specific to the hour, but, unless it's a holiday (when hours may be extended), you can expect these places to be open during daylight hours.

Urban Singapore Attractions

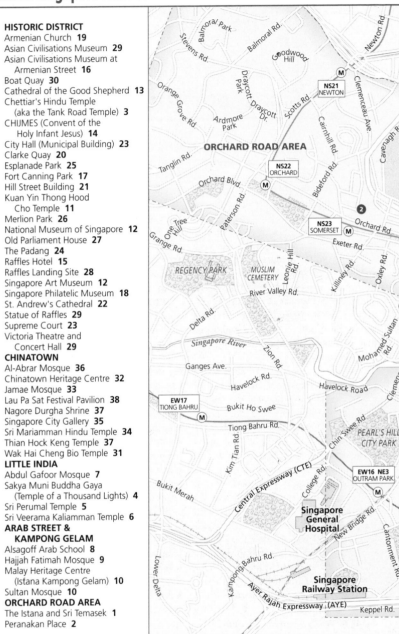

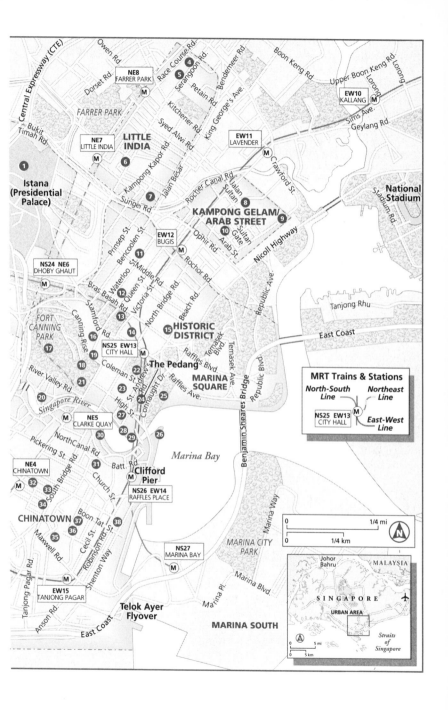

1 The Historic District

When Sir Stamford Raffles first sailed up the Singapore River he saw a small fishing and trading village along the banks and a thick overgrowth of jungle and mangrove forest creeping up a gentle hill that overlooked the harbor. Over the years to follow, the left bank of the river would become the nerve center for sea trade, and the right bank, at the foot of the hill, would be cleared for the center of government activity.

Raffles's Town Plan of 1822 had special plans for this district, referred to in this book as the Historic District but also called the City Centre. The center point was the **Padang,** a large field for sports and ceremonies. Around the field, government buildings were erected, each reflecting preferred British tastes of the day. European hotels popped up, as well as cultural centers, and the park along the marina became a lively focal point for the European social scene.

The oldest part of the city is Fort Canning Park, the hill where Raffles built his home. Its history predates Raffles, with excavation sites unearthing artifacts and small treasures from earlier trading settlements and a sacred shrine that's believed to be the final resting place of Iskander Shah, founder of the Sultanate of Malacca.

Armenian Church ✿   Of all colonial buildings, the Armenian Church (more formally called the Church of St. Gregory the Illuminator) is one of the most beautiful examples of early architectural style here. Designed by George Coleman, one of Singapore's most prolific and talented architects, it is his finest work. Although there were many alterations in the last century, the main style of the structure still dominates. The round congregation hall is powerful in its simplicity, its long louvered windows letting in cooling breezes while keeping out the imposing sunlight. Roman Doric columns support symmetrical porticos that protect the structure from rain. All in all, it's a wonderful achievement of combined European eclectic tastes and tropical necessity.

The first permanent Christian church in Singapore, it was funded primarily by the Armenian community, which was at one time quite powerful. Today, few Singaporeans can trace their heritage back to this influential group of immigrants. The church was consecrated in 1836, and the last appointed priest serving the parish retired in 1936. Although regular Armenian services are no longer held, other religious organizations make use of the church from time to time. The cemetery in the back of the church is the burial site of many prominent Armenians, including Ashgen Agnes Joachim, discoverer of the Vanda Miss Joachim, Singapore's national flower.

60 Hill St., across from the Grand Plaza Hotel. ✆ 65/6334-0141. Free admission. 15-min. walk from City Hall MRT.

Asian Civilisations Museum ✿✿✿   If you only have time for one museum, this is the one I recommend. This fantastic and well-executed exhibit of Southeast Asian culture highlights the history of the region and explores the Chinese, South Indian, and Islamic heritage that helped to shape regional cultures here. Well-planned galleries showcase fine arts, furniture, porcelain, jade, and other relics with excellent descriptions.

The Empress Place Building that houses the museum stood as a symbol of British colonial authority as sea travelers entered the Singapore River. The stately building housed almost the entire government bureaucracy around the year 1905 and was a government office until the 1980s, housing the Registry of Births and Deaths and the Citizenship Registry.

Don't forget to stop at the Museum Shop (✆ **65/6336-9050**) to browse exquisite ethnic crafts of the region. Also, check out the museum's website to find out more about their free lecture series.

Historic District Attractions

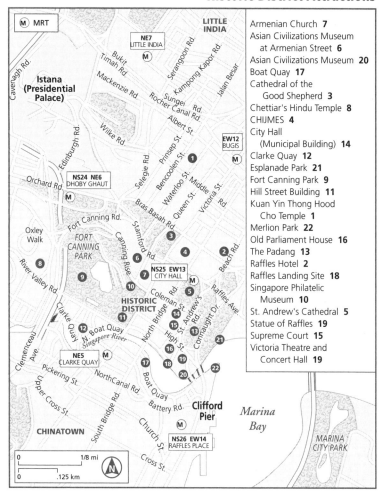

1 Empress Place. ② **65/6332-7798**. www.acm.org.sg. Adults S$5 (US$3.20/£1.65), children and seniors S$2.50 (US$1.60/85p); free on Fri from 7–9pm. Mon 1–7pm; Tues–Sun 9am–7pm (extended hours Fri until 9pm). Free guided tours in English Tues–Fri 11am and 2pm, with an extra tour on weekends at 3:30pm. 15-min. walk from City Hall MRT.

Asian Civilisations Museum at Armenian Street This small branch of the Asian Civilisations Museum (see above) is currently closed for a major renovation. At the time of this update no official information had been released about the focus of future exhibits, which are slated for launch in 2008. The quaint building was the former Tao Nan School, which dates from 1910.

39 Armenian St. ② **65/6332-3015**. www.acm.org.sg. Closed until 2008. 15-min. walk from City Hall MRT.

Cathedral of the Good Shepherd This cathedral was Singapore's first permanent Catholic church. Built in the 1840s, it unified many elements of a fractured parish. In the early days of the colony, the Portuguese Mission thought itself the fount of the Holy Roman Empire's presence on the island, and so the French bishop was reduced to holding services at the home of a Mr. McSwiney on Bras Basah Road, a dissenting Portuguese priest held forth at a certain Dr. d'Ameida's residence, and the Spanish priest was so reduced that we don't even know where he held his services. These folks were none too pleased with their makeshift houses of worship and so banded together to establish their own cathedral—the Cathedral of the Good Shepherd. Designed in a Latin cross pattern, much of its architecture is reminiscent of St Martin-in-the-Fields and St. Paul's in Covent Garden. The archbishop's residence, in contrast, is a simple two-story bungalow with enclosed verandas and a portico. Also on the grounds are the resident's quarters and the priests' residence, the latter more ornate in design, with elaborate plasterwork.

4 Queen St. (at the corner of Queen St. and Bras Basah Rd.). © **65/6337-2036.** Free admission. Open to the public during the day. 5-min. walk from City Hall MRT.

CHIJMES (Convent of the Holy Infant Jesus)   As you enter this bustling enclave of retail shops, restaurants, and nightspots, it's difficult to imagine this was once a convent which, at its founding in 1854, consisted of a lone, simply constructed bungalow. After decades of buildings and add-ons, this collection of unique yet perfectly blended structures—a school, a private residence, an orphanage, a stunning Gothic chapel, and many others—was enclosed within walls, forming peaceful courtyards and open spaces encompassing an entire city block. Legend has it the small door on the corner of Bras Basah and Victoria streets welcomed hundreds of orphan babies, girl children who just appeared on the stoop each morning, either born during inauspicious years or to poor families. In late 1983, the convent relocated to the suburbs, and some of the block was leveled to make way for the MRT Headquarters. Thankfully, most of the block survived and the Singapore government, in planning the renovation of this desirable piece of real estate, wisely kept the integrity of the architecture. For an evening out, the atmosphere at CHIJMES is exquisitely romantic.

A note on the name: CHIJMES is pronounced "Chimes"; the "Chij," as noted, stands for Convent of the Holy Infant Jesus, and the "mes" was just added on so they could pronounce it "Chimes."

30 Victoria St. © **65/6336-1818.** Free admission. 5-min. walk from City Hall MRT.

City Hall (Municipal Building)   During the Japanese occupation, City Hall was a major headquarters, and it was here in 1945 that Admiral Lord Louis Mountbatten accepted the Japanese surrender. In 1951, the Royal Proclamation from King George VI was read here declaring that Singapore would henceforth be known as a city. Fourteen years later, Prime Minister Lee Kuan Yew announced to its citizens that Singapore would henceforth be called an independent republic.

City Hall, along with the Supreme Court, was judiciously sited to take full advantage of its prime location. Magnificent Corinthian columns march across the front of the symmetrically designed building, while inside, two courtyards lend an ambience of informality to otherwise officious surroundings. For all its magnificence and historical fame, however, its architect, F. D. Meadows, relied too heavily on European influence. The many windows afford no protection from the sun, and the entrance leaves pedestrians unsheltered from the elements. In defining the very nobility of the Singapore government, it appears the Singaporean climate wasn't taken into consideration.

3 St. Andrew's Rd., across from the Padang. Entrance is not permitted. 5-min. walk from City Hall MRT.

Fort Canning Park   These days, Fort Canning Park is known for great views over Singapore, but in days past it served as the site of Raffles's home and the island's first botanic garden. Its history goes back even farther, though: Excavations have unearthed ancient brick foundations and artifacts that give credence to the island natives' belief that their royal ancestors lived and were buried on the site. Atop the hill, a mysterious *keramat,* or sacred grave, marks what is believed to be the burial site of Iskander Shah (also known as Parameswara), the Palembang ruler who came to Singapore in the late 1300s before settling in Malacca.

From the start Raffles chose this hill to build his home (at the site of the present-day lookout point), which later became a residence for Singapore's diplomats and governors. In 1860, the house was torn down to make way for Fort Canning, which was built to quell British fears of invasion but instead quickly became the laughingstock of the island. The location was ideal for spotting invaders from the sea, but defending Singapore? Not likely. The cannons' range was such that their shells couldn't possibly have made it all the way out to an attacking ship—instead, most of the town below would have been destroyed. In 1907, the fort was demolished for a reservoir. Today, the only reminders of the old fort are some of the walls and the Fort Gate, a deep stone structure. Behind its huge wooden door you'll find a narrow staircase that leads to the roof.

Raffles also chose this as the location for the first botanic garden on the island. The garden was short-lived due to lack of funding; however, the park still has a pretty interesting selection of plants and trees, like the cannonball tree with its large round seed pods, and the cotton tree, whose pods open to reveal fluffy white "cotton" that was commonly used for stuffing pillows and mattresses. In many parts, these plants are well marked along the pathways. Also look for the ASEAN sculpture garden; five members of the Association of Southeast Asian Nations each donated a work for the park in 1982 to represent the region's unity.

Fort Canning was also the site of a **European cemetery.** To make improvements in the park, the graves were exhumed and the stones placed within the walls surrounding the outdoor performance field that slopes from the Music and Drama Society building. A large Gothic monument was erected in memory of James Napier Brooke, infant son of William Napier, Singapore's first law agent, and his wife, Maria Frances, the widow of prolific architect George Coleman. Although no records exist, Coleman probably designed the cupolas as well as two small monuments over unknown graves. The Music and Drama Society building itself was built in 1938. Close by, in the wall, are the tombstones of Coleman and of Jose D'Almeida, a wealthy Portuguese merchant.

Inside the park, the **Battle Box** is an old World War II bunker displaying in wax dioramas and a multimedia show the surrender of Singapore. It's open Tuesday to Sunday from 10am to 6pm; adults S$8 (US$5.10/£2.65), children S$5 (US$3.20/ £1.65); © **65/6333-0510.**

The National Parks Board gives free guided tours of the park, but not the Battle Box, every last Saturday of the month (except Aug) at 4pm; call © **65/6332-1302** to register.

51 Canning Rise. © **65/6332-1302.** www.nparks.gov.sg. Free admission. Major entrances are from behind the Hill Street Building, Percival Rd. (Drama Centre), National Library Carpark, and Canning Walk (behind Park Mall). Dhoby Ghaut or City Hall MRT.

Hill Street Building   Originally built to house the British Police Force, the building was sited directly across from Chinatown for easy access to quell the frequent gang fights. Later it became home to the National Archives, and it is believed that inquisitions and torture were carried out in the basement during the Japanese occupation. Former National Archives employees have claimed to have seen ghosts of tortured souls sitting at their desks.

Today, this colorful building houses the Ministry of Information, Communications and the Arts (MITA), and the National Arts Council. Inside, check out ARTrium@ MITA, with seven galleries displaying Singaporean, Southeast Asian, and European fine arts. It's air-conditioned!

140 Hill St. at the corner of River Valley Rd., on Fort Canning Park. Free admission. 5-min. walk from Clarke Quay MRT.

Kuan Yin Thong Hood Cho Temple   It's said that whatever you wish for within the walls of Kuan Yin Temple comes true, so get in line and have your wish ready. It must work, as there's a steady stream of people on auspicious days of the Chinese calendar. The procedure is simple (watch others to catch on): Wear shoes easily slipped off before entering the temple and join the queue. When it is your turn, light several joss sticks, bow with them, and make a wish before placing them in the urn provided. Pick up the cylindrical container filled with wooden sticks and shake it until one stick falls out—each stick has a number. Give this number to the interpretation office and they will hand you a piece of paper with verses in Mandarin and English. This will tell you your general fortune, plus a clue as to whether your wish will come true. (For a small fee, interpreters outside can help with the translation.) Now for the payback: If your wish comes true, you're supposed to return to the temple and offer fruits and flowers to say thanks (oranges, pears, and apples are a thoughtful choice and jasmine petals are especially nice). So be careful what you wish for. After you're back home and that job promotion comes through, your new manager might nix a trip back to Singapore so you can bring fruits to this little temple! To be on the safe side, bring the goods with you when you make your wish.

Waterloo St., about 1½ blocks from Bras Basah Rd. Free admission. Open to the public during the day. 15-min. walk from Bugis MRT.

National Museum of Singapore ★★★   The once-little history museum, the former Singapore History Museum, closed its dusty halls in 2003 and has now reopened after a massive renovation. Now, this beautiful 120-year-old building has not only been restored, but has been expanded to more than twice its original size and features state-of-the-art multimedia exhibits designed to bring history to life and to make it accessible to all visitors. The History Gallery tells the story of Singapore from two points of view: from a historian's perspective and from the "man on the street." You decide which story you'd like to hear, then choose the corresponding audio headset that will guide you through the exhibit. The four Living Galleries show objects and elements of everyday Singaporean life: Food, Fashion, Film, and Photography. The museum conducts free guided tours in English Monday through Friday at 11am and 2pm, and on Saturday and Sunday at 11:30am and 3:30pm; the tour takes 1 to 1½ hours. The building itself is a gorgeous mix of colonial and contemporary architecture; a free tour that focuses just on the architecture is offered Friday through Sunday at 3:30pm.

93 Stamford Rd. ✆ 65/6332-3659. www.nationalmuseum.sg. Adults S$10 (US$6.40/£3.20), children and seniors S$5 (US$3.20/£1.60); free admission to the Living Galleries daily from 6–9pm. History Gallery daily 10am–6pm; Living Galleries daily 10am–9pm. 5-min. walk from Dhoby Ghaut or City Hall MRT.

Old Parliament House   The Old Parliament House is probably Singapore's oldest surviving structure, even though it has been renovated so many times it no longer looks the way it was originally constructed. It was designed as a home for John Argyle Maxwell, a Scottish merchant, but he never moved in. In 1822, Raffles returned to Singapore and was furious to find a residence being built on ground he'd allocated for government use. So the government took over Maxwell's house for its court and other offices. In 1939, when the new Supreme Court was completed, the judiciary moved into Maxwell's House (as it became officially known); then, in 1953, following a major renovation, the small structure was renamed Parliament House and was turned over to the legislature.

The original house was designed by architect George D. Coleman, who had helped Raffles with his Town Plan of 1822. Coleman's design was in the English neo-Palladian style. Simple and well suited to the Tropics, this style was popular at the time with Calcutta merchants. Major alterations have left very little behind of Coleman's design, replacing it with an eclectic French classical style, but some of his work survives.

Today, the building has been transformed once again—The Arts House at the Old Parliament has been lovingly restored, with spaces for visual and performance arts plus special cultural events. A couple of highbrow eateries offer a variety of Thai and Western cuisine. Singapore's parliament now operates out of the new Parliament Building just next door.

The bronze elephant in front of the Old Parliament House was a gift to Singapore in 1872 from His Majesty Somdeth Phra Paraminda Maha Chulalongkorn (Rama V), supreme king of Siam, as a token of gratitude following his stay the previous year.

1 Old Parliament Lane, at the south end of the Padang, next to the Supreme Court. ℂ 65/6332-6900. www.thearts house.com.sg. Free admission; extra charge for tickets to events. 15-min. walk from City Hall MRT.

The Padang   This large field has witnessed its share of historical events. Bordered on one end by the Singapore Recreation Club and on the other end by the Singapore Cricket Club, and flanked by City Hall, the area was once known as Raffles Plain. Upon Raffles's return to the island in 1822, he was angry that resident Farquhar had allowed merchants to move private residences into the prime area he had originally intended for government buildings. All building permits were rescinded, and the Padang became the official center point for the government quarters, around which the Esplanade and City Hall were built.

Today, the Padang is mainly used for public and sporting events—pleasant activities—but in the 1940s it felt more forlorn footsteps when the invading Japanese forced the entire European community onto the field. There they waited while the occupation officers dickered over a suitable location for the "conquered." They ordered all British, Australian, and Allied troops as well as European prisoners on the 22km (14-mile) march to Changi.

An interesting side note: Frank Ward, designer of the Supreme Court, had big plans for the Padang and surrounding buildings. He would have demolished the Cricket Club, Parliament House, and Victoria Hall & Theatre to erect an enormous government block if World War II hadn't arrived, ruining his chances.

St. Andrew's Rd. and Connaught Dr. Free admission. 5-min. walk from City Hall MRT.

Raffles Hotel ⭐⭐   Built in 1887 to accommodate the increasing upper-class trade, Raffles Hotel was originally only a couple of bungalows with 10 rooms, but, oh, the view of the sea was perfection. The owners, Armenian brothers named Sarkies, already had a couple of prosperous hotels in Southeast Asia (the Eastern & Oriental in Penang and the Strand in Rangoon) and were well versed in the business. It wasn't long before they added a pair of wings and completed the main building—and reading rooms, verandas, dining rooms, a grand lobby, the Bar and Billiards Room, a ballroom, and a string of shops. By 1899, electricity was turning the cooling fans and providing the pleasing glow of comfort.

As it made its madcap dash through the twenties, the hotel was the place to see and be seen. Vacancies were unheard of. Hungry Singaporeans and guests from other hotels, eager for a glimpse of the fabulous dining room, were turned away for lack of reservations. The crowded ballroom was jumping every night of the week. During this time Raffles's guest book included famous authors like Somerset Maugham, Rudyard Kipling, Joseph Conrad, and Noël Coward. These were indeed the glory years, but the lovely glimmer from the chandeliers soon faded with the stark arrival of the Great Depression. Raffles managed to limp through that dark time—and, darker still, through the Japanese occupation—and later pull back from the brink of bankruptcy to undergo modernization in the '50s. But fresher, brighter, more opulent hotels were taking root on Orchard Road, pushing the "grand old lady" to the back seat.

In the 1980s Raffles was brought back to its former glory. History-minded renovators selected 1915 as a benchmark and, with a few changes here and there, faithfully restored the hotel to that era's magnificence and splendor. Today, the hotel's restaurants and nightlife draw thousands of visitors daily to its open lobby, its theater playhouse, the Raffles Hotel Museum, and 65 exclusive boutiques. Its 15 restaurants and bars—especially the Tiffin Room, Raffles Grill, and Doc Cheng's, all reviewed in chapter 5—are a wonder, as is its famous Bar and Billiards Room and Long Bar.

1 Beach Rd. ℂ 65/6337-1886. City Hall MRT.

Raffles Landing Site　The polymarble statue at this site was unveiled in 1972. It was made from plaster casts of the original 1887 figure located in front of the Victoria Theatre and Concert Hall (see below) and stands on what is believed to be the site where Sir Stamford Raffles landed on January 29, 1819.

North Boat Quay. Free admission. 15-min. walk from City Hall MRT.

St. Andrew's Cathedral　Designed by George Coleman; erected on a site selected by Sir Stamford Raffles himself; named for the patron saint of Scotland, St. Andrew; and primarily funded by Singapore's Scottish community, the first St. Andrew's was the colonials' Anglican Church. Completed toward the end of the 1830s, its tower and spire were added several years later to accord the edifice more stature. By 1852, because of massive damage sustained from lightning strikes, the cathedral was deemed unsafe and torn down. The cathedral that now stands on the site was completed in 1860. Of English Gothic Revival design, the cathedral is one of the few standing churches of this style in the region. The spire resembles the steeple of the Salisbury Cathedral—another tribute from the colonials to Mother England. Not only English residents but Christian Chinese, Indians, Continental Europeans, and Malays consider this to be their center of worship.

The plasterwork of St. Andrew's inside walls used a material called Madras *chunam,* which, though peculiar, was a common building material here in the 1880s. A combination of shell lime (without the sand) was mixed with egg whites and coarse sugar or jaggery until it took on the consistency of a stiff paste. The mixture was thinned to a workable consistency with water in which coconut husks had steeped and was then applied to the surface, allowed to dry, and polished with rock crystal or smooth stones to a most lustrous patina. Who would've thought?

The original church bell was presented to the cathedral by Maria Revere Balestier, the daughter of famed American patriot Paul Revere. The bell is now in the archives of the Singapore History Museum.

11 St. Andrew's Rd., across from the Padang. © **65/6337-6104**. Free admission. Open during daylight hours. City Hall MRT.

Singapore Art Museum ✿   The Singapore Art Museum (SAM) officially opened in 1996 to house an impressive collection of over 6,500 pieces of art and sculpture, most of it by Singaporean and Malay artists. Limited space requires the curators to display only a small number at a time, but these are incorporated in interesting exhibits to illustrate particular artistic styles, social themes, or historical concepts. A large collection of Southeast Asian pieces rotates regularly, as well as visiting international exhibits. Besides the main halls, the museum offers up a gift shop with fine souvenir ideas, a cafe, a conservation laboratory, an auditorium, and the E-mage Gallery, where multimedia presentations include not only the museum's own acquisitions but other works from public and private collections in the region as well. Once a Catholic boys' school established in 1852, SAM has retained some visible reminders of its former occupants: above the front door of the main building you can still see inscribed "St. Joseph's Institution," and a bronze-toned, cast-iron statue of St. John Baptist de la Salle with two children stands in its original place.

71 Bras Basah Rd. © **65/6332-3222**. www.singart.com. Adults S$5 (US$3.20/£1.60), children and seniors S$2.50 (US$1.60/85p), free admission Fri 6–9pm. Sat–Thurs 10am–7pm; Fri 10am–9pm. Free guided tours in English Mon–Fri 11am and 2pm, with additional Sat–Sun tour at 3:30pm. 5-min. walk from City Hall MRT.

Singapore Philatelic Museum   This building, constructed in 1895 to house the Methodist Book Room, underwent a S$7-million (US$4.5-million/£2.3-million) restoration to become the Philatelic Museum in 1995. Exhibits include a fine collection of old stamps issued to commemorate historically important events, first-day covers, antique printing plates, postal service memorabilia, and private collections. Visitors can trace the development of a stamp from idea to the finished sheet, and you can even design your own. Free guided tours are available upon request.

23B Coleman St. © **65/6337-3888**. www.spm.org.sg. Adults S$5 (US$3.20/£1.65), children and seniors S$4 (US$2.50/£1.30). Mon 1–7pm; Tues–Sun 9am–7pm. 10-min. walk from Clarke Quay MRT.

Statue of Raffles   This sculpture of Sir Stamford Raffles was erected on the Padang in 1887 and moved to its present position after getting in the way of one too many cricket matches. During the Japanese occupation, the statue was placed in the Singapore History Museum (then the Raffles Museum) and was replaced here in 1945. The local joke is that Raffles's arm is outstretched to the Bank of China building, and his pockets are empty. (Translation: In terms of wealth in Singapore, it's Chinese 1, Brits 0.)

Behind the Victoria Theatre and Concert Hall, 9 Empress Place. Free admission. 15-min. walk from City Hall MRT.

Supreme Court   The Supreme Court stands on the site of the old Hotel de L'Europe, a rival of Raffles Hotel until it went bankrupt in the 1930s. The court's structure, a classical style favored for official buildings the world over, was completed in 1939. With its spare adornment and architectural simplicity, the edifice has a no-nonsense, utilitarian attitude, and the sculptures across the front, executed by the Italian sculptor Cavaliere Rodolpho Nolli, echo what transpires within. Justice is the most breathtaking, standing 2.7m (9 ft.) high and weighing almost 4 tons. Kneeling on either side of her are representations of Supplication and Thankfulness. To the far left are Deceit and Violence. To the far right, a bull represents Prosperity and two children hold wheat, to depict Abundance.

Two and a half million bricks were used in building this structure, but take a moment to note the stonework: It's fake! Really a gypsum type of plaster, it was applied by Chinese plasterers who molded it to give the appearance of granite. A dome, a copy of the one at St. Paul's Cathedral in London, covers an interior court-yard, which is surrounded by the four major portions of the Supreme Court building.

Visitors can go inside and take a peek at the Supreme Court Gallery, a historical exhibit of the courts system. You're also welcome to attend court hearings, provided appropriate dress and etiquette codes are observed.

1 St. Andrew's Rd., across from the Padang. © 65/6336-0644. Free admission. Mon–Fri 8:30am–5pm; Sat 8:30am–1pm. 10-min. walk from City Hall MRT.

Victoria Theatre and Concert Hall   Designed by colonial engineer John Bennett in a Victorian Revival style that was fashionable in Britain at the time, the theater por-tion was built in 1862 as the Town Hall. Victoria Memorial Hall was built in 1905 as a memorial to Queen Victoria, retaining the same style of the old building. The clock tower was added a year later. In 1909, with its name changed to Victoria Theatre, the hall opened with an amateur production of the *Pirates of Penzance*. Another notable performance occurred when Noël Coward passed through Singapore and stepped in at the last moment to help out a traveling English theatrical company that had lost a leading man. The building looks much the same as it did then, though of course the interiors have been modernized. It was completely renovated in 1979, conserving all the original details, and was renamed Victoria Concert Hall. It housed the Singapore Symphony Orchestra until the opening of the Esplanade–Theatres on the Bay, when they shifted to the larger digs.

9 Empress Place, at the southern end of the Padang. © **65/6339-6120**. Free admission to lobby areas. Concert tick-ets priced depending on performance and seat location. 15-min. walk from City Hall MRT.

ALONG THE RIVER

The Singapore River had always been the heart of life in Singapore even before Raf-fles landed, but for many years during the 20th century life here was dead—quite lit-erally. Rapid urban development that began in the 1950s turned the river into a giant sewer, killing all plant and animal life in it. In the mid-1980s, though, the government began a large and very successful cleanup project; and shortly thereafter, the buildings at Boat Quay and Clarke Quay, and later Robertson Quay, were restored. Now the areas on both banks of the river offer entertainment, food, and pubs day and night.

Boat Quay ⚐   Known as "the belly of the carp" by the local Chinese because of its shape, this area was once notorious for its opium dens and coolie shops. Nowadays, thriving restaurants boast every cuisine imaginable and the rocking nightlife offers up a variety of sounds—jazz, rock, blues, Indian, and Caribe—that are lively enough to get any couch potato tapping his feet. See chapters 5 and 8 for dining and nightlife suggestions. *Note:* pronounce quay like *key.*

Located on the south bank of the Singapore River between Cavenagh Bridge and Elgin Bridge. Free admission. 5-min. walk from Clarke Quay MRT.

Chettiar's Hindu Temple (aka the Tank Road Temple) One of the richest and grandest of its kind in Southeast Asia, the Tank Road Temple is most famous for a *thoonganai maadam,* a statue of an elephant's backside in a seated position. It's said that there are only four others of the kind, located in four temples in India.

The original temple was completed in 1860, restored in 1962, and practically rebuilt in 1984. The many sculptures of Hindu deities and the carved Kamalam-patterned rosewood doors, arches, and columns were executed by architect-sculptors imported from Madras, India, specifically for the job. The Hindu child god, Lord Muruga, rules over the temple and is visible in one form or another wherever you look. Also notice the statues of the god Shiva and his wife, Kali, captured in their lively dance competition. The story goes that Kali was winning the competition, so Shiva lifted his leg above his head, something a woman wasn't thought capable of doing. He won and quit dancing—good thing, too, because every time Shiva did a little jig he destroyed part of the world. Outside in the courtyard are statues of the wedding of Lord Muruga; his brother, Ganesh; another brother, Vishnu; and their father, Shiva; along with Brahma, the creator of all.

Used daily for worship, the temple is also the culmination point of Thaipusam, a celebration of thanks, and the Festival of Navarathiri (see chapter 3).

15 Tank Rd., close to the intersection of Clemenceau Ave. and River Valley Rd. ℂ 65/6737-9393. Free admission. 20-min. walk from Clarke Quay MRT.

Clarke Quay The largest of the waterfront developments, Clarke Quay was named for the second governor of Singapore, Sir Andrew Clarke. In the 1880s, a pineapple cannery, iron foundry, and numerous warehouses made this area bustle. Today, with 60 restored warehouses hosting restaurants and a shopping section known as Clarke Quay Factory Stores, the Quay still hops. **River House,** formerly the home of a *towkay* (company president), occupies the oldest building. In the evenings you can find the **Satay Club** here, a spot where satay sellers gather to sell the juicy little Malay meat kabobs dipped in yummy peanut chili sauce. Get up early on Sunday, forgo the comics section, and take in the **flea market,** which opens at 9am and lasts all day. You'll find lots of bargains on unusual finds.

Also here, **G-Max Reverse Bungy** (3E River Valley Rd.; ℂ 65/6338-1146; www. gmax.co.nz) will strap you and two buddies into a cage and fling you around at the end of giant bungee cords for only S$35 (US$22/£12) each. You'll go up 60m (197 ft.) high at 200kmph (124 mph). Woo! Stop by during weekdays from 3pm to 1am, and on weekends from noon until late.

River Valley Rd. west of Coleman Bridge. ℂ 65/6337-3292. www.clarkequay.com.sg. Free admission. Clarke Quay MRT.

Esplanade Park Esplanade Park and Queen Elizabeth Walk, two of the most famous parks in Singapore, were established in 1943 on land reclaimed from the sea. Several memorials are located here. The first is a fountain built in 1857 to honor **Tan Kim Seng,** who gave a great sum of money toward the building of a waterworks. Another monument, **the Cenotaph,** commemorates the 124 Singaporeans who died in World War I; it was dedicated by the Prince of Wales. On the reverse side, the names of those who died in World War II have been inscribed. The third prominent memorial is dedicated to **Major General Lim Bo Seng,** a member of the Singaporean underground resistance in World War II who was captured and killed by the Japanese. His memorial was unveiled in 1954 on the 10th anniversary of his death. At the far end of the park, the Esplanade–Theatres on the Bay opened in October 2002.

Fashioned after the Sydney Opera House, the unique double-domed structure is known locally as the Durians, because their spiky domes resemble halves of durian shells (the building itself is actually smooth—the "spikes" are sun shields).

Connaught Dr., on the marina, running from the mouth of the Singapore River along the Padang to the Esplanade–Theatres on the Bay. Daily until midnight. Free admission. 10-min. walk from City Hall MRT.

Merlion Park   The Merlion is Singapore's half-lion, half-fish national symbol, the lion representing Singapore's roots as the "Lion City" and the fish representing the nation's close ties to the sea. Bet you think a magical and awe-inspiring beast like this has been around in tales for hundreds of years, right? No such luck. Rather, he was the creation of some scheming marketers at the Singapore Tourism Board in the early 1970s. Despite the Merlion's commercial beginnings, he's been adopted as the national symbol and spouts continuously every day at the mouth of the Singapore River.

South bank, at the mouth of the Singapore River, adjacent to One Fullerton. Free admission. Daily 7am–10pm. 15-min. walk from either City Hall or Raffles Place MRT.

2 Chinatown & Tanjong Pagar

When the first Chinese junk landed in Singapore sometime around 1821, the sailors aboard rushed to the shore and prayed to Ma Po Cho, the Goddess of Heavenly Sages, for bringing them safely to their destination. Small shrines were built on the shore, which became the first stops for all Chinese sailors as they landed—many of these shrines still exist today.

The Chinese and other merchants set up warehouses along the western bank of the Singapore River, and business offices, residences, clan associations, and coolie houses filled the area behind Boat Quay. In 1822, when Raffles developed his Town Plan, he reserved this area for the Chinese to live.

As you tour Chinatown, you may be surprised to see a Hindu Temple and even a couple of Indian mosques. Although the area was predominantly Chinese, many Hindus and Muslims settled here, drawn by commerce.

For a long time, Chinatown remained basically as it always had, but the past 15 years have seen major changes by the Urban Redevelopment Authority, with schemes to renovate and preserve historic buildings and to clean up the streets. Unfortunately after shophouses were lovingly restored, the old calligraphers, cobblers, kite-makers, fortunetellers, and other craftspeople who'd inhabited them could no longer afford the rents. Sadly, many of these beautiful streets are now lined with souvenir shops.

Al-Abrar Mosque   This mosque, also called Masjid Chulia after the Chulias, the group of Indian moneylender immigrants who funded its construction (*masjid* is Malay for mosque), was originally erected as a thatched building in 1827, thus its Tamil name Kuchu Palli, which means "hut mosque." The building that stands today was built in the 1850s, and even though it faces Mecca, the complex conforms with the grid of the neighborhood's city streets. In the late 1980s, the mosque underwent major renovations that enlarged the mihrab and stripped away some of the ornamental qualities of the columns in the building. The one-story prayer hall was extended upward into a two-story gallery. Little touches like the timber window panels and fanlight windows have been carried over into the new renovations.

192 Telok Ayer St., near the corner of Telok Ayer St. and Amoy St., near Thian Hock Keng Temple. Free admission. 15-min. walk from either Raffles Place or Tanjong Pagar MRT.

Chinatown Attractions

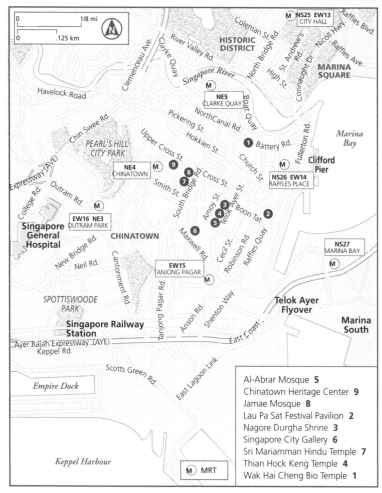

Chinatown Heritage Centre ★★ This block of old shophouses in the center of the Chinatown heritage district has been converted into a display that tells the story of the Chinese immigrants who came to Singapore to find work in the early days of the colony. Walk through rooms filled with period antiques replicating coolie living quarters, shops, clan association houses, and other places that were prominent in daily life. It reminded me of the museum on Ellis Island in New York City that walks visitors through the immigrant experience of the early 1900s. Like Ellis Island, this display also has detailed descriptions to explain each element of the immigrant experience.

48 Pagoda St. ℂ **65/6325-2878**. www.chinatownheritage.com.sg. Adults S$8.80 (US$5.65/£2.65), children S$5.30 (US$3.40/£1.75). Daily 9am–8pm. English-language tour every hour. 5-min. walk from Chinatown MRT.

Jamae Mosque   Jamae Mosque was built by the Chulias, Tamil Muslims who were some of the earlier immigrants to Singapore and who had a very influential hold over Indian Muslim life centered in the Chinatown area. The Chulias built not only this mosque, but the Al-Abrar Mosque and the Nagore Durgha Shrine as well. Jamae Mosque dates from 1827 but wasn't completed until the early 1830s. The mosque stands today almost exactly as it did then.

Although the front gate is typical of mosques you'd see in southern India, inside most of the buildings reflect the neoclassical style of architecture introduced in administrative buildings and homes designed by George Coleman and favored by the Europeans. There are also some Malay touches in the timber work. A small shrine inside, which may be the oldest part of the mosque, was erected to memorialize a local religious leader, Muhammad Salih Valinva.

18 South Bridge Rd., at the corner of South Bridge Rd. and Mosque St. Free admission. Chinatown MRT. 10-min. walk from Chinatown MRT.

Lau Pa Sat Festival Pavilion   Though it used to be well beloved, the locals think this place has become quite touristy. Once the happy little hawker center known as Telok Ayer Market, it began life as a wet market, selling fruits, vegetables, and other foodstuffs. Now it's part hawker center, part Western fast-food outlets.

It all began on Market Street in 1823, in a structure that was later torn down, redesigned, and rebuilt by G. D. Coleman. Close to the water, seafood could be unloaded fresh off the pier. After the land in Telok Ayer Basin was reclaimed in 1879, the market was moved to its present home. A new design by James MacRitchie kept the original octagonal shape and was constructed of 3,000 prefab cast-iron elements brought in from Europe.

In the 1970s, as the financial district began to develop, the pavilion was dominated by hawkers who fed the lunchtime business crowd. In the mid-1980s, the structure was torn down to make way for the MRT construction and then meticulously put back together, puzzle piece by puzzle piece. By 1989, the market was once again an urban landmark, but it sat vacant until Scotts Holdings successfully tendered to convert it into a festival market. At this time, numerous changes were made to the building, which was renamed Lau Pa Sat (Old Market) in acknowledgment of the name by which the market had been known by generations of Singaporeans. By the way, Lau Pa Sat is one of the few hawker centers that's open 24 hours, in case you need a coffee or snack before retiring.

18 Raffles Quay, located in the entire block flanked by Robinson Rd., Cross St., Shenton Way, and Boon Tat St. Free admission. Daily 24 hr. 10-min. walk from Raffles Place MRT.

Nagore Durgha Shrine   Although this is a Muslim place of worship, it is not a mosque, but a shrine, built to commemorate a visit to the island by a Muslim holy man of the Chulia people (Muslim merchants and moneylenders from India's Coromandel Coast), who was traveling around Southeast Asia spreading the word of Indian Islam. The most interesting visual feature is its facade: Two arched windows flank an arched doorway, with columns in between. Above these is a "miniature palace"—a massive replica of the facade of a palace, with tiny cutout windows and a small arched doorway in the middle. The cutouts in white plaster make it look like lace. From the corners of the facade, two 14-level minarets rise, with three little domed cutouts on each level and onion domes on top. Inside, the prayer halls and two shrines are painted and decorated in shockingly tacky colors.

Controversy surrounds the dates that the shrine was built. The government, upon naming the Nagore Durgha a national monument, claimed it was built sometime in the 1820s; however, Nagoreallauddeen, who is the 15th descendant of the holy man for whom the shrine is named, claims it was built many years before. According to Nagoreallauddeen, the shrine was first built out of wood and *attap* (a thatch roof made from a type of palm), and later, in 1815, was rebuilt from limestone, 4 years before the arrival of Sir Stamford Raffles. In 1818, rebuilding materials were imported from India to construct the present shrine. The government has no historical records to prove the previous existence of the shrine at that time. Nagoreallauddeen, who sits daily in the office just to the right in the entrance hall, is fighting to have his date made official and has covered the government plaque to the left of the front door, which declares the shrine a national monument. He'll tell you the whole story of the building and of his lineage if you ask, but he doesn't speak English, so try to grab a translator.

140 Telok Ayer St., at the corner of Telok Ayer St. and Boon Tat St. © 65/6324-0021. Free admission. 15-min. walk from either Raffles Place or Tanjong Pagar MRT.

Singapore City Gallery   This enormous exhibit is perhaps of real interest only to Singaporeans and civil planners, but if you're in the neighborhood, it's worth a pop inside to see the giant plan of the city in miniature. Very cool. If you have time, sift through 48 permanent exhibits and 25 interactive displays that paint a historical picture of the development of urban Singapore.

URA Centre, 45 Maxwell Rd. © 65/6321-8321. www.ura.gov.sg. Free admission. Mon–Fri 9am–5pm; Sat 9am–1pm. 10-min. walk from Tanjong Pagar MRT.

Sri Mariamman Hindu Temple   As the oldest Hindu temple in Singapore, Sri Mariamman has been the central point of Hindu tradition and culture. In its early years, the temple housed new immigrants while they established themselves and also served as social center for the community. Today, the main celebration here is the Thimithi Festival in October or November (see chapter 3). The shrine is dedicated to the goddess Sri Mariamman, who is known for curing disease (a very important goddess to have around in those days), but as is the case at all other Hindu temples, the entire pantheon of Hindu gods are present to be worshipped as well. On either side of the *gopuram* are statues of Shiva and Vishnu, while inside are two smaller shrines to Vinayagar and Sri Ararvan. Also note the sacred cows that lounge along the top of the temple walls.

The temple originated as a small wood-and-thatch shrine founded by Naraina Pillai, an Indian merchant who came to Singapore with Raffles's first expedition and found his fortune in trade. In the main hall of the temple is the small god that Pillai originally placed here.

244 South Bridge Rd., at the corner of South Bridge Rd. and Pagoda St. © 65/6223-4064. Free admission. 10-min. walk from Chinatown MRT.

Thian Hock Keng Temple ★★★   Thian Hock Keng, the "Temple of Heavenly Bliss," is one of the oldest Chinese temples in Singapore. Before land reclamation, when the shoreline came right up to Telok Ayer Road, the first Chinese sailors landed here and immediately built a shrine, a small wood-and-thatch structure, to pray to the goddess Ma Po Cho for allowing their voyage to be safely completed. For each subsequent boatload of Chinese sailors, the shrine was always the first stop upon landing.

Ma Po Cho, the Mother of the Heavenly Sages, was the patron goddess of sailors, and every Chinese junk of the day had an altar dedicated to her.

The temple that stands today was built in 1841 over the shrine with funds from the Hokkien community, led by the efforts of two Malacca-born philanthropists, Tan Tock Seng and Tan Kim Seng. All of the building materials were imported from China, except for the gates, which came from Glasgow, Scotland, and the tiles on the facade, which are from Holland. The doorway is flanked by two lions, a male with a ball to symbolize strength and a female with a cup to symbolize fertility. On the door are door gods, mythical beasts made from the combined body parts of many animals. Note the wooden bar that sits at the foot of the temple entrance (as do similar bars in so many Chinese temples). This serves a couple of purposes: First, it keeps out wandering ghosts, who cannot cross over the barrier. Second, it forces anyone entering the temple to look down as they cross, bowing their head in humility. Just inside the door are granite tablets that record the temple's history.

Ahead at the main altar is Ma Po Cho, and on either side are statues of the Protector of Life and the God of War. To the side of the main hall is a Gambler Brother statue, prayed to for luck and riches. From here you can see the temple's construction of brackets and beams, fitting snugly together and carved with war heroes, saints, flowers, and animals, all in red and black lacquer and gilded in gold. Behind the main hall is an altar to Kuan Yin, the Goddess of Mercy. On either side of her are the sun and moon gods.

To the left of the courtyard are the ancestral tablets. In keeping with Confucian filial piety, each represents a soul. The tablets with red paper are for souls still alive. Also in the temple complex are a pagoda and a number of outer buildings that at one time housed a school and community associations.

158 Telok Ayer St., ½ block beyond Nagore Durgha Shrine. 𝒞 **65/6423-4616**. Free admission. 15-min. walk from Tanjong Pagar MRT.

Wak Hai Cheng Bio Temple 🕹🕹   Like most of Singapore's Chinese temples, Wak Hai Cheng Bio had its start as a simple wood-and-thatch shrine where sailors, when they got off their ships, would go to express their gratitude for sailing safely to their destination. Before the major land-reclamation projects shifted the shoreline outward, the temple was close to the water's edge, and so it was named "Temple of the Calm Sea Built by the Guangzhou People." It's a Teochew temple, located in a part of Chinatown originally populated by this dialect group.

Inside the Taoist temple walls are two blocks, the one on the left devoted to Ma Po Cho, the Mother of Heavenly Sages, who protects travelers and ensures a safe journey. The one on the left is devoted to Siong Tek Kong, the god of business. Both are as important to the Chinese community today as they were way back when. Look for the statue of the Gambler Brother, with coins around his neck. The Chinese pray to him for wealth and luck; in olden days would put opium on his lips. This custom is still practiced today, only now they use a black herbal paste called *koyo,* which is conveniently legal.

Inside the temple you can buy joss sticks and paper for S$2.50 (US$1.50/85p). Three joss sticks are for heaven, your parents, and yourself, to be burned before the altar. Three corresponding packets of elaborately decorated paper and gold leaf are to be burned outside in the gourd-shaped kilns (gourd being a symbol of health). The joss or "wishing paper," four thin sheets stamped with black and red characters, has many meanings. The red sheet is for luck (red being particularly auspicious) and the other three are to wash away your sins, for a long life, and for your wishes to be carried to heaven. Even if you are not Taoist, you're more than welcome to burn the joss.

The temple itself is quite a visual treat, with ceramic figurines and pagodas adorning the roof, and every nook and cranny of the structure adorned with tiny three-dimensional reliefs that depict scenes from Chinese operas. The spiral joss hanging in the courtyard adds an additional picturesque effect.

30-B Phillip St., at the corner of Phillip St. and Church St. Free admission. 5-min. walk from Raffles Place MRT.

3 Little India

Little India did not develop as a community planned by the colonial authorities like Kampong Gelam or Chinatown, but came into being because immigrants to India were drawn to business developments here. In the late 1920s, the government established a brick kiln and lime pits here that attracted Indian workers, and the abundance of grass and water made the area attractive to Indian cattle traders.

Desire Paths (65 Kerbau Rd.; © **65/6392-1772**) will lease you a headset with an audio tour of Little India, guiding you through the streets and giving you all kinds of insight into this part of town. Headsets are available Tuesday through Saturday from 10am to 4pm for S$18 (US$12/£5.95) each.

A word of advice: If you visit Little India on a Sunday, be prepared for a mob scene the likes of Calcutta! Sunday is the only day off for Singapore's many immigrant Indian and Bangladeshi laborers, so Serangoon Road gets a little crazy.

Abdul Gafoor Mosque   This charming little mosque is resplendent, thanks to a loving restoration completed in 2003. Nestled behind a row of shophouses, you really can't see it until you arrive at the gate. Inside the compound, the bright yellow and green facade and minarets reflect an Indian Muslim architectural preference, most likely imported with the mosque's builder Sheik Abdul Gafoor. The original mosque on this site, called Al-Abrar Mosque, was constructed of wood in 1859, and is commemorated on a granite plaque within the compound above what could have been either an entrance gate or part of the mosque itself. The newer mosque on the site was built in 1907 and includes some unusual features, including ornate European-style columns and the sunburst above the main entrance. This "sundial" has 25 rays in Arabic calligraphy relief said to represent the 25 prophets in the Koran.

Inside the courtyard, an information office provides robes for those in shorts and sleeveless tops. As in every mosque, the main prayer hall is off-limits to non-Muslims.

41 Dunlop St., between Perak Rd. and Jalan Besar. © **65/6295-4209**. Free admission. 15-min. walk from Little India MRT.

Sakya Muni Buddha Gaya (Temple of a Thousand Lights)   Thai elements influence this temple, from the *chedi* (stupa) roofline to the huge Thai-style Buddha image inside. Often this temple is brushed off as strange and tacky, but all sorts of surprises are inside, making the place a veritable Buddha theme park. On the right side of the altar, statues of baby bodhisattvas receive toys and sweets from devotees. Around the base of the altar, murals depict scenes from the life of Prince Siddhartha (the Buddha) as he searches for enlightenment. Follow them around to the back of the hall and you'll find a small doorway to a chamber under the altar. Another Buddha image reclines inside, this one shown at the end of his life, beneath the Yellow Seraka tree. On the left side of the main part of the hall is a replica of a footprint left by the Buddha in Ceylon. Next to that is a wheel of fortune; for S50¢ (US30¢/15p) you get one spin.

336 Race Course Rd., 1 block past Perumal Rd. © **65/6294-0714**. Free admission. 5-min. walk from Farrer Park MRT.

An Introduction to Hindu Temples

The *gopuram* is the giveaway—the tiered roof piled high with brightly colored statues of gods and goddesses. Definitely a Hindu temple. So what are they all doing up there? It's because in India, what with the caste system and all, the lower classes were at one time not permitted inside the temple, so having these statues on the outside meant they could still pray without actually entering. Furthermore, although each temple is dedicated to a particular deity, all the gods are represented, in keeping with the Hindu belief that although there are many gods, they are all one god. So everyone is up there, in poses or scenes that depict stories from Hindu religious lore. Sometimes there are brightly colored flowers, birds, and animals as well— especially sacred cows. So why are some of them blue? It's because blue is the color of the sky, and to paint the gods blue meant that they, like the sky, are far-reaching and ever present.

There's no special way to pray in these temples, but by custom, most will pray first to Ganesh, the god with the elephant head, who is the remover of obstacles, especially those that can hinder one's closeness to God. Another interesting prayer ritual happens in the temple's main hall around a small dais that holds nine gods, one for each planet. Devotees who need a particular wish fulfilled will circle the dais, praying to their astrological planet god for their wish to come true.

The location of Hindu temples is neither by accident nor by Raffles's Town Plan. By tradition, they must always be built near a source of fresh water so that every morning, before prayer, all of the statues can be bathed. The water runs off a spout somewhere outside the main hall, from which devotees take the water and touch their heads.

Non-Hindus are welcome in the temples to walk around and explore. **Temple etiquette** asks that you first remove your shoes, and if you need to point to something, out of respect, please use your right hand, and don't point with your index finger (use your knuckle instead).

Sri Perumal Temple   Sri Perumal Temple, built in 1855, is devoted to the worship of Vishnu. As part of the Hindu trinity, Vishnu is the sustainer, balancing out Brahma the creator and Shiva the destroyer. When the world is out of whack, he rushes to its aid, reincarnating himself to show mankind that there are always new directions for development.

On the first tier to the left of the front entrance on the *gopuram,* statues depict Vishnu's nine reincarnations. Rama, the sixth incarnation, is with Hanuman, the monkey god, who helped him in the fierce battle to free his wife from kidnapping. Krishna, shown reclining amid devotees, is the eighth incarnation and a hero of many Hindu legends, most notably the Bhagavad-Gita. Also up there is the half-human and half-bird Garuda, Vishnu's steed. Inside the temple are altars to Vishnu, his two wives, and Garuda.

During Thaipusam, the main festival celebrated here (see chapter 3), male devotees who have made vows over the year carry *kavadi*—huge steel racks decorated with flowers and fruits and held onto their bodies by skewers and hooks—to show their thanks and devotion, while women carry milk pots in a parade from Sri Perumal Temple to Chettiar's Temple on Tank Road.

397 Serangoon Rd., ½ block past Perumal Rd. Free admission. Best times to visit are daily 7–11am or 5–7:30pm. 5-min. walk from Farrer Park MRT.

Sri Veerama Kaliamman Temple 🐦🐦   This Hindu temple is primarily for the worship of Shiva's wife, Kali, who destroys ignorance, maintains world order, and blesses those who strive for knowledge of God. The box on the walkway to the front entrance is for smashing coconuts, a symbolic smashing of the ego, asking God to show "the humble way." The coconuts have two small "eyes" at one end so they can "see" the personal obstacles to humility they are being asked to smash.

Inside the temple in the main hall are three altars, the center one for Kali (depicted with 16 arms and wearing a necklace of human skulls) and two altars on either side for her two sons—Ganesh, the elephant god, and Murugan, the four-headed child god. To the right is an altar with nine statues representing the nine planets. Circle the altar and pray to your planet for help with a specific trouble.

Around the left side of the main hall, the first tier of the *gopuram* tells the story of how Ganesh got his elephant head. A small dais in the rear left corner of the temple compound is an altar to Sri Periyachi, a very mean looking woman with a heart of gold. She punishes women who say and do things to make others feel bad. She also punishes men—under her feet is an exploiter of ladies.

Here's a bit of trivia: Red ash, as opposed to white, is applied to the forehead after prayers are offered in a temple devoted to a female god.

On Serangoon Rd. at Veerasamy Rd. Free admission. Daily 8am–noon and 5:30–8:30pm. 10-min. walk from Little India MRT.

4 Arab Street & Kampong Gelam

Kampong Gelam is the traditional heart of Singaporean Muslim life. Since early colonial days the area has attracted Muslims from diverse ethnic backgrounds, fusing them into one community by their common faith and lifestyle. The name Kampong Gelam comes from the Malay word *kampong,* meaning village, and *gelam,* a particular kind of tree that at one time grew abundantly in the area.

In 1819, the British made a treaty with Sultan Hussein Shah, then sultan of Singapore, to cede the island to the British East India Trading Company. As part of the agreement, the sultan was offered a stipend and given Kampong Gelam as settlement for his palace and subjects. Sultan Hussein built his palace, Istana Kampong Gelam, and sold off parcels of land for burial grounds, schools, mosques, and farms. Trade grew in the area, as a wave of merchants and tradesmen moved in to serve and provision the large numbers of pilgrims who debarked from here on their journey to Mecca each year.

Although the ethnic Arab population in Singapore has never reached large proportions, their influence is immediately obvious through such street names as Bussorah, Muscat, Baghdad, and of course, Arab Street, the center of modern Kampong Gelam—a neat little shopping enclave for textiles and regional handicrafts. Note that the shops along Arab Street close on Sundays.

Alsagoff Arab School   Built in 1912, the school was named for Syed Ahmad Alsagoff, a wealthy Arab merchant and philanthropist who was very influential in

Singapore's early colonial days and who died in 1906. It is the oldest girls' school in Singapore, and was the island's first Muslim school.

121 Jalan Sultan, across from Sultan Plaza. 15-min. walk from Bugis MRT.

Hajjah Fatimah Mosque ✦✦   Hajjah Fatimah was a wealthy businesswoman from Malacca and something of a local socialite. She married a Bugis prince from Celebes, and their only child, a daughter, married Syed Ahmed Alsagoff, son of Arab trader and philanthropist Syed Abdul Rahman Alsagoff. Hajjah Fatimah had originally built a home on this site, but after it had been robbed a couple of times and later set fire to, she decided to find a safer home and built a mosque here instead.

Inside the high walls of the compound are the prayer hall, an ablution area, gardens and mausoleums, and a few other buildings. You can walk around the main prayer halls to the garden cemeteries, where flat square headstones mark the graves of women and round ones mark the graves of men. Hajjah Fatimah is buried in a private room to the side of the main prayer hall, along with her daughter and son-in-law.

The minaret tower in the front was designed by an unknown European architect and could be a copy of the original spire of St. Andrew's Cathedral. The tower leans a little, a fact that's much more noticeable from the inside. On the outside of the tower is a bleeding heart—an unexpected place to find such a downright Christian symbol. It's a great example of what makes this mosque so charming—all the combined influences of Moorish, Chinese, and European architectural styles.

4001 Beach Rd., past Jalan Sultan. 📞 **65/6297-2774**. Free admission. 20-min. walk from Bugis MRT.

Malay Heritage Centre (Istana Kampong Gelam) ✦✦   When the Malay Heritage Centre opened its doors in 2004, it became the first museum dedicated to the history, culture, and arts of this often-marginalized ethnic group. The Centre has lovingly displayed exhibits that offer a glimpse into Singapore's early Malay settlements, the sultan's royal family, Malay arts, and 20th-century Malay life.

There's a bit of irony here. The museum is housed in the Istana Kampong Gelam, the former royal palace that housed the descendants of the original sultan that oversaw Singapore. In 1819, Sultan Hussein signed away his rights over the island in exchange for the land at Kampong Gelam plus an annual stipend for his family. After the Sultan's death, the family fortunes began to dwindle and disputes broke out among his descendants. In the late 1890s, they went to court, where it was decided that because no one in the family had the rights as the successor to the sultanate, the land should be reverted to the state. The family was allowed to remain in the house, but because they didn't own the property they lost the authority to improve the buildings. Over the years the compound fell into a very sad state of dilapidation. Eventually, Sultan Hussein's family was given the boot by the government to make way for this museum heralding the value of the Malay, and the Sultan's, cultural contribution to Singapore. Hmm.

Every Wednesday at 3:30pm and Sunday at 11:30am there's a cultural show with live music, costumes, and dancing.

The house to the left before the main gate of the Istana compound is called **Gedong Kuning,** or Yellow Mansion. It was the home of Tenkgu Mahmoud, the heir to Kampong Gelam. When he died, it was purchased by local Javanese businessman Haji Yusof, the belt merchant. Today it houses a Malay restaurant, Tepak Sireh (📞 **65/6393-4373;** daily 11:30am–2:30pm and 6:30–9:30pm).

An Introduction to Mosques

To appreciate what's going on in the mosques in Singapore, here's a little background on some of the styles and symbols behind these exotic buildings. I have also included some tips that will help non-Muslims feel right at home.

The rule of thumb for mosques is that they all face Mecca. Lucky for these buildings (and for Singaporean urban planners), most of the major mosques in Singapore have managed to fit within the grid of city streets quite nicely, with few major angles or corners jutting into the surrounding streets. One fine example of a mosque that obeys the Mecca rule but disregards zoning orders is Sultan Mosque in Kampong Gelam. A peek around the back will reveal how the road is crooked to make way for the building.

The mosques in Singapore are a wonderful blend of Muslim influences from around the world. The grand Sultan Mosque has the familiar onion dome and Moorish stylings of the Arabic Muslim influence. The smaller but fascinating Hajjah Fatimah Mosque is a real blend of cultures, from Muslim to Chinese to even Christian—testimony to Islam's tolerance of other cultural symbols. On the other hand, the mosques in Chinatown, such as Jamae Mosque and the Nagore Durgha Shrine, are Saracenic in flavor, a style that originated in India in the late 19th century, mixing traditional styles of Indian and Muslim architecture with British conventionality.

Each mosque has typical features such as a **minaret,** a narrow tower from which the call to prayer was sounded (before recorded broadcasts), and a **mihrab,** a niche in the main hall which indicates the direction of Mecca and in front of which the imam prays, his voice bouncing from inside and resonating throughout the mosque during prayers. You will also notice that there are no statues to speak of, in accordance to Muslim laws which forbid images of Allah and the Prophet Mohammed. Some mosques will have a *makam,* a burial site within the building for royalty and esteemed benefactors. This room is usually locked but sometimes can be opened upon request. To the side of the main prayer hall there's always an **ablution area,** a place for worshipers to wash the exposed parts of their bodies before prayers, to show their respect. This is a custom for all Muslims, whether they pray in the mosque or at home.

When visiting the mosques in Singapore, and anywhere else for that matter, there are some important rules of **etiquette** to follow. Appropriate dress is required. For both men and women, shorts are prohibited, and you must remove your shoes before you enter. For women, please do not wear short skirts or sleeveless, backless, or low-cut tops (although modern Singaporean Muslims do not require women to cover their heads before entering). *Also remember:* Never enter the main prayer hall. This area is reserved for Muslims only. Women should also tread lightly around this area, as it's forbidden for women to enter. No cameras or video cameras are allowed, and remember to turn off cellular phones and pagers. Friday is the Sabbath day, and you should not plan on going to the mosques between 11am and 2pm on this day.

85 Sultan Gate. ℂ 65/6391-0450. Adults S$3 (US$1.90/£1), children S$2 (US$1.30/65p). Culture show; S$10 (US$6.40/£3.30) adults, S$5 (US$3.20/£1.65) children. Mon 1–6pm; Tues–Sun 10am–6pm. 15-min. walk from Bugis MRT.

Sultan Mosque ⟨★⟩   Though more than 80 mosques exist on the island of Singapore, Sultan Mosque is the real center of the Muslim community. The mosque that stands today is the second Sultan Mosque to be built on this site. The first was built in 1826, partially funded by the East India Company as part of their agreement to leave Kampong Gelam to Sultan Hussein and his family in return for sovereign rights to Singapore. The present mosque was built in 1928 and was funded by donations from the Muslim community. The Saracenic flavor of the onion domes, topped with crescent moons and stars, is complemented by Mogul cupolas. Funny thing, though: The mosque was designed by an Irish guy named Denis Santry, who was working for the architectural firm Swan and McLaren.

Other interesting facts about the mosque: Its dome base is a ring of black bottles; the carpeting was donated by a prince of Saudi Arabia and bears his emblem; and at the back of the compound, North Bridge Road has a kink in it, showing where the mosque invaded the nicely planned urban grid pattern. Also, if you make your way through the chink where the back of the building almost touches the compound wall, peer inside the *makam* to see the royal graves. They open the makam doors on Friday mornings and afternoons.

Sultan Mosque, like all the others, does not permit shorts, miniskirts, low necklines, or other revealing clothing to be worn inside. However, they do realize that non-Muslim travelers like to be comfortable as they tour around and provide cloaks free of charge. They hang just to the right as you walk up the stairs.

3 Muscat St. ℂ 65/6293-4405. Free admission. Daily 9am–1pm and 2–4pm. No visiting is allowed during Mass congregation Fri 11:30am–2:30pm. 15-min. walk from Bugis MRT.

5 Orchard Road Area

In the beginning Orchard Road was just that, orchards and plantations. But as Singapore began to attract international settlers, this area transformed into an enclave where wealthy Europeans built their homes. Today, Orchard Road still represents affluence and luxury even though colonial homesteads have been replaced with glitzy malls and high-rise hotels. And true to its roots, the Orchard Road area still has one of the highest concentrations of western expatriate residences on the island.

The Istana and Sri Temasek   In 1859, the construction of Fort Canning necessitated the demolition of the original governors' residence, and the autocratic and unpopular governor-general Sir Harry St. George Ord proposed this structure be built as the new residence. Though the construction of such a large and expensive edifice was unpopular, Ord had his way, and design and construction went through, with the building mainly performed by convicts under the supervision of Maj. J. F. A. McNair, the colonial engineer and superintendent of convicts.

In its picturesque landscaped setting, Government House echoed Anglo-Indian architecture, but its symmetrical and cross-shaped plan also echoed the form of the traditional Malay *istana* (palace). During the occupation, the house was occupied by Field Marshal Count Terauchi, commander of the Japanese Southern Army, and Major General Kawamura, commander of the Singapore Defense Forces. With independence, the building was renamed the Istana and today serves as the official residence of the president of the Republic of Singapore. Used mainly for state and ceremonial occasions, the grounds are open to every citizen on selected public holidays, though they're not generally open for visits. The house's domain includes several other houses of senior colonial civil servants. The colonial secretary's residence, a typical 19th-century bungalow, is also gazetted a monument and is now called Sri Temasek.

Orchard Rd., between Claymore and Scotts roads. Free admission. 5-min. walk from Dhoby Ghaut MRT.

Peranakan Place Emerald Hill was once nothing more than a wide treeless street along whose sides quiet families lived in typical terrace houses(residential units similar to shophouses, with a walled courtyard in the front instead of the usual "five-foot way." Toward Orchard Road, the terrace houses turned into shophouses, with their first floors occupied by small provisioners, seamstresses, and dry-goods stores.

As Orchard Road developed, so did Emerald Hill—the buildings were all renovated. The shophouses close to Orchard Road became restaurants and bars and the street was closed off to vehicular traffic. Now it's an alfresco cafe, landscaped with a veritable jungle of potted foliage and peopled by colorful tourists—much different from its humble beginnings.

But as you pass Emerald Hill, don't just blow it off as a tourist trap. Walk through the cafe area and out the back onto Emerald Hill. All of the terrace houses have been redone, and magnificently. The facades have been freshly painted and the tiles polished, and the dark-wood details add a contrast that is truly elegant. When these places were renovated, they could be purchased for a song, but as Singaporeans began grasping at their heritage in recent years, their value shot up, and now these homes fetch huge sums.

For a peek inside some of these wonderful places (and who doesn't like to see how the rich live?), go to a bookstore and look at *Living Legacy: Singapore's Architectural Heritage Renewed,* by Robert Powell. Gorgeous photographs take you inside a few of these homes and some other terrace houses and bungalows around the island, showing off the traditional interior details of these buildings and bringing their heritage to life.

Intersection of Emerald Hill and Orchard Rd. Free admission. 5-min. walk from Somerset MRT.

6 Attractions Outside the Urban Area

The famous image of Singapore, promulgated by the tourism board and recognizable to business travelers everywhere, is of the towering cityscape along the water's edge—but there's a reason they call this place the Garden City. Not only are there picturesque gardens and parks nestled within the urban jungle, but the urban jungle is nestled within real jungle. While it's true that most of the wooded areas have been replaced by suburban housing, it's also true that thousands of acres of secondary rainforest have survived the migration of Singaporeans to the suburbs. Better yet, there are still some areas with primary rainforest, some of which are accessible by paths.

Singapore has spectacular **gardens,** from the well-groomed Botanic Gardens to **nature preserves** like Bukit Timah and Sungei Buloh, where tropical rainforest and mangrove swamps are close enough to the city that you can visit them on a morning or afternoon visit. Outside the city center you'll also find **historic sites and temples** like the edifying Changi Prison Museum and the Siong Lim Temple, as well as **museums** and **science centers.**

Attractions Outside the Urban Area

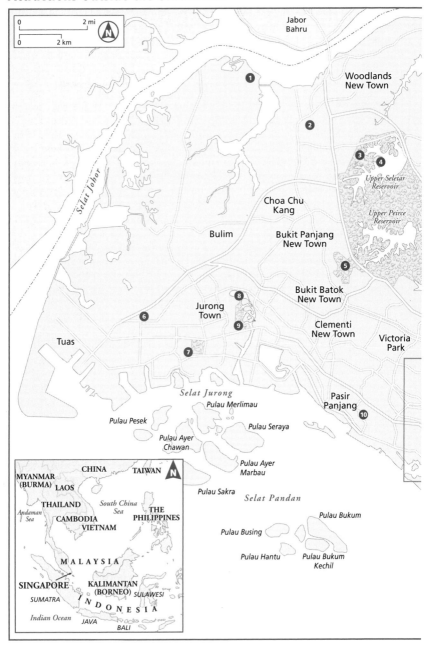

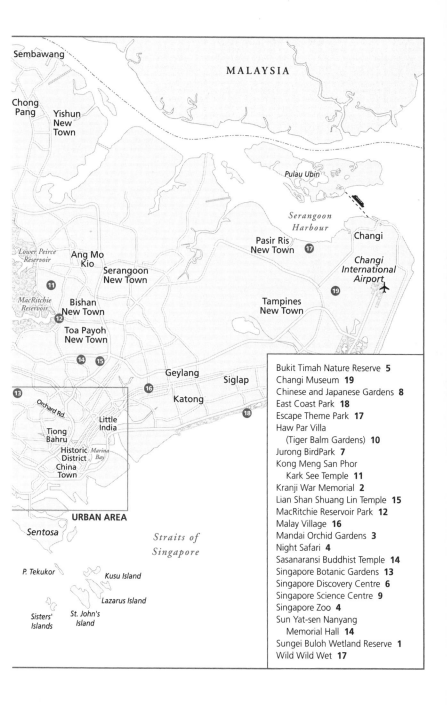

MALAYSIA

Sembawang

Chong Pang

Yishun New Town

Pulau Ubin

Serangoon Harbour

Pasir Ris New Town **17**

Changi

Lower Peirce Reservoir

Ang Mo Kio

Serangoon New Town

11

Changi International Airport

MacRitchie Reservoir

Bishan New Town

12

Toa Payoh New Town

Tampines New Town

19

14 **15**

Geylang

Siglap

13

Orchard Rd.

16

Katong

18

Tiong Bahru

Little India

Historic District

Marina Bay

China Town

URBAN AREA

Sentosa

Straits of Singapore

P. Tekukor

Kusu Island

Lazarus Island

Sisters' Islands

St. John's Island

Bukit Timah Nature Reserve **5**
Changi Museum **19**
Chinese and Japanese Gardens **8**
East Coast Park **18**
Escape Theme Park **17**
Haw Par Villa
(Tiger Balm Gardens) **10**
Jurong BirdPark **7**
Kong Meng San Phor
Kark See Temple **11**
Kranji War Memorial **2**
Lian Shan Shuang Lin Temple **15**
MacRitchie Reservoir Park **12**
Malay Village **16**
Mandai Orchid Gardens **3**
Night Safari **4**
Sasanaransi Buddhist Temple **14**
Singapore Botanic Gardens **13**
Singapore Discovery Centre **6**
Singapore Science Centre **9**
Singapore Zoo **4**
Sun Yat-sen Nanyang
Memorial Hall **14**
Sungei Buloh Wetland Reserve **1**
Wild Wild Wet **17**

WESTERN SINGAPORE ATTRACTIONS

The attractions grouped in this section are on the west side of Singapore, beginning from the Singapore Botanic Gardens at the edge of the urban area all the way out to the Singapore Discovery Centre past Jurong. Transportation can be problematic in this part of the island; as the MRT system rarely goes directly to any of the main sights, taxis can be hard to find, and bus routes get more complex. Keep the telephone number for taxi booking handy. Sometimes ticket sales people at each attraction can help and make the call for you.

Bukit Timah Nature Reserve 🐒🐒 Bukit Timah Nature Reserve is pure primary rainforest. Believed to be as old as 1 million years, it's the only place on the island with vegetation that exists exactly as it was before the British settled here. The park is more than 81 hectares (202 acres) of soaring canopy teeming with mammals and birds and a lush undergrowth with more bugs, butterflies, and reptiles than you can shake a vine at. Here you can see more than 700 plant species, many of which are exotic ferns, plus mammals like long-tailed macaques, squirrels, and lemurs. There's a visitor center and four well-marked paths, one of which leads to Singapore's highest point. At 163m (535 ft.) above sea level, don't expect a nosebleed, but some of the scenic views of the island are really nice. Also at Bukit Timah is Hindhede Quarry, which filled up with water at some point, so you can take a dip and cool off during your hike. The National Parks Board gives free guided tours on the first Sunday of the month at 9:30 and 10:30am; call ☎ **65/6554-5127** to register.

177 Hindhede Dr. ☎ **6488-5736**. www.nparks.gov.sg Free admission. Daily 8:30am–6:30pm. Newton MRT, then bus no. 171 to park entrance.

Chinese and Japanese Gardens Situated on two islands in Jurong Lake, the gardens are reached by an overpass and joined by the Bridge of Double Beauty. The **Chinese Garden** dedicates most of its area to "northern style" landscape architecture, the style of Imperial gardens, integrating brightly colored buildings with the surroundings. The Stoneboat is a replica of the stone boat at the Summer Palace in Beijing. Inside the Pure Air of the Universe building are courtyards and a pond, and there is a seven-story pagoda, the odd number of floors symbolizing continuity.

I like the Garden of Beauty, in Suzhou style, representing the southern style of landscape architecture. Southern gardens were built predominantly by scholars, poets, and men of wealth. Sometimes called Black-and-White gardens, these smaller gardens had more fine detail, featuring subdued colors as the plants and elements of the rich natural landscape gave them plenty to work with. Inside the Suzhou garden are 2,000 pots of *penjiang* (bonsai) and displays of small rocks.

While the Chinese garden is more visually stimulating, the **Japanese Garden** is intended to evoke feeling. Marble-chip paths let you hear your own footsteps and meditate on the sound. They also serve to slow the journey for better gazing. The Keisein, or "Dry Garden," uses white pebbles to create images of streams. Ten stone lanterns, a small traditional house, and a rest house are nestled between two ponds with smaller islands joined by bridges.

Toilets are situated at stops along the way, as well as benches to have a rest or to just take in the sights. Paddle boats can be rented for S$5 (US$3.20/£1.65) per hour just outside the main entrance.

1 Chinese Garden Rd. ☎ **65/6261-3632**. Free admission; admission to bonsai garden: Adults S$2 (US$1.30/65p), children S$1 (US60¢/35p). Daily 6am–11pm. Chinese Garden MRT.

Haw Par Villa (Tiger Balm Gardens) 🜛 In 1935, brothers Haw Boon Haw and Haw Boon Par—creators of Tiger Balm, the camphor and menthol rub that comes in those cool little pots—took their fortune and opened Tiger Balm Gardens as a venue for teaching traditional Chinese values. They made more than 1,000 statues and life-size dioramas depicting Chinese legends and historical tales and illustrating morality and Confucian beliefs. Many of these were gruesome and bloody and some of them were really entertaining. But Tiger Balm Gardens suffered a horrible fate. In 1985, it was converted into an amusement park and reopened as Haw Par Villa. Most of the statues and scenes were taken away and replaced with rides. Well, business did not exactly boom. In fact, the park lost money fast. But recently, in an attempt to regain some of the original Tiger Balm Garden edge, they replaced many of the old statues, some of which are a great backdrop for really kitschy vacation photos, and ditched the rides. They also decided to open the gates free of charge.

262 Pasir Panjang Rd. © 65/6774-0300. Free admission. Daily 9am–7pm. Buona Vista MRT and transfer to bus no. 200.

Jurong BirdPark 🜛 *Kids* Jurong BirdPark, with a collection of 8,000 birds from more than 600 species, showcases Southeast Asian breeds plus other colorful tropical beauties, some of which are endangered. The more than 20 hectares (50 acres) can be easily walked or, for a couple dollars extra, you can ride the panorail for a bird's-eye view (so to speak) of the grounds. I enjoy the Waterfall Aviary, the world's largest walk-in aviary. It's an up-close-and-personal experience with African and South American birds, plus a pretty stroll through landscaped tropical forest. This is where you'll also see the world's tallest man-made waterfall, but the true feat of engineering here is the panorail station, built inside the aviary. Another smaller walk-in aviary is for Southeast Asian endangered bird species; at noon every day this aviary experiences a man-made thunderstorm. The daily guided tours and regularly scheduled feeding times are enlightening. Other bird exhibits are the flamingo pools, the World of Darkness (featuring nocturnal birds), and the penguin parade, a favorite for Singaporeans, who adore all things arctic.

The **World of Hawks** show, at 10am and 4pm, features birds of prey either acting out their natural instincts or performing falconry tricks. The **All-Star Birdshow** takes place at 11am and 3pm, with trained parrots that race bikes and birds that perform all sorts of silliness, including staged birdie misbehaviors.

2 Jurong Hill. © 65/6265-0022. www.birdpark.com.sg. Adults S$16 (US$10/£5.30), children under 12 S$8 (US$5.10/£2.65). Daily 9am–6pm. Boon Lay MRT and transfer to bus no. 194 or 251.

Singapore Botanic Gardens 🜛🜛 In 1822, Singapore's first botanic garden was started at Fort Canning by Sir Stamford Raffles. After it lost funding, the present Botanic Garden came into being in 1859 thanks to the efforts of a horticulture society; it was later turned over to the government for upkeep. More than just a garden, this space occupied an important place in the region's economic development when "Mad" Henry Ridley, one of the garden's directors, imported Brazilian rubber tree seedlings from Great Britain. He devised improved latex-trapping methods and led the campaign to convince reluctant coffee growers to switch plantation crops. The garden also pioneered orchid hybridization, breeding a number of internationally acclaimed varieties.

Carved out within the tropical setting lies a rose garden, sundial garden with pruned hedges, banana plantation, spice garden, and sculptures by international artists dotted throughout. As you wander, look for the Cannonball tree (named for its cannonball-shaped fruit), Para rubber trees, teak trees, bamboos, and a huge array of palms, including the sealing wax palm—distinguished by its bright scarlet stalks—and the rumbia palm, which bears the pearl sago. The fruit of the silk-cotton tree is a pod filled with silky stuffing that was once used for stuffing pillows. Flowers like bougainvilleas and heliconias add beautiful color.

The **National Orchid Garden** is 3 hectares (7½ acres) of gorgeous orchids growing along landscaped walks. The English Garden features hybrids developed here and named after famous visitors to the garden—there's the Margaret Thatcher, the Benazir Bhutto, the Vaclav Havel, and more. The gift shops sell live hydroponic orchids in test tubes for unique souvenirs.

The gardens have three lakes. Symphony Lake surrounds an island band shell for "Concert in the Park" performances by the local symphony and international entertainers like Chris de Burg. Call visitor services at the number below for performance schedules.

The National Parks Board gives free guided tours on the second Saturday of the month at 9am, 10am, 11am, and 4pm; and free guided tours of the Orchid Garden on the third Saturday of the month at 9am, 10am, 11am, and 4pm. Register 15 minutes before the walk at the Visitor Centre near Nassim Gate.

Main entrance at corner of Cluny Rd. and Holland Rd. ✆ 65/6471-7361. www.nparks.gov.sg. Free admission. Daily 5am–midnight. The National Orchid Garden adults S$5 (US$3.20/£1.65), children under 12 and seniors S$1 (US60¢/35p). Daily 8:30am–7pm. Orchard MRT then bus no. 7, 105, 106, or 174 from Orchard Blvd.

Singapore Discovery Centre *(Kids*   This cool display of the latest military technology has hands-on exhibits that cannot be resisted—1 of 19 interactive information kiosks, for instance, lets you design tanks and ships. Airborne Rangers, a virtual-reality experience, lets you parachute from a plane and manipulate your landing to safety. In the motion simulator, feel your seat move in tandem with the fighter pilot on the screen. The Shooting Gallery is a computer-simulated combat firing range using real but decommissioned M16 rifles. IMAX features roll at the five-story iWERKS Theatre regularly, in two and three dimensions. When you get hungry, there's a fast-food court. You can also have a 30-minute bus tour of the neighboring Singapore Air Force Training Institute free with SDC admission. Inquire about tour times at the front counter.

510 Upper Jurong Rd. ✆ 65/6792-6188. www.sdc.com.sg. Adults S$10 (US$6.40/£3.30), children under 12 S$6 (US$3.80/£2). Tues–Fri and Sun 9am–6pm; Sat 9am–8pm. MRT to Boon Lay; transfer to SBS no. 192 or 193.

Singapore Science Centre *(Kids*   The center features hands-on exhibits in true science-center spirit. Interestingly the 7,500 sq. m (80,729 sq. ft.) of exhibits directly relate to the science syllabuses of the local school system, from primary school level all the way through junior college. The galleries are all clearly marked to explain their interactive use, and study sheets are also available. The Technology Gallery is one of the more interesting exhibits if you can wrestle the kids away from the machines. There's a Virtual Voyages simulation theater plus the Omni Theatre planetarium, which has a projection booth encased in glass so you can check out how it works. Best to avoid visits during weekends and school holiday times in June and December.

15 Science Centre Rd., off Jurong Town Hall Rd. ✆ 65/6425-2500. www.science.edu.sg. Adults S$6 (US$3.80/£2), children under 16 S$3 (US$1.90/£1). Tues–Sun and public holidays 10am–6pm. Jurong East MRT to bus no. 66 or 335.

CENTRAL & NORTHERN SINGAPORE ATTRACTIONS

The northern part of Singapore contains most of the island's nature reserves and parks. Here's where you'll find the Singapore Zoo, in addition to some sights with historical and religious significance. Despite the presence of the **MRT** in the area, there is not any simple way to get from attraction to attraction with ease. Bus transfers to and from MRT stops are the way to go—or you could stick to taxicabs.

Kong Meng San Phor Kark See Temple   The largest and most modern religious complex on the island, this place, called Phor Kark See for short, is comprised of prayer and meditation halls, a hospice, gardens, and a vegetarian restaurant. The largest building is the Chinese-style Hall of Great Compassion. There is also the octagonal Hall of Great Virtue and a towering pagoda. For S50¢ (US30¢/15p) you can buy flower petals to place in a dish at the Buddha's feet. Compared to other temples on the island, Phor Kark See seems shiny—having only been built in 1981. As a result, the religious images inside carry a strange, almost artificial, cartoon air about them.

88 Bright Hill Dr., located in the center of the island to the east of Bukit Panjang Nature Preserve (Bright Hill Dr. is off Ang Mo Kio Ave.). ℂ 65/6453-4046. Take MRT to Bishan, then take bus No. 410.

Kranji War Memorial   Kranji Cemetery commemorates the men and women who fought and died in World War II. Prisoners of war in a camp nearby began a burial ground here, and after the war it was enlarged to provide space for all the casualties. The Kranji War Cemetery is the site of 4,000 graves of servicemen, while the Singapore State Cemetery memorializes the names of over 20,000 who died and have no known graves. Stones are laid geometrically on a slope with a view of the Strait of Johor. The memorial itself is designed to represent the three arms of the services.

Woodlands Rd., located in the very northern part of the island. Daily 7am–6pm. Kranji MRT.

Lian Shan Shuang Lin Temple   This temple, in English "the Twin Groves of the Lotus Mountain Temple," has a great story behind its founding. One night in 1898, Hokkien businessman Low Kim Pong and his son had the same dream(of a golden light shining from the west. The following day, the two went to the western shore and waited until, moments before sundown, a ship appeared carrying a group of Hokkien Buddhist monks and nuns on their way to China after a pilgrimage to India. Low Kim Pong vowed to build a monastery if they would stay in Singapore. They did.

Laid out according to feng shui principles, the buildings include the Dharma Hall, a main prayer hall, and drum and bell towers. They are arranged in *cong lin* style, a rare type of monastery design with a universal layout so that no matter how vast the grounds are, any monk can find his way around. The entrance hall has granite wall panels carved with scenes from Chinese history. The main prayer hall has fantastic details in the ceiling, wood panels, and other woodcarvings. In the back is a shrine to Kuan Yin, goddess of mercy.

Originally built amid farmland, the temple became surrounded by suburban highrise apartments in the 1950s and 1960s, with the Toa Payoh Housing Development Board New Town project and the Pan-Island Expressway creeping close by.

184-E Jalan Toa Payoh. ℂ 65/6259-6924. Free admission. Located in Toa Payoh New Town. Toa Payoh MRT to bus no. 232, 237, or 238.

MacRitchie Nature Trail   Of all the nature reserves in Singapore, the Central Catchment Nature Reserve is the largest at 2,000 hectares (5,000 acres). Located in the center of the island, it's home to four of Singapore's reservoirs: MacRitchie, Seletar, Pierce, and Upper Pierce. The rainforest here is secondary forest, but the animals don't care; they're just as happy with the place. There's one path for walking and jogging (no bicycles allowed) that stretches 3km (1.75 miles) from its start in the southeast corner of the reserve, turning to the edge of MacRitchie Reservoir, then letting you out at the Singapore Island Country Club. The National Parks Board gives free guided tours on the second Sunday of the month at 9:30 and 10:30am; to register, call ☎ **65/6554-5127.**

Central Catchment Nature Reserve. ☎ **65/6468-5736.** www.nparks.gov.sg. Free admission. From Orchard Rd. take bus no. 132 from the Orchard Parade Hotel. From Raffles City take bus no. 130. Get off at the bus stop near Little Sisters of the Poor. Next to Little Sisters of the Poor, follow the paved walkway, which turns into the trail.

Mandai Orchid Gardens   Owned and operated by Singapore Orchids Pte. Ltd. to breed and cultivate hybrids for international export, the gardens double as an STB tourist attraction. Arranged in English garden style, orchid varieties are separated in beds that are surrounded by grassy lawn. Tree-growing varieties prefer the shade of the covered canopy. On display is Singapore's national flower, the Vanda Miss Joaquim, a natural hybrid in shades of light purple. Behind the gift shop is the Water Garden, where a stroll will reveal many houseplants common to the West, as you would find them in the wild.

Mandai Lake Rd., on the route to the Singapore Zoo. ☎ **65/6269-1036.** Adults S$3 (US$1.90/£1), children under 12 S$1 (US60¢/35p). Mon 8am–6pm; Tues–Sun 8am–7pm. Ang Mo Kio MRT bus no. 138.

Night Safari ★★★ (Kids)   Singapore takes advantage of its unchanging tropical climate and static ratio of daylight to night to bring you the world's first open-concept zoo for nocturnal animals. Here, as in the zoological gardens, animals live in landscaped areas, their barriers virtually unseen by visitors. These areas are dimly lit to create a moonlit effect, and a guided tram leads you through "regions" designed to resemble the Himalayan foothills, the jungles of Africa, and, naturally, Southeast Asia. Some of the free-range prairie animals come very close to the tram. The 45-minute ride covers almost 3.5km (2 miles) and has regular stops to get off and have a rest or stroll along trails for closer views of smaller creatures.

Staff, placed at regular intervals along the trails, help you find your way, though it's almost impossible to get lost along the trails; however, it is nighttime, you are in the forest, and it can be spooky. The guides are there more or less to add peace of mind (and all speak English). Flash photography is strictly prohibited, and be sure to bring plenty of insect repellent. Check out the bathrooms; they're all open-air, Bali style.

Singapore Zoo, 80 Mandai Lake Rd., at the western edge of the Bukit Panjang Nature Reserve, on the Seletar Reservoir. ☎ **65/6269-3411.** www.zoo.com.sg. Adults S$20 (US$13/£6.60), children under 12 S$10 (US$6.40/£3.30). Combination Zoo and Night Safari ticket: adults S$28 (US$18/£9.25), children S$14 (US$9/£4.60). Daily 7:30pm–midnight. Ticket sales close at 11pm. Entrance Plaza, restaurant, and fast-food outlet open 6:30–11:30pm. Ang Mo Kio MRT to bus no. 138.

Sasanaransi Buddhist Temple   Known simply as the Burmese Buddhist Temple, it was founded by a Burmese expatriate to serve the overseas Burmese Buddhist community. His partner, an herbal doctor also from Burma, traveled home to buy a 10-ton block of marble from which was carved the 3.3m-tall (11-ft.) Buddha image that sits in the main hall, surrounded by an aura of brightly colored lights. The original temple was off Serangoon Road in Little India and was moved here in 1991 at the request of the Housing Development Board. On the third story is a standing Buddha image in gold and murals of events in the Buddha's life.

14 Tai Gin Rd., located next to the Sun Yat-sen Villa near Toa Payoh New Town. Daily 6:30am–9pm. Chanting Sun 9:30am, Wed 8pm, and Sat 7:30pm. Take MRT to Toa Payoh, then take a taxi.

Singapore Zoo ★★ Kids

They call themselves the Open Zoo because, rather than coop the animals in jailed enclosures, they let them roam freely in landscaped areas. Beasts of the world are kept where they are supposed to be using psychological restraints and physical barriers that are disguised behind waterfalls, vegetation, and moats. Some animals are grouped with other species to show them coexisting as they would in nature. For instance, the white rhinoceros is neighborly with the wildebeest and ostrich—not that wildebeests and ostriches make the best company, but certainly contempt is better than boredom. Guinea and pea fowl, Emperor tamarins, and other creatures are free-roaming and not shy; however, if you spot a water monitor or long-tailed macaque, know that they're not zoo residents—just locals looking for a free meal. Major zoo features are the Primate Kingdom, Wild Africa, the Reptile Garden, the children's petting zoo, and underwater views of polar bears, sea lions, and penguins. Daily shows include primate and reptile shows at 10:30am and 2:30pm, and elephant and sea lion shows at 11:30am and 3:30pm. You can take your photograph with an orangutan, chimpanzee, or snake, and there are elephant and camel rides, too.

Zoo literature includes half-day and full-day agendas to help make the most of your visit. The best time to arrive, however, is at 9am, to have breakfast with an orangutan, which feasts on fruits and puts on a hilarious and very memorable show. If you miss that, you can also have tea with it at 4pm. Another good time to go is just after a rain, when the animals cool off and get frisky. See also the Night Safari listing, above.

80 Mandai Lake Rd., at the western edge of the Bukit Panjang Nature Reserve, on the Seletar Reservoir. 🕿 65/ 6269-3411. www.zoo.com.sg. Adults S$15 (US$9.60/£4.95), children under 12 S$7.50 (US$4.80/£2.50). Combination Zoo and Night Safari ticket: adults S$28 (US$18/£9.25), children S$14 (US$9/£4.65). Daily 8:30am–6pm. Ang Mo Kio MRT to bus no. 138.

Sungei Buloh Wetland Reserve ★

Located to the very north of the island and devoted to the wetland habitat and mangrove forests that are so common to the region, 87-hectare (218-acre) Sungei Buloh is out-of-the-way, and not the easiest place to get to; but it's a beautiful park, with constructed paths and boardwalks taking you through tangles of mangroves, soupy marshes, grassy spots, and coconut groves. Of the flora and fauna, the most spectacular sights here are the birds, of which there are somewhere between 140 and 170 species in residence or just passing through for the winter. Of the migratory birds, some have traveled from as far as Siberia to escape the cold months from September to March. Bird observatories are set up at different spots along the paths. Also, even though you're in the middle of nowhere, Sungei Buloh has a visitor center, a cafeteria, and souvenirs. Go early to beat the heat. The National Parks Board gives free guided tours every Saturday at 9 and 10am, and 3 and 4pm; call to registration.

301 Neo Tiew Crescent. 🕿 65/6794-1401. Adults S$1 (US60¢/35p), children and seniors S50¢ (US30¢/15p). Mon–Sat 7:30am–7pm; Sun and public holidays 7am–7pm. Audiovisual show Mon–Sat 9am, 11am, 1pm, 3pm, and 5pm; hourly Sun and public holidays. Kranji MRT to bus no. 925. Stop at Kranji Reservoir Dam and cross causeway to park entrance.

Sun Yat-sen Nanyang Memorial Hall ★

Dr. Sun Yat-sen visited Singapore eight times to raise funds for his revolution in China and made Singapore his headquarters

The Peranakans of Katong

If you'd like to experience local culture that's a bit off the beaten track, come to Katong. This neighborhood came to prominence before World War II, when Peranakans and Eurasians, families of mixed heritage, populated this area outside of the city center along the east coast of the island. Many Peranakans, because of their mixed Chinese and Malay heritage, rose to financial power and were known to build lavish homes (many of which still line the streets of Katong), furnishing them with ornate, Chinese-inspired interiors, and they dress with opulent flair.

Peranakan antique furniture sports detailed woodcarvings in classic Chinese design but with unbelievably gaudy mother of pearl inlay everywhere. Their pottery also follows Chinese aesthetics with pretty floral, phoenix, and dragon patterns but in vivid colors more representative of Malay tastes—bright yellows, pinks, and greens.

Peranakan ladies wore the *sarong kebaya*, a two-piece outfit consisting of a brightly colored cotton sarong topped with a delicately embroidered fitted blouse pinned with silver or gold broaches. Peranakan ladies (called Nonyas) were also known for their dainty beaded slippers. The outfit is really quite elaborate, but if you think it's a thing of the past you'll be surprised to see how many local women still wear full traditional costume to weddings and other special events.

To visit Katong, start by taking a taxi to the corner of East Coast and Joo Chiat roads (don't worry, there are plenty of taxis here to bring you back to town). This is the epicenter of a boom in Peranakan heritage appreciation that has seen restaurants, a clothier, and an antiques house find cheers from locals who are keen to see this heritage survive. From this junction you can find **Kim Choo Kueh Chang** (109 and 111 East Coast Rd.; ℂ **65/6440-5590**), a place for traditional Nonya glutinous rice dumplings—the tetra-pack-shaped bundles wrapped in *pandan* leaves you may see hanging in bunches in food stalls around the island. Here you can buy and try, and also see how they are made.

Just next door is **Rumah Bebe** (113 East Coast Rd.; ℂ **65/6774-3652**), a boutique that specializes in fantastic quality sarongs and *kebayas* with all

for gaining the support of overseas Chinese in Southeast Asia. A wealthy Chinese merchant built the villa around 1880 for his mistress, and a later owner permitted Dr. Sun Yat-sen to use it. The house reflects the classic bungalow style, which is becoming endangered in modern Singapore. Its typical bungalow features include a projecting carport with a sitting room overhead, verandas with striped blinds, second-story cast-iron railings, and first-story masonry balustrades. A covered walkway leads to the kitchen and servants' quarters in the back.

Inside, the life of Dr. Yat-sen is traced in photos and watercolors, from his birth in southern China through his creation of a revolutionary organization.

12 Tai Gin Rd., near Toa Payoh New Town. ℂ **65/6256-7377**. Adults S$3 (US$1.90/£1), children and seniors S$2 (US$1.30/65p). Tues–Sun 9am–5pm. Toa Payoh MRT to bus No. 45.

the accessories. Proprietress Bebe Seet, a well-known pillar of the Peranakan community, is the local authority on traditional beaded slippers, selling her handmade creations, giving demonstrations, and teaching the art of beading. You can even custom order a pair.

Also here, stop into **True Blue Cuisine** (117 East Coast Rd.; ℭ **65/6440-0449**), reviewed in chapter 5, to try the best Nonya cuisine in a setting that is practically a museum dedicated to cultural artifacts.

You'll notice these shops are newly renovated, freshly painted, and quite welcoming. If you prefer your cultural experience a bit more down-and-dirty, backtrack down East Coast Road to the next block. At the junction of East Coast and Ceylon roads is the heart of the *laksa* wars. On two street corners, opposite each other, about four open-air hawker stalls fight over who has the best *laksa* in Singapore. This local specialty, a rich, spicy coconut based soup with noodles, prawns, fishcake, and cockles, is delicious, and you'll find the best right here. I usually go for the *laksa* at **No. 49** (no phone). Pull up a stool and eat on the sidewalk. (A hidden treasure—if you walk half a block down Ceylon Rd. you'll find an old but recently renovated Sri Lankan Hindu temple dedicated to Ganesh, the elephant-headed god. If you're dressed modestly, they'll welcome you in for a look-see.)

If you follow East Coast Road in the opposite direction you'll find two older establishments. **The Katong Antique House** (208 East Coast Rd.; ℭ **65/6345-8544**) is operated by Peter Wee, the president of the local Peranakan heritage association. It's a very small display, but everything's authentic and for sale, as opposed to the objects at the museum, in case you wanted to take a bit of Peranakan heritage home.

Next door is my favorite Nonya restaurant, **The Peranakan Inn** (210 East Coast Rd.; ℭ **65/6440-6195**), a simple coffee shop–style restaurant with authentic home-style food at very reasonable prices. What you lack in decor you gain in authenticity.

EASTERN SINGAPORE ATTRACTIONS

The east coast leads from the edge of Singapore's urban area to the tip of the eastern part, at Changi Point. Eastern Singapore is home to Changi International Airport, nearby Changi Prison, and the long stretch of East Coast Park along the shoreline. The **MRT** heads east in this region, but swerves northward at the end of the line. A popular **bus line** for east coast attractions not reached by MRT is bus no. 2, which takes you to Changi Prison, Changi Point, Malay Village, and East Coast Park.

Changi Museum ⭐ Upon successful occupation of Singapore, the Japanese marched all British, Australian, and Allied European prisoners to Changi by foot, where they lived in a prison camp for 3 years, suffering overcrowding, disease, and malnutrition. Prisoners were cut off from the outside world except to leave the camp for labor duties. The hospital conditions were terrible; some prisoners suffered public beatings, and many died. In an effort to keep hope alive, they built a small chapel from wood and attap. Years later, at the request of former POWs and their families and friends, the government built this replica.

The museum displays sketches by W. R. M. Haxworth and secret photos taken by George Aspinall—both POW's who were imprisoned here. Displayed with descriptions, the pictures, along with writings and other objects from the camp, bring this period to life, depicting the day-to-day horror with a touch of high morale.

1000 Upper Changi Rd., in the same general area as the airport. (C) 65/6214-2451. www.changimuseum.com. Free admission. Guided tour or audio tour headset rental: Adult S$8 (US$5.10/£2.65), children S$4 (US$2.60/£1.30). Daily 9:30am–4:30pm. Tanah Merah MRT to bus no. 2.

East Coast Park   East Coast Park is a narrow strip of reclaimed land, 8.5km (5¼ miles) long, tucked in between the shoreline and East Coast Parkway, and serves as a hangout for Singaporean families on the weekends. Moms and dads barbecue under the trees while the kids swim at the beach, which is nothing more than a narrow lump of grainy sand sloping into yellow-green water that has more seaweed than a sushi bar. Paths for bicycling, in-line skating, walking, or jogging run the length of the park and are crowded on weekends and public and school holidays. On Sundays, you'll find kite flyers in the open grassy parts. The lagoon is the best place to go for bicycle rentals, canoeing, and windsurfing. If you go to the MacDonald's Carpark C entrance, you'll find beach cafes, some sea kayak rentals, plus in-line skates and bicycle rentals as well. A couple of outfits, listed in "Sports & Recreation," later in this chapter, offer equipment rentals and instruction. The park is also home to **UDMC Seafood Centre** (reviewed in chapter 5), located not far from the lagoon.

East Coast Pkwy. Free admission. Bus no. 36 to Marine Parade and use the underpass to cross the highway.

Escape Theme Park *Kids*   If you think your kids will pass out at the sight of another museum, Singapore's newest and best amusement park will keep them occupied. There are rides for small kiddies and families, plus exciting ones for big kiddies as well. The go-kart circuit is happening. They also have carnival games with prizes, plus snacks and beverages. If it gets too hot, visit Wild Wild Wet, below. A beach and good seafood hawker fare are also nearby.

Downtown East 1, Pasir Ris Close. (C) 65/6581-9112. www.escapethemepark.com.sg. Adult S$17 (US$11/£5.45), children S$8.30 (US$5.30/£2.75). Sat–Sun and public and school holidays 10am–8pm. Pasir Ris MRT.

Malay Village   In 1985, Malay Village opened in Geylang as a theme village to showcase Malay culture. It's always been a sort of tatty display, but since the opening of the Malay Heritage Centre in Kampong Gelam 2 years ago, it's grown even more obscure and has almost completely dropped off the Singapore Tourism Board's radar. There's a small cultural display and lots of shops that cater to the local Malay community in Geylang, a neighborhood with a strong Malay heritage. While not nearly as shiny as the new center, there's something more authentic about Malay Village, probably because it's in the heart of a residential district.

I've also had some interesting experiences here—Malay Village still hosts the **Kuda Kepang,** a fascinating traditional Malay dance, on Saturday nights at 8pm, free of charge. It's a long performance but worth the wait because at the end the dancers are put in a trance and walk on glass, eat glass, and rip coconuts to shreds with their teeth (see "Frommer's Favorite Singapore Experiences," in chapter 1, for details). Arrive early because the place gets packed—but with locals, not tourists.

39 Geylang Serai, in the suburb of Geylang. (C) **65/6748-4700**. Free admission. Daily 10am–10pm. 10-min. walk from Paya Lebar MRT.

Wild Wild Wet *(Kids)*   Beat the heat at this water park, with flumes, raft slides, wave pool, plus lots of water activities for children. Locker rooms and food and beverage facilities are all convenient, plus water safety is provided by trained lifeguards. This park and neighboring Escape Theme Park both opened in 2003, so the facilities haven't gotten that worn and tatty look that older theme parks take on after a while.

Downtown East 1, Pasir Ris Close. (C) **65/6581-9128**. www.wildwildwet.com. Adults S$13 (US$8.30/£4.25), children S$8.80 (US$5.60/£2.90). Mon and Wed–Fri 1–7pm; Sat–Sun and public and school holidays 10am–7pm. Pasir Ris MRT.

7 Sentosa Island

In the 1880s, Sentosa was a hub of British military activity, with hilltop forts built to protect the harbor from sea invasion from all sides. Today, it has become a weekend getaway spot and Singapore's answer to Disneyland. Tomorrow it will be the site of one of Singapore's new "integrated resorts"—hotels, resorts, amusement and entertainment parks, plus gambling casinos, slated for opening in 2010. In the meantime, Sentosa is spending gobs of money to upgrade all existing facilities to meet the bar raised by the coming attractions.

If you're spending the day, there are numerous restaurants and a couple of food courts. For a unique dining option, consider **Sky Dining,** aboard a glass-bottomed cable car, where you can spend a couple hours eating a three-course Western meal (set menus S$88/US$56/£29 or S$158/US$101/£52 for two; children's set S$20/US$6.40/£3.60). It's especially popular on Valentine's Day or for birthdays and wedding proposals. Meals are pretty tasty, provided by the Jewel Box restaurant. For more information call (C) **65/6377-9688,** or visit www.mountfaber.com.sg.

For overnights, the **Shangri-La's Rasa Sentosa Resort and Spa** and the **Sentosa Resort & Spa** (see chapter 4) are popular hotel options. For general Sentosa inquiries, call (C) **1800/736-8672** or see www.sentosa.com.sg.

GETTING THERE

Island admission is S$2 (US$1.30/65p) each for adults and children payable at the Visitors' Centre upon entry, with tickets to additional attractions and activities purchased separately once inside.

The most entertaining way to get there is to take the cable car. From the Cable Car Towers ((C) **65/6270-8855**) they make the trip daily from 8:30am to 11pm at a cost of S$9.90 (US$6.30/£3.25) adults and S$4.50 (US$2.90/£1.50) children one-way or S$11 (US$7/£3.60) adults and S$5.50 (US$3.50/£1.80) children round-trip. The view is okay (but too far from the city to see skyline) and the ride is especially fun for kids. The cable cars also extend up Mt. Faber on the Singapore side. If you choose to take a cable car up to the top, you can take it back down again. Otherwise, if you choose to alight at this stop you can take a taxi back to civilization.

The new Sentosa Express opened in January 2007. This light-rail train operates between VivoCity at the HarbourFront MRT station and Sentosa, with stops at the beach, major attractions, and the future site of the integrated resort. Pick up the train to Sentosa at Vivo City, 3rd level, where you can purchase tickets for S$3 (US$1.90/ 90p), which includes all-day rides, plus Sentosa admission.

A bus that operates from the HarbourFront Bus Terminal (near HarbourFront MRT) operating daily from 7am to 11pm; with extended hours until 12:30am on Friday, Saturday, and the eve of public holidays, that costs S$1 (US60¢/35p) per person, paid upon arrival at Sentosa. Or any city taxi can take you there; just pay the entrance fee after you cross the causeway, and the driver can drop you anywhere you'd like to go within the island.

GETTING AROUND

Once on Sentosa, a free bus system with four color-coded routes snakes around the island.

SEEING THE SIGHTS

The most notable attractions that you get free with your Sentosa admission are the **Fountain Gardens and Musical Fountain,** staging fountain, lights, and laser shows nightly (aimed at junior audiences); the **Dragon Trail Nature Walk,** a 1.5km (1-mile) stroll through secondary rainforest to see dragon sculptures and local flora and fauna; and the **beaches.**

Sentosa has three beaches. At **Siloso Beach,** deck chairs, beach umbrellas, and a variety of **watersports equipment** like pedal boats, aqua bikes, fun bugs, canoes, surfboards, and banana boats are available for hire at nominal charges. Bicycles are also available for hire. Shower and changing facilities, food kiosks, and snack bars are at rest stations. **Palawan Beach** has a greater assortment of beachside bars and restaurants, while **Tanjong Beach** is the quietest and most laid-back of the three.

Several attractions on Sentosa charge separate entrance fees; they include the **Sentosa Luge & Skyride** (S$8/US$5.10/£2.65 per ride; Mon–Thurs 10am–6pm, Sat–Sun 10am–7pm), **Sijori WonderGolf** (adults S$8–S$10/US$5.10–US$6.40/ £2.65–£3.30, children S$4–S$7/US$2.60–US$4.50/£1.30–£2.30; daily 9am–7pm), **Sentosa 4D Magix** motion cinema (adults S$16/US$10/£5.30, children S$9.50/ US$6.10/£3.15; daily 10am–9pm), and the **Carlsberg Sky Tower** (adults S$10/ US$6.40/£3.30, children S$6/US$3.80/£3.30; daily 9am–9pm.) The best attractions, in my opinion, are as follows:

Fort Siloso   Fort Siloso guarded Keppel Harbour from invasion in the 1880s. It's one of three forts built on Sentosa, and it later became a military camp in World War II. The buildings have been outfitted to resemble a barracks, kitchen, laundry, and military offices as they looked back in the day. In places, you can explore the underground tunnels and ammunition holds, but they're not as extensive as you would hope they'd be.

✆ **65/6275-0388.** Adults S$8 (US$5.10/£2.65), children S$5 (US$3.20/£1.65). Daily 10am–6pm.

Images of Singapore *✫✫*   Images of Singapore is without a doubt one of the main reasons to come to Sentosa. There are three parts to this museum/exhibit: the Pioneers of Singapore, the Surrender Chambers—which have been there as far as I can remember—and Festivals of Singapore, a recent addition.

Pioneers of Singapore is an exhibit of beautifully constructed life-size dioramas that place figures like Sultan Hussein, Sir Stamford Raffles, Tan Tock Seng, and Naraina Pillai, to name just a few, in the context of Singapore's timeline and note their contributions to its development. Also interesting are the dioramas depicting scenes from

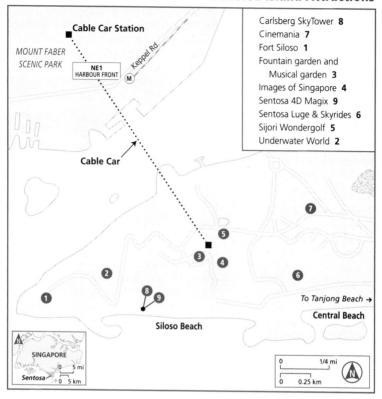

Carlsberg SkyTower **8**
Cinemania **7**
Fort Siloso **1**
Fountain garden and
    Musical garden **3**
Images of Singapore **4**
Sentosa 4D Magix **9**
Sentosa Luge & Skyrides **6**
Sijori Wondergolf **5**
Underwater World **2**

Cable Car Station

MOUNT FABER
SCENIC PARK

NE1
HARBOUR FRONT

Cable Car

To Tanjong Beach →

Central Beach

Siloso Beach

SINGAPORE

Sentosa

0   5 mi
0   5 km

0   1/4 mi
0   0.25 km

the daily routines of the different cultures as they lived during colonial times. It's a great stroll that brings history to life.

The powers that be have tried to change the name of the **Surrender Chambers** to the Sentosa Wax Museum, but it still hasn't caught on because the Surrender Chambers are oh-so-much more than just a wax museum. The gallery leads you through authentic footage, photos, maps, and recordings of survivors to chronologically tell the story of the Pacific theater activity of World War II and how the Japanese conquered Singapore. The grand finale is a wax museum depicting, first, a scene of the British surrender and, last, another of the Japanese surrender.

The newest addition, **Festivals of Singapore,** is another life-size diorama exhibit depicting a few of the major festivals and traditions of the Chinese, Malay, Indian, and Peranakan cultures in Singapore.

© 65/6275-0388. Adults S$10 (US$6.40/£3.30), children S$7 (US$4.50/£2.30). Daily 9am–7pm.

Underwater World ★ *Kids*   Underwater World is without a doubt one of the most visited attractions on Sentosa. Everybody comes for the tunnel: 83m (272 ft.) of transparent acrylic tube through which you glide on a conveyor belt, gaping at sharks, stingrays, eels, and other creatures of the sea drifting by, above and on both sides. At 11:30am, 2:30pm, and 4:30pm daily, a scuba diver hops in and feeds them by hand.

In smaller tanks you can view other unusual sea life like the puffer fish and the mysteriously weedy and leafy sea dragons. The price also includes admission to the Dolphin Lagoon, with pink dolphin shows daily at 11am, 1pm, 3:30pm, and 5pm. Then there's the latest display of bamboo shark embryos, developing within egg cases—what's keeping you?

© 65/6275-0388. www.underwaterworld.com.sg. Adults S$20 (US$13/£6.45), children S$13 (US$8/£4.15). Daily 9am–9pm.

8 Organized Tours

Although touring Singapore is simple enough for DIY travelers, visitors with little time, or who want to delve deeper into local sights, can take advantage of convenient organized activities.

COACH TOURS

Tour East (© 65/6738-2622) organizes typical half-day coach tours of the city (adults S$30/US$19/£9.90, children S$15/US$9.60/£4.95), and full-day coach excursions to some of the main attractions around the island (adults S$70/US$45/£23, children S$35/US$22/£12), some with meals included. The Peranakan Trail takes visitors out to Katong, a suburban neighborhood that is the focal point of Peranakan heritage (adults S$40/US$26/£13, children S$20/US$13/£6.60).

For something different, go for the **DUCKTour** (© 65/6338-6877; www.ducktours.com.sg) a combined coach and boat tour in an amphibious vehicle, a decommissioned military craft, that circles you around the Historic District for a tour of the harbor. The hour-long tour starts every hour, departing from the Suntec City Mall Galleria, with additional transfers from the DUCKTours office on Orchard Road (at the corner of Cairnhill Rd.) Reservations are highly recommended and tours cost S$33 (US$21/£11) adults, S$17 (US$11/£5.60) children ages 4 to 12, and S$2 (US$1.30/65p) kids under 3. DUCKTours also operates the **HiPPO Tour** aboard an open-top double-decker bus, cruising Orchard Road, Little India, Kampong Gelam, Chinatown, and the Historic District. Pick it up at the DUCKTours office on Orchard Road or at Suntec City, then get on and off at sights that interest you along the way. The day ticket costs S$33 (US$21/£11) adults, S$13 (US$8.30/£4.30) children 4 to 12, and S$2 (US$1.30/65p) for kids under 3. Call DUCKTours for information.

WALKING TOURS

The **National Museum of Singapore** (© 65/6332-4075; www.nhb.gov.sg) usually offers a selection of tours that I highly recommend. The Overview of Singapore History & Culture is a half-day historical look at the city's ethnic enclaves with guide Geraldine Lowe, Singapore's local authority on history and heritage. The Cemetery Tour takes you outside the city to see a side of local culture that is rarely explored. At the time of writing tours were temporarily on hold until after the festivals surrounding the reopening of the museum cool down (it was tough to get any info at all!). Tours were expected to resume in early 2007; call for details.

Singapore Walks (© 65/6325-1631; www.singaporewalks.com) is another reputable outfit that organizes guided walking tours of the Historic District, Chinatown, Little India, Kampong Gelam, and other neighborhoods Monday through Saturday. Call them to find out the meeting time and place for the tour you want; adults pay S$18 (US$12/£5.95), children tour for S$12 (US$7.70/£3.95).

RIVER TOURS & CRUISES

Singapore Explorer (© **65/6339-6833;** www.singaporeexplorer.com.sg) operates boats up and down the Singapore River and into the harbor from 9am to 11pm daily. A bumboat ride with recorded info about the riverside sights costs adults S$12 (US$7.70/£3.95) and children S$6 (US$3.80/£2). If you want to ride in an air-conditioned glass-top boat, tickets for adults are S$15 (US$9.60/£4.95), children S$6 (US$3.80/£2). They also offer a wine-and-dine cruise, but I say spend your time and money savoring the best food in one of the restaurants reviewed in chapter 5. The boats can be picked up from Clarke Quay or the Raffles Place MRT Jetty.

The *Imperial Cheng Ho,* operated by **Watertours** (© **65/6533-9811;** www.watertours.com.sg) is a huge boat modeled after the sort of Chinese junk that Admiral Cheng Ho might have sailed when he explored this region in the 15th century. A 2½-hour cruise takes you past the Singapore skyline, the mouth of the Singapore River, then out past Sentosa with a stop on Kusu Island. I recommend the Morning Glory Cruise at 10am (adults S$25/US$16/£8.25, children S$12/US$7.70/£3.95). There's also a High Tea Cruise at 2:30pm (adults S$29/US$19/£9.60, children S$14/US$9/£4.60) and a dinner cruise at 5:30pm (adults S$53/US$34/£17, children S$27/US$17/£8.90). Watertours can arrange hotel transfer with your booking.

TRISHAW TOUR

These cycle rickshaws were once a staple form of public transportation. Now they're only permitted on busy streets with special permits, and only for guided tours. **Singapore Explorer** (© **65/6339-6833;** www.singaporeexplorer.com.sg) coordinates regular outings through Chinatown from 10am to 7pm daily. You can either call ahead to book a ride, or you can just show up at the corner of Sago and Terrenganu streets; you'll see the collection of trishaws under cover. The half-hour trip takes you through Chinatown's quaint streets for a charge of S$36 (US$23/£12) per person. You can also combine the trishaw tour with a half-hour bumboat trip for only S$2 (US$1.30/65p) extra. Singapore Explorer can arrange pick up from anywhere if you book in advance.

9 The Surrounding Islands

Sixty smaller islands surround Singapore, some of which are open for full- or half-day trips. The ferry rides are cool and breezy, and they provide interesting up-close views of some of the larger ships docked in the harbor. The islands themselves are small and, for the most part, don't have a lot going on. The locals basically see them as little escapes from the everyday grind—peaceful respites for the family.

KUSU & ST. JOHN'S ISLANDS

Kusu Island and St. John's Island are both located to the south of Singapore proper, about a 15- to 20-minute ferry ride to Kusu, 25 to 30 minutes to St. John's.

Its name meaning "Tortoise Island" in Chinese, many popular legends exist about how **Kusu Island** came to be. The most popular ones involve shipwrecked people, either fishermen or monks, who were rescued when a tortoise turned himself into an island. Kusu Island was originally two small islands and a reef, but in 1975, reclaimed land turned it into a (very) small getaway island. There are two places of worship: a Chinese temple and a Malay shrine. The Chinese temple becomes a zoo during "Kusu Season" in October, when thousands of Chinese devotees flock here to pray for health, prosperity, and luck. There are two swimming lagoons (the one to the north has a pretty view of Singapore Island), picnic tables, toilets, and public telephones.

Historically speaking, **St. John's Island** is an unlikely place for a day trip. As far back as 1874, this place was a quarantine for Chinese immigrants sick with cholera; in the 1950s, it became a deportation holding center for Chinese Mafia thugs; and later, it was a rehab center for opium addicts. Today you'll find a mosque, holiday camps, three lagoons, bungalows, a cafeteria, a huge playing field, and basketball. It's much larger than Kusu Island, but not large enough to fill a whole day of sightseeing. Toilets and public phones are available.

Ferries leave at regular intervals from the Marina South Pier (© **65/1800-736-8672;** take the MRT to Marina Bay then bus no. 402 to the pier. The boat makes a circular route, landing on both islands. Adult tickets cost S$11 (US$7/£3.65), and tickets for children under 12 are S$8 (US$5.10/£2.65). *Tip:* Pack a lunch and bring drinks, sunblock, and mosquito repellent.

PULAU UBIN 🐐

My favorite island getaway has to be Ubin. Located off the northeast tip of Singapore, Pulau Ubin remains the only place in Singapore where you can find life as it used to be before urban development. Lazy kampong villages pop up alongside trails perfect for a little more rugged bicycling. It's truly a great day trip for those who like to explore nature and rural scenery. Rumors have it that during the occupation the Japanese brought soldiers here to be tortured, and so some believe the place is haunted.

To get to Ubin, take bus no. 2 to Changi Village (or just take a cab—the bus ride is long). Walk past the food court down to the water and find the ferry. There's no ticket booth, so you should just approach the captain and buy your ticket from him—it'll cost you about S$2 (US$1.30/65p). The boats leave regularly, but only when they've got enough passengers to justify a trip, with the last one returning from the island as late as 11pm (make sure you double-check with the ferryman so you don't get stranded!).

Once you're there, bicycle-rental places along the jetty can provide you with bikes and island maps at reasonable prices. A few coffee shops cook up rudimentary meals, and you'll also find public toilets and coin phones in the more populated areas.

10 Sports & Recreation

BEACHES

Besides the beach at East Coast Park (see "Attractions Outside the Urban Area," earlier in this chapter) and those on Sentosa Island (see above) you can try the smaller beach at Changi Village, called Changi Point. From the shore, you have a panoramic view of Malaysia, Indonesia, and several smaller islands that belong to Singapore. The beach is calm and frequented mostly by locals who set up camps and barbecues to hang out all day. There are kayak rentals along the beach, and in Changi Village you'll find, in addition to a huge hawker center, quite a few international restaurants and pubs to hang out in and have a fresh seafood lunch when you get hungry. To get there take SBS bus no. 2 from either the Tanah Merah or Bedok MRT stations.

On Kusu and St. John's Islands there are quiet swimming lagoons, a couple of which have quite nice views of the city.

BICYCLE RENTAL

Bicycles are not for rent within the city limits, and traffic does not really allow for cycling on city streets, so sightseeing by bicycle is not recommended for city touring.

If you plan a trip out to **Sentosa,** cycling provides a great alternative to that island's tram system and gets you closer to the parks and nature there. For a little light cycling, most people head out to **East Coast Park,** where rentals are inexpensive, the scenery is nice on cooler days, and there are plenty of great stops for eating along the way. One favorite place where the locals go for mountain-biking sorts of adventures (and to cycle amid the old kampong villages) is **Pulau Ubin,** off the northeast coast of Singapore.

AT EAST COAST PARK   Bicycles can be rented at East Coast Park from **SDK Recreation** (℡ **65/6445-2969**), near McDonald's at Carpark C; open 7 days from about 11am to 8 or 9pm. Rentals are S$4 to S$6 (US$2.60–US$3.80/£1.30–£2) per hour, depending on the type and quality bike you're looking for. Identification may be requested, or leave a S$50 (US$32/£17) deposit.

ON SENTOSA ISLAND   Try a couple places on Siloso Beach off Siloso Road, a short walk from Underwater World (see "Sentosa Island," earlier in this chapter). There's a kiosk at Sakae Sushi (℡ **65/6271-6385**) and another at Costa Sands (℡ **65/6275-2471**). Both are open 7 days from around 10am to 6:30 or 7pm. Rental for a standard bicycle is S$4 (US$2.60/£1.30) per hour. A mountain bike goes for S$8 (US$5.10/£2.65) per hour. Identification is required.

IN PULAU UBIN   When you get off the ferry, there are a number of places to rent bikes. The shops are generally open between 8am and 6pm and will charge between S$5 and S$8 (US$3.20–US$5.10/£1.65–£2.65) per hour, depending on which bike you choose. Most rental agents will have a map of the island for you—take it. Even though it doesn't look too impressive, it'll be a great help.

GOLF

Golf is big in Singapore, and although there are quite a few clubs, many are exclusively for members only. However, many places are open for limited play by nonmembers. All will require you bring an international par certificate. Most hotel concierges will be glad to make arrangements for you, and this may be the best way to go. Also, it's really popular for Singaporeans to go on day trips to Malaysia for the best courses.

Changi Golf Club   This 9-hole walking course is par 34 and nonmembers may play at this private club only on weekdays (walk-ins okay, but advance booking recommended). They may even be able to set you up with other players. The course opens at 7:30am. Last tee is 4:30pm.

20 Netheravon Rd. ℡ **65/6545-5133**. Greens fees S$40 (US$26/£13); caddy fees S$10 (US$6.40/£3.30). Mon–Fri 7:30am–4:30pm.

Seletar Base Golf Course   A public course, Seletar's 9-hole, par-36 course is open 7 days a week. Very low-cost golf cart and equipment rentals are available with deposit. First tee is at 7am except for Monday and Thursday, when first tee is at 11am. Last tee is 5:30pm.

244 Oxford St., 3 Park Lane. ℡ **65/6481-4745**. Greens fees Mon–Fri S$30 (US$19/£9.90), Sat–Sun S$40 (US$27/£13). Tues–Wed and Fri–Sun 7am–5:30pm; Mon and Thurs 11am–5:30pm.

Sentosa Golf Club   The best idea if you're traveling with your family and want to get in a game, Sentosa's many activities will keep the kids happy while you practice your swing guilt-free at one of the club's two 18-hole 72-par courses. This private course charges much more for nonmembers than other courses (and weekend play for nonmembers is restricted to Sun afternoon), it's a beautiful championship course and a relaxing time away from the city. Advance phone bookings are required.

27 Bukit Manis Rd., Sentosa Island. © 65/6275-0022. Greens fees Mon–Fri S$231 (US$148/£76); Sun S$315 (US$202/£104). Daily 7am–7pm.

SCUBA DIVING

The locals are crazy about scuba diving but are more likely to travel to Malaysia and other Southeast Asian destinations for good underwater adventures. The most common complaint is that the water surrounding Singapore is really silty—sometimes to the point where you can barely see your hand before your face. See chapters 10 through 12 for scuba activities in Malaysia.

SEA CANOEING

Rubber sea canoes and one- or two-person kayaks can be rented at Siloso Beach on Sentosa, the beach at East Coast Park (near MacDonald's Carpark C), and the beach at Changi Point. Prices range from S$6 to S$12 (US$3.80–US$7.70/£2–£3.95) per hour, depending on the type of craft you rent. Life jackets are provided. These places don't have phones so just go to the beach and scout out the rental places on the sand.

TENNIS

Quite a few hotels in the city provide tennis courts for guests, many floodlit for night play (which allows you to avoid the daytime heat), and even a few that can arrange lessons, so be sure to check out the hotel listings in chapter 4. If your hotel doesn't have tennis facilities, ask your concierge for help to arrange a game at a facility outside the hotel. Many hotels have signing agreements with sister hotel properties or special rates with independent fitness centers within the city.

WATER-SKIING & WAKEBOARDING

The Kallang River, located to the east of the city, has hosted quite a few international water-skiing tournaments. If this is your sport, contact the Cowabunga Ski Centre, the authority in Singapore. Located at **Kallang Riverside Park,** 10 Stadium Lane (© **65/6344-8813;** www.extreme.com.sg), they'll arrange lessons for adults and children plus water-skiing and wakeboarding trips. Beginner courses will set you back S$130 (US$83/£43), while more experienced skiers and boarders can hire a boat plus equipment for 4 hours for S$300 (US$192/£99) on weekdays and S$360 (US$230/£119) on weekends. It's open Tuesday through Friday noon to 7pm and Saturday, Sunday, and public holidays 9am to 7pm. Call in advance for a reservation.

WINDSURFING & SAILING

You'll find both windsurfing boards and sailboats for rent at the lagoon in East Coast Park, which is where these activities primarily take place. The largest and most reputable firm to approach has to be the **Pasta Fresca Seasport Centre** at 1212 East Coast Pkwy. (© **65/6449-5118**). For S$24 (US$15/£7.90) an hour you can rent a Laser, or for S$22 (US$14/£7.25) an hour you can rent windsurf gear. Expect to leave around S$20 (US$13/£6.60) deposit.

7

Singapore Shopping

In Singapore, shopping is a sport, and from the practiced glide through haute couture boutiques to skillful back-alley bargaining to win the best prices on Asian treasures, it's always exciting, with something to satiate every pro shopper's appetite.

The focal point of shopping in Singapore is **Orchard Road,** a very long stretch of glitzy shopping malls packed with Western clothing stores, from designer apparel to cheap chic, and many other mostly imported finds. Singaporeans have a love-hate relationship with Orchard Road. As the shopping malls developed, they brought hip styles into the reach of everyday Singaporeans, adding a cosmopolitan sheen to Singapore style. But Orchard Road also ushered in a new culture of obsessive consumerism.

Even to outsiders, Orchard Road is a drug; however, most of the clothing and accessories shops sell Western imports, and although the prices may be bargain-basement for Japanese visitors, the rest of us will find that the prices of Western brand-name fashions are no less expensive than at home. And it's all the same stuff you can get at home, too.

Another myth about shopping in Asia is that consumer electronics, cameras, and computer hardware and software are a steal. Although some good bargains can be found if you hunt well, be careful if the offer sounds too good to be true—it usually is. By and large, prices here are comparable to those of the West.

For shopping with a local flavor, there are still some nifty shopping areas—**Little India, Arab Street,** and **Chinatown**—where shopping for unusual handicrafts is as much a main attraction as the sights. Anybody who's been around Singapore long enough will tell you that most of the really juicy bargains went the way of the dodo when the huge shopping malls came to town, but if you know the value of certain items that you'd like, some comparison shopping may save you a little money. In this chapter, I'll give you some tips on where to find the better merchandise, competitive prices, and memorable shopping experiences.

Take note: I am an *expert* shopper and have shopped just about everywhere in Singapore, with the help of my mother, also a shopping expert. The shops that I have singled out for this book are the best of the best; my family and I have purchased goods and services from virtually every one of them. We know you will find the same satisfaction that we have.

1 Singapore Shopping: The Ground Rules

HOURS   Shopping malls are generally open from 10am to 9pm Monday through Saturday, with some stores keeping shorter Sunday hours. The malls sometimes remain open until 10pm on holidays. Smaller shops are open from around 10am to 5pm Monday through Saturday but are almost always closed on Sundays. Hours will vary from shop to shop. Arab Street is closed on Sundays.

PRICES Almost all of the stores in shopping malls have fixed prices. Sometimes these stores will have seasonal sales, especially in July, when they have the month-long **Great Singapore Sale,** during which prices are marked down, sometimes up to 50% or 75%. In the smaller shops and at street vendors, prices are sometimes not marked, and vendors will quote you higher prices than the going rate in anticipation of the bargaining ritual. These are the places to find good prices, if you negotiate well.

BARGAINING In Singapore, many shopkeepers cling to the old tradition of not fixing prices on their merchandise, instead making every item's purchase a little performance piece by insisting their customers bargain for it. For Westerners who are unaccustomed to this tradition, bargaining can be embarrassing and frustrating at first—after all, Westerners are accustomed to accepting fixed prices without an argument, and if you don't know the protocol, you can't be sure what to do. All it takes is a little practice, though, and soon you'll be bargaining with the best of 'em. I've seen many travelers go into their first market like lambs to the slaughter, only to loosen up after a few encounters and begin to enjoy the process for the sport it really is.

The most important thing to remember when bargaining is to keep a friendly, good-natured banter between you and the seller. Getting him or her mad won't save you a dime, and if you get 'em really riled up, they won't sell you anything at any price and will just throw you out. But don't let that scare you; just be nice and patient, and you'll get where you want to go.

One important tip for bargaining is to first have an idea of the value of what you're buying. This can be difficult for unusual items, but a little comparison shopping here may help you out. Try to look like you live in Singapore. A lot of the local European and North American residents shop at these places, so you won't look out of place. If a salesperson asks you where you are from, don't smile and say London or San Francisco, but try "Holland Village," the neighborhood where many Western expatriates live. If they think you're an expat, many times they'll give you a better price in the hopes of getting a repeat customer.

A simple "How much?" is the place to start, to which they'll reply with their top price. Let the bidding begin! It's always good to come back with a little smile and ask, "Is that your best price?" They'll probably come down a bit, but if it's obvious they're trying to soak you, tell them you'll pay a price that's about half of what they had originally offered; otherwise, just knock about 30% or 40% off. The standard reaction from them will always be to look at you like you're a crazy person for even suggesting such a discount—but don't falter! This is standard technique. For each little bit their price comes down, bring yours up just a bit until you reach a price you like. If you're having trouble talking them down, try these strategies: When buying more than one item, ask for a generous discount on the less expensive item. If you've seen it cheaper elsewhere, tell them. Or you can pull the old, "But I only have $20" ploy. (Just make sure you don't turn around and ask them to change a $50!) Try anything, even if it's just a wink and a little, "Don't you have any special discounts for ladies shopping on Wednesdays?"

Some people have said that once you start the bargaining ritual, it's rude to walk away and not purchase the item. Well, I see it this way: It's my money, and if I still don't feel comfortable shelling it out, then I won't do it under any feeling of obligation. (However, if you've spent hours negotiating over a high-priced item, and the owner agrees to your offer, it will be considered harsh to walk away after going through all that trouble.) Besides, the final bargaining strategy is to just politely say, "No, thank you" and walk away. You'll be surprised at how fast prices can come down as you're walking out the door.

GLOBAL REFUND SCHEME   When you shop in stores that display the blue "Tax Free Shopping" logo, the government will refund the goods and services tax (GST) you pay on purchases totaling S$100 (US$64/£33) or more. Upon request, the sales clerk will fill out a Tax Free Shopping Cheque, which you retain with your receipt. If you've purchased that S$100 (US$64/£33) worth at the same store but on different dates, you can still claim the refund for all of the items. When you leave Singapore, present your checks at Customs along with your passport and let them see the goods you've purchased to show that you're taking them out of the country with you. Customs will stamp the forms, which you then present at any of the Global Refund Counters in the airport for an on-the-spot cash refund (in Singapore dollars), a check, a direct transfer of the amount to your credit card account, or an airport shopping voucher. To qualify you must spend at least S$300 (US$192/£99) overall, and you can't receive a refund of more than S$500 (US$320/£165) per person. You can also claim cash or credit refunds anytime during your stay at one of four downtown counters: Centrepoint Shopping Centre Customer Service Counter, Level 1, 176 Orchard Rd.; Funan Digitalife Mall, Information Counter Level 2, 109 North Bridge Rd.; Sim Lim Square, Information Counter, Level 1, 1 Rochor Canal Rd.; and Wisma Atria, Customer Service Centre, Level 1, 435 Orchard Rd. If you chose to claim your refund downtown, you only need to show receipts; however, goods and all paperwork still must be shown upon departure at the airport. For complete details, call the Global Refund Scheme hot line at ℭ **65/6225-6238;** www.globalrefund.com.

Another company, Premier Tax Free (www.premiertaxfree.com), also offers GST refunds with kiosks at the airport.

CLOTHING SIZES   Those of you used to shopping in big-and-tall stores will unfortunately find little ready-to-wear clothing in Singapore that'll fit you—but that doesn't mean you can't take advantage of the many excellent tailors around town. Shopping for ready-made clothing in standard sizes can be confusing, because clothing made in Singapore is generally for export and everything else is imported from outside. This means that clothing in local shops can reflect American, British, or Continental sizes, depending on which country it came from or was intended for. The chart below may help you figure out your size, but really the only way to be sure if it's your size is to try it on.

Ladies' Dress Sizes								
U.S.	8	10	12	14	16	18		
U.K.	30	32	34	36	38	40		
Continental	36	38	40	42	44	46		
Ladies' Shoes								
U.S.	5	5½	6	6½	7	7½	8	8½	9
U.K.	3½	4	4½	5	5½	6	6½	7	7½
Continental	35	35	36	37	38	38	38	39	40

Urban Singapore Shopping

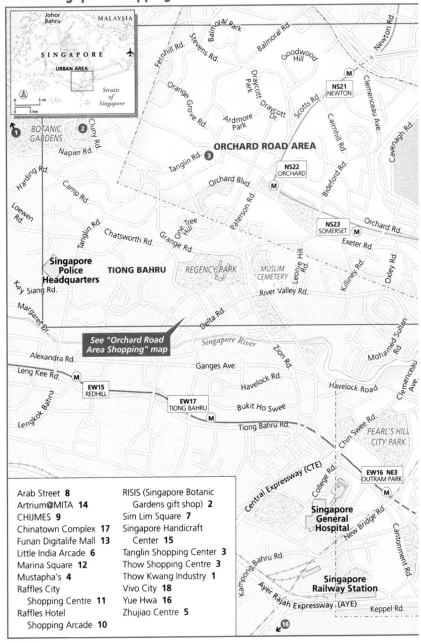

Arab Street **8**
Artrium@MITA **14**
CHIJMES **9**
Chinatown Complex **17**
Funan Digitalife Mall **13**
Little India Arcade **6**
Marina Square **12**
Mustapha's **4**
Raffles City
    Shopping Centre **11**
Raffles Hotel
    Shopping Arcade **10**

RISIS (Singapore Botanic
    Gardens gift shop) **2**
Sim Lim Square **7**
Singapore Handicraft
    Center **15**
Tanglin Shopping Center **3**
Thow Shopping Centre **3**
Thow Kwang Industry **1**
Vivo City **18**
Yue Hwa **16**
Zhujiao Centre **5**

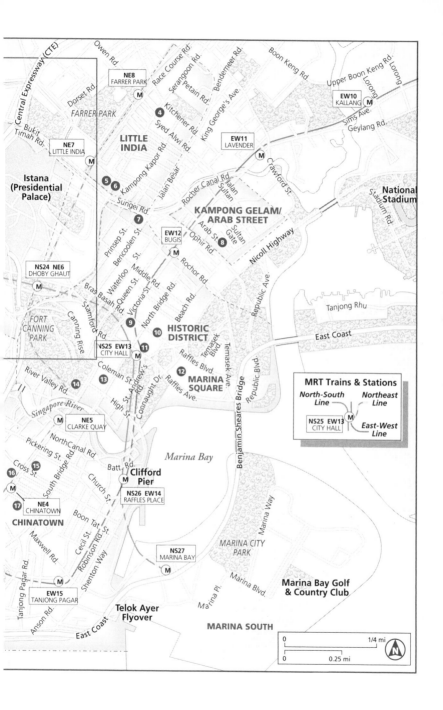

Central Expressway (CTE)

Owen Rd.

NE8
FARRER PARK
Ⓜ

Race Course Rd.

Serangoon Rd.

Petain Rd.

Bendemeer Rd.

Boon Keng Rd.

Upper Boon Keng Rd.

Lorong

Lorong

EW10
KALLANG
Ⓜ

Sims Ave.

Geylang Rd.

Dorset Rd.

FARRER PARK

④

Kitchener Rd.

Syed Alwi Rd.

King George's Ave.

Bukit Timah Rd.

NE7
LITTLE INDIA
Ⓜ

LITTLE
INDIA

EW11
LAVENDER
Ⓜ

Crawford St.

National
Stadium

Istana
(Presidential
Palace)

⑤ ⑥

Kampong Kapor Rd.

Jalan Besar

Rocher Canal Rd.

Jalan Sultan

Stadium Rd.

Sungei Rd.

⑦

KAMPONG GELAM/
ARAB STREET

Arab St.

Sultan Gate

Nicoll Highway

EW12
BUGIS
Ⓜ

Ophir Rd.

⑧

Prinsep St.

Bencoolen St.

Waterloo St.

Queen St.

Middle Rd.

North Bridge Rd.

Rochor Rd.

Beach Rd.

Republic Ave.

Tanjong Rhu

NS24 NE6
DHOBY GHAUT
Ⓜ

Bras Basah Rd.

Stamford Rd.

Victoria St.

FORT
CANNING
PARK

Canning Rise

⑨

⑩ HISTORIC
DISTRICT

Temasek Blvd.

East Coast

NS25 EW13
CITY HALL
Ⓜ ⑪

Coleman St.

St. Andrew's Rd.

Raffles Blvd.

Temasek Ave.

Republic Blvd.

River Valley Rd.

⑭

⑬

High St.

Connaught Dr.

Raffles Ave.

⑫ MARINA
SQUARE

Benjamin Sheares Bridge

Singapore River

Ⓜ NE5
CLARKE QUAY

North Canal Rd.

Pickering St.

South Bridge Rd.

Batt. Rd.

Church St.

Marina Bay

MRT Trains & Stations

North-South   Northeast
Line   Line

NS25 EW13   Ⓜ
CITY HALL   *East-West
                              Line*

Cross St.

⑮

⑯
Ⓜ

⑰ NE4
CHINATOWN
Ⓜ

CHINATOWN

Boon Tat St.

Cecil St.

Robinson Rd.

Ⓜ Clifford
Pier

NS26 EW14
RAFFLES PLACE

Marina Bay

MARINA CITY
PARK

Marina Way

Maxwell Rd.

Tanjong Pagar Rd.

Shenton Way

NS27
MARINA BAY
Ⓜ

Marina Blvd.

Marina Bay Golf
& Country Club

EW15
TANJONG PAGAR

Anson Rd.

Telok Ayer
Flyover

East Coast

Ma'rina Pl.

MARINA SOUTH

0 ————————— 1/4 mi

0 ————————— 0.25 mi

Ⓝ

Men's Suits									
U.S. & U.K.	34	36	38	40	42	44	46	48	
Continental	44	46	48	50	52	54	56	58	

Men's Shirts									
U.S. & U.K.	14	14½	15	15½	16	16½	17	17½	
Continental	36	37	38	39	40	41	42	43	

Men's Shoes										
U.S.	7	7½	8	8½	9	9½	10	10½	11	11½
U.K.	6½	7	7½	8	8½	9	9½	10	10½	11
Continental	39	40	41	42	43	43	44	44	45	45

Children's Clothes							
U.S.	2	4	6	8	10	13	15
U.K.	1	2	5	7	9	10	12
Continental	1	2	5	7	9	10	12

2 The Shopping Scene, Part 1: Western-Style Malls

Orchard Road is the biggie, as I've said, but other good mall spots are at Marina Bay, Bugis Junction, Raffles City, and at Raffles Hotel. The hottest thing on the shopping mall scene is **Vivo City** (1 HarbourFront Walk; © **65/6377-6860**). Opened in November 2006, it's Singapore's biggest shopping mall with 300 retailers, plus dining, entertainment, even a rooftop sun deck with a bandshell and kiddie wading pool. Walking distance from the HarbourFront MRT station, the mall is positioned in an area that will boom with the new Sentosa Integrated Resort opening up in 2010.

ORCHARD ROAD AREA

The malls on Orchard Road are a tourist attraction in their own right, with smaller boutiques and specialty shops intermingled with huge department stores. Takashimaya and Isetan have been imported from Japan. **John Little** is the oldest department store in Singapore, followed by **Robinson's. Tangs** is historic, having grown from a cart-full of merchandise nurtured by the business savvy of local entrepreneur C. K. Tang. Boutiques range from the younger styles of Stussy and Guess? to the sophisticated fashions of Chanel and Salvatore Ferragamo. You'll also find antiques, Oriental carpets, art galleries and curio shops, HMV music stores, Kinokuniya and Borders bookstores, video arcades, and scores of restaurants, local food courts, fast-food joints, and coffeehouses—even a few discos, which open in the evenings (see chapter 8). It's hard to say when Orchard Road is not crowded, but it's definitely a mob scene on weekends, when folks have the free time to come and hang around, looking for fun.

Centrepoint Centrepoint is home to Robinson's department store, which first opened in Singapore in 1858. Here you'll find about 150 other shops, plus fast-food outlets, and a Times bookstore. 176 Orchard Rd. © **65/6235-6629**.

Far East Plaza At this crowded mall, the bustle of little shops will sell everything from CDs to punk fashions, luggage to camera equipment, eyewear to souvenirs. Mind yourself here: Most of these shops do not display prices, but rather gauge the

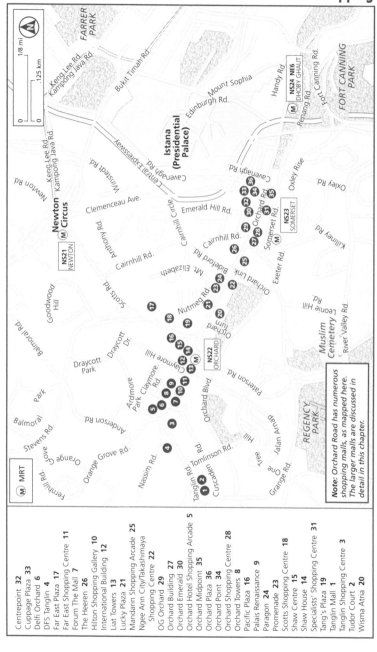

Note: Orchard Road has numerous shopping malls, as mapped here. The larger malls are discussed in detail in this chapter.

price depending on how wealthy the customer appears. If you must shop here, use your shrewdest bargaining powers. It may pay off to wear an outfit that has seen better days. 14 Scotts Rd. ② 65/6374-2325.

The Heeren Thanks to the opening of a Singapore branch of Britain's HMV music stores, the Heeren is the big hangout for teens. The front entrance of the mall hums with towers of video monitors flashing and blaring the latest in American and British chart toppers. There is also a nice cafe to the side, with a garden for enjoying a cup of coffee, tea, or a snack. 260 Orchard Rd. ② 65/6733-4725.

Hilton Shopping Gallery The shopping arcade at the Hilton International Hotel is the most exclusive shopping in Singapore. Gucci, Donna Karan, Missoni, and Louis Vuitton are just a few of the international design houses that have made this their Singapore home. 581 Orchard Rd. ② 65/6737-2233.

Lucky Plaza The map of this place will take hours to decipher, as more than 400 stores are here (no kidding). It's basically known for sportswear, camera equipment, watches, and luggage. If you buy electronics, please make sure you get an international warranty with your purchase. Also, like Far East Plaza, Lucky Plaza is a notorious rip-off problem for travelers. Make sure you come here prepared to fend off slick sales techniques. It may also help to take the government's advice and avoid touts and offers that sound too good to be true. 304 Orchard Rd. ② 65/6235-3294.

Ngee Ann City/Takashimaya Shopping Centre Takashimaya, a major Japanese department store import, anchors Ngee Ann City's many smaller boutiques. Alfred Dunhill, Chanel, Coach, Tiffany & Co., Royal Copenhagen, and Waterford and Wedgwood boutiques are found here, along with many other local and international fashion shops. 391 Orchard Rd. ② 65/6739-9323.

Palais Renaissance Shops here include upmarket boutiques like Prada, Versus, and DKNY. 390 Orchard Rd. ② 65/6737-1520.

Paragon Another upmarket shopping mall, with tenants including Diesel, Emanuel Ungaro, Escada, and Ferragamo. 290 Orchard Rd. ② 65/6738-5535.

Shaw House The main floors of Shaw House are taken up by Isetan, a large Japanese department store with designer boutiques for men's and women's fashions, accessories, and cosmetics. On the fifth level, the Lido Theatre screens new releases from Hollywood and around the world. 350 Orchard Rd. ② 65/6235-1150.

Specialists' Shopping Centre The anchor store in this smaller shopping mall is John Little, Singapore's oldest department store, which opened in 1845. The prices, however, are very up-to-date. 277 Orchard Rd. ② 65/6737-8222.

Tanglin Mall ✿ This mall has a few charming boutiques filled with regional handicrafts for home and neat ethnic fashions from Singapore's neighboring countries. 163 Tanglin Rd. ② 65/6736-4922.

Tanglin Shopping Centre ✿✿ Tanglin Shopping Centre is unique and fun. You won't find many clothing stores here, but you'll find shop after shop selling antiques, art, and collectibles—from curios to carpets. 19 Tanglin Rd. ② 65/6373-0849.

Tangs Once upon a time, C. K. Tang peddled goods from an old cart in the streets of Singapore. An industrious fellow, he parlayed his business into a small department store. A hit from the start, Tangs has grown exponentially over the decades and now competes with the other international megastores that have moved in. But Tang's is truly Singaporean, and its history is a local legend. 320 Orchard Rd. *C* **65/6737-5500.**

Wisma Atria   Wisma Atria caters to the younger set. Here you'll find everything from Nine West to a Levi's store mixed in with numerous eyewear, cosmetics, and high- and low-fashion boutiques, all under one roof. 435 Orchard Rd. *C* **65/6235-2103.**

MARINA BAY

The Marina Bay area arose from a plot of reclaimed land and now boasts the giant Suntec City convention center and all the hotels, restaurants, and shopping malls that have grown up around it. Shopping in the Marina Bay area is popular for everyone because of its convenience, with the major malls and hotels all interconnected by covered walkways and pedestrian bridges, making it easy to get around with minimal exposure to the elements.

Marina Square   Marina Square is a huge complex that, in addition to a wide variety of shops, has a cinema, fast-food outlets and cafes, pharmacies, and convenience stores. 6 Raffles Blvd. *C* **65/6335-2613.**

Millenia Walk   Smaller than Marina Square, Millenia Walk has more upmarket boutiques like Fendi, Guess?, and Liz Claiborne, to name a few. 9 Raffles Blvd. *C* **65/6883-1122.**

Suntec City Mall   Tons of shops selling fashion, sports equipment, books, CDs, plus restaurants and food courts, and a cinema adjacent to the Suntec Convention Centre. 3 Temasek Blvd. *C* **65/6821-3668.**

AROUND THE CITY CENTER

Although the Historic District doesn't have as many malls as the Orchard Road area, it still has some good shopping. Raffles City can be overwhelming in its size but convenient because it sits right atop the City Hall MRT stop. One of my favorite places to go, however, is the very upmarket Raffles Hotel Shopping Arcade, where I like to window-shop and dream about actually being able to afford some of the stuff on display.

Parco Bugis Junction   Here you'll find restaurants—both fast food and fine dining—mixed in with clothing retailers, most of which sell fun fashions for younger tastes. 230 Victoria St. *C* **65/6334-8831.**

Raffles City Shopping Centre   Raffles City sits right on top of the City Hall MRT station, which makes it a very well-visited mall. Men's and women's fashions, books, cosmetics, and accessories are sold in shops here, along with gifts. 252 North Bridge Rd. *C* **65/6338-7766.**

Raffles Hotel Shopping Arcade   These shops are mostly haute couture; however, there is the Raffles Hotel gift shop for interesting souvenirs. For golfers, there's a Jack Nicklaus signature store. 328 North Bridge Rd. *C* **65/6337-1886.**

3 The Shopping Scene, Part 2: Multicultural Shopping

The most exciting shopping has got to be in all the ethnic enclaves throughout the city. Down narrow streets, bargains are to be had on all sorts of unusual items. If you're stuck for a gift idea, read on. Chances are I'll mention something for even the most difficult person on your list.

CHINATOWN

For Chinese goods, nothing beats **Yue Hwa** ✿✿, 70 Eu Tong Sen St. (© **65/6538-4222**), a five-story Chinese emporium that's an attraction in its own right. The superb inventory includes all manner of silk wear (robes, underwear, blouses), embroidery and house linens, bolt silks, tailoring services (for perfect mandarin dresses!), cloisonné (enamel work) jewelry and gifts, pottery, musical instruments, traditional Chinese clothing for men and women (from scholars' robes to coolie duds!), jade and gold, cashmere, art supplies, herbs—I could go on and on. Prices are terrific. Plan to spend some time here.

For one-stop souvenir shopping, you can tick off half your list at **Chinatown Point,** aka the **Singapore Handicraft Center,** 133 New Bridge Rd. (© **6534-0112**). With dozens of small shops that sell mainly Chinese handicraft items from carved jade to imported Chinese classical instruments, and lacquerware. The best gifts there include hand-carved chops (Chinese seals) with a few shops offering good selections of carved stone, wood, bone, glass, and ivory chops ready to be carved to your specifications. Simple designs are affordable, although some of the more elaborate chops and carvings fetch a handsome sum. You can also commission a personalized Chinese scroll painting or calligraphy piece.

My all-time favorite gift idea? Spend an afternoon learning the traditional Chinese tea ceremony at the **Tea Chapter,** 9–11 Neil Rd. (© **65/6226-1175**), and pick up a tea set—they have a lovely selection of tea pots, cups, and accessories, as well as quality teas for sale. When you return home, you'll be ready to give a fabulous gift—not just a tea set, but your own cultural performance as well. Another neat place to visit is **Kwong Chen Beverage Trading,** 16 Smith St. (© **65/6223-6927**), for some Chinese teas in handsome tins. Although the teas are really inexpensive, they're packed in lovely tins—great to buy lots to bring back as smaller gifts. For serious tea aficionados or those curious about Traditional Chinese Medicine (TCM), stop by **Eu Yan Sang** (269 South Bridge Rd.; © **65/6223-6333**; www.euyansang.com.sg) where they have stocks of very fine (and expensive) teas, plus herb and herbal remedies for health. For something a little more unusual, check out **Siong Moh Paper Products,** 39 Mosque St. (© **65/6224-3125**), which also carries a full line of ceremonial items. Pick up some joss sticks (temple incense) or joss paper (books of thin sheets of paper, stamped in reds and yellows with bits of gold and silver leaf). Definitely a conversation piece, as is the Hell Money, stacks of "money" that believers burn at the temple for their ancestors to use in the afterlife. Perfect for that friend who has everything? Also, if you duck over to **Sago Lane** while you're in the neighborhood, there are a few souvenir shops that sell Chinese kites and Cantonese Opera masks—cool for kids.

ARAB STREET

Over on Arab Street, shop for handicrafts from Malaysia and Indonesia. I go for sarongs at **Hadjee Textiles,** 75 Arab St. (© **65/6298-1943**), for their stacks of folded sarongs in beautiful colors and traditional patterns. They're perfect for traveling, as they're lightweight, but can serve you well as a dressy skirt, a bedsheet, beach blanket, window shade, bath towel, or whatever you need—when I'm on the road I can't live without mine. Buy a few here and the prices really drop. If you're in the market for a more masculine sarong, **Goodwill Trading,** 56 Arab St. (© **65/6298-3205**), specializes in *pulicat,* or the plaid sarongs worn by Malay men. For modern styles of batik, check out **Basharahil Brothers,** 101 Arab St. (© **65/6296-0432**), for their very interesting designs, but don't forget to see their collection of fine silk batiks in the back.

For batik household linens, you can't beat **Maruti Textiles,** 93 Arab St. (℗ **65/6392-0253**), where you'll find high-quality place mats and napkins, tablecloths, pillow covers, and quilts from India. The buyer for this shop has a good eye for style.

I've also found a few shops on Arab Street that carry **handicrafts** from Southeast Asia. For antiques and curios, try **Gim Joo Trading,** 16 Baghdad St. (℗ **65/6293-5638**), a jumble of the unusual, some of it old. A departure from the more packed and dusty places here, **Suraya Betawj,** 67 Arab St. (℗ **65/6398-1607**), carries gorgeous Indonesian and Malaysian crafted housewares in contemporary design—the type you normally find for huge prices in shopping catalogs back home.

Other unique treasures include the large assortment of fragrance oils at **Aljunied Brothers,** 91 Arab St. (℗ **65/6293-2751**). Muslims are forbidden from consuming alcohol in any form (a proscription that includes the wearing of alcohol-based perfumes as well), so these oil-based perfumes re-create designer scents plus other floral and wood creations. Check out their delicate cut-glass bottles and atomizers as well. Finally, for the crafter in your life, **Kin Lee & Co.,** 109 Arab St. (℗ **65/6291-1411**), carries a complete line of patterns and accessories to make local Peranakan beaded slippers. In vivid colors and floral designs, these traditional slippers were always made by hand, to be attached later to a wooden sole. The finished versions are exquisite, plus they're fun to make.

LITTLE INDIA

I have a ball shopping the crowded streets of Little India. The best shopping is on Serangoon Road, where Singapore's Indian community shops for Indian imports and cultural items. The absolute best place to start is **Mustapha's** ✿✿, 320 Serangoon Rd./145 Syed Alwi Rd., at the corner of Serangoon and Syed Alwi roads (℗ **65/6299-2603**), but be warned, you can spend the whole day there—and night, too, because Mustapha's is open 24 hours every day. This maze of a department store fills two city blocks full of imported items from India. Granted, much of it is everyday stuff, but the real finds are rows of saris and silk fabrics; two floors of jaw-dropping gold jewelry in Indian designs; an entire supermarket packed with spices and packets of instant curries; ready-made Indian-style tie-dye and embroidered casual wear; incense and perfume oils; cotton tapestries and textiles for the home—the list goes on. And prices can't be beat, seriously.

Little India offers all sorts of small finds, especially throughout **Little India Arcade** (48 Serangoon Rd.) and just across the street on Campbell Lane at **Kuna's,** 3 Campbell Lane (℗ **65/6294-2700**). Here you can buy inexpensive Indian costume jewelry like bangles, earrings, and necklaces in exotic designs and a wide assortment of decorative dots (called *pottu* in Tamil) to grace your forehead. Indian handicrafts include brass work, woodcarvings, dyed tapestries, woven cotton household linens, small curio items, very inexpensive incense, colorful pictures of Hindu gods, and other ceremonial items. Look here also for Indian cooking pots and household items.

Across the street from Little India Arcade, the second floor of **Zhujiao Centre** is packed with stall after stall of inexpensive *salwar kameez,* or Punjabi suits, the three-piece outfits—long tunic over pants, with matching shawl—worn by northern Indian ladies. Don't be afraid to bargain for the best price.

Punjab Bazaar, #01–07 Little India Arcade, 48 Serangoon Rd. (℗ **65/6296-0067**), carries a more upmarket choice of *salwar kameez,* in many styles and fabrics. If nothing strikes your fancy at Punjab Bazaar, try **Roopalee Fashions,** a little farther down at 84 Serangoon Rd. (⑦ **65/6298-0558**). Both shops carry sandals, bags, and other accessories to complement your new outfit.

4 Best Buys A to Z

ANTIQUES   A 5-minute walk north of Orchard Road is the mellow **Tanglin Shopping Centre** (Tanglin Rd.), whose quiet halls are just packed with little antiques boutiques. Tanglin is a quiet place, which adds to the museum feel as you stroll past window displays of paintings, tapestries, and curios made of jade or brass—all kinds of quality collectibles and gifts. A couple of good shops to visit are **Antiques of the Orient,** #02–40 Tanglin Shopping Centre (⑦ **65/6734-9351**), selling old prints and maps, and **Aspara,** #02–30 Tanglin Shopping Centre (⑦ **65/6735-5018**), with an interesting collection of Chinese and Burmese antiques. There are many more—this is a place to really explore.

If you continue along Tanglin Road you'll find **Tudor Court,** with a few more interesting shops inside, including **Antiquity Hands of the Hills** (⑦ **65/6735-5332**), with textiles, jewelry, and curio items from Tibet.

To get an eyeful of some local furnishings in antique Indonesian, Chinese, and Peranakan styles, take a taxi out to **Dempsey Road** and walk up the hill to the warehouses. Inside each warehouse are dealers like the **Shang Antique,** full of Chinese antiques and Burmese teak at Blk. 16, #01–04/05 Dempsey Rd. (⑦ **65/6388-8838**), and the **Renaissance Art Gallery,** with displays of Chinese figurines, Southeast Asian Buddha images, and chests at Blk. 15, #01–06 Dempsey Rd. (⑦ **65/6474-0338**). More than a dozen places are here, each specializing in different wares. Some have large furniture pieces, from carved teak Indonesian-style reproduction furniture to authentic pieces from mainland China. Some have smaller collectible items, like carved scale weights from the old opium trade or collections of Buddha images. Oriental carpet shops are also mixed in. The stores on Dempsey Road are all open daily from around 11am to 6:30pm, though they close for a short lunch break at midday. As with all of the antiques shops in Singapore, they'll help you locate a reliable shipper to send your purchases home.

ASIAN FASHION   You can find *cheongsam,* those cute little sleeveless shifts with the Mandarin collars and frog closures, in ready-made polyester styles at souvenir shops all over Chinatown. When you're ready to get serious, go to **Yue Hwa,** 70 Eu Tong Sen St. (⑦ **65/6538-4222**), where they hire expert *cheongsam* tailors from Hong Kong who fit the dress perfectly to your body, help you select your fabric from a wide range of pure Chinese silks, and choose your own preferred style. Expect to drop about S$450 (US$288/£149) for a full-length *cheongsam,* a small price to pay for a drop-dead sexy, one-of-a-kind formal dress.

If Bollywood blockbusters make you drool, you'll die for **Stylemart,** 149–151 Selegie Rd. (⑦ **65/6338-2073**). Specializing in tailored Indian formalwear, they have rows of Indian-style brocade silks that are simply edible and an enormous collection of breathtakingly exotic beaded silks to make your eyes twinkle. They will fashion anything you want—traditional or modern dresses, gowns, pantsuits, anything—out of the stuff. A simple formal gown with shawl in silk brocade will start at S$500 (US$320/£165). Pay more for beaded styles. It's worth it.

The true authentic Singaporean style is that of the Nonyas, Peranakan ladies who wear the traditional *sarong kebaya.* These ladies pair fine sarongs with delicate lace blouses (*kebaya*) closed with silver or gold brooches and accessorized with beaded slippers and a bag. Still today you will see Singaporean ladies don *sarong kebaya* for weddings and special parties. If you'd like to outfit yourself in one, the place to go is **Rumah Bebe** (113 East Coast Rd.; ℂ 65/6247-8781), located in Katong, the heart of Peranakan culture. Proprietress Bebe Seet is a local *sarong kebaya* expert. Her shop sells fine batiks (much nicer than the ordinary ones on Arab St.), and matching blouses. She also specializes in beaded slippers, teaching classes out of the back of her shop. Her sarongs start at S$60 (US$38/£20), with *kebayas* starting at about S$125 (US$80/£41). Her handmade shoes will set you back a few hundred bucks.

ELECTRONICS   At **Funan Digitalife Mall,** 109 North Bridge Rd. (ℂ 65/6336-8325), you can find computers and accessories—there are many, many shops, each with special offers and deals, so compare when you shop. At **Sim Lim Square,** 1 Rochor Canal Rd. (ℂ 65/6332-5839), not only can you find computers, but office and home electronics as well. Bargain hard here—prices are not marked.

If you're in the market for photographic equipment, the best place to go is **Cathay Photo,** #01–05, #01–07/08, #01–11/14 Peninsula Plaza, 111 North Bridge Rd. (ℂ 65/6337-4274).

EYEGLASSES   Eyeglasses? Why would anyone want to buy eyeglasses on his vacation? Because in Singapore they're dirt-cheap, that's why. For the price of one pair of frames with prescription lenses in the United States, I can get a pair of prescription glasses, a pair of prescription sunglasses, contact lenses, and even have my old frames relensed. If you can beat that at home, do it. If not, take advantage while you can.

They're so inexpensive because the government does not have as strict regulations on optometry as do countries in the West. However, the larger prescription firms are very good at what they do, and many shops carry the latest frames from international designers. At **Capitol Optical** you'll get the best price on generic frames, but not cheap quality in the lenses. Centrally located branches are at #03–132 Far East Plaza (ℂ 65/6736-0365); #01–77 Lucky Plaza (ℂ 65/6734-4166); and 435 Orchard Rd. #03–39 Wisma Atria (ℂ 65/6732-2401).

FABRICS   Exquisite fabrics like Chinese silk, Thai silk, batiks, and inexpensive gingham are very affordable and the selections are extensive. Most fabrics are sold by the meter and there is no standard width, so make sure you inquire when you're purchasing off the bolt. Be sure to check out **Arab Street.** I adore the selection of silks from India, Thailand, Japan, and Europe at **Poppy Fabric,** 111 Arab St. (ℂ 65/6296-6352). Buy modern batik fabrics at **Basharahil Bros.,** 101 Arab St. (ℂ 65/6296-0432), and be sure to take a peek at their batik silks in the back—just gorgeous!

For other finds, a few shops along Serangoon Road in Little India have some fine Indian silks. The largest selection is at **Mustapha's,** 320 Serangoon Rd. (ℂ 65/6299-2603).

FINE ART   As Singaporeans' wealth increases, so does appreciation of the arts, so you'll get to see a multitude of successful galleries cropping up, many of which feature the works of local and regional artists. Late-19th-century Chinese oil paintings, watercolors, and brush paintings blend agreeably with contemporary artworks by well-known and new-to-the-scene artists from ASEAN (Association of Southeast Asian Nations) countries as well as the United States and Europe. Rich antique embroideries, carved jade and wooden pieces, and calligraphy (an art unto itself) beg to be admired.

Six Galleries are packed into the **Artrium@MITA** (The Ministry of Information, Communications and The Arts), 140 Hill St., including **Gajah Gallery,** with regional fine arts (ℂ 65/6737-4202) and **Soobin Gallery** (ℂ 65/6837-2777).

Artfolio's exhibits at #02–12 **Raffles Hotel Arcade,** 328 North Bridge Rd. (✆ **65/ 6334-4677**), always make me wish I were rich enough to collect. If you're in the market for fine arts from the mainland (China, that is).

Tanglin Shopping Centre also has a ton of art galleries. For contemporary Southeast Asian art, visit **Hakaren Art Gallery,** #01–49, 02–43 Tanglin Shopping Centre (✆ **65/6733-3382**). **Kwan Hua Art Gallery,** #02–65 Tanglin Shopping Centre (✆ **65/6735-5663**), carries a collection of Chinese brush paintings and oils.

JEWELRY Jewelry can be a bargain. Gold, which is sold at the day's rate, is fashioned into modern Western styles and into styles that suit Chinese and Indian tastes. *Note:* Chinese and Indian jewelers only work with 18-karat quality and above, usually 22- and 24-karat designs—Chinese gold tends to be bright yellow while Indian gold has a reddish hue to it. Loose stones, either precious or semiprecious, are abundant in many reputable shops and can be set for you.

For contemporary upmarket jewels and settings, the most trusted dealer in Singapore is **Larry Jewelry (S) Pte. Ltd.,** #01–8 Raffles City Shopping Centre, 252 North Bridge Rd. (✆ **65/6336-9648**), but be prepared to drop some serious cash.

Peek in the window displays of the gold shops along Serangoon Road and you'll see all kinds of Indian-style gold necklaces and bangles. Each Indian ethnic group has its own traditional patterns, all of them featuring intricate filigree. The selection at **Mustapha's,** 320 Serangoon Rd. (✆ **65/6299-2603**), is absolutely mind-blowing. I can't imagine the staggering value of all their merchandise. Don't forget there are two levels here; the best stuff is downstairs.

For Chinese jade try **Yue Hwa,** 70 Eu Tong Sen St. (✆ **65/6538-4222**). Jade is tough for Westerners to buy, because it's hard to discern a good piece from a bad one. Yue Hwa has fixed prices, but the quality is always dependable.

A unique gift or souvenir, a gold-plated orchid is something you don't find every day. The process was developed in the 1970s and is exclusive to Singapore. Different orchid species make up brooches, earrings, and pendants at local jewelry designer **RISIS, Singapore Botanic Gardens** gift shop, 1 Cluny Rd. (✆ **65/6475-2319**), and #01–084 Suntec City Mall, 3 Temasek Blvd. (✆ **65/6338-8250**).

MEN'S TAILORING There are some fine men's tailors for suits and slacks made to fit, but beware touts along Orchard Road. If you can get a cheap price, chances are you're getting a cheap suit. **Justmen's** (19 Tanglin Rd., #01–36/39 Tanglin Shopping Centre; ✆ **65/6737-4800**) is an institution within the expatriate community here. They are well versed in current fashions, carry the best selection of fine fabrics, and can fit your measurements perfectly—this will probably be one of the best suits you've ever had. The prices are a steal, starting from S$650 (US$416/£215) for a two-piece suit.

ORIENTAL CARPETS Once you've walked on a hand-knotted **Nain** in your bare feet, trailed your fingers along the pile of an antique **Heriz,** or admired the sensuous colors of a **Tabriz,** you'll never look at broadloom again with the same forbearance. If luxury Oriental carpets seem too expensive for your pocketbook, Singapore prices will surprise you.

Ask anyone in Singapore where to shop for carpets, and he'll send you to **Hassan's Carpets,** #03–01/06 Tanglin Shopping Centre (✆ **65/6737-5626**), which has been a fixture in Singapore for generations. Proprietor Suliman Hamid is the local authority on carpets, having advised on and supplied the carpets for the restoration of Raffles Hotel. He and his staff know the background of every rug and have wonderful stories to tell. They forego the hard sales pitch for more civilized discourse on carpet appreciation. It's an afternoon well spent.

If you still want to see more carpets, you can take a taxi out to Dempsey Road where you'll find a few warehouses filled with stock.

PEWTER   Royal Selangor, the famous Malaysian pewter manufacturer since 1885, rode high on the Malaysian tin business at the turn of the 20th century, pewter being a tin alloy. This firm is based in Kuala Lumpur and has eight showrooms in Singapore. If you're really into pewter, you can visit the Royal Selangor Pewter Centre, 3A River Valley Rd., 01–01 Clarke Quay (✆ **65/6268-9600;** www.royalselangor.com.sg), where they have an exhibit of the history of pewter works in the region with pewtersmith demonstrations daily from 9am to 9pm for S$2 (US$1.30/65p) entry. For S$30 (US$19/£9.90), you can sign up for a half-hour hands-on pewtersmith workshop. If you just want to shop, you can also stop in at their showrooms at #02–38 Raffles City Shopping Centre (✆ **65/6339-3958**); #02–40 Paragon, 290 Orchard Rd. (✆ **65/ 6235-6633**); and #02–127 Marina Square (✆ **65/6339-3115**).

POTTERY   Antique porcelain items can be found in the many small shops along Pagoda and Trenagganu streets in Chinatown. But the ultimate in pottery shopping is a place the locals refer to as the "pottery jungle." **Thow Kwang Industry Pte. Ltd.** is a taxi ride away at 85 Lorong Tawas off Jalan Bahar (✆ **65/6265-5808**). This backwoods place has row after row of pots, lamps, umbrella stands—you name it. There's even a room with antique pieces.

SHOES   You can seriously go nuts over cheap shoes here. We're talking prices from S$9.90 to S$39 (US$6.30–US$25/£3.25–£13) for cute little sandals, dressy shoes, and work pumps. Granted, they're not Ferragamo, but at these prices you can literally buy a pair of shoes to match every outfit in your closet. Unfortunately, if you're bigger than a size 8, finding your size will be tough. Otherwise, my two favorite places for shoes on the cheap-cheap are the shoe departments at **Seiyu,** Parco Bugis Junction (✆ **65/6337-3606**), and **OG,** Orchard Point (✆ **65/6317-2222**).

SOUTHEAST ASIAN HANDICRAFTS   At **Lim's,** 211 Holland Ave., #02–01 Holland Road Shopping Centre (✆ **65/6467-1300**) and #02–154/155 Vivo City (✆ **65/6376-9468**), you'll find items for the home from all over Southeast Asia; think Pier One Imports, only cheaper. Vietnamese lacquerware and handbags, Indonesian teakwood carvings and batik linens, Thai silk pillow covers and tableware, Chinese pottery and arts, the list goes on and on. Prices are very reasonable, and the merchandise is all of good quality. It's located in Holland Village, an expat neighborhood outside the city center, but it's worth the trip. It can be tricky to find—enter the building through the sliding glass doors next to the Cold Storage grocery store and head up the narrow escalator to the second level.

I'm a big fan of local clothing designer Peter Hoe's boutique, **Olathe,** at 30 Victoria St., #01–05 CHIJMES (✆ **65/6339-6880**). This Malaysian fabric and clothing designer fashions very handsome individual fabric patterns pieced together in styles to suit Western wardrobes. His collection of regional silver jewelry is also worth noting as is his home decor collection next door.

8

Singapore After Dark

What do you want to do tonight? Do you want to go out for a cultural experience and find a traditional dance or music performance or a Chinese opera, or do you want to put on your finery and rub elbows with society at the symphony? If it's live performance you're looking for, you have your choice not only of the local dance and theater troupes but of the many West End and Broadway shows that come through on international tours. Or you may want to try a local performance—smaller theater groups have lately been hitting nerves and funny bones through stage portrayals of life in the Garden City. Singapore has been transforming itself into a center for the arts in this part of the world and is striving to achieve the level of sophistication you'd come to expect from a Western city.

If partying it up is more your speed, all kinds of nighttime revelry are going on. Society may seem puritanical during the daylight hours, but at night, the clubs get crazy.

Increasingly, Singapore's nightlife has been clustering around nightlife hubs. On of the earliest hub, **Boat Quay,** is a strip of renovated shophouses along the Singapore River that turns into a veritable parade of small bars, karaoke lounges, discos, and cafes after 9pm. As you stroll along the river, you can hear the hip-hop, reggae, jazz, blues, rap, techno, disco—you name it—pouring from each door.

Upriver, **Clarke Quay** has recently had a shot in the arm from the Ministry of

Sound, which opened in 2005 (covered later in this chapter). In December 2006, a handful of new clubs opened up, promising to be the ultimate trend-setters in all the land. But at the time of writing they were really too new for me to decide if they're a hit or not. Check it out at www.the-cannery.com.sg. Try at your own risk.

Farther upriver, near Robertson Quay, find **Mohamed Sultan Road,** a hub of clubs and bars that popped up in the mid-'90s. While the bars here still hop on weekends, most of their glitter has faded to newer joints elsewhere.

Also opened in late 2006, the **St. James Power Station,** 3 Sentosa Gateway (© **65/6270-7676;** www.stjamespowerstation.com.sg) looks very promising, with 9 different clubs, serving up everything from Mandarin pop to karaoke to world music to live bands and DJ dance music. The nearly 5,600-sq-m (60,000 sq.-ft.) space occupies Singapore's first coal-fired power station, built in 1927. With the opening of Vivo City, Singapore's biggest shopping mall, just next door, plus the building of the integrated resort across the water, St. James Power Station has a bright future.

Then there's **Orchard Road.** The area around the Scotts Road and Orchard Road intersection has a tremendous number of nightclubs, each with its own favorite clientele and all with high admission prices. Also fun, and with a high concentration of nightlife options, is **CHIJMES.**

1 Tips on Singapore Nightlife

INFORMATION Major cultural festivals are highly publicized by the **Singapore Tourism Board (STB),** who will give you complete details at their Visitors Centres (see p. 30 for locations) or on their website (www.stb.com.sg). Another good resource is the Life! section of *Straits Times,* which lists events for each day, plus theater and cinema listings. The freebie *I-S Magazine* promotes Singapore's clubbing lifestyle.

TICKETS Two ticket agents, **TicketCharge** and **Sistic,** handle bookings for almost all theater performances, concert dates, and special events. You can find out about schedules before your visit through their websites: www.ticketcharge.com.sg and www.sistic.com.sg. When in Singapore, stop by one of their centrally located outlets to pick up a schedule or call them for more information. Call TicketCharge at $\mathcal{C}$ 65/ 6296-2929 or head for Centrepoint, Forum The Shopping Mall, Funan The IT Mall, Marina Square Shopping Centre, or Tanglin Mall. For **Sistic** bookings call $\mathcal{C}$ 65/ 6348-5555, or see them at the Victoria Concert Hall Box Office, Parco Bugis Junction, Raffles Shopping Centre, Scotts, Specialists' Shopping Center, Suntec Mall, or Wisma Atria.

HOURS Theater and dance performances can begin anywhere between 7:30 and 9pm. Be sure to call for the exact time, and don't be late—at Esplanade they don't let latecomers in. Many bars open in the late afternoon, a few as early as lunchtime. Disco and entertainment clubs usually open around 6pm but generally don't get lively until 10 or 11pm. Closing time for bars and clubs is at 1 or 2am on weekdays, 3 or 4am on weekends. A few have extended hours until 6am.

DRINK PRICES Because of the government's added tariff, alcoholic beverage prices are high everywhere, whether in a hotel bar or a neighborhood pub. "House pour" drinks (generics) are between S$8 and S$14 (US$5.10–US$9/£2.65–£4.60). A glass of house wine will cost between S$10 and S$15 (US$6.40–US$9.60/£3.30–£4.95), depending whether it's a red or a white. Local draft beer (Tiger), brewed in Singapore, is around S$10 (US$6.40/£3.30). Hotel establishments are, on average, the most expensive venues, while stand-alone pubs and cafes are better value. Almost every bar and club has a happy hour in the early evenings and discounts can be up to 50% off for house pours and drafts. Most of the disco and entertainment clubs charge covers, but they will usually include one or more drinks. Hooray for ladies' nights— usually Wednesdays—when those of the feminine persuasion get in for free and sometimes even drink for free, too.

DRESS CODE Many clubs will require smart casual attire. Feel free to be trendy, but stay away from shorts, T-shirts, sneakers, and torn jeans. Be forewarned that you may be turned away if not properly dressed. Many locals dress up for a night on the town, usually in elegant garb or fashionista threads.

SAFETY You'll be fairly safe out during the wee hours in most parts of the city, and even a single woman alone has little to worry about. Occasionally, groups of young men may catcall, but by and large those groups are not hanging out in the more cosmopolitan areas. You can always get home safely in a taxi, which fortunately isn't too hard to find even late at night, with one exception: When Boat Quay clubs close, there's usually a mob of revelers scrambling for cabs. (Note that after midnight, a 50% surcharge is added to the fare, so make sure you don't imbibe your ride home!)

Urban Singapore Nightlife

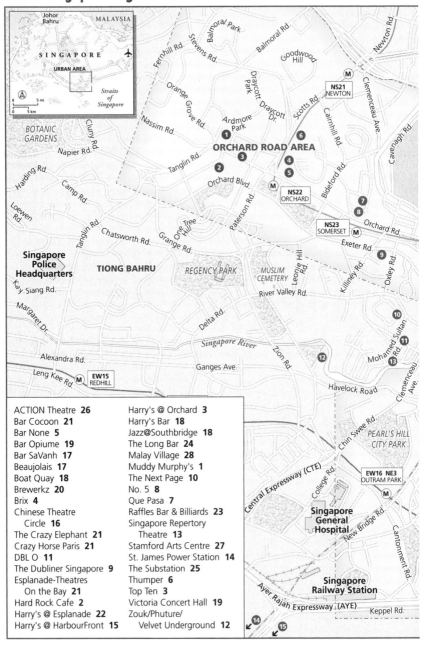

ACTION Theatre **26**
Bar Cocoon **21**
Bar None **5**
Bar Opiume **19**
Bar SaVanh **17**
Beaujolais **17**
Boat Quay **18**
Brewerkz **20**
Brix **4**
Chinese Theatre
  Circle **16**
The Crazy Elephant **21**
Crazy Horse Paris **21**
DBL O **11**
The Dubliner Singapore **9**
Esplanade-Theatres
  On the Bay **21**
Hard Rock Cafe **2**
Harry's @ Esplanade **22**
Harry's @ HarbourFront **15**

Harry's @ Orchard **3**
Harry's Bar **18**
Jazz@Southbridge **18**
The Long Bar **24**
Malay Village **28**
Muddy Murphy's **1**
The Next Page **10**
No. 5 **8**
Que Pasa **7**
Raffles Bar & Billiards **23**
Singapore Repertory
  Theatre **13**
Stamford Arts Centre **27**
St. James Power Station **14**
The Substation **25**
Thumper **6**
Top Ten **3**
Victoria Concert Hall **19**
Zouk/Phuture/
  Velvet Underground **12**

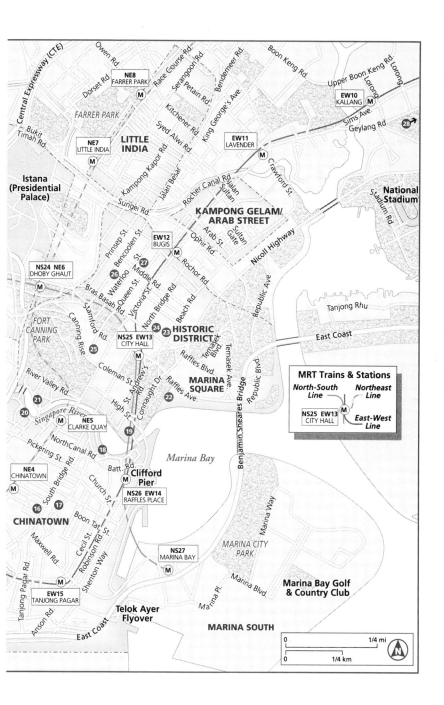

2 The Bar & Club Scene

Singaporeans love to go out at night, whether it's to lounge around in a cozy wine bar or to jump around on a dance floor until 3am. This city has become pretty eclectic in its entertainment choices, so you'll find everything from live jazz to acid jazz, from polished cover bands to internationally acclaimed guest DJs. The nightlife is happening. Local celebrities and the young, wealthy, and beautiful are the heroes of the scene, and their quest for the "coolest" spot keeps the club scene on its toes.

BARS

The **Hard Rock Cafe** in Singapore, #02–01 HPL House, 50 Cuscaden Rd. (© **65/ 6235-5232**), is just like the one in your hometown, so why bother on vacation? The resident band is pretty good and, of course, so are the burgers, but beyond that it's not much more than a tourist pickup joint.

Bar Cocoon The IndoChine group of restaurants also operates several chic bars throughout the city. With the feel of a luxe opium den, you'll be enveloped in stylish contemporary Southeast Asian decor and groovy textural music. A sensual place to meet for a cocktail before dinner, to relax for a night cap, or to just loll away the hours with mixed cocktails. Also check out sister bars: **Bar Opiume,** 1 Empress Place, Asian Civilisations Museum (© **65/6339-2876**) and **Bar SaVanh,** 49A Club St. (© **65/ 6323-0145**). Hours are Sunday to Thursday 5pm to 3am and Friday and Saturday 5pm to 6am. 3A Merchant's Court, Clarke Quay, River Valley Rd. #01–02. © 65/6557-6268.

Brix In the basement of the Grand Hyatt Regency, Brix hosts a good house band and international visiting groups as well. A pickup joint of sorts, it's a bit more sophisticated than others. The Music Bar features live jazz and R&B, while the Wine & Whiskey Bar serves up a fine selection of wine, Scotch, and cognac. Hours are Sunday to Thursday 7pm to 2am; Friday and Saturday 7pm to 3am. Happy hour nightly, from 7 to 9pm. Basement, Grand Hyatt Singapore, 10 Scotts Rd. © 65/6416-7292. Cover charge after 9pm S$35 (US$22/£12).

Coastes In urban Singapore you can almost forget that technically you're on a tropical island. When that happens, trek out to Coastes, an open-air bar where you can step off the sun deck and into the sand. Cold beer and exotic cocktails are served at shady tables or at lounge chairs under the sun while you chill out to cool Ibiza party music. Coastes also serves pizza, burgers, and pasta for lunch and dinner daily. On a clear day the sunset is great. Hours are Monday to Thursday 10am to midnight; Friday 10am to 1am, Saturday 9am to 1am and Sunday 9am to midnight. 50 Siloso Beach Walk, #01–05/06, Sentosa Island. © 65/6274-9668.

The Crazy Elephant Crazy Elephant is the city's address for blues-rock. Hang out in cooling breezes blowing off the river while listening to classic rock and blues by resident bands. This place has hosted, in addition to some excellent local and regional guitarists, international greats such as Rick Derringer, Eric Burdon, and Walter Trout. It's an unpretentious place to chill out and have a cold one. Beer is reasonably priced as well. Hours are Sunday to Thursday 5pm to 1am; Friday and Saturday 5pm to 2am with daily happy hour 5 to 9pm. 3E River Valley Rd., #01–03/04 Traders Market, Clarke Quay. © 65/6337-1990.

The Dubliner Singapore Located in a restored colonial building, Dubliner's got great atmosphere, with vaulted ceilings, tiled floors and pretty plasterwork, and outdoor seating on the veranda. It's also a pretty decent Irish pub, with a friendly staff and a cast of regulars from the local expat crowd. Sports matches are broadcast regularly (mainly soccer), and there's variety of cold beer on tap. Hours are Sunday to Thursday 11am to 1am and Friday and Saturday 11am to 2am; daily happy hour runs 5 to 8pm. Winsland Conservation House, 165 Penang Rd. ℂ **65/6735-2220.**

The Long Bar　Here's a gem of a bar, even if it is touristy and expensive. With tiled mosaic floors, large shuttered windows, and punkah fans moving in waves above, Raffles Hotel has tried to retain much of the charm of yesteryear, so you can enjoy a Singapore Sling in its birthplace and take yourself back to when history was made. And truly, the thrill at the Long Bar is tossing back one of these sweet juicy drinks while pondering the Singapore adventures of all the famous actors, writers, and artists who came through here in the first decades of the 20th century. If you're not inspired by the poetry of the moment, stick around and get juiced for the pop/reggae band at 9pm, which is quite good. Hours are Sunday to Thursday 11am to 1am, Friday and Saturday 11am to 2am. Happy hour nightly 6 to 9pm, with special deals on pitchers of beer and some mixed drinks. A Singapore Sling is S$21 (US$13/£6.95), and a Sling with souvenir glass costs S$32 (US$20/£10). Raffles Hotel Arcade, Raffles Hotel, 1 Beach Rd. ℂ **65/6337-1886.**

Muddy Murphy's　This is another popular Irish bar in Singapore. A favorite sports hangout, with big-screen viewing of international soccer and rugby matches, and live bands on weekends (otherwise it's canned Irish music). The ambience is created by the mostly Irish imported trappings around the place. Occasionally they'll even have an Irish band. There is a limited menu for lunch, dinner, and snacks. Hours are Sunday to Thursday 11am to 1am; Friday and Saturday 11am to 3am. Happy hour is daily 11am to 7:30pm (happy hour begins earlier, but the discount is not as great as other places). #B1–01/06 Orchard Hotel Shopping Arcade, 442 Orchard Rd. ℂ **65/6735-0400.**

The Next Page　Few bars stand out for ambience like the Next Page, which is a freaky Chinese dream in an old Singaporean shophouse. Creep through the *pintu pagar* front door into the main room, its old walls of crumbling stucco washed in sexy Chinese red and lanterns glowing crimson in the air shaft rising above the island bar. The crowd is mainly young professionals who by late night have been known to dance on the bar (and not only on weekends). The back has a bit more space for seating, darts, and a pool table. A small snack menu is available. Open daily 3pm to 3am. Happy hour daily 3 to 9pm. 17 Mohamed Sultan Rd. ℂ **65/6235-6967.**

No. 5　Down Peranakan Place are a few bars, one of which is No. 5, a cool, dark place just dripping with Southeast Asian ambience, from its old shophouse exterior to its partially crumbling interior walls hung with rich woodcarvings. The hardwood floors and beamed ceilings are complemented by seating areas cozied with Oriental carpets and kilim throw pillows. Upstairs is more conventional table-and-chair seating. The glow of the skylighted air shaft and the whirring fans above make this an ideal place to stop for a cool drink on a hot afternoon. In the evenings, be prepared for a lively mix of people. Open Monday to Thursday noon to 2am, Friday and Saturday noon to 3am, Sunday 5pm to 2am. Happy hour daily noon to 9pm. 5 Emerald Hill. ℂ **65/6732-0818.**

MICROBREWERIES

Brewerkz　Brewerkz, with outside seating along the river and an airy contemporary style inside—like a giant IKEA warehouse built around brewing kettles and copper pipes—brews the best house beer in Singapore. The bar menu features five tasty brew selections from recipes created by their English brew master: Nut Brown Ale, Red Ale, Wiesen, Bitter, and Indian Pale Ale (which, by the way, has the highest alcohol content). Their American cuisine lunch, dinner, and snack menu is also very good—I recommend planning a meal here as well. Open Sunday to Thursday 5pm to 1am, Friday and Saturday 5pm to 3am. Happy hour is held daily 3 to 9pm with two-for-one beers. #01–05 Riverside Point, 30 Merchant Rd. ⒸⒸ **65/6438-7438.**

JAZZ BARS

Harry's Bar The official after-work drink stop for finance professionals from nearby Shenton Way, Harry's biggest claim to fame is that it was bank-buster Nick Leeson's favorite bar. But don't let the power ties put you off. Harry's is a cool place, from airy riverside seating, to cozy tables next to the stage. Harry's is known for its live jazz and R&B music, which is always good. Of all the choices along Boat Quay, Harry's remains the classiest; and even though it's also the most popular, you can usually get a seat. Upstairs, the wine bar is very laid-back, with plush sofas and dimly lit seating areas. Recently, Harry's outposts have been opening all over the city: **Harry's @ Esplanade,** Esplanade Mall #01–05/07, 8 Raffles Ave. (Ⓒ **65/6334-0132**), **Harry's @ HarbourFront,** HarbourFront Centre, #0–1-64 Maritime Square (Ⓒ **65/6271-8234**), **Harry's @ Orchard,** Orchard Towers, #01–05 and #02–08/09, 1 Claymore Dr. (Ⓒ **65/6736-7330**), **Harry's @ Holland V,** Holland Village, 27 Lorong Mambong (Ⓒ **65/6467-4222**), and two branches at **Changi Airport.** Open Sunday to Thursday 11am to 1am, Friday and Saturday 11am to 2am. Happy hour daily 11am to 9pm. 28 Boat Quay. Ⓒ **65/6538-3029.**

Jazz@Southbridge This is really the only true jazz bar in Singapore. Most other "jazz" joints mix in a bit of blues and rock to attract a wider audience. But owner Eddie Chan wouldn't allow such a thing! The resident band is fun and very good. The place gets crowded and smoky, but people are friendly, especially if you want to talk about music. When visiting performers play, a door cover is charged. Open Tuesday to Sunday from 5:30pm until 1am (sometimes later). 82B Boat Quay. Ⓒ **65/6327-4671.**

Raffles Bar & Billiards Talk about a place rich with the kind of elegance only history can provide. Raffles Bar & Billiards began as a bar in 1896 and over the decades has been transformed to perform various functions as the hotel's needs dictated. In its early days, legend has it that a patron shot the last tiger in Singapore under a pool table here. Whether or not the tiger part is true, one of its two billiards tables is an original piece, still in use after 100 years. In fact, many of the fixtures and furniture here are original Raffles antiques, including the lights above the billiards tables and the scoreboards, and are marked with small brass placards. In the evenings, a jazzy little trio shakes the ghosts out of the rafters, while the well-heeled lounge around enjoying single malts, cognacs, coffee, port, champagne, chocolates, and imported cigars. Expect to drop a small fortune. Open daily 11:30am to 12:30am. Raffles Hotel, 1 Beach Rd. Ⓒ **65/6331-1746.**

CLUBS

Bar None In Singapore's trendy club scene, nightclubs have been known to come and go. Bar None is one place that has enjoyed steady success, probably because they do a great job keeping up with their patrons' needs, with regularly scheduled theme parties and comedy nights. Resident band Jive Talking is a hot club band in town, playing a high-voltage mix of R&B, Top 40, and rock. Be prepared to queue up on weekends. On some Mondays, Bar None opens its stage to local indie bands. Hours are Tuesday to Sunday 7pm to 3am, Monday 7pm to 2am. Happy hour is 7 to 9pm. Basement Marriott Hotel, 320 Orchard Rd. ⓒ **65/6831-4656**. Cover Fri S$25 men (US$16/£8.25), S$20 women (US$13/£6.60), includes 1 drink.

DBL O   Singapore's cheapest club has S$12 (US$7.70/£6.95) jugs of bottom-shelf mixed drinks and draft beer all night, every night (a jug is about four drinks). A cavernous place with a light-up wall and Top 40 dance music, it's very popular with those who want to hang out without the pretenses of some of the newer fashion-victim clubs. Two bars within the club have a garden terrace and pool tables. Open Wednesday to Friday 8pm to 3am and Saturdays 8pm to 4am. 11 Unity St. #01–24 Robertson Walk. ⓒ **65/6735-2008**. Cover charges vary for men and women depending on the night from S$15 to S$25 (US$9.60–US$16/£4.95–£8.25).

Ministry of Sound   Sister club to London's famed Ministry of Sound, this one is sprawling, at 3,700 sq. m (40,000 sq. ft). Importing the best DJs from the global clubbing scene, MoS has hot music, an audio system that is one of the best in Singapore, and very trippy digital projections and visual effects around the club. Too bad on weekends the queue is horribly long to get inside and the service staff is too few to cater to the crowds. Go if you must. Open Wednesday to Saturday from 9pm to 4am; happy hours vary from night to night. Block C, The Cannery, River Valley Road, #01 (02–07) and #02 (01–08), Clarke Quay. ⓒ **65/6235-2292**. Cover charges range from S$12 to S$25 (US$7.70–US$16/ £6.95–£8.25) depending on your gender, the night of the week, and the time of your arrival.

Thumper   Every time I update this book, there's a New Hot Spot, which is full of spark, but by the time I make my next update it has either fallen asleep or is gone. Thumper's held ground, though, with a steady stream of high-profile celebs keeping it hip. It does have one timeless feature, a really nice outdoor terrace for happy hour cocktails as the sun sets over Scotts Road. In the early evenings, you'll hear live soul singers, and later in the evening a live funk band gets the dance floor moving. Open Monday and Tuesday 6pm to 2am, Wednesday and Thursday 6pm to 3am, and Friday and Saturday 6pm to 4am. There is a happy hour daily 11am to 9pm. Goodwood Park Hotel, 22 Scotts Rd. ⓒ **65/6735-0827**. Cover charge varies, includes 1 drink.

Top Ten   It's the most notoriously sleazy joint in Singapore and throws a wild party every night of the week. The huge space is like an auditorium, with multilevel loungey seating areas looking down onto one of Singapore's best soundstages and dance floors. A cover band plays three sets of pop and rock 7 days a week, but people don't come here for the decor or the music: Top Ten is a pickup joint for Thai working girls. Other clubs in the building, called Orchard Towers, host ladies from other parts of the region, which is how the building got its unofficial name . . . Four Floors of Whores. No joke. Open daily 5pm to 3am with a happy hour daily 9 to 11pm. #04–35/36 Orchard Towers, 400 Orchard Rd. ⓒ **65/6732-3077**. Cover Fri–Sat S$18 (US$12/£5.95), includes 1 drink.

Zouk/Phuture/Velvet Underground   Singapore's first innovative danceteria, Zouk introduced the city to house music, which throbs nightly in its cavernous disco, comprising three warehouses joined together. They play the best in modern music, so even if you're not much of a groover you can still have fun watching the party from the many levels that tower above the dance floor. If you need a bit more intimacy in your nightlife, Velvet Underground (VU), within the Zouk complex, drips in red velvet and soft lighting—a good complement to the more soulful sounds spinning here. The newer addition to Zouk, Phuture, draws a younger, more hip-hop–loving crowd than VU. Including the outdoor wine bar, Zouk is your one-stop shop for a party; in

Singapore, this place is legendary. All clubs are open daily 6pm to 3am. 17 Jiak Kim St. ℂ 65/6738-2988. Cover charges vary. Pay the highest cover of the three clubs (S$12–S$28/US$7.70–US$18/£3.95–£9.25) and freely hop between clubs; otherwise, pay extra moving from one to the next.

GAY NIGHTSPOTS

Singapore's gay clubbing scene is alive and well but still very underground. Bars come and go, so to get the absolute latest happenings you'll have to go beyond mainstream media. The Web has listings at **www.utopia-asia.com** where you'll find the best updated information about the most recent parties and hangouts. For the latest info, I'd recommend one of the chat rooms suggested at the address above, and talk to the experts. Velvet Underground, part of the Zouk complex (see above), welcomes a mixed clientele of gays, lesbians, and straight folks.

WINE BARS

Beaujolais   This little gem, in a shophouse built on a hill, is tiny, but its charm makes it a favorite for loyal regulars. Two tables outside (on the Five-Foot-Way, which serves more as a patio than a sidewalk) and two tables inside don't seem like much room, but there's more seating upstairs. They believe that wine should be affordable, and so their many labels tend to be more moderately priced per glass and bottle. Hours are Monday to Friday 11am to 1am and Saturday and Sunday 6pm to midnight; happy hours runs from opening until 9pm. 1 Ann Siang Hill. ℂ 65/6224-2227.

Que Pasa   One of the more mellow stops along Peranakan Place, this little wine bar serves up a collection of some 70 to 100 labels with plenty of atmosphere and a nice central location. It's another bar in a shophouse, but this one has as its centerpiece a very unusual winding stairway up the air shaft to the level above. Wine bottles and artwork line the walls. In the front you can order tapas and cigars. The upstairs VIP club looks and feels like a formal living room, complete with wing chairs and board games. Hours are Sunday to Thursday 6pm to 2am, Friday and Saturday 6pm to 3am. 7 Emerald Hill. ℂ 65/6235-6626.

3 The Performing Arts

Professional and amateur theater companies, dance troupes, opera companies, and musical groups offer a wide variety of not only Asian performances, but Western as well. Broadway road shows don't stop in San Francisco, where the road ends, but continue on to include Singapore in their itineraries, and international stars like Domingo, Pavarotti, Yo Yo Ma, Wynton Marsalis, and Michael Jackson have come to town. International stars make up only a small portion of the performance scene, though. Singapore theater comprises four distinct language groups—English, Chinese, Malay, and Tamil—and each maintains its own voice and culture.

CLASSICAL PERFORMANCES

The **Singapore Symphony Orchestra** performs regularly in its new home at Esplanade—Theatres On the Bay, with regular special guest appearances by international celebrities. For information about the orchestra, check out www.sso.org.sg, or for performance dates see www.esplanade.com.

The **Singapore Lyric Opera,** Stamford Arts Centre, 155 Waterloo St. #03–06 (ℂ **65/6336-1929**), also appears regularly. Call for upcoming schedules, or call Sistic (ℂ **65/6348-5555**).

The **Singapore Chinese Orchestra,** the only professional Chinese orchestra in Singapore, has won several awards for its classic Chinese interpretations. They perform every 2 weeks at a variety of venues (including outdoor concerts at the Botanic Gardens). Contact them c/o People's Association, Block B, Room 5, No. 9 Stadium Link (℃ **65/6440-3839;** www.sco.com.sg). Buy tickets through Sistic.

THEATER

Most international companies will perform at the new **Esplanade—Theatres On the Bay** (1 Esplanade Dr., 10-min. walk from City Hall MRT; ℃ **65/6828-8222;** www.esplanade.com). Smaller shows are staged at the **Victoria Concert Hall,** 2nd floor Victoria Memorial Hall, 11 Empress Place (℃ **65/6338-6125**). **Sistic** (℃ **65/6348-5555**) handles bookings for both venues.

A few local companies are quite noteworthy. Granted, theater is new to Singaporeans; however, many local playwrights have emerged to capture life here (with some hilarious interpretations), using local stage talents. **ACTION Theatre,** 42 Waterloo St. (℃ **65/6837-0842**), is one of the best companies to capture poignant and funny social themes, many of which cross cultural barriers. **The Necessary Stage,** 278 Marine Parade Rd., #B1–02 Marine Parade Community Building (℃ **65/6440-8115**), blazed trails for the local performing arts scene after staging productions that touched tender nerves for the community, including a startlingly frank monologue by the first Singaporean to publicly declare his struggle with AIDS. The **Singapore Repertory Theatre,** DBS Arts Centre, 20 Merbau Rd., Robertson Quay (℃ **65/6733-0005**), is another company to watch; in recent years they've staged local productions of perennial favorites like *The Glass Menagerie* and *Little Shop of Horrors.* Also check out the many events at the **Substation,** 45 Armenian St. (℃ **65/6337-7800;** www.substation.org), which offers its space to many smaller troupes, plus performance artists.

CULTURAL SHOWS

Once upon a time, **Cantonese opera** could be seen under tents on street corners throughout the city. These days, local and visiting companies still perform, but very sporadically. For a performance you can count on, the **Chinese Theatre Circle,** 5 Smith St. (℃ **65/6323-4862**), has a 2-hour show on Fridays and Saturdays with excerpts from the most famous and beloved tales and explanations of the craft. Come at 7pm for the show with "dinner" (chicken nuggets, really; tickets are S$35/US$22/£12) or at 8pm to catch the last half with tea only (S$20/US$13/£6.60).

If you're looking for something relevant to Malay culture, **Malay Village,** 39 Geylang Serai (℃ **65/6748-4700**), has a program on weekends that I think is highly commendable. Every Saturday they perform the *Kuda Kepang,* a traditional dance from Johor in southern Malaysia. Featuring male dancers on wooden horses, this long performance is well worth the wait. During the grand finale, the dancers walk on glass, eat glass, and tear coconuts with their teeth. It's all real, and highly recommended.

9

Planning Your Trip to Malaysia

Compared with spicy Thailand to the north and cosmopolitan Singapore to the south, Malaysia is a relative secret to many from the West, and most travelers to Southeast Asia skip over it, opting for more heavily traversed routes.

Boy, are they missing out. Those who venture here wander through streets awash with international influences from colonial times and trek through mysterious rainforests and caves, sometimes without another tourist in sight. They relax peacefully under palms on lazy white beaches that fade into blue, blue waters. They spy the bright colors of batik sarongs hanging to dry in the breeze. They hear the melodic drone of the Muslim call to prayer seeping from exotic mosques. They taste culinary masterpieces served in modest local shops—from Malay with its deep mellow spices to succulent seafood punctuated by brilliant chili sauces. In Malaysia, I'm always thrilled to witness life without the distracting glare of the tourism industry, and I leave impressed by how accessible Malaysia is to outsiders while remaining true to its heritage.

Malaysia just doesn't get the tourism press it deserves, but it's not because foreign travelers aren't welcome. True, the Malaysian Tourism Board has almost no international advertising campaign—and you'll be hard-pressed to get any useful information out of them—but everyone from government officials in Kuala Lumpur to boat hands in Penang seems delighted to see the smiling face of a traveler who has discovered just how beautiful their country is.

Chapter 10 covers the major destinations of peninsular Malaysia. We begin with the country's capital, Kuala Lumpur (KL), then tour the peninsula's west coast—the cities of Johor Bahru, Malacca (Melaka), the hill resorts at Cameron and Genting Highlands, plus islands like the popular Penang, secluded Pangkor, and luxurious Langkawi. Chapter 11 takes you up the east coast of the peninsula, through resort areas in Kuantan, Cherating, and Terengganu, plus the small and charming Tioman and Redang Islands. My coverage also includes Taman Negara National Park, peninsular Malaysia's largest national forest. Finally, in chapter 12, we cross the South China Sea to the island of Borneo, where the Malaysian states of Sarawak and Sabah feature Malaysia's most impressive forests as well as unique and diverse cultures.

Malaysia is accessible to the rest of the world through its international airport in Kuala Lumpur. Or if you want to hop from another country in the region, daily flights to Malaysia's many smaller airports give you access to all parts of the country, and you can also travel by car, bus, or train from Singapore or Thailand. In this section, I'll run through your options and get you started.

1 Malaysia's Regions in Brief

Malaysia's territory covers peninsular Malaysia—bordering Thailand in the north just across from Singapore in the south—and two states on the island of Borneo, Sabah and Sarawak, approximately 240km (150 miles) east across the South China Sea. All 13 of its states total 329,749 sq. km (127,316 sq. miles) of land. Of this area Peninsular Malaysia makes up about 132,149 sq. km (51,023 sq. miles) and contains 11 of Malaysia's 13 states: Kedah, Perlis, Penang, and Perak are in the northwest; Kelantan and Terengganu are in the northeast; Selangor, Negeri Sembilan, and Melaka are about midway down the peninsula on the western side; Pahang, along the east coast, sprawls inward to cover most of the central area (which is mostly forest preserve); and Johor covers the entire southern tip from east to west, with two vehicular causeways linking it to Singapore, just over the Strait of Johor. Kuala Lumpur, the nation's capital, appears on a map to be located in the center of the state of Selangor, but it is actually a federal district similar to Washington, D.C., in the United States.

On Borneo, Sarawak and Sabah share the landmass with Indonesia's Kalimantan. Also sharing the island, in a tiny nook on the Sarawak coast, is the tiny oil-rich Sultanate of Brunei Darussalam.

Back on the peninsula, the major cities can be found closer to the coastline, many having built on old trade or mining settlements, usually near one of Malaysia's many rivers.

THE LAY OF THE LAND

Tropical evergreen forests, estimated to be some of the oldest in the world, cover more than 70% of Malaysia. The country's diverse terrain allows for a range of forest types, such as montane forests, sparsely wooded tangles at higher elevations; lowland forests, the dense tropical jungle type; mangrove forests along the waters' edge; and peat swamp forests along the waterways. On the peninsula, three national forests—Taman Negara (or "National Forest") and Kenong Rimba Park, both inland, and Endau Rompin National Park, located toward the southern end of the peninsula—are the most convenient to get to, especially Taman Negara, a short trip from KL, which has well-developed facilities and regular guided nature tours. Sabah and Sarawak step up the adventure quotient with countless rainforests, peculiar wildlife, and fascinating indigenous cultures.

Malaysia is surrounded by the South China Sea on the east coast and the Strait of Malacca on the west, and the waters off the peninsula vary in terms of sea life (and beach life). The waters off the east coast house a living coral reef, good waters, and gorgeous tropical beaches, while more southerly parts host beach resort areas. By way of contrast, the surf in southern portions of the Strait of Malacca is choppy

---

Tips Abbreviating Malaysia

The first tip here is that people are always abbreviating Kuala Lumpur to KL. Okay, that's pretty obvious. But these people will abbreviate everything else they can get away with. So, Johor Bahru becomes JB, Kota Bharu KB, Kota Kinabalu KK—you get the picture. Malaysia itself is often shortened to M'sia and Singapore to S'pore. To make it easier for you, the only shortened version I've used in this book is KL.

and cloudy from shipping traffic—hardly ideal for diving or for the perfect Bali Hai vacation. But once you get as far north as Penang, the waters become beautiful again. Meanwhile, the sea coast of Sabah and Sarawak counts numerous resort areas that are ideal for beach vacationing and scuba diving.

2 Visitor Information

The **Malaysia Tourism Board (MTB)** (www.tourismmalaysia.gov.my) can provide some information by way of pamphlets and advice before your trip, but keep in mind they are not as sophisticated as the Singapore Tourism Board. Much of the information they provide is vague, broad-stroke descriptions with few concrete details that are useful for the traveler—a lot of it quite outdated.

Within Malaysia, each state or tourist destination has its own tourism board that operates a website and local offices for tourist information. These are your best bets, as they have on-the-ground knowledge that's more current. For each destination, I have provided websites, telephone contacts, and locations of information offices.

3 Entry Requirements & Customs

ENTRY REQUIREMENTS

To enter the country you must have a valid passport. Citizens of the United States do not need visas for tourism and business visits, and upon entry are granted a Social/Business Visit Pass good for up to 3 months. Citizens of Canada, Australia, New Zealand, and the United Kingdom can also enter the country without a visa and will be granted up to 30 days pass upon entry. For other countries, please consult the nearest Malaysian consulate before your trip for visa regulations. Also note: Travelers holding Israeli passports are not permitted to travel within Malaysia (likewise, Malaysians are forbidden from traveling to Israel).

For information on obtaining a passport please see "Passports" in the "Fast Facts: Singapore" section, in chapter 3.

If you are arriving from an area in which yellow fever has been reported, you will be required to show proof of yellow fever vaccination. Contact your nearest MTB office to research the specific areas that fall into this category.

CUSTOMS REGULATIONS

With regard to currency, you can bring into the country as many foreign currency notes or traveler's checks as you please, but you are not allowed to leave the country with more foreign currency or traveler's checks than you had when you arrived.

Social visitors can enter Malaysia with 1 liter of hard alcohol and 1 carton of cigarettes without paying duty—anything over that amount is subject to local taxes. Prohibited items include firearms and ammunition, daggers and knives, and pornographic materials. Be advised that, similar to Singapore, Malaysia enforces a very strict drug-abuse policy that includes the death sentence for convicted drug traffickers.

Peninsular Malaysia

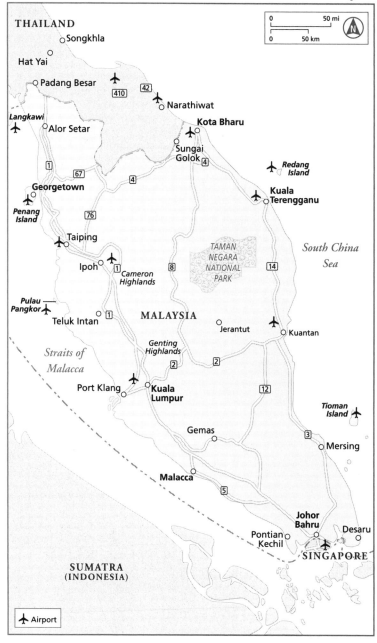

Money

CURRENCY

Malaysia's currency is the **Malaysian ringgit.** Prices are marked as RM (a designation I've used throughout this book). Notes are issued in denominations of RM1, RM2, RM5, RM10, RM20, RM50, RM100, RM500, and RM1,000. One ringgit is equal to 100 sen. Coins come in denominations of 1, 5, 10, 20, and 50 sen, and there's also a 1-ringgit coin.

In 2005 Malaysia ended a 7-year peg of the ringgit at RM3.80 to US$1. Now, the country uses a managed float system that measures the currency against a basket of several major currencies. At the time of writing, 1 ringgit was worth US28¢ and UK14p—this is the conversion rate I've used for this guide.

Currency can be changed at banks and hotels, but you'll get a more favorable rate if you go to one of the money-changers that seem to be everywhere; in shopping centers, in little lanes, and in small stores—just look for signs. They are often men in tiny booths with a lit display on the wall behind them showing the exchange rate. All major currencies are generally accepted, and there is never a problem with the U.S. dollar.

ATMs

Kuala Lumpur, Penang, and Johor Bahru have quite a few automated teller machines (ATMs) scattered around, but they are few and far between in the smaller towns and nonexistent on smaller islands and remote beach areas. In addition, some ATMs do not accept credit cards or debit cards from your home bank. I have found that debit cards on the MasterCard/Cirrus or Visa/Plus networks are almost always accepted at **Maybank,** with at least one location in every major town. Cash is dispensed in ringgit deducted from your account at the day's rate.

CREDIT CARDS

Credit cards are widely accepted at hotels and restaurants, and at many shops as well. Most popular are American Express, MasterCard, and Visa. Some banks may

Malaysian Ringgit Conversion Chart

RM	US$	UK£	euro€
0.10	0.03	0.01	0.02
0.20	0.06	0.03	0.04
0.50	0.14	0.07	0.11
1.00	0.28	0.14	0.21
2.00	0.56	0.29	0.43
5.00	1.41	0.72	1.07
10.00	2.82	1.45	2.15
20.00	5.64	2.89	4.29
50.00	14.10	7.23	10.73
100.00	28.20	14.46	21.45
500.00	141.00	72.33	107.25
1,000.00	282.00	144.66	214.49

East Malaysia

also be willing to advance cash against your credit card, but you have to ask around because this service is not available everywhere.

In Malaysia, to report a lost or stolen card, call **American Express** at its head office in Kuala Lumpur (☎ **03/2161-4000**); for **MasterCard** call ☎ **800/804-594;** and for **Visa** call ☎ **800/800-159.** Both numbers are toll-free from anywhere in the country. For more on credit cards and what to do if your wallet gets stolen, see Chapter 3, "Planning Your Trip to Singapore."

TRAVELER'S CHECKS

Generally, travelers to Malaysia will never go wrong with American Express and Thomas Cook traveler's checks, which can be cashed at banks, hotels, and licensed money changers. Unfortunately, they are often not accepted at smaller shops. Even in some big restaurants and department stores, many cashiers don't know how to process these checks, which might lead to a long and frustrating wait. For more on traveler's checks see chapter 3.

What Things Cost in Kuala Lumpur	RM	US$	UK£
Taxi from the airport to city center	67.40–180.40	18.90–50.50	9.40–25.30
Local telephone call (3 min.)	0.20	0.06	0.03
Double room at an expensive hotel (J. W. Marriott)	700.00	196.00	98.00
Double room at a moderate hotel (Meliá Kuala Lumpur)	400.00	112.00	56.00
Double room at an inexpensive hotel (Swiss-Inn)	155.00	43.40	21.70
Dinner for one at an expensive restaurant (Scalini's)	70.00–100.00	19.60–28.00	9.80–14.00
Dinner for one at a moderate restaurant (Restoran Saray)	50.00–70.00	14.00–19.60	7.00–9.80
Dinner for one at an inexpensive restaurant (Top Hat)	40.00	11.20	5.60
Glass of beer	15.00–20.00	4.20–5.60	2.10–2.80
Coca-Cola	2.00–6.00	0.60–1.70	0.30–0.80
Cup of coffee at common coffee shop	1.50	0.40	0.20
Cup of coffee in a hotel	6.00	1.70	0.80
Roll of 36-exposure color film	15.00	4.20	2.10
Admission to the National Museum	2.00	0.60	0.30
Movie ticket	10.00	2.80	1.40

5 When to Go

There are **two peak seasons** in Malaysia, one in winter and another in summer. The peak winter tourist season falls roughly from the beginning of December to the end of January, covering the major winter holidays—Christmas, New Year's Day, Chinese New Year. Hari Raya Puasa, celebrating the end of Ramadan, shifts dates from year to year. If you plan to travel to Malaysia around October, I highly recommend calling MTB to find out exactly when this holiday will fall.

Singapore's school holidays occur from mid-May through to the end of June, and again during November and December, when families are likely to flock to Malaysia's seaside resorts, particularly the budget and mid-priced properties. I hate to say it, but I've heard numerous complaints about resort holidays that have become nightmares when guests have to wrestle to get to the breakfast buffet and must suffer screaming children around the pool. Malaysia's schoolchildren are cut loose for about 1 to 2 weeks in March, May, and August with a longer break from mid-November through December.

The peak summer season falls in the months of June, July, and August, and can last into mid-September. During this period hotels are booked solid with families from the Middle East as this is school holiday season for many of the region's countries. After September it's quiet again until December. Both seasons experience approximately equal tourist traffic, but in summer months that traffic may ebb and flow.

CLIMATE

Climate considerations will play a role in your plans. If you want to visit any of the east coast resort areas, the low season is between November and March, when the monsoon tides make the water too choppy for watersports and beach activities. During this time many island resorts will close. On the west coast, the rainy season is from April through May, and again from October through November.

The temperature is basically static year-round. Daily averages range from 67°F to 90°F (21°C–32°C). Temperatures in the hill resorts get a little cooler, averaging 67°F (21°C) during the day, 50°F (10°C) at night.

HOLIDAYS

During Malaysia's official public holidays, expect government offices to be closed, as well as some shops and restaurants, depending on the ethnicity of the shop owner or restaurant owner. During **Hari Raya Puasa** and **Chinese New Year** you can expect many shop and restaurant closings. However, look out for special sales and celebrations. Also count on public parks, shopping malls, and beaches to be more crowded during public holidays, as locals will be taking advantage of their time off.

Official public holidays fall as follows: New Year's Day (Jan 1), Chinese New Year (Feb 7–8, 2008), Prophet Muhammad's Birthday (Mar), Labor Day (May 1); Wesak Day (May 1, 2007; May 19, 2008), King's Birthday (June 2); National Day (Aug 31), Hari Raya Aidil Fitri (also called Hari Raya Puasa, Oct 13–14, 2007; Oct 2–3, 2008), Deepavali (Nov 8, 2007; Oct 27, 2008), Hari Raya Haji (Dec 20–21, 2007; Dec 9–10, 2008) and Christmas (Dec 25). *Note:* Please confirm all 2008 dates listed above before you plan your trip; at the time of writing, dates beyond 2007 could not be confirmed by any authority. In addition, each state has a public holiday to celebrate the birthday of the state sultan.

6 Travel Insurance

See chapter 3, "Planning Your Trip to Singapore," for information about trip-cancellation insurance, medical insurance, and lost-luggage insurance.

7 Health & Safety

STAYING HEALTHY

The **tap water** in KL is supposedly potable, but I don't recommend drinking it—in fact, I don't recommend drinking tap water anywhere in Malaysia. Bottled water is inexpensive enough and readily available at convenience stores and food stalls. Food prepared in hawker centers is generally safe—I have yet to experience trouble and I'll eat almost anywhere. If you buy fresh fruit, wash it well with bottled water and carefully peel the skin off before eating it.

Malaria has not been a major threat in most parts of Malaysia, even Malaysian Borneo. **Dengue fever,** on the other hand, which is also carried by mosquitoes, remains a constant threat in most areas, especially rural parts. Dengue, if left untreated, can cause fatal internal hemorrhaging, so if you come down with a sudden fever or skin rash, consult a physician immediately. There are no prophylactic treatments for dengue; the best protection is to wear plenty of insect repellent—the breed of mosquito that

Tips Travel Warning

Under U.S. law, insurance companies are not required to cover any medical expenses incurred in countries on the **State Department's Travel Advisory List,** even if their policies indicate they will cover out-of-country medical expenses. Some supplemental carriers (such as the ones listed in chapter 3) will sell travelers coverage for these areas. You can view the Travel Advisory List at http://travel.state.gov.

carries dengue bites during the day as opposed to malaria-carrying ones that bite at night. Choose a product that contains DEET or is specifically formulated to be effective in the Tropics.

In 2003, SARS seemed to skip right over Malaysia, but **Avian Influenza,** or Bird Flu, has found its way here, particularly in the northern state of Kelantan. The United States Centers for Disease Control (CDC) advises travelers to Malaysia to avoid contact with live or raw poultry.

STAYING SAFE

Malaysia has been having a terrible problem with thievery. "Snatch thieves" are becoming bolder and bolder, riding on motorcycles through heavily populated areas in KL, Johor Bahru, and other cities, snatching handbags from women's shoulders. Some victims have been dragged and seriously injured. When you're out, don't wear your handbag on your side that's facing the street, or better yet, don't carry a handbag at all.

The first thing I do when I check into a hotel is put my passport, international tickets, extra cash, and traveler's checks, plus any credit or ATM card I do not have immediate plans to use, straight into the safe, either in my room or behind the hotel's front desk.

Be careful when traveling on overnight trains and buses where there are great opportunities for theft (many times by fellow tourists, believe it or not). Keep your valuables close to you as you sleep.

For further health and insurance and safety information, see chapter 3.

8 Specialized Travel Resources

For additional, generalized information for travelers with special needs, please see chapter 3, "Planning Your Trip to Singapore."

TRAVELERS WITH DISABILITIES

Traveling in developing countries is a daunting task for disabled individuals, and Malaysia is no exception. While Malaysian Airlines and some luxury hotels have facilities for guests in wheelchairs, most every attraction, shopping mall, restaurant, and mode of public transportation provide no accessibility at all. In urban centers, sidewalks are either non-existent, buckled, or cluttered. At the time of writing there were no inbound tour operators specializing in tours for travelers with disabilities.

GAY & LESBIAN TRAVELERS

In conservative Malaysia, homosexuality is illegal, though the law is never enforced with regards to tourists. To find out current, destination-specific travel advice for gays and lesbians, visit www.utopia-asia.com.

SENIOR TRAVEL

Seniors have few discounts in Malaysia, except at some attractions, where they might pay a bit less—but it's usually such a small discount that it's hardly worth pulling out your passport. However, Malaysia offers great incentives to lure potential retirees to the country; check out www.retiringinmalaysia.com for incentives on purchasing a house, car, and education, as well as details on tax breaks.

WOMEN TRAVELERS

As a woman traveler who has been to all corners of Malaysia and back again by myself, I can honestly say I have never once felt threatened. However, my travel philosophy is "When in Rome . . ." Like Malay women, I wear long skirts or pants, and shirts that cover the tops of my arms. I always carry a scarf in my bag in case etiquette requires I cover my head. I find many doors open to me when the locals feel I am respectful of their ways.

JEWISH TRAVELERS

Travelers with Israeli passports are not permitted to enter Malaysia. If you are of Jewish heritage and carry a passport from a country other than Israel, I recommend you downplay your heritage. Former prime minister Dr. Mahathir Mohammed has been known to make anti-Semitic comments in pubic, sentiments that unfortunately carry over into the general population.

ECOTOURISM

Malaysia's rainforests are disappearing at an alarming rate thanks to logging and clearing, and its coral reefs are beginning to show signs of abuse. Unfortunately these natural wonders are some of the country's best attractions. The companies I have listed in this book, especially those in Sabah and Sarawak, operate with a sensitivity to the environment and its preservation.

9 Getting There

BY PLANE

Malaysia has six international airports—at Kuala Lumpur, Penang, Langkawi, Kota Kinabalu, Kuching, and Johor Bahru—and 14 domestic airports at locations that include Kota Bharu, Kuantan, and Kuala Terengganu. Specific airport information is listed with coverage of each city.

A passenger service charge, or **airport departure tax,** is levied on all flights. A tax of RM5 ($1.40/70p) for domestic flights and RM40 ($11/£5.60) for international flights is usually included in your ticket price.

Few Western carriers fly directly to Malaysia. If **Malaysian Airlines (www. malaysiaairlines.com)** does not have suitable routes from your home country, you'll have to contact another airline to work out a route that connects. I have found Malaysia Airlines service to be of a very good standard, not to mention that they have possibly the lowest rates to Southeast Asia from North American destinations.

From the United States, Malaysia Airlines (© 800/552-9264) flies from Los Angeles and Newark/NYC.

From Canada, North American carriers will have to connect with a Malaysian Airlines flight, either in East Asia or in Europe.

From the United Kingdom, Malaysia Airlines (© 0870/607-9090) flies from London's Heathrow Airport to KL.

From Australia, Malaysia Airlines (© 1300/655-324) flies directly to Kuala Lumpur from Perth, Adelaide, Brisbane, Sydney, and Melbourne.

From New Zealand, Malaysia Airlines (© 0800/777-747) flies to KL from Auckland.

BY TRAIN

FROM SINGAPORE The **Keretapi Tanah Melayu Berhad (KTM),** Malaysia's rail system, runs express and local trains that connect the cities along the west coast of Malaysia with Singapore to the south and Thailand to the north. Trains depart daily from the **Singapore Railway Station** (✆ **65/6222-5165**) on Keppel Road in Tanjong Pagar, not far from the city center. Trains to Kuala Lumpur depart daily for fares from S$34–S$68 (US$9.50–US$19/£11–£22). The trip takes around 6 hours on an *ekspres* train—avoid the 10am mail train if you want to reach there before your next birthday). Kuala Lumpur's KL Sentral railway station (✆ **03/2267-1200**) is a 10-minute taxi ride from the center of town and is connected to the Putra LRT, KL Monorail city public transportation trains, and the Express Rail Link (ERL) to Kuala Lumpur International Airport (KLIA).

FROM THAILAND   KTM's international service departs from the **Hua Lamphong Railway Station** (✆ **662/223-7010** or 662/223-7020) in Bangkok, with operations to Hua Hin, Surat Thani, Nakhon Si Thammarat, and Hat Yai in Thailand's southern peninsula. The final stop in Malaysia is at Butterworth (Penang), so passage to KL will require you to catch a connecting train onward. The daily service departs at 3:15pm and takes approximately 22 hours from Bangkok to Butterworth. There is no first- or third-class service on this train, only air-conditioned second class; upper berth goes for about US$20, and lower is US$23.

For a fascinating journey from Thailand, you can catch the **Eastern & Orient Express (E&O)** (www.orient-express.com), which operates a route between Chiang Mai and Bangkok, Kuala Lumpur, and Singapore. Traveling in the luxurious style for which the Orient Express is renowned, you'll finish the entire journey in about 42 hours. Your entry-level cabin is Pullman, priced at approximately US$1,375 per person double occupancy, with State and Presidential Suite also available. All fares include meals on the train. Overseas reservations

for the E&O Express can be made through a travel agent or, from the United States and Canada call on the east coast ✆ **1631/847-3716** and on the west coast ✆ **1480/595-7602,** from Australia ✆ **1800/000-395,** and from the United Kingdom ✆ **0845/077-2222.** From Singapore, Malaysia, and Thailand contact the E&O office in Singapore at ✆ **65/6392-3500.**

BY BUS

From Singapore, there are many bus routes to Malaysia. If you want to travel on land, I personally prefer the bus over the train from Singapore to Kuala Lumpur. Executive coaches operated by **Grassland Express** have huge seats that recline, serve a box lunch on board, and show movies. They also have express buses to Malacca, Genting Highlands, Penang, and more. Call them in Singapore at ✆ **65/6292-1166.** Buses depart from Golden Mile Complex, 5001 Beach Rd. for the 5-hour trip (S$30–S$42/US$19–US$27/£9.90–£14 one-way).

Buses to Johor Bahru and Malacca can be picked up at the Ban Sen terminal at the corner of Queen and Arab streets. Call ✆ **65/6292-8149** for buses to Johor Bahru (S$2.40/US$1.50/80p) and ✆ **65/6293-5915** for buses to Malacca (S$11/US$7/£3.60).

From Thailand, you can grab a bus in either Bangkok or Hat Yai (in the southern part of the country) heading for Malaysia. I don't recommend the bus trip from Bangkok. It's just far too long a journey to be confined to a bus. You're better off taking the train. From Hat Yai, many buses leave regularly to northern Malaysian destinations, particularly Butterworth (Penang). Also be warned the U.S. Department of State does not recommend U.S. citizens travel in Southern Thailand due to terrorist violence.

BY TAXI (FROM SINGAPORE)

From the Johor-Singapore bus terminal at Queen and Arab streets, the **Singapore Johor Taxi Operators Association** (© **65/6296-7054**) can drive you to Johor Bahru for S$40 (US$26/£13).

BY CAR

Major international car rental agencies operating in Singapore will rent cars that you can take over the causeway to Malaysia, but be prepared to pay a small fortune. They're much cheaper if you rent within the country. At Kuala Lumpur International Airport, find **Avis** at Counter B-16 at the arrival hall in the main terminal (© **03/8776-4540**). There's another branch at the international airport in Penang (**04/643-9633**), or make a booking through www. avis.com.

10 Getting Around

The modernization of Malaysia has made travel here—whether it's by plane, train, bus, taxi, or self-driven car—easier and more convenient than ever. Malaysia Airlines has service to every major destination within the peninsula and East Malaysia, and now budget carrier AirAsia connects all major towns for cheap. Buses have a massive web of routes between every city and town. Train service up the western coast and out to the east provides even more options. And a unique travel offering—the outstation taxi—is available to and from every city on the peninsula. All the options make it convenient enough for you to plan to hop from city to city and not waste too much precious vacation time.

By and large, all the modes of transportation between cities are reasonably comfortable. Air travel can be the most costly of the alternatives, followed by outstation taxis, then buses and trains.

BY PLANE

Malaysia Airlines (© **1300/883-000;** www.malaysiaairlines.com) links from its hub in Kuala Lumpur to the cities of Johor Bahru, Kota Bharu, Kota Kinabalu, Kuala Terengganu, Kuantan, Kuching, Langkawi, Penang, and other smaller cities not covered in this volume. Malaysian Airline's national hot line (© **1300/ 883-000**) can be dialed from anywhere in the country. Individual airport information is provided in sections for each city that follows. One-way domestic fares can average RM100 to RM400 ($28–$112/ £14–£56).

AirAsia, a new budget airline, competes with Malaysia Airlines with incredibly affordable rates. It links all the country's major cities with fares that on average run from RM40 and up ($11/£5.60)—seriously. Call their KL office at © **03/8775-4000,** or visit their website at www.airasia.com.

Berjaya Air (© **03/2145-2828;** www. berjaya-air.com) operates a small fleet of aircraft that services the peninsula's island resorts, with flights that link KL to Pangkor, Langkawi, Tioman, and Redang islands, with another flight between Singapore and Tioman.

BY TRAIN

The **Keretapi Tanah Melayu Berhad (KTM)** provides train service throughout peninsular Malaysia. Trains run from north to south between the Thai border and Singapore, with stops between including Butterworth (Penang), Kuala Lumpur, and Johor Bahru. There is a second line that branches off at Gemas, midway between Johor Bahru and KL, and heads northeast to Tempas near Kota Bharu. Fares range from RM64 ($18/ £8.95) for first-class between Johor Bahru and KL, to RM85 ($24/£12) for first-class passage between Johor Bahru and

Butterworth. Train station information is provided for each city under individual city headings in the following chapters.

BY BUS

Malaysia's intercity coach system is extensive and inexpensive, but I don't really recommend it. With the exception of executive coach services between KL and Singapore, which are excellent, standard coaches get dirtier and dirtier each year, maintenance issues are a question mark, and road safety is a roll of the dice. Still, if you must, for each city covered, I've listed bus terminal locations, but scheduling information must be obtained from the bus company itself.

BY TAXI

You can take special hired cars, called **outstation taxis,** between every city and state on the peninsula. Rates depend on the distance you plan to travel. They are fixed and stated at the beginning of the trip but many times can be bargained down. In Kuala Lumpur, go to the second level of the Puduraya Bus Terminal to find cabs that will take you outside the city or call the **Kuala Lumpur Outstation Taxi Service Station** (© **03/2078-0213**). A taxi from KL to Malacca will cost you approximately RM140 ($39/£20), KL to Cameron Highlands RM220 ($62/£31), KL to Butterworth or Johor Bahru RM300 ($84/£42). Outstation taxi stand locations are included under each individual city heading in the following chapters. These cars are usually basic older-model sedans.

Also, within each of the smaller cities, feel free to negotiate with unmetered taxis for hourly, half-day, or daily rates. It's an excellent way to get around for sightseeing and shopping without transportation hassles. Hourly rates are anywhere from RM15 to RM25 ($4.20–$7/£2.10–£3.50).

BY CAR

The cities along the west coast of the peninsula are linked by the North–South Highway. There are rest areas with toilets, food outlets, and emergency telephones at intervals along the way. There is also a toll that varies depending on the distance you're traveling.

Driving along the east coast of Malaysia is actually much more pleasant than driving along the west coast. The highway is narrower and older, but it takes you through oil palm and rubber plantations, and the essence of *kampung* Malaysia permeates throughout. As you near villages you'll often have to slow down and swerve past cows and goats, which are really quite oblivious to oncoming traffic. You have to get very close to honk at them before they move.

The speed limit on highways is 110kmph (68 mph). On the minor highways the limit ranges from 70 to 90kmph (43–56 mph). Do not speed, as there are traffic police strategically situated around certain bends.

Distances between major towns are: from KL to Johor Bahru, 368km (221 miles); from KL to Malacca, 144km (86 miles); from KL to Kuantan, 259km (155 miles); from KL to Butterworth, 369km (221 miles); from Johor Bahru to Malacca, 224km (134 miles); from Johor Bahru to Kuantan, 325km (195 miles); from Johor Bahru to Mersing, 134km (80 miles); from Johor Bahru to Butterworth, 737km (442 miles).

To rent a car in Malaysia, you must produce a driver's license from your home country that shows you have been driving at least 2 years. There are desks for major car-rental services at the international airports in Kuala Lumpur and Penang, and additional outlets throughout the country (see individual city sections in later chapters for this information).

11 Tips on Accommodations, Dining & Shopping

TIPS ON ACCOMMODATIONS

Peak months of the year for hotels in western peninsular Malaysia are December through February and July through September. For the east coast, the busy times are July through September. You will need to make reservations well in advance to secure your room during these months.

TAXES & SERVICE CHARGES All the nonbudget hotels charge a 10% service charge and 5% government tax. As such, there is no need to tip. But bellhops still tend to be tipped at least RM2 (60¢/30p) per bag, and car jockeys or valets should be tipped at least RM4 ($1.10/55p) or more.

TIPS ON DINING

Malaysian food seems to get its origins from India's rich curries, influenced by Thailand's herbs and spices. You'll find delicious blends of coconut milk and curry, shrimp paste and chilies, accented by exotic flavors of galangal (similar to turmeric), lime, and lemon grass. Sometimes pungent, a few of the dishes have a deep flavor from fermented shrimp paste that is an acquired taste for Western palates. By and large, Malaysian food is delicious, but in multicultural Malaysia, so is the Chinese food, the Peranakan food, the Indian food—the list goes on. The Chinese brought their own flavors from their points of origin in the regions of southern China. Teochew, Cantonese, and Szechuan are all styles of Chinese cuisine that you'll find throughout the country. Peranakan food is unique to Malacca, Penang, and Singapore. The Peranakans, or "Straits Chinese," combined local ingredients with some traditional Chinese dishes to create an entirely new culinary form. And Indian food, both northern and southern, can be found in almost every city, particularly in the western part of the peninsula. And, of course, you'll find gorgeous fresh seafood almost everywhere.

I strongly recommend eating in a hawker stall when you can, especially in Penang, which is famous for its local cuisine.

Also, many Malaysians eat with their hands and off banana leaves when they are having *nasi padang* or *nasi kandar* (rice with mixed dishes). This is absolutely acceptable. If you choose to follow suit, wash your hands first and try to use your right hand because the left is considered unclean (traditionally, it's the hand used to wash after a visit to the toilet). Although almost all of the food you encounter in a hawker center will be safe for eating, it is advisable to go for freshly cooked hot or soupy dishes. Don't risk the precooked items.

Also, avoid having ice in your drink in the smaller towns because it might come from a dubious water supply. If you ask for water, either make sure it's boiled or buy mineral water.

TAXES & SERVICE CHARGES A 10% service charge and 5% government tax are levied in proper restaurants, but hawkers charge a flat price.

TIPS ON SHOPPING

Shopping is a huge attraction for tourists in Malaysia. In addition to modern fashions and electronics, there are great local handicrafts. In each city section in the following chapters, I've listed some great places to go for local shopping.

For **handicrafts,** prices can vary. There are many handicraft centers, such as Karyaneka, with outlets in cities all over the country, where goods can be priced a bit higher but where you are assured of good quality. Alternatively, you could hunt out bargains in markets and at roadside stores in little towns, which can be much more fun.

Batik is one of the most popular arts in Malaysia, and the fabric can be purchased just about anywhere in the country. Batik can be fashioned into outfits and scarves or purchased as sarongs. Another beautiful Malaysian textile craft is *songket* weaving. These beautiful cloths are woven with metallic threads. Sometimes *songket* cloth is patterned into modern clothing, but usually it is sold as sarongs.

Traditional woodcarvings have become popular collectors' items. Carvings by *orang asli* groups in peninsular Malaysia and by the indigenous tribes of Sabah and Sarawak have traditional uses in households or are employed for ceremonial purposes to cast off evil spirits and cure illness. They have become much sought after by tourists.

Malaysia's **pewter products** are famous. Selangor Pewter is the brand that seems to have the most outlets and representation. You can get anything from a picture frame to dinner sets.

Silver designs are very refined, and jewelry and fine home items are still made by local artisans, especially in the northern parts of the peninsula. In addition, craft items such as *wayang kulit* (shadow puppets) and *wau* (colorful Malay kites) make great gifts and souvenirs.

12 Etiquette & Customs

The mix of cultural influences in Malaysia is the result of centuries of immigration and trade with the outside world, particularly with Arab nations, China, and India. Early groups of incoming foreigners brought wealth from around the world, plus their own unique cultural heritages and religions. Further, once imported, each culture remained largely intact; that is, none have truly been homogenized. Traditional temples and churches exist side by side with mosques.

Likewise, **traditional art forms** of various cultures are still practiced in Malaysia, most notably in the areas of dance and performance art. Chinese opera, Indian dance, and Malay martial arts are all very popular cultural activities.

Silat, originating from a martial arts form (and still practiced as such by many), is a dance performed by men and women. Religious and cultural festivals are open for everyone to appreciate and enjoy. Unique arts and traditions of indigenous people distinguish Sabah and Sarawak from the rest of the country.

Traditional **Malaysian music** is very similar to Indonesian music. Heavy on rhythms, its constant drum beats underneath the light repetitive melodies of the stringed gamelan (no relation at all to the Indonesian metallophone gamelan, with its gongs and xylophones) will entrance you with its simple beauty.

Questions of etiquette in Malaysia are very similar to those in Singapore, so see chapter 3 for more information.

FAST FACTS: Malaysia

American Express The main office for American Express is located in KL at Menara Maybank, Ground Level banking hall, Jalan Perak (☏ **1300/886-688**).

Business Hours Banks are open from 10am to 3pm Monday through Friday and 9:30 to 11:30am on Saturday. Government offices are open from 8am to 12:45pm and 2 to 4:15pm Monday through Friday and from 8am to 12:45pm on Saturday. Smaller shops like provision stores may open as early as 6 or

6:30am and close as late as 9pm, especially those near the wet markets. Many such stores are closed on Saturday evenings and Sunday afternoons and are busiest before lunch. Other shops are open 9:30am to 7pm. Department stores and shops in malls tend to open later, about 10:30 or 11am until 8:30 or 9pm throughout the week. Note that in Kuala Terengganu and Kota Bharu the weekday runs from Saturday to Wednesday.

Dentists & Doctors All hotels and resorts have qualified physicians on call who speak English. These doctors will come directly to your room for treatment. If your condition is serious, he or she can help you to check in to a local hospital. Call ⓒ **999** for emergencies.

Drug Laws As in Singapore, the death sentence is mandatory for drug trafficking (defined as being in possession of more than 15g of heroin or morphine, 200g of marijuana or hashish, or 40g of cocaine). For lesser quantities you'll be thrown in jail for a very long time and flogged with a cane.

Electricity The voltage used in Malaysia is 220–240 volts AC (50 cycles). Three-point square plugs are used, so buy an adapter if you plan to bring any appliances. Also, many larger hotels can provide adapters upon request.

Embassies While in Malaysia, should you need to contact an official representative from your home country, the following contact information in Kuala Lumpur can help you out: United States Embassy, ⓒ **03/2168-5000**; Canadian High Commission, ⓒ **03/2718-3333**; Australian High Commission, ⓒ **03/2146-5555**; New Zealand High Commission, ⓒ **03/2078-2533**; and the British High Commission, ⓒ **03/2148-2122.**

Internet Service is available to all of the nation, and I have found Internet cafes in the most surprisingly remote places. Although the major international hotels will have access for their guests in the business center, charges can be very steep. I used to recommend Internet cafes in each city but found that these small places came and went overnight, making it impossible for me to provide accurate information for this book. Wherever you are, your best bet is to ask your concierge or the local tourism information office for the best places close by. Usage costs only about RM5 to RM10 ($1.40–$2.80/70p–£1.40).

Language The national language is Malay, or Bahasa Malaysia, although English is widely spoken. Chinese dialects and Tamil are also spoken.

Liquor Laws Liquor is sold in pubs and supermarkets in all big cities, or in provision stores. If you're going to an island, your resort will have limited alcohol selections, so you may wish to bring your own. In Terengganu and Kelantan, liquor is strictly limited to a handful of Chinese restaurants. Pubs and other nightspots should officially close by 1am nationwide, but there are places in KL that stay open later.

Newspapers & Magazines English-language papers the *New Straits Times, The Star, The Sun,* and *The Edge* can be bought in hotel lobbies and magazine stands. Of the local KL magazines, *Day & Night* has great listings and local "what's happening" information for travelers.

Postal Services Post office locations in each city covered are provided in each section. Overseas airmail postage rates are as follows: RM0.50 (10¢/5p) for postcards and RM1.50 (40¢/20p) for a 100-gram letter.

Taxes Hotels add a 5% government tax to all hotel rates, plus an additional 10% service charge. Larger restaurants also figure the same 5% tax into your bill, plus a 10% service charge, whereas small coffee shops and hawker stalls don't charge anything above the cost of the meal. Although most tourist goods (such as crafts, camera equipment, sports equipment, cosmetics, and select small electronic items) are tax-free, a small, scaled tax is issued on various other goods such as clothing, shoes, and accessories that you'd buy in the larger shopping malls and department stores.

Telephone **To place a call from your home country to Malaysia:** Dial the international access code (011 in the U.S. and Canada; 0011 in Australia; or 00 in the U.K., Ireland, and New Zealand), plus the country code (60), plus the Malaysia area code (Cameron Highlands 5, Desaru 7, Genting Highlands 9, Johor Bahru 7, Kuala Lumpur 3, Kuala Terengganu 9, Kota Bharu 9, Kota Kinabalu 88, Kuantan 9, Kuching 82, Langkawi 4, Malacca 6, Mersing 7, Penang 4, Tioman 9), followed by the six-, seven-, or eight-digit phone number (for example, from the U.S. to Kuala Lumpur, you'd dial 011-60-3/0000-0000).

To place a direct international call from Malaysia: Dial the international access code (00), plus the country code of the place you are dialing (U.S. and Canada 1, Australia 61, Republic of Ireland 353, New Zealand 64, U.K. 44), plus the area/city code and the residential number.

To reach the international operator: Dial © **108.**

To place a call within Malaysia: You must use area codes if calling between states. Note that for calls within the country, area codes are preceded by a zero (Cameron Highlands 05, Desaru 07, Genting Highlands 09, Johor Bahru 07, Kuala Lumpur 03, Kuala Terengganu 09, Kota Bharu 09, Kota Kinabalu 088, Kuantan 09, Kuching 082, Langkawi 04, Malacca 06, Mersing 07, Penang 04, Tioman 09).

Television Guests in larger hotels will sometimes get satellite channels such as HBO, Star TV, or CNN. Another in-house movie alternative, Vision Four, preprograms videos throughout the day. Local TV stations TV2, TV5, and TV7 show English-language comedies, movies, and documentaries.

Time Malaysia is 8 hours ahead of Greenwich Mean Time, 16 hours ahead of U.S. Pacific Standard Time, 13 ahead of Eastern Standard Time, and 2 hours behind Sydney. It is in the same zone as Singapore. There is no daylight saving time.

Tipping People here don't really tip, but you might want to give your bellhop something. In a nicer hotel, at least RM5 ($1.40/70p) per bag should be fine. In a budget hotel, they'll probably be shocked.

Toilets To find a public toilet, ask for the *tandas*. In Malay, *lelaki* is male and *perempuan* is female. Be prepared for pay toilets. Coin collectors sit outside almost every public facility, taking RM0.20 (5¢/2p) per person, RM0.30 (8¢/3p) if you want paper. Once inside, you'll find that your money doesn't go for cleaning crews. Public toilets are pure filth. They smell horrible and the floors are always an inch deep with stagnant water. While most toilets are of the "squatty-potty" variety (a porcelain bowl set into the floor), even if you find a seat-style toilet bowl, the locals always place their feet on the seat to squat. The best toilets are in hotels, upmarket shopping malls, and restaurants.

Water Water in Kuala Lumpur is supposed to be potable, but most locals boil the water before drinking it—and if that's not a tip-off, I don't know what is. I advise against drinking the tap water anywhere in Malaysia. Hotels will supply bottled water in your room. If they charge you for it, expect inflated prices. A 1.5-liter bottle goes for RM7 ($2/£1) in a hotel minibar, but RM2 (60¢/30p) at 7-Eleven.

10

Peninsular Malaysia: Kuala Lumpur & the West Coast

The most popular destinations in Malaysia dot the west coast of the country's peninsula. If you have little time, you can stick to this central corridor and still experience fascinating Malaysian heritage and gorgeous outdoors without traveling too far.

Kuala Lumpur, the nation's capital, lies about midway between the northern border with Thailand and the tip of the peninsula, before you reach Singapore. For a newcomer, the city's museums, shopping, and delicious dining choices make it a good introduction to Malaysia's culture. Kuala Lumpur is a great jumping-off point for discovering Malaysia's jungles as well.

The sleepy town of **Malacca,** a 2½-hour drive south of the capital city, has remarkably retained much of its old-world charm, with evidence of previous Portuguese, Dutch, and British colonial administrations mixed with the cultures of the Arabs, Indians, and Chinese who settled and traded here centuries ago.

Pulau Pangkor, or Pangkor Island, is a secluded island hideaway with delicious tropical resorts dripping with Southeast Asian ambience, a mere half-hour's flight from Kuala Lumpur.

Farther north, **Penang** is perhaps Malaysia's most popular destination. Once the seat of British colonial power in the region, Penang still bears signs of its former inhabitants. Georgetown, the main town on the island, bustles with charm—narrow streets, old shophouses, curious places of worship, and terrific street food. If you stay in Penang's resort area, you can enjoy the stimulating culture and the relaxing beach in one destination.

Finally, north of Penang, **Langkawi** has the greatest collection of stunning beach resorts to choose from. In the Andaman Sea, it also has the best waters of all the west coast attractions—blue and crystal clear.

1 Kuala Lumpur ★★

Kuala Lumpur (or KL as it is commonly known) is more often than not a traveler's point of entry to Malaysia. As the capital it is the most modern and developed city in the country, with contemporary high-rises and world-class hotels, glitzy shopping malls, and international cuisine.

The city began sometime around 1857 as a small mining boomtown created by the Industrial Revolution's hunger for raw materials. Fueled by tin mining in the nearby Klang River valley, the town grew under the business interests of three officials: a local Malay ruler, a British resident, and a Chinese headman (Kapitan China). The industry and village attracted Chinese laborers, Malays from nearby villages, and Indian

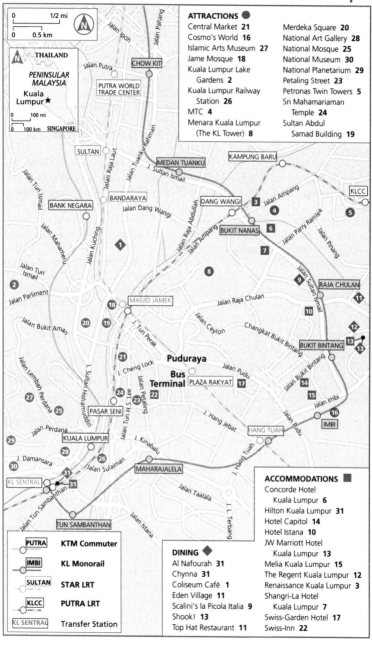

ATTRACTIONS ●

Central Market **21**
Cosmo's World **16**
Islamic Arts Museum **27**
Jame Mosque **18**
Kuala Lumpur Lake
  Gardens **2**
Kuala Lumpur Railway
  Station **26**
MTC **4**
Menara Kuala Lumpur
  (The KL Tower) **8**

Merdeka Square **20**
National Art Gallery **28**
National Mosque **25**
National Museum **30**
National Planetarium **29**
Petronas Twin Towers **5**
Petaling Street **23**
Sri Mahamariaman
  Temple **24**
Sultan Abdul
  Samad Building **19**

ACCOMMODATIONS ■

Concorde Hotel
  Kuala Lumpur **6**
Hilton Kuala Lumpur **31**
Hotel Capitol **14**
Hotel Istana **10**
JW Marriott Hotel
  Kuala Lumpur **13**
Melia Kuala Lumpur **15**
The Regent Kuala Lumpur **12**
Renaissance Kuala Lumpur **3**
Shangri-La Hotel
  Kuala Lumpur **7**
Swiss-Garden Hotel **17**
Swiss-Inn **22**

DINING ◆

Al Nafourah **31**
Chynna **31**
Coliseum Café **1**
Eden Village **11**
Scalini's la Picola Italia **9**
Shook! **13**
Top Hat Restaurant **11**

PUTRA KTM Commuter
IMBI KL Monorail
SULTAN STAR LRT
KLCC PUTRA LRT
KL SENTRAL Transfer Station

immigrants who followed the British; as the town grew, colonial buildings that housed local administrative offices were erected around Merdeka Square, bounded by Jalan Sultan Hishamuddin and Jalan Kuching. The town, and later the city, spread outward from this center.

Life in 19th-century KL had many difficult starts and stops—tin was subject to price fluctuations, the Chinese were involved in clan "wars," but worst of all, malaria was killing thousands. Still, in the late 1800s KL overcame its hurdles to become the capital of the state and eventually of the Federated Malay States. Its development continued to accelerate, with a brief setback during the Japanese World War II occupation, until 1957, when newly independent Malaysia declared Kuala Lumpur its national capital.

Today the original city center at **Merdeka Square** is the core of KL's history. Buildings like the Sultan Abdul Samad Building, the Royal Selangor Club, and the Old Kuala Lumpur Railway Station are gorgeous examples of British style peppered with Moorish flavor. South of this area is KL's **Chinatown.** Along Jalan Petaling and surrounding areas are markets, shops, food stalls, and the bustling life of the Chinese community. There's also a **Little India** in KL, around the area occupied by Masjid Jame, where you'll find flower stalls, Indian Muslim and Malay costumes, and traditional items. Across the river you'll find **Lake Gardens,** a large sanctuary that houses Kuala Lumpur's bird park, butterfly park, and other attractions and gardens. Modern Kuala Lumpur is rooted in the city's **"Golden Triangle,"** bounded by Jalan Ampang, Jalan Tun Razak, and Jalan Imbi. This section is home to most of KL's hotels, office complexes, shopping malls, and sights like the KL Tower and the Petronas Twin Towers, the tallest buildings in the world from 1998 to 2004, when Taipei 101 stole the title.

ESSENTIALS
VISITOR INFORMATION

In Kuala Lumpur, the Malaysia Tourism Board has several offices. The largest is at the **MTC,** the **Malaysia Tourist Centre** (see "Attractions," later in this chapter), located on 109 Jalan Ampang (© **03/2164-3929**) and open daily from 8am to 10:30pm. In addition to a tourist information desk, MTC also has a money changer; ATM; tourist police post; travel agent booking for Taman Negara trips, city tours, and limited hotel bookings; souvenir shops; an amphitheater; and Transnasional bus ticket bookings.

Vision KL Magazine is offered for free in many hotel rooms and has listings for events in KL and around the country, plus ads for restaurants and shops. At newsstands it costs RM6.80 ($1.90/95p).

GETTING THERE

BY PLANE   The **Kuala Lumpur International Airport (KLIA)** (© **03/8776-4386**), located in Sepang, 53km (32 miles) outside the city, opened in 1998. KLIA is a huge complex with business centers, dining facilities, a fitness center, medical services, shopping, post offices, and an airport hotel operated by **Pan Pacific** (© **03/8787-3333**). Although there are money changers, they are few and far between, so hop on the first queue you see and don't assume there's another one just around the corner.

GETTING INTO TOWN FROM THE AIRPORT

BY TAXI   City taxis are not permitted to pick up fares from the airport (although you will find illegal gypsy cabs—avoid them!), but **special airport taxis** (© **03/8787-3678**) operate round-the-clock, charging RM92 ($26/£13) for a premier car (Mercedes) and RM67 ($19/£9.45) for a standard vehicle (the locally built Proton). Vans with seating capacity up to eight can also be hired for RM180 ($51/£25). Coupons must be purchased at the arrival concourse.

An **express coach** (© 03/2730-2000) connects KLIA to KL Sentral train station, where you can catch a cab to the city's major hotels. It costs RM35 ($9.80/£4.90) for a ticket, so you may as well take the Express Rail Link, listed below. It's faster.

The **Express Rail Link** (© 03/2267-8000) runs between KLIA and KL Sentral train station from 5am to 1am daily. Trains depart every 15 minutes and take 28 minutes to complete the journey. Tickets cost RM35 ($9.80/£4.90) for adults and RM15 ($4.20/£2.10) for children. From KL Sentral, taxis are always on hand and use a coupon system (about RM7/$2/£1 or RM8/$2.20/£1.10 to central parts of the city), or you can catch one of the city's commuter trains to a station near your hotel.

BY TRAIN   I love KL's shiny new train station, **KL Sentral.** Not only does it serve as a clean, safe, and orderly base from which to take the train, it's also a hub for local commuter train services around the city; it's got tons of facilities, money changers, ATMs, fast food, and shops; and it's got an easy taxi coupon system (about RM7/$2/£1 or RM8/$2.20/£1.10 to central parts of the city)—cabs are really easy to find here. For KL Sentral information, call © 03/2267-1200.

BY BUS   If you're arriving in KL by bus, be warned, different bus companies drop off at different locations around the city. In chapter 9, "Planning Your Trip to Malaysia," I recommended **Grassland Express** buses from Singapore (© 65/6292-1166). These buses will drop you off either at the Puduraya Bus Terminal in the center of town or on Jalan Imbi just opposite the Times Square shopping mall—a much preferable location. KL has three official bus terminals that handle inter-city bus departures and arrivals to all parts of the country: the aforementioned Puduraya Terminal on Jalan Pudu, Putra Terminal on Jalan Tun Ismail, and Pekililing Terminal on Jalan Ipoh. If you arrive at Puduraya, the biggest of the three, good luck! It's congested—both with toxic fumes and traffic jams: one of the reasons I avoid standard bus travel in Malaysia. Taxis—another less-than-pleasant mode of transportation (see below) can usually be found at any of these terminals.

GETTING AROUND

Kuala Lumpur is a prime example of a city that was not planned, per se, from a master graph of streets. Rather, because of its beginnings as an outpost, it grew as it needed to, expanding outward and swallowing up rural surroundings. The result is a tangled web of streets too narrow to support the traffic of a capital city. Cars and buses weave through one-way lanes, with countless motorbikes sneaking in and out, sometimes in the opposite direction of traffic or up on the sidewalks. Expect traffic jams in the morning rush between 6 and 9am, and again between 4 and 7pm. At other times, taxis are a convenient way of getting around, but the commuter train system, if they're going where you need to, is perhaps the best value and easiest route. City buses are hot and crowded with some very confusing routes. Walking can also be frustrating. Many sidewalks are in poor condition, with buckled tiles and gaping gutters. The heat can be prohibitive as well. However, areas within the colonial heart of the city, Chinatown, Little India, and some areas in the Golden Triangle are within walking distance of each other.

BY TAXI   If you ask me, KL cabbies should have their tires slashed. If you can get one to stop, the driver will almost always refuse to use the meter (which is against the law), quoting what seems to be the standard—RM10 ($2.80/£1.15), usually for a trip that normally costs RM4 ($1.10/55p). If it's raining, expect that quote to double. I usually don't dicker over the price because it's only a buck and a half. It's just frustrating when cab after cab passes you by. In some places within the city, taxi stands try to solve this problem. Be prepared for taxis to pull over, roll down the window, and hear the pleas from the queue before deciding upon which passenger to take, regardless of the order of the queue. Somewhere there are numbers to call for taxi booking—what a joke! Maybe they'll show, and maybe they won't. Don't even waste your time. Technically, the metered fare is RM2 (60¢/30p) for the first 2km and an additional RM0.10 (3¢/1p) for each 200m after that. Between midnight and 6am you'll be charged an extra 50% of the total fare.

BY BUS I don't recommend travel on city buses. They're cheap but not dependable, with city routes that will get newcomers lost for sure. It's not the most relaxing way to get around.

BY RAIL KL has a network of mass transit trains that snake through the city and out to the suburbs, and it'll be worth your time to become familiar with them, because taxis are sometimes unreliable and traffic jams can be unbearable. Trouble is, there are five train routes and each one is operated by a different company. How confusing! The lines don't seem to connect in any logical way.

The four lines that are most useful to visitors are the **Putra LRT,** the **Star LRT,** the **KL Monorail,** and the **ERL Express Rail Link** to the airport. The latter route is explained under "Getting into Town from the Airport," above.

The **Kelana Jaya Line,** formerly called Putra LRT, has stops at Bangsar (featured in the section "Kuala Lumpur After Dark," later in this chapter), KL Sentral (train station), Pasar Seni (Chinatown), Masjid Jamek, Dang Wangi, and KLCC shopping center. The **Ampang & Sri Petaling Line,** formerly called the Star LRT, is only convenient if you need to get to the Putra World Trade Centre. It also stops at Masjid Jamek and Plaza Rayat. Average trips on both lines will cost around RM2 (60¢/30p).

The **KL Monorail** provides good access through the main hotel and shopping areas of the city, including stops at KL Sentral, Imbi, Bukit Bintang (the main shopping strip), and Raja Chulan (along Jalan Sultan Ismail, where many hotels are). Fares run between RM1.20 (30¢/15p) and RM 2.50 (70¢/35p).

As a rough guide all lines operate between 5 or 6am until around midnight, with trains coming every 10 minutes or so. Tickets can be purchased at any station either from the stationmaster or from single-fare electronic ticket booths.

ON FOOT The heat and humidity can make walking between attractions pretty uncomfortable. However, sometimes the traffic is so unbearable that you'll get where you're going much faster by strapping on your tennis shoes and hiking it.

FAST FACTS: KUALA LUMPUR

The **area code** for Kuala Lumpur is 03, and the city's phone numbers have an eight-digit format. Numbers in the rest of the country have seven digits.

The main office for **American Express** is located in KL at Menara Maybank, Ground Level banking hall, Jalan Perak (© **1300/886-688**). You'll also find headquarters for all Malaysian and many international banks, most of which have outlets along Jalan Sultan Ismail, plus ATMs at countless locations thought the city. Look for money changers in just about every shopping mall; they're a better bargain than banks or hotel cashiers.

KL's **General Post Office,** on Jalan Sultan Hishamuddin in the enormous Pos Malaysia Komplex Dayabumi (© **03/2274-1122**), can be pretty overwhelming. If you can, try to use your hotel's mail service for a much easier time. Internet service in KL will run about RM3 to RM6 (80¢–$1.70/40p–85p) per hour for usage. Internet cafes come and go, popping up in backpacker areas like Chinatown and the streets around BB Plaza off Jalan Bukit Bintang.

If you have a medical **emergency,** the number to dial is ☎ **999.** This is the same number for **police and fire emergencies** as well.

WHERE TO STAY

Following the financial crisis of 1997, occupancy levels in KL's hotels took a nosedive, driving prices of even the most deluxe accommodations to rock-bottom. Well, they're back to pre-crisis levels, which is bad news for you, the traveler. International business-class properties like the Four Seasons, Hilton, Sheraton, and Mandarin Oriental fill their rooms every night with corporate travelers who are charged corporate rates to their corporate expense accounts. The hotels I've selected here represent only those properties I think are best for leisure travelers. Even the very expensive hotels I've chosen have qualities that extend beyond the business center.

If you plan to travel to KL in July and August and want to stay in an upmarket hotel, you'll need to book your room well in advance. KL's super-peak season falls during these months, when travelers from the Middle East take a break from scorching temperatures back home. Malaysia is the perfect tropical holiday spot for Muslim travelers from around the world, and the Malaysia Tourism Board has done an excellent job of attracting the Middle Eastern market in particular, extending restaurant and cafe hours, and even shopping mall hours into the wee hours of the morning.

VERY EXPENSIVE

The Regent Kuala Lumpur ☆ Of the best five-star properties in Kuala Lumpur, nobody delivers first-class accommodations with the finesse of the Regent. A landmark along KL's fashionable Jalan Bukit Bintang shopping strip, The Regent has an ever-bustling lobby to match the excitement along the sidewalks outside—the lobby lounge is filled night and day. Surprisingly, the staff always seems polite and professional despite the barrage. The Regent's guest rooms are spacious, quiet, and cool, with huge plush beds covered in soft cozy cotton sheets and down comforters. Bathrooms are large, marble affairs with plenty of counter space. The outdoor pool is a palm-lined free-form escape, and the fitness center is state-of-the-art, with sauna, steam, spa, and Jacuzzi. In the plot directly next to the hotel construction began on a new, mammoth shopping and apartment complex. Ask about it when you make your booking: nobody wants to hear driving piles when they're trying to nap.

160 Jalan Bukit Bintang, 55100 Kuala Lumpur. ☎ **800/545-4000** in the U.S. and Canada, 800/022-800 in Australia, 800/440-800 in New Zealand, 800/917-8795 in the U.K., or 03/2141-8000. Fax 03/2142-1441. www.regenthotels.com. 468 units. RM700 ($196/£98) double; from RM950 ($266/£133) suite. AE, DC, MC, V. 5 min. walk to Bukit Bintang Monorail station. **Amenities:** 3 restaurants; bar and lobby lounge; outdoor pool; 2 squash courts; 24-hr. fitness center w/Jacuzzi, sauna, steam, and massage; concierge; limousine service; business center; 24-hr. room service; babysitting; same-day laundry service; dry cleaning; nonsmoking rooms; executive-level rooms. *In room:* A/C, TV w/satellite programming and in-house movie, minibar, coffee/tea-making facilities, hair dryer, safe.

Shangri-La Hotel Kuala Lumpur ☆☆☆ In 2003 Shangri-La emerged from a massive face-lift which enhanced its "tropical oasis in the city" ambience. I'm a big fan of Shangri-La, an Asian hotel chain that seeks to create luxury accommodations within lush gardens—something different from the typically faceless city tower of most urban hotels. Complete renovations to the guest rooms included new carpets, soft upholstered furniture, drapes, and bed linens in bright, natural colors and textures. Flatscreen TVs and broadband access come standard (although Internet usage is extra). Of all the upmarket hotels in the city, the Shang has the most attractive facilities for leisure travelers, with a pretty landscaped outdoor pool and fitness center stocked with the latest equipment.

11 Jalan Sultan Ismail, 50250 Kuala Lumpur. © 800/942-5050 in the U.S. and Canada, 800/222-448 in Australia, 0800/442-179 in New Zealand, or 03/2032-2388. Fax 03/2070-1514. www.shangri-la.com. 701 units. RM810 ($227/£113) double; from RM1,420 ($398/£199) suite. AE, DC, MC, V. 10-min. walk to Bukit Nanas Monorail station. **Amenities:** 5 restaurants; outdoor pool; outdoor lighted tennis courts; fitness center w/Jacuzzi, steam, sauna, and massage; concierge; limousine service; salon; babysitting; 24-hr. room service; same-day dry cleaning; laundry service; nonsmoking rooms; executive level rooms. *In room:* A/C; TV w/satellite programming and in-house movie; Internet access; minibar; coffee/tea-making facilities; hair dryer, safe.

EXPENSIVE

Hilton Kuala Lumpur 𝒢𝒢𝒢 The absolute hottest hotel in KL, and probably one of the most innovative hotels in the world—forget anything you've ever experienced in a Hilton. From the airy, art-filled public spaces to the rooftop lagoon pool, everything is done with edgy style and sophistication. Large rooms have sleek contemporary decor, with a desk area wired for work, mood lighting, stocked minibar with a coffee plunger and heavy mugs and a 42-inch plasma TV. A "magic button" handles all service requests, and three "lifestyle boxes" provide little extras like desk accessories, bath treats, and games. Bathrooms are great! Deep tubs, wide "rain" showerheads and a mini LCD screen TV built into the shaving mirror! The hotel's fitness center is operated by the very competent Clarke Hatch company and the rooftop pool and Bali spa are great escapes. Hilton hotels use the best rate of the day system, so I've listed a general rate during peak season below, as opposed to rack rates listed for other properties.

3 Jalan Stesen Sentral, 50470 Kuala Lumpur. © 800/HILTONS in the U.S. and Canada, 800/293-229 in Australia, 800/ 448-002 in New Zealand, 0875/90-90-90 in the U.K., or 03/2264-2264. Fax 03/2264-2266. www.hilton.com. 542 units. RM425 ($119/£60) double; from RM690 ($193/£97) suite. AE, DC, MC, V. Opposite KL Sentral station. **Amenities:** 5 restaurants; 2 bars; outdoor pool; fitness center; spa; concierge; limousine service; business center; 24-hr. room service; babysitting; same-day laundry service; dry cleaning; nonsmoking rooms; executive-level rooms. *In room:* A/C, TV w/satellite programming and in-house movie, minibar, coffee/tea-making facilities, hair dryer, safe.

Hotel Istana 𝒢 Fashioned after a Malay palace, Hotel Istana is rich with Moorish architectural elements, and *songket* weaving patterns are featured in decor elements throughout. The guest rooms were recently refurbished with Malaysian touches like handwoven carpets and upholstery in local fabric designs, capturing the exotic flavor of the culture without sacrificing modern comfort and convenience. Located on Jalan Raja Chulan, Istana is in a favorable Golden Triangle location, within walking distance to shopping and some of the sights in that area.

73 Jalan Raja Chulan, 50200 Kuala Lumpur. © 03/2141-9988. Fax 03/2144-0111. www.hotelistana.com.my. 516 units. RM550 ($154/£77) double; from RM740 ($207/£104) suite. AE, DC, MC, V. 5-min. walk to Raja Chulan Monorail station. **Amenities:** 4 restaurants; lobby lounge; outdoor pool; 2 outdoor lighted tennis courts; 2 squash courts; fitness center w/Jacuzzi, sauna, steam, and massage; concierge; limousine service; business center; 24-hr. room service; babysitting; same-day laundry service; dry cleaning; executive-level rooms. *In room:* A/C, TV w/satellite programming and in-house movie, minibar, coffee/tea-making facilities, hair dryer, safe.

JW Marriott Hotel Kuala Lumpur 𝒢 Opened in 1997, the Marriott is finding itself overshadowed by some of the city's newer properties. But the small lobby area still allows for a very dramatic entrance, complete with wrought-iron filigree and marble. The modern guest rooms have a European flavor, decorated in deep greens and reds with plush carpeting, large desks, and a leather executive chair that are all beginning to show wear. If you've stayed at Marriott in other locations, this one might disappoint you. It's not their hottest property, yet the staff is very motivated and enthusiastic. Another great plus: the hotel is next door to some of the most upmarket and trendy shopping complexes in the city. Similar to the Regent, this hotel is adjacent to what appeared to be a new construction site, so ask about noise pollution when booking.

183 Jalan Bukit Bintang, 55100 Kuala Lumpur. (C) **800/228-9290** in the U.S. and Canada, 800/251-259 in Australia, 800/221-222 in the U.K., or 03/2715-9000. Fax 03/2715-7000. www.marriott.com. 518 units. RM700 ($196/£98) double; RM6,000 ($1,680/£840) suite. AE, DC, MC, V. 10-min. walk to Bukit Bintang Monorail station. **Amenities:** 4 restaurants; lounge and cigar bar; outdoor pool; outdoor lighted tennis court; fitness center w/Jacuzzi, sauna, and steam; new spa w/massage and beauty treatments; concierge; limousine service; business center; salon; 24-hr. room service; babysitting; same-day laundry service; dry cleaning; executive-level rooms; shopping mall w/designer boutiques adjacent. *In room:* A/C, TV w/satellite programming, dataport, minibar, coffee/tea-making facilities, hair dryer, safe.

Renaissance Kuala Lumpur Hotel ★★ *Value*
The Renaissance offers a terrific value for the money. It's basically two hotels in one: the posh Renaissance Wing and the New World Wing, its budget neighbor, with both properties sharing all hotel facilities. Each wing has its own entrance, connected in the middle where the ballroom and banquet rooms are housed. Guest rooms in the Renaissance Wing have an "official" feel to them—very bold and impressive, and completely European in style. In fact, you'll never know you're in Malaysia. The New World Wing is contemporary, with simpler decor, but is no less comfortable. The enormous outdoor pool, which sits between the two hotel towers, is second only to Shangri-La's (reviewed above).

Corner of Jalan Sultan Ismail and Jalan Ampang, 50450 Kuala Lumpur. (C) **800/HOTELS-1** in the U.S. and Canada, 800/251-259 in Australia, 800/441-035 in New Zealand, or 03/2162-2233. Fax 03/2163-1122. 910 units. Renaissance Wing: RM695 ($195/£97); from RM1,400 ($392/£196) suite. New World Wing: RM625 ($175/£88) double, from RM950 ($175/£133) suite. AE, DC, MC, V. 5-min. walk to Bukit Nanas Monorail and Dang Wangi LRT stations. **Amenities:** 3 restaurants; lounge; large landscaped outdoor pool; outdoor lighted tennis court; fitness center w/sauna and massage; concierge; limousine service; business center; shopping arcade; salon; 24-hr. room service; babysitting; same-day laundry service; dry cleaning; nonsmoking rooms; executive-level rooms. *In room:* A/C, TV w/satellite programming and in-house movie, minibar, coffee/tea-making facilities, hair dryer, safe.

MODERATE

Concorde Hotel Kuala Lumpur ★★ *Value*
Concorde is one of my favorites in this price category for its central location and quality accommodations at an incredible price. Although rooms are not as large as those in more expensive hotels, they're well outfitted with desks, side chairs, comfortable beds, and tidy bathrooms in an up-to-date style that can compete with the best of them. Concorde has a small outdoor pool with a charming cafe and small fitness center. The lobby lounge is noisy at night because it's popular. Hard Rock Cafe is also on the premises, one of the more fun clubs in town.

2 Jalan Sultan Ismail, 50250 Kuala Lumpur. (C) **03/2144-2200.** Fax 03/2144-1628. www.concorde.net/kl. 570 units. RM250 ($70/£35) double; from RM1,000 ($280/£140) suite. AE, DC, MC, V. 5-min. walk to Bukit Nanas Monorail station and 10-min. walk to Dang Wangi LRT station. **Amenities:** 3 restaurants; lobby lounge and Hard Rock Cafe; small outdoor pool; fitness center w/sauna, steam, and massage; concierge; limousine service; business center; shopping arcade; salon; 24-hr. room service; babysitting; same-day laundry service; dry cleaning; executive-level rooms. *In room:* A/C, TV w/satellite programming and in-house movie, minibar, coffee/tea-making facilities, safe.

Meliá Kuala Lumpur ★ *Value*
This tourist-class hotel had nothing special to boast until recently. The opening of a KL Monorail station just outside, combined with the mind-bogglingly enormous Times Square shopping and entertainment complex across the street, has certainly added great value. The small lobby is functional, with space for tour groups and a very active and efficient tour desk. Newly renovated guest rooms

have light wood furnishings, contemporary fixtures, wall desks with a swivel arm for extra space, and big-screen TVs. Bathrooms, although small, are well-maintained with good counter space. Mealtimes in the hotel's coffee shop can be a little crowded.

16 Jalan Imbi, 55100 Kuala Lumpur. ✆ 03/2142-8333. Fax 03/2142-6623. www.solmelia.com. 301 units. RM500 ($140/£70) double; from RM1,200 ($336/£168) suite. AE, DC, MC, V. Imbi Monorail station. **Amenities:** 2 restaurants; bar and karaoke lounge; small outdoor pool; health center w/massage; tour desk; small business center; shopping arcade; salon; 24-hr. room service; babysitting; same-day laundry service; dry cleaning; nonsmoking rooms. In room: A/C, TV w/satellite programming and in-house movie, minibar, coffee/tea-making facilities, iron.

Swiss-Garden Hotel   For midrange prices, Swiss-Garden offers reliable comfort, okay location, and affordability that attracts many leisure travelers to its doors. It also knows how to make you feel right at home, with a friendly staff (the concierge is on the ball) and a hotel lobby bar that actually gets patronized (by travelers having cool cocktails at the end of a busy day of sightseeing). The guest rooms are simply furnished, but are neat and comfortable. Swiss-Garden is just walking distance from KL's lively Chinatown district, and close to the Puduraya bus station (which unfortunately makes traffic ugly at rush hour). Facilities include an outdoor pool, a small spa, and a fitness center.

117 Jalan Pudu, 55100 Kuala Lumpur. ✆ 03/2141-3333. Fax 03/2141-5555. www.swissgarden.com. 310 units. RM200 ($56/£28) double; from RM350 ($98/£49) suite. AE, DC, MC, V. **Amenities:** 2 restaurants; lobby lounge; small outdoor pool; small fitness center; spa w/massage; concierge; limousine service; business center; 24-hr. room service; babysitting; same-day laundry service; dry cleaning; nonsmoking rooms. In room: A/C, TV w/satellite programming and in-house movie, minibar, coffee/tea-making facilities, hair dryer, safe.

INEXPENSIVE

Hotel Capitol ★ Value   A top pick for a budget hotel, Capitol is located in an up-and-coming part of the city's popular Golden Triangle district, close to the junction of Jalan Sultan Ismail and Jalan Bukit Bintang. In the surrounding lanes you'll find small eateries and shops for necessities, and a short hop away is the Times Square megamall. The place has been nicely refurbished, with a minimalist lobby that's function over frills. Inside the refurbished guest rooms, the wooden furniture seems like it's been around a while, but the upholstery, bedding, carpeting, and drapes are all fresh. The big tiled bathroom also has a long bathtub. There are no leisure facilities to speak of, but if you've come to KL to sightsee, you won't miss them.

Jalan Bulan, off Jalan Bukit Bintang, 55100 Kuala Lumpur. ✆ 800/448-8355 in the U.S. and Canada, 800/221-176 in Australia, or 03/2143-7000. Fax 03/2143-0000. 225 units. RM250 ($70/£35) double. AE, DC, MC, V. 10-min. walk to Imbi Monorail station. **Amenities:** Restaurant; limited room service; same-day laundry service; nonsmoking rooms. In room: A/C, TV w/satellite programming and in-house movies, minibar, coffee/tea-making facilities, hair dryer, safe.

Swiss-Inn   This mini-size hotel is one of KL's most popular budget places. Tucked away in the heart of Chinatown, Swiss-Inn's best asset is its location, amid the jumble of vibrant nightmarket hawkers. The place is small and offers almost no facilities. Higher-priced rooms have a small window, a bit more space (but are still compact) and are somewhat better maintained. Budget rooms, on lower floors, are very small, the cheapest having no windows at all. The beige carpeting can use a deep cleaning, the walls can use a fresh coat of paint, and the bathrooms some new grout work. On my last visit, housekeeping wasn't up to snuff, which added to the problem. Still, they often have good promotional rates. Make sure you reserve your room early because this place runs at high occupancy year-round. The cafe, hidden behind market stalls, is an interesting place to have a beer and people-watch.

62 Jalan Sultan, 50000 Kuala Lumpur. ✆ 03/2072-3333. Fax 03/2031-6699. www.swissgarden.com/hotel/sikl. 110 units. RM180 ($50/£25) double. AE, DC, MC, V. **Amenities:** Restaurant; bar; tour desk; Internet terminals for guest use (extra charge); limited room service; babysitting; same-day laundry service; dry cleaning; nonsmoking rooms. *In room:* A/C, TV w/in-house movie, coffee/tea-making facilities.

WHERE TO DINE

Kuala Lumpur, like Singapore, is very cosmopolitan. Here you'll not only find delicious and exotic cuisine, but you'll find it served in some pretty trendy settings.

Al Nafourah ★★★ LEBANESE   Dripping with the magical allure of a desert oasis, Al Nafourah is pure Arabian Nights. With Moorish arches, twinkling lanterns, carved screens, silken hangings, mosaic tiles, and woven carpets throughout, the restaurant also has booths in private nooks for extra romance. The Lebanese cuisine is some of the best around, with lamb, chicken, and fish dishes in tangy herbs and warm flatbreads straight from a wood-fire oven. Outside on the terrace, sit back and drink a heady coffee and smoke from a hookah while taking in belly dance performances. A truly memorable evening.

Le Meridien Kuala Lumpur, 2 Jalan Stesen Sentral. ✆ 03/2263-7888. Reservations recommended. Main courses RM25–RM80 ($7–$22/£3.50–£11). AE, DC, MC, V. Daily noon–2:30pm and 6:30–10:30pm.

Chynna ★★ CANTONESE   Chynna is pure dinner theater: From the Madam Wong–style red lanterns to the Old China antique replica furnishings, you'll think you're in a highly stylized Shanghai of yesteryear. For fun, there's a show kitchen where you can watch delectable dim sum morsels being prepared, or you can just sit at your table and watch the tea master refill your cup with acrobatic moves. Pure genius! The delicious lunch dim sum menu is extensive with most dishes between RM8 and RM12 ($2.20–$3.40/£1.10–£1.70). Dinner is standard Cantonese fare, with an extensive menu of soups and rice and noodle dishes.

Hilton Kuala Lumpur, 3 Jalan Stesen Sentral. ✆ 03/2264-2264. Reservations recommended. Small dishes RM28–RM56 ($7.80–$16/£3.90–£7.85). AE, DC, MC, V. Daily noon–2:30pm and 6:30–10:30pm.

Coliseum Cafe *Finds* WESTERN/LOCAL   What can I say about Coliseum? Okay, the place is 86 years old, and so is the staff (seriously, some have worked here their whole lives). Located in the grottiest hotel I've ever witnessed, with stained white walls, worn tile floors, and threadbare linens, this is KL's authentic "greasy spoon." It sounds dreadful, but the place is legendary, and someday it will be gone and there will never be anything else like it. It used to be *the place* for the starched-shirt colonial types to get real Western food back in the day. Now it's a favorite with the locals, who come for enormous sizzling steaks (which fill the place with greasy smoke), baked crabmeat served in the shell, and the house favorite caramel custard pudding. Actually, the food is quite nice, and the prices are terrific for the steaks, which I highly recommend ordering. You either get this place or you don't.

98–100 Jalan Tuanku Abdul Rahman. ✆ 03/2692-6270. Reservations not accepted. Main courses RM10–RM34 ($2.80–$9.50/£1.40–£4.75). MC. Daily 8am–10pm.

Eden Village SEAFOOD   Uniquely designed inside and out to resemble a Malay house, Eden Village has great local atmosphere. It was once KL's most famous "fancy place" for a night out. Now it's visited by as many tourists as locals but still retains some authenticity. Waitresses are clad in traditional *sarong kebaya* and serve up popular dishes like braised shark's fin in a clay pot with crabmeat and roe, and the Kingdom of the Sea (a half lobster baked with prawns, crab, and cuttlefish). Terrace seating is the best in the house.

260 Jalan Raja Chulan. © 03/2141-4027. Reservations recommended. Main courses RM18–RM100 and up ($5–$28/£2.50–£14). AE, MC, V. Lunch Mon–Sat noon–3pm; dinner daily 7pm–midnight.

Feast Village ★★ INTERNATIONAL   I'm one of those people who can never decide what I want to eat. This is the place for me! Located in the basement of Starhill Gallery, the city's most exclusive shopping mall, Feast Village isn't a single restaurant, but a cluster of 13 restaurants arranged like a small Malay village. As you stroll along stone and timber pathways, you'll pass cafes that serve seafood, steaks, Malay, Chinese, Thai, Korean, Indian, and more. Within each cafe, the menu is unique and so is the decor. Wander, smell the smells, read the menus, check out the sights, and find the perfect food for your mood.

Basement, Starhill Gallery, 181 Jalan Bukit Bintang. © 03/2782-3800. Reservations not required. Main courses vary from outlet to outlet. AE, DC, MC, V. Most outlets daily noon–2:30pm and 6:30–10:30pm.

Scalini's la Piccola Italia ★★ ITALIAN   Four chefs from Italy create the dishes that make Scalini's a favorite among KL locals and expatriates. From a very extensive menu you can select pasta, fish, and meat, as well as a large selection of pizzas. The specials are superb and change all the time. Some of the best dishes are salmon with creamed asparagus sauce and ravioli with goat cheese and zucchini. Scalini's has a large wine selection (which is actually part of the romantic decor) with labels from California, Australia, New Zealand, France, and, of course, Italy.

19 Jalan Sultan Ismail. © 03/2145-3211. Reservations recommended. Main courses RM28–RM56 ($7.90–$16/£3.90–£7.85). AE, DC, MC, V. Sun–Thurs noon–2:30pm and 6–10:30pm; Fri noon–2:30pm and 6–11pm; Sat 6–11pm.

Shook! JAPANESE/CHINESE/ITALIAN/WESTERN GRILL   This place is unique for a number of reasons. First, Shook! is located on the ground floor of a shopping center, in a cavernous space decorated in a sort of Zen minimalism with splashes of color. Above, escalators glide shoppers to floors over the glass stage where the pop and jazz band plays nightly. Second, the menu features four different types of cuisine that are prepared in four separate show kitchens. It will take a few minutes to read the menu, which offers a mind-boggling selection of Japanese, Chinese, Italian, and Western grill specialties. Very inventive. A good spot if your party can't agree on where to eat—something for everyone. One caveat: The waitstaff sometimes seem lost in Shook's enormity.

Starhill Centre, Lower Ground Floor, 181 Jalan Bukit Bintang. © 03/2716-8535. Main courses RM20–RM200 ($5.60–$56/£2.80–£28). AE, DC, MC, V. Daily noon–2:30pm and 6:30–10:30pm.

Top Hat Restaurant ★★★ Finds ASIAN MIX   Let me tell you about my favorite restaurant in Kuala Lumpur. First, Top Hat has a unique atmosphere. In a 1930s bungalow that was once a school, the place winds through room after room, its walls painted in bright hues and furnished with an assortment of mix-and-matched teak tables, chairs, and antiques. Second, the menu is fabulous. While a la carte is available, Top Hat puts together set meals featuring Nonya, Malacca Portuguese, traditional Malay, Thai, Western, even vegetarian recipes. They're all brilliant. Desserts are huge and full of sin.

No. 7 Jalan Kia Peng. © 03/2142-8611. Reservations recommended. Main courses RM28–RM60 ($7.80–$17/£3.90–£8.40). Set meals RM30–RM100 ($8.40–$28/£4.20–£14). AE, DC, MC, V. Lunch Mon–Fri noon–2:30pm; dinner daily 6–10:30pm.

ATTRACTIONS

Most of Kuala Lumpur's historic sights are located in and around the Merdeka Square/ Jalan Hishamuddin area, while many of the gardens, parks, and museums are out at Lake Gardens. Taxi fare between the two locations should run you about RM5 ($1.40/70p).

City tours can be booked through **Tour Fifty-one,** located at the MTC (Malaysia Tourism Centre) on Jalan Ampang (✆ **03/2161-8830**). They coordinate a half-day coach tour for RM50 ($14/£7) adults and RM30 ($8.40/£4.20) children. It swings by most of the places listed here but is rushed.

Central Market ✪   The original Central Market, built in 1936, used to be a wet market, but the place is now a cultural center (air-conditioned!) for local artists and craftspeople selling antiques, crafts, and curios. It's fantastic for buying Malaysian and Asian crafts and souvenirs, with two floors of shops to choose from. The Central Market also stages evening performances (7:45pm on weekends) of Malay martial arts, Indian classical dance, or Chinese orchestra. Call for performance information.

Jalan Benteng. ✆ **03/2274-6542**. Daily 10am–10pm. Shops open until 8:30 or 9pm.

Cosmo's World Theme Park ✪✪✪ *Kids*   I don't care if you have kids or not, Cosmo's rocks. The world's largest indoor amusement park is literally built into the walls of this 900-outlet shopping mall. You don't even need to ride the looping roller coaster to feel that thrill in the pit of your stomach. Just stand and watch it overhead as it flashes by. It really takes your breath away. There are saner rides, too, plus a host of kiddie rides. Highly recommended for families with bored kids.

Berjaya Times Square Shopping Mall, No. 1 Jalan Imbi. ✆ **03/2117-3118**. Adults RM25 ($7/£3.50); children RM15 ($4.20/£2.10). Daily 10am–10pm.

Islamic Arts Museum ✪✪   The seat of Islamic learning in Kuala Lumpur, the center has displays of Islamic texts, artifacts, porcelain, and weaponry in local and visiting exhibits.

Jalan Lembah Perdana. ✆ **03/2274-2020**. Adults RM12 ($3.40/£1.70); children RM6 ($1.70/85p). Daily 10am–6pm.

Jame Mosque (Masjid Jame)   The first settlers landed in Kuala Lumpur at the spot where the Gombak and Klang rivers meet, and in 1909 a mosque was built here. Styled after an Indian Muslim design, it is one of the oldest mosques in the city. It is supposed to be opened to the public, but many foreigners, even those properly attired, have been shooed away at the gate.

Jalan Tun Terak. Free admission.

Kuala Lumpur Lake Gardens (Taman Tasik Perdana)   Built around an artificial lake, the 92-hectare (229-acre) park has plenty of space for jogging and rowing, and has a playground for the kids. It's the most popular park in Kuala Lumpur. Inside the Lake Gardens find the **Kuala Lumpur Bird Park** ✪ (Jalan Perdana; ✆ **03/2273-5423;** www.birdpark.com.my; adults RM30/$8.40/£4.20, children RM22/$6.20/£3.10; daily 9am–6pm) nestled in beautifully landscaped gardens, with over 3,000 birds within a huge walk-in aviary. Quite impressive. **Kuala Lumpur Orchid Garden** (Jalan Perdana; ✆ **03/2693-5399;** weekend and public holiday admission adults RM1/30¢/15, free for children; free weekday admission for all; daily 9am–6pm) has a collection of over 800 orchid species from Malaysia, and thousands of international varieties. The **Kuala Lumpur Butterfly Park** (Jalan Cenderasari; ✆ **03/2693-4799;**

adults RM15/$4.20/£2.10, children RM8/$2.20/£1.10; daily 9am–6pm) has over 6,000 butterflies belonging to 120 species making their home in this park, which has been landscaped with more than 15,000 plants to simulate the butterflies' natural rainforest environment. There are also other small animals and an insect museum.

Enter through Jalan Parliament. Free admission. Daily 9am–6pm.

Kuala Lumpur Railway Station Built in 1910, the KL Railway Station is a beautiful example of Moorish architecture.

Jalan Sultan Hishamuddin. Daily 7:30am–10:30pm.

Malaysia Tourist Centre (MTC) At MTC you'll find an exhibit hall, tourist information services for Kuala Lumpur and Malaysia, and other travel-planning services. On Tuesdays, Thursdays, Saturdays, and Sundays there are cultural shows at 2pm, featuring Malaysian dance and music. Shows are RM5 ($1.40/70p) for adults, free for children.

Jalan Ampang. ℭ 03/2164-3929. Free admission. Daily 9am–6pm.

Menara Kuala Lumpur Standing 421m (1,389 ft.) tall, this concrete structure is the third-tallest tower in the world, and the views from the top reach to the far corners of the city and beyond. At the top, the glass windows are fashioned after the Shah Mosque in Isfahan, Iran.

Bukit Nanas. ℭ 03/2020-5448. Adults RM10 ($2.80/£1.40); children RM5 ($1.40/70p). Daily 9am–10pm.

Merdeka Square Surrounded by colonial architecture with an exotic local flair, the square was once the site of British social and sporting events. These days, Malaysia holds its spectacular Independence Day celebrations on the field, which is home to the world's tallest flagpole, standing at 100m (330 ft.).

Jalan Raja. Free admission.

National Art Gallery The building that now houses the National Art Gallery was built as the Majestic Hotel in 1932 and has been restored to display contemporary works by Malaysian artists. There are also international exhibits.

Jalan Temerloh off Jalan Tun Razak. ℭ 03/4025-4990. Free admission. Daily 10am–6pm.

National Mosque (Masjid Negara) Built in a modern design, the most distinguishing features of the mosque are its 73m (243-ft.) minaret and the umbrella-shaped roof, which is said to symbolize a newly independent Malaysia's aspirations for the future. Could be true, as the place was built in 1965, the year Singapore split from Malaysia.

Jalan Sultan Hishamuddin (near the KL Railway Station). Free admission. Daily 9am–6pm.

National Museum (Muzim Negara) 🞜🞜 Located at Lake Gardens, the museum has more than 1,000 items of historical, cultural, and traditional significance, including art, weapons, musical instruments, and costumes.

Jalan Damansara. ℭ 03/2282-6255. Admission adults RM2 (60¢/30), children under 12 free. Daily 9am–6pm.

National Planetarium *Kids* The National Planetarium has a Space Hall with touch-screen interactive computers and hands-on experiments, a Viewing Gallery with binoculars for a panoramic view of the city, and an Ancient Observatory Park with models of Chinese and Indian astronomy systems. The Space Theatre has two different outer-space shows at 11am, 2pm, and 4pm for an extra charge of RM3 (80¢/40p) for adults and RM2 (60¢/30p) for children.

Lake Gardens. ℂ **03/2273-5484**. Admission to exhibition hall adults RM1 (30¢/15p), children free. Tues–Sun 10am–4pm.

Petaling Street 🎯 This is the center of KL's Chinatown district. By day, stroll past hawker stalls, dim sum shops, wet markets, and all sorts of shops, from pawnshops to coffin makers. At night, a crazy bazaar (which is terribly crowded) pops up—look for designer knockoffs, fake watches, and pirated VCDs (video CDs) here.

Petronas Twin Towers 🎯 Standing at an awesome 452m (1,482 ft.) above street level, with 88 stories, the towers were the tallest buildings in the world from 1998 to 2004 (when Taipei 101 snatched the title). From the outside, the structures are designed with the kind of geometric patterns common to Islamic architecture, and on levels 41 and 42 the two towers are linked by a bridge. Visitors are permitted on the viewing deck on the bridge from 10am to 8pm every day except Mondays and public holidays; otherwise, the building is accessible only if you are conducting business inside.

Kuala Lumpur City Centre. ℂ **03/2051-7770**. Free admission.

Sri Mahamariaman Temple With a recent face-lift (Hindu temples must renovate every 12 years), this bright temple livens the gray street scene around it. It's a beautiful temple tucked away in a narrow street in KL's Chinatown area, which was built by Thambusamy Pillai, a pillar of old KL's Indian community.

Jalan Bandar. Free admission.

Sultan Abdul Samad Building In 1897 this exotic building was designed by Regent Alfred John Bidwell, a colonial architect responsible for many of the buildings in Singapore. He chose a style called "Muhammadan" or "neo-Saracenic," which combines Indian Muslim architecture with Gothic and other Western elements. Built to house government administrative offices, today it is the home of Malaysia's Supreme Court and High Court.

Jalan Raja. Free admission.

GOLF

People from all over Asia flock to Malaysia for its golf courses, many of which are excellent standard courses designed by pros. The **Kuala Lumpur Golf & Country Club,** 10 Jalan 1/70D Off Jalan Bukit Kiara (ℂ **03/2093-1111**), has 2 courses, 18 holes each, par 71 and 72, designed by R. Nelson and R. Wright, with greens fees of RM189 ($53/£27) weekdays. The club is closed to nonmembers on weekends and holidays. **Suajana Golf & Country Club,** Km 3, Jalan Lapangan Terbang Sultan Abdul Aziz Shah, 46783 Subang Selangor (ℂ **03/7846-1466;** fax 03/7846-7818), has two 18-hole courses, each par 72, designed by Ronald Fream, with greens fees of RM223 ($62/£31) weekdays, RM353 ($99/£49) weekends and holidays.

SHOPPING

Kuala Lumpur is a truly great place to shop. In recent years, mall after mall has risen from city lots, filled with hundreds of retail outlets selling everything from haute couture to cheap chic clothing, electronic goods, jewelry, and arts and crafts. The **major shopping malls** are located in the area around Jalan Bukit Bintang and Jalan Sultan Ismail. There are also a few malls along Jalan Ampang. Suria KLCC, just beneath the Petronas Twin Towers, is KL's most upmarket mall, while Berjaya Times Square wins the prize for excess with 900 shops, food and entertainment outlets, plus the world's largest indoor amusement park.

Still the best place for Malaysian handicrafts, the huge **Central Market** on Jalan Benteng (© **03/2274-6542**) keeps any shopper saturated for hours. There you'll find a jumble of local artists and craftspeople selling their wares in the heart of town. It's also a good place to find Malaysian handicrafts from other regions of the country. One specific shop I like to recommend for Malaysian handicrafts is **KL Craft Complex,** Section 3 Jalan Conlay (© **03/2162-7533**), with its warehouse selection of assorted goods from around the country, all of it fine quality. Don't forget to walk through the gardens to see the artists' village. In the bungalows toward the side of the building you'll find some of Malaysia's finest contemporary artists displaying their works for sale. And wear comfy shoes; you may need to walk back to the main road to get a cab.

Another favorite shopping haunt in KL is **Chinatown,** along Petaling Street. Day and night, it's a great place to wander and bargain for knockoff designer clothing and accessories, sunglasses, T-shirts, souvenirs, fake watches, and pirated videos.

Pasar malam (**night markets**) are very popular evening activities in KL. Whole blocks are taken up with these brightly lit and bustling markets packed with stalls selling everything you can dream of. They are likely to pop up anywhere in the city. Two good bets for catching one: Go to Jalan Haji Taib after dark until 10pm. On Saturday nights, head for Jalan Tuanku Abdul Rahman.

KUALA LUMPUR AFTER DARK

There's nightlife to spare in KL, from fashionable lounges to sprawling discos to pubs perfect for lounging. Basically, you can expect to pay about RM11 to RM20 ($3.10–$5.60/£1.55–£2.80) for a pint of beer, depending on what and where you order. Although quite a few pubs are open for lunch, most clubs won't open until about 6 or 7pm. These places must all close by 1 or 2am, so don't plan on staying out too late. Nearly all have a happy hour, usually between 5 and 7pm, when drink discounts apply on draft beers and "house-pour" (lower shelf) mixed drinks. Generally, you're expected to wear dress-casual clothing for these places, but avoid old jeans, tennis shoes, and very revealing outfits.

The center of nightlife, if you want to browse, begins at the corner of Jalan Sultan Ismail and Jalan P. Ramlee. Walk along P. Ramlee and you'll find bars of all kinds, plus cafes and coffee shops.

For a little live music with your drinks, the **Hard Rock Cafe,** Jalan Sultan Ismail next to Concorde Hotel (© **03/2715-5555**), hosts the best of the regional bands, which play nightly for a crowd of locals, tourists, and expatriates who take their parties very seriously.

The biggest dance club in town is **Zouk,** fashioned after the ultra-successful Zouk in Singapore. It's at 113 Jalan Ampang, down the street from MTC (© **03/2171-1997**). There's a cover charge of anywhere between RM25 and RM40 ($7–$11/£3.50–£5.60), depending on what's going on inside.

Bangsar, just outside the city limits, is 2 or 3 blocks of bars, cafes, and restaurants that cater to a variety of tastes (in fact, so many expatriates hang out there, they call it Kweiloh Lumpur, "Foreigner Lumpur" in Mandarin). Every taxi driver knows where it is. Get in and ask to go to Jalan Telawi Tiga in Bangsar (fare should be no more than RM5 or RM6 ($1.40 or $1.70/70p or 85p), and once there it's very easy to catch a cab back to town. During the week, it's kinda quiet.

SIDE TRIPS FROM KUALA LUMPUR

TAMAN NEGARA NATIONAL PARK ✦✦✦

Malaysia's most famous national park, **Taman Negara,** covers 434,300 hectares (1,085,750 acres) of primary rainforest estimated to be as old as 130 million years and encompasses within its borders **Gunung Tahan,** peninsular Malaysia's highest peak at 2,187m (7,175 ft.) above sea level.

Prepare to see lush vegetation and rare orchids, some 250 bird species, and maybe, if you're lucky, some barking deer, tapir, elephants, tigers, leopards, and rhinos. As for primates, there are long-tailed macaques, leaf monkeys, gibbons, and more. Malaysia has taken the preservation of this forest seriously since the early part of the century, so Taman Negara showcases efforts to keep this land in as pristine a state as possible while still allowing humans to appreciate the splendor.

There are outdoor activities for any level of adventurer. Short **jungle walks** to observe nature are lovely, but then so are the hard-core 9-day treks or climbs up Gunung Tahan. There are also overnight trips to night hides where you can observe animals up close. The jungle canopy walk is the longest in the world, and at 25m (83 ft.) above ground, the view is spectacular. There are also rivers for rafting and swimming, fishing spots, and a couple of caves.

If you plan your trip through one of the main resort operators, they can arrange, in addition to accommodations, all meals, treks, and a coach transfer to and from Kuala Lumpur. Prices vary wildly, depending on the season you plan your visit, your level of comfort desired, and the extent to which you wish to explore the forests. The best time to visit the park is between the months of April and September; other times it will be a tad wet, and that's why it's called a rainforest.

Mutiara Taman Negara Resort ✦, well established in the business of hosting visitors to the park, is the best accommodations in terms of comfort. It organizes trips for 3 days and 2 nights or for 4 days and 3 nights, as well as an a la carte deal where you pay for lodging and activities separately. Accommodations come in many styles: a bungalow suite for families; chalet and chalet suite, both good for couples; standard guesthouse rooms in a motel-style longhouse; and dormitory hostels for budget travelers. To get an idea of pricing, a 3-day, 2-night package runs about RM765 ($214/£107) per person, double occupancy in a chalet, with air-conditioning with attached bathroom, plus full board meals and activities. What it doesn't include is bus transfer from KL (RM80/$22/£11 per person round-trip) and the boat upriver from the park entrance (RM56/$16/£7.85 per person round-trip). A la carte activities include a 3-hour jungle trek, a 1½-hour night jungle walk, the half-day Lata Berkoh river trip with swimming, a 2-hour cave exploration, and a trip down the rapids in a rubber raft (Kuala Tahan, Jerantut, 27000 Pahang; ✆ **09/266-3500,** Kuala Lumpur Sales Office 03/2145-5585).

GENTING HIGHLANDS

The "City of Entertainment," as Genting is known locally, serves as Malaysia's answer to Las Vegas, complete with bright lights (which can be seen from Kuala Lumpur) and gambling. And although most people come here for the casino, there's a wide range of other activities, although most of them seem to serve the purpose of entertaining the kids while you bet their college funds at the roulette wheel. Honestly, I'll bet there's a more exciting place to gamble closer to where you live—this place holds little appeal for anyone but locals. Still, if you itch to place a bet . . .

Genting has four hotels of varying prices within the resort. Rates vary depending on the season, so be prepared for higher rates during the winter holidays. **Genting Hotel** is the best choice—a newer property that's linked directly to the casino. Week-day rates are from RM235 ($66/£33) for double occupancy, and weekend rates are from RM335 ($94/£47) double occupancy.

The 24-hour casino charges a refundable deposit of RM200 ($56/£28) entry for people over 21 years of age. Outside of the casino, there's also a pond, a bowling alley, and an indoor heated pool. The **Awana Golf and Country Club** (✆ 03/6101-3025) is the premier golf course in these hills. For children, the Genting Theme Park covers 9300 sq. m (100,000 sq. ft.) of mostly rides, plus many Western fast-food eating out-lets, games, and other attractions.

For buses from Kuala Lumpur, call **Genting Highlands Transport,** operating buses every half-hour from 6:30am to 9pm daily from KL Sentral train station. The cost for one-way is RM7.40 ($2.10/£1.05) and the trip takes 1 hour. The bus lets you off at the foot of the hill, where you take the cable car to the top (price included with bus ticket). For bus information, call ✆ 03/2279-8989.

You can also get there by hiring an **outstation taxi.** The cost is RM40 ($11/£5.60) and a taxi can be arranged by calling the **Puduraya** outstation taxi stand at ✆ 03/2078-0213.

The **Genting Highlands Resort** is owned and operated by Resorts World Berhad, who'll be glad to provide you with hotel reservations if you call ✆ 03/2718-1118.

CAMERON HIGHLANDS

Located in the hills, this colonial-era resort town has a cool climate, which makes it the perfect place for weekend getaways by Malaysians and Singaporeans who are sick of the heat. If you've been in the region awhile, you might also appreciate the respite.

The climate is also very conducive to agriculture. After the area's discovery by British surveyor William Cameron in 1885, the major crop here became tea, which is still grown today. The area's lovely gardens supply cities throughout the region with vegetables, flowers, and fruit year-round. Among the favorites here are the strawber-ries, which can be eaten fresh or transformed into yummy desserts in the local restau-rants. At the many commercial flower nurseries you can see chrysanthemums, fuchsias, and roses growing on the terraces. Rose gardens are prominent here.

Temperatures in the highlands average 70°F (21°C) during the day and 50°F (10°C) at night. There are paths for treks though the countryside and to peaks of sur-rounding mountains. Two waterfalls, the Robinson Falls and Parit Falls, have pools at their feet where you can have a swim.

There are **no visitor information services** here. They've been closed for a very long time, and have no immediate plans for reopening. You'll find banks with ATMs and money-changing services along the main road in Tanah Rata, the main town.

The best choice for accommodations here is the **Smokehouse Hotel.** Situated between Tanah Rata and Brinchang towns, this picturesque Tudor mansion has pretty gardens outside and a charming old-world ambience inside. Built in 1937 as a coun-try house in the heyday of colonial British getaways, its conversion into a hotel has kept the place happily in the 1930s. Guest suites have four-poster beds and antique furnishings, with some of the wear that one might expect from an old inn. The hotel encourages guests to play golf at the neighboring course, sit for afternoon tea with strawberry confections, or trek along nearby paths (for which they'll provide a picnic basket). It's all a bizarre escape from Malaysia, but a charming one (Tanah Rata,

Cameron Highlands, Pahang Darul Makmur; © 05/491-1215; fax 05/491-1214; RM460–RM730/$129–$204/£64–£102 suite).

Most of the sights can be seen in a day, but it's difficult to plan your time well. In Cameron Highlands I recommend trying one of the sightseeing outfits in either Brinchang or Tanah Rata. **C. S. Travel & Tours,** 47 Main Rd., Tanah Rata (© 05/491-1200), is a highly reputable agency that will plan half-day tours for RM20 ($5.60/ £2.80) or full days starting from RM80 ($22/£11). On your average tour you'll see the Boh tea plantation and factory, flower nurseries, rose gardens, strawberry farms, butterfly farms, and the Sam Poh Buddhist Temple. You're required to pay admission to each attraction yourself (about RM5/$1.40/70p). They also provide trekking and overnight camping tours in the surrounding hills with local trail guides.

If you want to hit around some balls, **Padang Golf,** Main Road between Tanah Rata and Brinchang (© 05/491-1126), has 18 holes at par 71, with greens fees around RM53 ($15/£7.35) on weekdays and RM84 ($24/£12) on weekends. They also provide club rentals, caddies, shoes, and carts.

To get to Cameron Highlands, **Kurnia Bistari Express Bus** (© 05/491-2978) operates between Kuala Lumpur and Tanah Rata daily for around RM17 ($4.80/ £2.40) one-way. They don't accept bookings in Kuala Lumpur, asking you to just show up at Puduraya bus terminal to buy your ticket and board the next bus. The bus terminal is in the center of town along the main drag. Just next to it is the taxi stand. It's a two-horse town; you can't miss either of them. Outstation taxis from KL will cost RM220 ($62/£31) for the trip. Call © 03/2078-0213 for booking. Taxis are cheaper on the way back because they don't have to climb the mountains.

2 Johor Bahru

Johor Bahru, the capital of the state of Johor, is at the southern tip of the Malaysian peninsula, where Malaysia's north-south highway comes to its southern terminus. Because it's just over the causeway from Singapore, a very short jump by car, bus, or train, it's a popular point of entry to Malaysia. Johor Bahru, or "JB," is not the most fascinating destination in Malaysia. If you want a good side trip from Singapore, there are more interesting sights in Malacca (see below) or better beaches on Tioman (see chapter 11).

The Malaysia Tourism Board office in Johor Bahru is at the **Johor Tourist Information Centre (JOTIC),** centrally located on Jalan Ayer Molek, on the second floor (© 07/223-4935). You can also find information at www.tourismjohor.com.

The **Sultan Ismail Airport/Senai International Airport,** 30 to 40 minutes outside the city (© 07/599-4737), has regular flights through Malaysia Airlines to and from major cities in Malaysia (© 1300/883-000; www.malaysiaairlines.com). **AirAsia** (© 1300/889-933; www.airasia.com) also uses JB as a hub to major destinations throughout Malaysia.

Buses to and from other parts of Malaysia are based at the Larkin Bus Terminal off Jalan Garuda in the northern part of the city. Taxis are available at the terminal to take you to the city. If you're coming from Singapore, the **Singapore–Johor Express** (© 65/6292-8149) operates every 10 minutes between 6:30am and midnight from the Ban Sen Terminal at Queen Street near Arab Street, Singapore. The cost for the half-hour trip is S$2.40 (US70¢/35p). If you take the bus, you can choose to get off at the Malaysian immigration checkpoint, which is more or less in the center of town, instead of going all the way to Larkin.

The **Keretapi Tanah Melayu Berhad (KTM)** trains arrive and depart from the Johor Bahru Railway Station at Jalan Tun Abdul Razak, opposite Merlin Tower (© 07/223-4727). Catch express trains from **KL Sentral** (© 03/2267-1200) twice daily for RM33 to RM64 ($9.20–$18/£4.60–£9), depending on the class you travel. From the **Singapore Railway Station** (© 65/6222-5165), on Keppel Road in Tanjong Pagar, the short trip is S$2.90 (US80¢/40p).

If you find yourself in JB overnight, the **Hyatt Regency** (Jalan Sungai Chat; © 800/233-1234 or 07/222-1234; fax 07/223-2718; http://johorbahru.regency.hyatt.com; RM235/$66/£33 double) is the top pick in terms of quality. JB has some good food, which you can try at the Tepian Tebrau Stalls in Jalan Skudai (along the seafront) and the hawker stalls near the Central Market. The dish that puts Johor Bahru on the map, *ikan bakar* (barbecued fish with chilies), is out of this world at the Tepian Tebrau stalls.

The sights in Johor Bahru are few, but there is an interesting museum inside the old *istana*. The **Royal Abu Bakar Museum,** also called the Istana Bakar, is a gorgeous royal palace built by Sultan Abu Bakar in 1866. Today it houses the royal collection of international treasures, costumes, historical documents, fine art from the family collection, and relics of the sultanate. It's at Jalan Tun Dr Ismail (© 07/223-0555; adults RM5/$1.40/70p, children under 12 RM4/$1.10/55p; Sat–Thurs 9am–4pm). The saracenic flavor of the **Bangunan Sultan Ibrahim (State Secretariat Building)** on Jalan Abdul Ibrahim makes it feel older than it truly is. Built in 1940, today it houses the State Secretariat.

3 Malacca (Melaka) ⓥ

Malacca's attraction is its cultural heritage, around which a substantial tourism industry has grown. If you're visiting, a little knowledge of history will help you appreciate all there is to see.

Malacca was founded around 1400 by Parameswara, called **Iskander Shah** in the Malay Annals. After he was chased from Palembang in southern Sumatra by invading Javanese, he set up a kingdom in Singapore (Temasek), and after being overthrown by invaders there, ran up the west coast of the Malay peninsula to Malacca, where he settled and established a port city. As the site was in a favorable spot to take advantage of the two monsoons that dominated shipping routes, Malacca soon drew the attention of Arab and Chinese traders, both of whom maintained very close relations for trade and political advantage. It was the early Arab merchants who introduced Islam to Malaysia. After Parameswara's death in 1414, his son, Mahkota Iskander Shah, converted to Islam and popularized the faith throughout the area.

During the 15th century, Malacca was ruled by a succession of wise sultans who expanded the wealth and stability of the economy; built up the administration's coffers; extended the sultanate to the far reaches of the Malay peninsula, Singapore, and parts of northern Sumatra; and thwarted repeated attacks by the Siamese. The success of the empire drew international attention.

The Portuguese were eyeing the port and formulating plans to dominate the east-west trade route, to establish the naval supremacy of Portugal and promote Christianity in the region. They struck in 1511 and conquered Malacca in a battle that lasted only a month. After the defeat, the sultanate fled to Johor while the Portuguese looted the city and sent its riches off to Lisbon.

Malacca

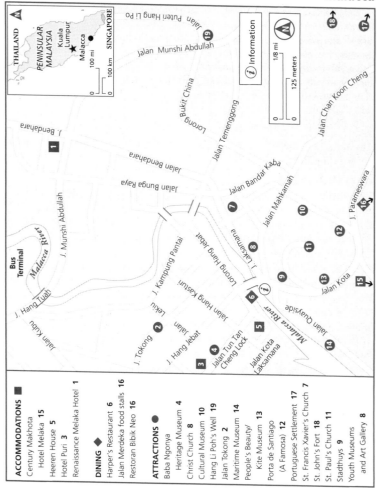

ACCOMMODATIONS ■
Century Makhota
Hotel Melaka **15**
Heeren House **5**
Hotel Puri **3**
Renaissance Melaka Hotel **1**

DINING ◆
Harper's Restaurant **6**
Jalan Merdeka food stalls **16**
Restoran Bibik Neo **16**

ATTRACTIONS ●
Baba Nyonya
  Heritage Museum **4**
Christ Church **8**
Cultural Museum **10**
Hang Li Poh's Well **19**
Jalan Tokong **2**
Maritime Museum **14**
People's Beauty/
  Kite Museum **13**
Porta de Santiago
  (A Famosa) **12**
Portuguese Settlement **17**
St. Francis Xavier's Church **7**
St. John's Fort **18**
St. Paul's Church **11**
Stadthuys **9**
Youth Museums
  and Art Gallery **8**

The Portuguese were the first of a chain of ruling foreign powers who would struggle in vain to retain the early economic success of the city. The foreign conquerors had a major strike against them: Their staunch Christianity alienated the locals and repelled Arab traders. The city quickly became nothing more than a sleepy outpost.

In 1641, the Dutch, with the help of Johor, conquered Malacca and controlled the city until 1795. Again, the Dutch were unsuccessful in rebuilding the glory of past prosperity in Malacca, and the city continued to sleep.

In 1795, the Dutch traded Malacca to the British in return for Bencoolen in Sumatra, being far more concerned with their Indonesian interests anyway. Malacca became a permanent British settlement in 1811, but by this time had become so poor and alienated that it was impossible to bring it back to life.

Today, Malacca is a sleepy backwater. The historic heart of town is distinctive with narrow one-way lanes hugged by old colonial-style shophouses built by the Dutch and British and later inhabited by wealthy Chinese and Peranakan (Straits-born Chinese) families. The buildings that stand out, however, are the bright red structures, a church and administrative buildings built by the Dutch during their rule. Just steps away are the remains of a Portuguese fort and church, and also close by you'll find English churches as well.

ESSENTIALS
VISITOR INFORMATION
The **Malacca Tourism Centre** is on Jalan Kota at the Town Square next to the bridge (© **06/281-4803**).

GETTING THERE
BY TRAIN Malacca doesn't have a proper train station, but the **KTM** stops at Tampin (© **06/441-1034**), 38km (24 miles) north of the city. It's not the most convenient way in and out of Malacca, but if you decide to stop en route between Kuala Lumpur and Johor Bahru, you can easily catch a waiting taxi to your hotel in town for RM40 ($11/£5.60).

BY BUS From Singapore, contact **Grassland Express** at © **65/6293-1166**. A bus departs at 8am daily for the 4½-hour trip (S$27/US$17/£8.90). From **KL's Puduraya Bus Terminal** on Jalan Pudu, **Transnasional** (© **03/6201-3463**) has hourly buses between 8am and 10pm for about RM9.50 ($2.70/£1.35). The trip takes about 2½ hours.

The bus station in Malacca is at Jalan Kilang, within the city. Taxis are easy to find from here.

BY TAXI **Outstation taxis** can bring you here from Kuala Lumpur for RM140 ($39/£20). The outstation taxi stand in Malacca is at the bus terminal on Jalan Kilang.

GETTING AROUND
Most of the historic sights around the town square are well within walking distance. For other trips **taxis** are the most convenient way around, but are at times difficult to find. They're also not as clearly marked as in KL or Johor Bahru. They are not metered, so be prepared to bargain. Basically, no matter what you do, you'll always be charged a higher rate than a local. Tourists are almost always quoted at RM10 ($2.80/£1.40) for local trips. Malaysians pay RM5 ($1.40/70p). If you're feeling sporty, you can bargain for a price somewhere in between.

Trishaws (bicycle rickshaws) are all over the historic areas of town, and in Malacca they're renowned for being very, very garishly decorated (which adds to the fun!). Negotiate for hourly rates of about RM20 ($5.60/£2.80) for two people.

FAST FACTS: MALACCA
Malacca's **area code** is 06. Major **banks** are located in the historic center of town, with a couple along Jalan Putra. **Internet** places come and go. Your best bet is to ask your hotel's concierge or the Malacca Tourism Centre (see above) for the nearest cafes.

WHERE TO STAY
Malacca is not very large, and most of the places to stay are well within walking distance of attractions, shopping, and restaurants.

Century Mahkota Hotel Melaka   Along the waterfront, the hotel is walking distance from sightseeing, historic areas, shopping, and commercial centers. Rooms are more like holiday apartments, with mini-kitchens and up to three bedrooms for family living—a big hit with Malaysian and Singaporean families. Each apartment has a tiled main room with clean cooking space at one end and simple rattan furnishings at the other—only bedrooms are air-conditioned. The views are of either the pools, the shopping mall across the street, or the muddy reclaimed seafront. The sprawling complex includes two outdoor pools and facilities for children, and is across from the largest shopping mall in Malacca. This place gets especially crowded during the school holidays in June and December.

Jalan Merdeka, 75000 Malacca. ℂ 06/281-2828. Fax 06/281-2323. 617 units. RM178–RM408 ($50–$114/£25–£57) 1- to 3-bedroom apt. AE, DC, MC, V. **Amenities:** 3 restaurants; lounge and piano bar; 2 outdoor pools; outdoor lighted tennis courts; squash courts; fitness center w/sauna and massage; children's playground; game room; tour desk; car-rental desk; shuttle; business center; 24-hr. room service; babysitting; same-day laundry service; dry cleaning. *In room:* TV w/satellite programming, coffee/tea-making facilities, hair dryer.

Heeren House ✦✦   This is the place to stay in Malacca for a taste of the local culture. Started by a local family, the small guesthouse is a renovated 100-year-old building furnished in traditional Peranakan and colonial style and located right in the heart of historical European Malacca. All the bedrooms have views of the Malacca River, and outside the front door of the hotel is a winding stretch of old buildings housing antiques shops. Just walk out and wander. Small rooms have very basic amenities. The rooms on the second floor are somewhat larger. Laundry service is available, and there's a cafe and gift shop on the premises. Everybody is nice as pie. Reserve well in advance.

1 Jalan Tun Tan Cheng Lock, 75200 Malacca. ℂ 06/281-4241. Fax 06/281-4239. 7 units. RM139 ($39/£20) double; RM239 ($67/£33) family suite. No credit cards. **Amenities:** Restaurant; same-day laundry service; souvenir shop. *In room:* A/C, TV.

Hotel Puri *Value*   In olden days, Jalan Tun Tan Cheng Lock was known as "Millionaire Row" for all the wealthy families that lived here. This old "mansion" has been converted into a guesthouse, its tiled parlor has become a lobby, and the courtyard is where breakfast is served each morning. Although Hotel Puri isn't big on space, it is big on value (discount rates can be pretty low). Rooms are very clean, and while not overly stylish, are comfortable enough for any weary traveler. A friendly and responsive staff adds to the appeal.

118 Jalan Tun Tan Cheng Lock, 75200 Malacca. ℂ 06/282-5588. Fax 06/281-5588. 50 units. RM127 (US$36/£18) double; RM265 ($74/£37) triple; suites from RM322 ($90/£45). AE, MC, V. **Amenities:** Restaurant; tour desk; limited room service; babysitting; same-day laundry service. *In room:* A/C, TV w/satellite programming, fridge, coffee/tea-making facilities, hair dryer.

Renaissance Melaka Hotel ✦   Renaissance is one of the more posh hotels in Malacca, and, according to business travelers, is the most reliable place for quality accommodations—but aside from the pieces of Peranakan porcelain and art in the public areas, you could almost believe you weren't in Malacca at all. The hotel is, however, situated in a good location, though you'll still need a taxi to most of the sights. Renovations in 2002 upgraded the guest rooms, which are fairly large and filled with Western comforts. Don't expect much from the views, as the hotel is in a more business-minded part of the city. No historical landmarks to gaze upon here. Facilities include an outdoor pool; fitness center with massage, sauna, and steam; two indoor squash courts; a tour operator desk; and a beauty salon. Golf is located nearby.

Jalan Bendahara, 75100 Malacca. (©) **800/228-9898** in the U.S. and Canada, 800/251-259 in Australia, 800/441-035 in New Zealand, 800/181-737 in the U.K., or 06/284-8888. Fax 06/284-9269. 294 units. RM480 ($134/£67) double; from RM620 ($174/£87) suite. AE, MC, V. **Amenities:** 3 restaurants; bar and lobby lounge; outdoor pool; golf nearby; squash courts; fitness center w/sauna, steam, and massage; concierge; tour desk; limousine service; business center; salon; 24-hr. room service; babysitting; same-day laundry service; dry cleaning; executive-level rooms. *In room:* A/C, TV w/satellite programming and in-house movie, minibar, coffee/tea-making facilities, safe.

WHERE TO DINE

In Malacca you'll find the typical mix of authentic Malay and Chinese food, and as the city was the major settling place for the Peranakans in Malaysia, their unique style of food is featured in many of the local restaurants.

A good recommendation for a quick bite at lunch or dinner if you're strolling in the historic area is the long string of open-air food stalls along Jalan Merdeka, just between Mahkota Plaza Shopping and Warrior Square. **Mama Fatso's** is especially good for Chinese-style seafood and Malay sambal curry. A good meal will run you about RM35 to RM40 ($9.80–$11/£4.90–£5.60) per person.

Try local Peranakan cuisine at **Restoran Bibik Neo** (No. 6, ground floor, Jalan Merdeka, Taman Melaka Raya; © **06/281-7054**), a small coffee shop that's about as authentic as you can get. *Ikan assam* with eggplant is a tasty mild fish curry that's very rich and tart, and I always go for the *otak-otak* (pounded fish and spices baked in a banana leaf).

For a taste of Portuguese Malacca, the **Portuguese Settlement** has some open-air food stalls by the water, where in the evenings hawkers sell an assortment of dishes inspired by these former colonial rulers, including many fresh seafood offerings. Saturday nights are best when, at 8pm, there's a cultural show with music and dancing. Other times it may be slow business. (Jalan d'Albuquerque off Jalan Ujon Pasir; dinner from RM15/$4.20/£2.10–RM20/$5.60/£2.80 per person; no credit cards.)

My favorite place in town is **Harper's Restaurant** (Harper's Building, Jalan Hang Jebat; © **06/282-8800**), which serves Nyonya, Chinese, and Western food in a terrific riverside ambience. This combination watering hole and bistro has a relaxed Asian feel, with open-air verandas and cane furnishings. Simple but atmospheric. The menu serves local dishes that can be adjusted for Western tastes upon request (if you need less chili, for example), and a selection of steaks prepared in Western style. Prices range from RM20 ($5.60/£2.80) for simple Asian small dishes to up to RM45 ($13/£6.30) for the surf and turf. They're open daily from 10am to 1:30am, but the Asian kitchen is only open from noon to 2:30pm and 6 to 10:30pm. Western food is served anytime between noon and 11:30pm. Visa and MasterCard are accepted.

ATTRACTIONS

To get the most out of Malacca, it's best to have a bit of knowledge about the history of the place, which I've explained briefly in the intro to this section. Most of the preserved historical sites are on both sides of the Malacca River. Start at **Stadthuys** (the old town hall, pronounced "stat-highs") and you'll see most of Malacca pretty quickly.

MUSEUMS

Baba Nyonya Heritage Museum ⭐ Called "Millionaire's Row," Jalan Tun Tan Cheng Lock is lined with row houses that were built by the Dutch and later bought by wealthy Peranakans; the architectural style reflects their East-meets-West lifestyle. The Baba Nyonya Heritage Museum sits at nos. 48 and 50 as a museum of Peranakan heritage. The entrance fee includes a guided tour.

48_50 Jalan Tun Tan Cheng Lock. © 06/283-1273. Adults RM8 ($2.20/£1.10), children RM4 ($1.10/55p). Daily 10am–12:30pm and 2–4:30pm.

Cultural Museum (Muzium Budaya) ★ A replica of the former palace of Sultan Mansur Syah (1456–77), this museum was rebuilt according to historical descriptions to house a fine collection of cultural artifacts such as clothing, weaponry, and royal items. The gardens are quite nice.

Kota Rd., next to Porta de Santiago. © 06/282-6526. Adults RM2 (60¢/30p), children RM0.50 (10¢/5p). Daily 9am–5:30pm.

Maritime Museum and the Royal Malaysian Navy Museum These two museums are located across the street from one another but share admission fees. The Maritime Museum is in a restored 16th-century Portuguese ship, with exhibits dedicated to Malacca's history with the sea. The Navy Museum is a modern display of Malaysia's less-pleasant relationship with the sea.

Quayside Rd. © 06/282-6526. Admission adults RM3 (80¢/40p), children RM1 (30¢/15p). Daily 9am–5:30pm.

The People's Museum, the Museum of Beauty, the Kite Museum, and the Governor of Melaka's Gallery This strange collection of displays is housed under one roof. The People's Museum is the story of development in Malacca. The Museum of Beauty is a look at cultural differences of beauty throughout time and around the world. The Kite Museum features the traditions of making and flying *wau* (kites) in Malaysia, and the governor's personal collection is on exhibit at the Governor's Gallery.

Kota Rd. © 06/282-6526. Admission adults RM2 (60¢/30p), children RM0.50 (10¢/5p). Daily 9am–5:30pm.

Stadthuys—The Museums of History & Ethnography and the Museum of Literature ★ The Stadthuys Town Hall was built by the Dutch in 1650, and it's now home to the Malacca Ethnographical and Historical Museum, which displays customs and traditions of all the peoples of Malacca, and takes you through the rich history of this city. Behind Stadthuys, the Museum of Literature includes old historical accounts and local legends. Admission price is for both exhibits.

Located at the circle intersection of Jalan Quayside, Jalan Laksamana, and Jalan Chan Koon Cheng. © 06/282-6526. Admission adults RM5 ($1.40/70p), children RM2 (60¢/30p). Daily 9am–5:30pm.

Youth Museums and Art Gallery In the old General Post office are these displays dedicated to Malaysia's youth organizations and to the nation's finest artists. An unusual combination.

Laksamana Rd. © 06/282-6526. Admission adults RM2 (60¢/30p), children RM0.50 (10¢/5p). Tues–Sun 9am–5:30pm.

HISTORICAL SITES

Christ Church The Dutch built this place in 1753 as a Dutch Reform Church, and its architectural details include such wonders as ceiling beams cut from a single tree and a Last Supper glazed tile motif above the altar. It was later consecrated as an Anglican church, and Mass is still performed today in English, Chinese, and Tamil.

Located on Jalan Laksamana. Free admission.

Hang Li Poh's Well Also called "Sultan's Well," Hang Li Poh's Well was built in 1495 to commemorate the marriage of Chinese Princess Hang Li Poh to Sultan Mansor Shah. It is now a wishing well, and folks say that if you toss in a coin, you'll someday return to Malacca.

Located off Jalan Laksamana Cheng Ho (Jalan Panjang). Free admission.

Jalan Tokong ⊛   Not far from Jalan Tun Tan Cheng Lock is Jalan Tokong, called the "Street of Harmony" by the locals because it has three coexisting places of worship: the Kampong Kling Mosque, the Cheng Hoon Teng Temple, and the Sri Poyyatha Vinayar Moorthi Temple.

Porta de Santiago (A Famosa) ⊛   Once the site of a Portuguese fortress called A Famosa, all that remains today of the fortress is the entrance gate, which was saved from demolition by Sir Stamford Raffles. When the British East India Company demolished the place, Raffles realized the arch's historical value and saved it. The fort was built in 1512, but the inscription above the arch, "Anno 1607," marks the date when the Dutch overthrew the Portuguese.

Located on Jalan Kota, at the intersection of Jalan Parameswara. Free admission.

Portuguese Settlement and Portuguese Square   The Portuguese Settlement is an enclave once designated for Portuguese settlers after they conquered Malacca in 1511. Some elements of their presence remain in the Lisbon-style architecture. Later, in 1920, the area was a Eurasian neighborhood. In the center of the settlement, Portuguese Square is a modern attraction with Portuguese restaurants, handicrafts, souvenirs, and cultural shows. It was built in 1985 in an architectural style to reflect the surrounding flavor of Portugal.

Located down Jalan d'Albuquerque off of Jalan Ujon Pasir in the southern part of the city. Free admission.

St. Francis Xavier's Church   This church was built in 1849 and dedicated to St. Francis Xavier, a Jesuit who brought Catholicism to Malacca and other parts of Southeast Asia.

Located on Jalan Laksamana. Free admission.

St. John's Fort   The fort, built by the Dutch in the late 18th century, sits on top of St. John's Hill. Funny how the cannons point inland, huh? At the time, threats to the city came from land. It was named after a Portuguese church to St. John the Baptist, which originally occupied the site.

Located off Lorong Bukit Senjuang. Free admission.

St. Paul's Church   The church was built by the Portuguese in 1521, but when the Dutch came in, they made it part of A Famosa, converting the altar into a cannon mount. The open tomb inside was once the resting place of St. Francis Xavier, a missionary who spread Catholicism throughout Southeast Asia, and whose remains were later moved to Goa.

Located behind Porta de Santiago. Free admission.

SHOPPING

Antiques hunting has been a major draw to Malacca for decades. Distinct Peranakan and teak furniture, porcelain, and household items fetch quite a price these days, due to a steady increase in demand for these rare treasures. The area down and around Jalan Hang Jebat and Jalan Tun Tan Cheng Lok called **Jonker Walk** sports many little antiques shops that are filled with as many gorgeous items as any local museum. You'll also find handmade crafts, ready-made batik clothing, and other souvenirs. Whether you're buying or just looking, it's a fun way to spend an afternoon.

For crafts and souvenirs, you'll also find a row of shops along the lane beside Stadthuys. Most prices seem fair, but you may need to do a little bargaining.

4 Pangkor

Pangkor's claim to fame is the spectacular, award-winning Pangkor Laut Resort, nestled on its own private island—without a doubt one of Malaysia's finest. Pangkor's main island supports a wee village and some smaller resorts. For a while, the Pan Pacific group operated a fine resort here, but they ran out of steam, leaving behind a worn-out facility that's become badly mismanaged. Other than that, there's not much to see.

If the exclusivity of seclusion is exciting for you, then Pangkor is your place. If you feel you need to break up the resort experience with something else, Langkawi (later in this chapter) to the north has luxury resorts that are all that, plus overnight trips to Penang.

The easiest way to get to Pangkor is to hop a flight. **Berjaya Air** (© **03/2145-8689;** www.berjaya-air.com) flies five times a week, and the trip is only 30 minutes. Compared to a 3½-hour drive from KL, then a ferry ride to the island, it saves a lot of hassle.

Pangkor Laut Resort ★★★   This little village comprises private wooden Malay-style chalets perched atop stilts, connected by wooden boardwalks over the green sea. Pangkor Laut creates an effect that is rustic and natural, yet uncompromisingly sophisticated and luxurious. Each roomy villa is adorned with warm wood interiors, uncluttered contemporary wood furnishings, king-size beds, and writing tables with Malaysian arts and textiles throughout. Each has a private sun deck furnished with chaise longues. There's no TV, but each villa comes with its own CD sound system on which you can play CDs from the resort's library. Spa and sea villas sit on stilts, with big picture windows that open out over the water. Lower-priced hill and garden villas are housed in double-story buildings, hill villas commanding the best sea views. Spa villas connect directly to the resort's delicious full-service Spa Village, a seaside collection of landscaped buildings and pavilions where you can select a range of treatments developed from Malay, Chinese, Indian and other traditional Asian natural beauty and health secrets. You won't get bored with dining options either. Pangkor Laut has seven outlets serving either food or beverages. Activities include chartered cruises, sailing, windsurfing, kayaking, and jungle trekking, and golf can be arranged on the mainland. If you take your seclusion seriously, Pangkor Laut has eight full-service private residences on the property as well.

Pangkor Laut Island, 32200 Lumut, Perak. © **05/699-1100.** Fax 05/699-1200. www.pangkorlautresort.com. 148 units. RM1,200–RM1,750 ($336–$490/£168–£245) villa. AE, DC, MC, V. **Amenities:** 4 restaurants; 3 lounges; TV room; 2 outdoor pools; 3 outdoor lighted tennis courts; 2 squash courts; fitness center; spa; Jacuzzi; watersports equipment; concierge; 24-hr. room service; babysitting; same-day laundry service; jungle trekking. *In room:* A/C; minibar, coffee/tea making facilities, hair dryer, safe.

5 Penang ★★★

Penang is unique in Malaysia because, for all intents and purposes, Penang has it all. Tioman Island (see chapter 11) may have beaches and forests, but it has no shopping or historical sights to speak of. And although Malacca has historical sights and museums, it hasn't a grain of decent sand. Penang has all of it: fun beaches, beautiful resorts, rich history, diverse culture, and delicious food. If you only have a short time to visit Malaysia but want to take in as wide an experience as you can, Penang is a good choice.

Penang gets its name from the Malay word *pinang,* in reference to the areca plant, which grew on the island in abundance. The nut of the tree, commonly called *betel,* was chewed habitually throughout the East (and in some parts still is). In the 15th century it was a quiet place populated by small Malay communities, attracting the interest of some southern Indian betel merchants. By the time Francis Light, an agent for the British East India Company, arrived in 1786, the island was already on the maps of European, Indian, and Chinese traders. Light landed on the northeast part of the island, where he began a settlement after an agreement with the sultan of Kedah, on the mainland. He called the town **Georgetown,** after George III. One story claims that to gain the help of the locals for clearing the site, he shot a cannon-load of coins into the jungle.

Georgetown became Britain's principal post in Malaya, attracting Europeans, Arabs, northern and southern Indians, southern Chinese, and Malays from the mainland and Sumatra to trade and settle. But it was never extremely profitable for England, especially when in 1819 Sir Stamford Raffles founded a new trading post in Singapore. Penang couldn't keep up with the new port's success.

In 1826 Penang, along with Malacca and Singapore, formed a unit called the Straits Settlements, over which Penang was voted the seat of government by a narrow margin. Finally in 1832, Singapore stole its thunder when authority shifted there. In the late 1800s Penang got a big break. Tin mines and rubber plantations on mainland Malaya were booming, and with the opening of the railway between KL and **Butterworth** (the town on the mainland just opposite the island), Penang once again thrived. Singapore firms scrambled to open offices in Butterworth.

The Great Depression hit Penang hard. So did the Japanese occupation from 1941 to 1945, when the island was badly bombed. But since Malaysia's independence in 1957, Penang has had relatively good financial success.

Today the state of Penang is made up of the island and a small strip of land on the Malaysian mainland. Georgetown is the seat of government for the state. Penang Island is 285 sq. km (171 sq. miles) and has a population of a little more than 1 million. Surprisingly, the population is mostly Chinese (59%), followed by Malays (32%), and Indians (7%).

Georgetown reminds me of the way Singapore looked before massive government redevelopment and restoration projects "sanitized" the old neighborhoods. Georgetown's grid of narrow streets are still lined with shophouses that bustle with activity. Historic churches, temples, and mosques mingle with the city's newer architecture.

West of Georgetown, along Penang's northern shore, you'll find a number of popular resorts, sprawling complexes along strips of sandy beaches. Unfortunately, because Penang is located in the Strait of Malacca, the waters are not the idyllic crystal-clear azure you hope for in a tropical holiday. Yes, you've got sun, sand, and seasports, but no snorkeling or scuba. In my opinion, if you really want it all, enjoy the waters and sea life while you stay at one of the luxury resorts on Langkawi to the north (covered later in this chapter), and hop on a ferry to Georgetown for a day trip of sightseeing.

ESSENTIALS
VISITOR INFORMATION

The main **Malaysia Tourism Board (MTB)** office is located at no. 10 Jalan Tun Syed Sheh Barakbah (© 04/261-9067), just across from the clock tower by Fort Cornwallis. There's another information center at **Penang International Airport** (© 04/643-0501) and a branch on the third level at **KOMTAR** (Kompleks Tun Abdul Razak) on Jalan Penang (© 04/261-4461).

Penang Island

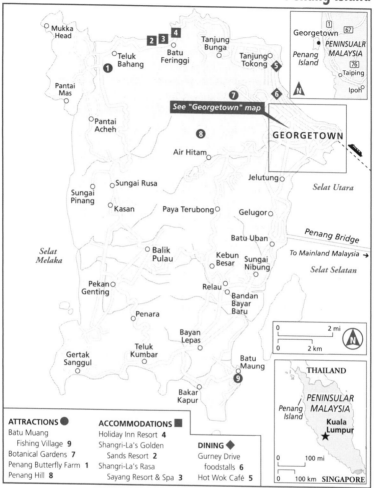

Georgetown [1] [67]

PENINSUALR MALAYSIA

Penang Island

[76]

Taiping

Ipoh

Mukka Head

Teluk Bahang ❶

Batu Feringgi ❷ ❸ ❹

Tanjung Bunga

Tanjung Tokong ❺

❼ ❻

See "Georgetown" map

GEORGETOWN

Pantai Mas

Pantai Acheh

❽

Air Hitam

Jelutung

Selat Utara

Sungai Rusa

Sungai Pinang

Kasan

Paya Terubong

Gelugor

Batu Uban

Penang Bridge

To Mainland Malaysia →

Selat Melaka

Balik Pulau

Kebun Besar

Sungai Nibung

Selat Selatan

Pekan Genting

Relau

Bandan Bayar Baru

Penara

Bayan Lepas

Gertak Sanggul

Teluk Kumbar

Batu Maung

❾

Bakar Kapur

| 0 | | 2 mi |
| 0 | | 2 km |

THAILAND

PENINSULAR MALAYSIA

Penang Island

Kuala Lumpur ★

| 0 | | 100 mi |
| 0 | | 100 km | SINGAPORE |

ATTRACTIONS ●
Batu Muang
  Fishing Village **9**
Botanical Gardens **7**
Penang Butterfly Farm **1**
Penang Hill **8**

ACCOMMODATIONS ■
Holiday Inn Resort **4**
Shangri-La's Golden
  Sands Resort **2**
Shangri-La's Rasa
  Sayang Resort & Spa **3**

DINING ◆
Gurney Drive
  foodstalls **6**
Hot Wok Café **5**

GETTING THERE

BY PLANE   **Penang International Airport** (☎ **04/643-4411**) has flights that connect from all over the world. **Malaysia Airlines** (☎ **1300/883-000;** www.malaysia airlines.com) has about 20 flights each day from KL, plus connecting flights from all over the country and region. Other airlines that service Penang are **Singapore Airlines, Thai Airways, Cathay Pacific,** and the popular budget carrier, **AirAsia** (☎ **1300/ 889-933;** www.airasia.com).

The airport is 20km (12 miles) from the city. To get into town, you must purchase fixed-rate coupons for taxis (RM38/$11/£5 to Georgetown; RM60/$17/£8 to Batu Feringgi). There are also car rentals at the airport; choose **Avis** (☎ **04/643-9633**).

BY TRAIN   By rail, the overnight trip from KL to Butterworth takes 10 hours and costs RM85 ($24/£12) first-class passage, or as low as RM17 ($4.80/£2) for economy class. The prices vary quite greatly depending on if you choose upper or lower berth, and what class passage you take. Call **KL Sentral** (© **03/2267-1200**) for schedule information.

The train will let you off at the **Butterworth Railway Station** (© **04/323-7962**), on Jalan Bagan Dalam (near the ferry terminal) in Butterworth, on the Malaysian mainland. From there, you can take a taxi to the island or head for the ferry close by.

BY BUS Many buses will bring you to Butterworth or Georgetown, but I really only recommend it if you're a glutton for punishment. Transnasional stopped their executive coach service, and if you take a standard coach the trip will be horrible.

BY FERRY The ferry to Penang is nestled between the Butterworth Railway Station and the Butterworth bus terminal. It operates 24 hours a day and takes 20 minutes from pier to pier. From 6am to midnight ferries leave every 10 minutes. From midnight to 1:20am boats run every half-hour, and from 1:20 to 6am they run hourly. Purchase your passage by dropping RM1.20 (30¢/15p) exact change in the turnstile (there's a change booth if you don't have it). Fare is paid only on the trip to Penang. The return is free. The ferry lets you off at Weld Quay.

BY TAXI The **outstation taxi** stand is in Butterworth next to the bus terminal (© **04/323-2045**). Fares to Butterworth from KL will be about RM300 ($84/£42).

GETTING AROUND

BY TAXI Taxis are abundant, but be warned they do not use meters, so you must agree on the price before you ride. Most trips within the city are between RM3 and RM6 (80¢–$1.70/40p–85p). If you're staying out at the Batu Feringgi beach resort area, expect taxis to town to run RM20 ($5.60/£2.80), RM30 ($8.40/£4.20) at night. The ride is about 15 or 20 minutes, but can take 30 minutes during rush hour.

BY BUS Buses also run all over the island and are well used by tourists who don't want to spring RM20 ($5.60/£2.80) every time they want to go to the beach. The dark blue no. 93 and the white with blue no. 202 both operate between KOMTAR in Georgetown and the beach resorts at Batu Feringgi. Fare is anywhere under RM3 (80¢/40p). Get exact change from your hotel's cashier before you set off and ask the bus driver about the exact fare to your destination.

CAR RENTAL If you want to drive, call Avis at the Penang International Airport at © **04/643-9633.** They can also provide a car with driver for RM80 ($22/£11) per hour, for a minimum booking of 4 hours. If you plan to visit areas off Penang Island, the rate will increase.

BY BICYCLE & MOTORCYCLE Along Batu Feringgi there are bicycles and motorcycles (little 100cc scooters, really) available for rent. I don't recommend hiring the scooters. You can never be certain of their maintenance record and Penang's drivers are careless about watching your back. A sad number of visitors are injured or worse because of scooter accidents.

BY TRISHAW In Georgetown it's possible to find some trishaw action for about RM20 ($5.60/£2.80) an hour. It's kitschy and touristy and I completely recommend it for traveling between in-town sights, at least for an hour or two. Bargain hard; these guys are skilled negotiators.

ON FOOT I think everyone should walk at least part of the time to see the sights of Georgetown because in between each landmark and exhibit there's so much more

Georgetown

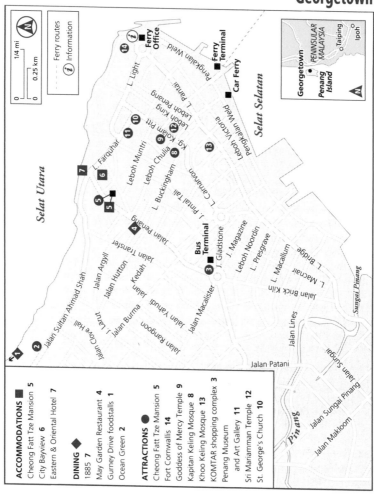

ACCOMMODATIONS ■
Cheong Fatt Tze Mansion 5
City Bayview 6
Eastern & Oriental Hotel 7

DINING ◆
1885 7
May Garden Restaurant 4
Gurney Drive foodstalls 1
Ocean Green 2

ATTRACTIONS ●
Cheong Fatt Tze Mansion 5
Fort Cornwallis 14
Goddess of Mercy Temple 9
Kapitan Keling Mosque 8
Khoo Keling Mosque 13
KOMTAR shopping complex 3
Penang Museum
and Art Gallery 11
Sri Mariamman Temple 12
St. George's Church 10

to see. A taxi, even a trishaw, will whisk you right by back alleys where elderly hair-cutters set up alfresco shops, bicycle repairmen sit fixing tubes in front of their stores, and Chinese grannies fan themselves in the shade. Georgetown is stimulating, with the sights of old trades still being plied on these living streets, the noise of everyday life, and the exotic smells of an old Southeast Asian port. Give yourself at least a day here. Start wandering early in the morning, by the waterfront, down the back alleys, before the heat of the sun takes hold—the lighting is perfect for photography and you will find fantastic subjects here.

FAST FACTS: PENANG

Penang's **area code** is 04. The **banking center** of Georgetown is in the downtown area (close to Ft. Cornwallis) on Leboh Pantai, Leboh Union, and Leboh Downing, but you'll find ATMs in KOMTAR and other smaller shopping plazas as well. **Internet** cafes come and go, so it's best to ask your hotel's concierge for the closest place to your hotel. If you're in town, Chulia Street, the main drag for backpacker tourists, has Internet access in a few places.

WHERE TO STAY

Although Georgetown has many hotels right in the city for convenient sightseeing, most visitors choose to stay at one of the beach resorts 30 minutes away at Batu Feringgi. Trips back and forth can be a bother (regardless of the resorts' free shuttle services), but if you're not staying in a resort, most of the finer beaches are off-limits.

Cheong Fatt Tze Mansion ★★ *Finds*   Hands down the most unique and memorable hotel experience in all of Malaysia—to sleep inside the walls of one of Asia's most carefully restored heritage homes, the huge and opulent mansion of 19th-century millionaire Cheong Fatt Tze. The lobby is a simple desk in the courtyard, inside the only facilities to speak of are a courtyard breakfast area, a library, and a TV room (guest rooms do not have TVs). Guest rooms are each distinctive in shape and decor, all with plank floors, charming architectural detail, and furnished in antiques and replicas of the period. Double rooms have either twin beds or one king-size. Suites are also available. All are air-conditioned and have private bathrooms, though they are pretty small and bare. The experience is described by the management as an "owner-hosted homestay," which is quite accurate. Don't expect the professional polish of the Shangri-La, but then, with so much beauty around you, who cares?

13 Leith St., 10200 Penang. ✆ 04/262-0006. www.cheongfatttzemansion.com. 16 units. RM350 ($98/£49) double; suites from RM420 ($118/£59). AE, DC, MC, V. **Amenities:** Breakfast area w/tea and beverage service; library; TV room; valet service; laundry service; nonsmoking rooms. *In room:* A/C, coffee/tea-making facilities.

The City Bayview Hotel, Penang   This city hotel is perfect for those who visit Penang for its cultural treasures rather than its beaches. A good budget choice, it has a number of fair dining venues, including a rooftop revolving restaurant with excellent views of the island. Choose from guest rooms in the newer wing, completed in 1999, or those in the old wing, which have been recently refurbished. Either choice offers cool rooms in neutral tones, not as elegant as many, but comfortable and definitely offering value for the money.

25-A Farquhar St., Georgetown, 10200 Penang. ✆ 04/263-3161. Fax 04/263-4124. 320 units. RM425 ($119/£60) double, from RM828 ($232/£116) suite. AE, DC, MC, V. **Amenities:** 3 restaurants; club w/live entertainment; lobby lounge; outdoor pool; concierge; limousine service; business center; 24-hr. room service; babysitting; same-day laundry service; dry cleaning; nonsmoking rooms. *In room:* A/C, TV w/in-house movie, minibar, coffee/tea-making facilities, hair dryer, safe.

Eastern & Oriental Hotel (E&O)   E&O first opened in 1884, established by the same Sarkies brothers who were behind Raffles Hotel in Singapore. Closed for many, many years (it was desperately in need of an overhaul) it reopened in April 2001. It is without a doubt the most atmospheric hotel in Penang, with manicured lawns and tropical gardens flanking a white colonial-style mansion, a lacelike facade, and Moorish minarets. Accommodations are all suites, with cozy sitting nooks and sleeping quarters separated by pocket sliding doors. You can expect molding details around every door and paned window, Oriental carpets over polished plank floorboards, and Egyptian cotton linens dressing each poster bed. Dining along the hotel's many verandas is gorgeous. One caveat—no beach, but the pool in the seafront garden is very pretty.

10 Farquhar St., 10200 Penang. ⓒ **04/222-2000**. Fax 04/261-6333. www.e-o-hotel.com. 101 units. RM900–RM2,050 ($252–$574/£126–£287). AE, DC, MC, V. **Amenities:** 2 restaurants; English-style pub; outdoor pool; small fitness center w/sauna; concierge; limousine service; 24-hr. room service; same-day laundry service; dry cleaning. *In room:* A/C, TV w/satellite programming, minibar, coffee/tea-making facilities.

Golden Sands Resort by Shangri-La

Shangri-La has been operating resorts on Penang longer than anyone else, and because it got here first you can bet it laid claim to the best beach. Shangri-La has two neighboring properties on this site, Golden Sands and its more exclusive sister, Rasa Sayang. A newer resort, Golden Sands is priced lower than the Rasa Sayang, so it attracts more families. The beach, pool area, and public spaces fill up fast in the morning, and folks are occupied all day with beach sports like parasailing and jet-skiing, and pool games. For the younger set, a kids' club keeps small ones busy while Mom and Dad do "boring stuff." Rooms are large with full amenities, and the higher-priced categories have views of the pool and sea.

Batu Feringgi Beach, 11100 Penang. ⓒ **800/942-5050** in the U.S. and Canada, 800/222-448 in Australia, 800/442-179 in New Zealand, or 04/881-1911. Fax 04/881-1880. www.shangri-la.com. 395 units. RM700 ($196/£98) double; RM1,750 ($490/£245) suite. AE, DC, MC, V. **Amenities:** 3 restaurants; lobby lounge; 2 outdoor lagoon-style pools; outdoor lighted tennis courts; watersports equipment and activities; children's center; game room; concierge; tour desk; car-rental desk; limousine service; shuttle service to Shangri-La Hotel in Georgetown; business center; salon; 24-hr. room service; babysitting; same-day laundry service; dry cleaning; self-service launderette. *In room:* A/C, TV w/satellite programming and in-house movie, fridge, coffee/tea-making facilities, hair dryer, safe.

Holiday Inn Resort Penang *Kids*

This is a recommended choice for families, but be warned this resort has little appeal for vacationing couples or singles sans children. For families it has everything—special Kidsuites have a separate room for the wee ones with TV, video, and PlayStation, some with bunk beds—choose from jungle, treasure island, or outer space themes. Holiday Inn also has a Kids Club, fully supervised day-care with activities and games and a lifeguard. Older kids can join in beach volleyball, water polo, bike tours, and an assortment of watersports arranged by the staff. Guest rooms are in two blocks: a low-rise structure near the beach and a high-rise tower along the hillside, connected by a second-story walkway. Naturally, the beachside rooms command the greater rate. Beachside rooms also have better ambience and slightly larger space with wood floors and details, while tower rooms have less charm. The lack of dining options gets tiring.

72 Batu Feringgi, 11100 Penang. ⓒ **04/881-1601**. Fax 04/881-1389. www.penang.holiday-inn.com. 362 units. RM450–RM550 ($126–$154/£63–£77) hill-view double; RM530–RM650 ($148–$182/£74–£91) seaview double; RM800 ($224/£112) Kidsuite; from RM800 ($224/£112) suite. AE, DC, MC, V. **Amenities:** Restaurant; lobby lounge; outdoor pool and children's pool; outdoor lighted tennis courts; fitness center; watersports equipment rentals; children's club; game room; concierge; tour desk; limousine service; 24-hr. room service; massage; babysitting; same-day laundry service; dry cleaning. *In room:* A/C, TV w/satellite programming and in-house movie, minibar, coffee/tea-making facilities, hair dryer, iron, safe.

Shangri-La's Rasa Sayang Resort & Spa ✦✦✦

Rasa Sayang reopened in 2006 after an RM10.5-million ($3-million/£1.5-million) renovation that saw the original buildings gutted and reformed into a state-of-the-art resort facility to compete with the deluxe resorts of Langkawi to the north. This was the original resort to be built along Batu Feringgi, so it commands the best beach of all the resorts, with 12 hectares (30 acres) of grounds—enough for a par-3 executive golf course, three pools, and plenty of gardens. Standard rooms are gorgeous, most with sea views, in contemporary style and natural tones, deep wood built-ins, and big fluffy beds. In the Rasa Wing, guest rooms have private verandas and gardens, or balconies with tubs outside.

Rasa Sayang also launched the Shangri-La's new spa brand, CHI, with decor and treatments based on Chinese principles of yin and yang and the five elements: metal, wood, water, fire, and earth. Guests here can also share facilities with sister property Golden Sands.

Batu Feringgi Beach, 11100 Penang. *(©* **800/942-5050** in the U.S. and Canada, 800/222-448 in Australia, 800/442-179 in New Zealand, or 04/888-8888. Fax 04/881-1880. www.shangri-la.com. 304 units. RM1,491 ($418/£209) double; RM2,266 ($635/£317) Rasa Wing double. AE, DC, MC, V. **Amenities:** 4 restaurants; 2 bars; 3 outdoor lagoon-style pools; fitness center; spa; outdoor lighted tennis courts; watersports equipment and activities; concierge; tour desk; car-rental desk; limousine service; shuttle service to Shangri-La Hotel in Georgetown; business center; salon; 24-hr. room service; babysitting; same-day laundry service; dry cleaning; self-service launderette. *In room:* A/C, TV w/satellite programming and in-house movie, fridge, coffee/tea-making facilities, hair dryer, safe.

WHERE TO DINE

The 1885 ★★ CONTINENTAL   If you're celebrating a special occasion while in Penang, The 1885 will make the experience beyond memorable. The nostalgic romance of the E&O Hotel, its colonial architecture, interiors, and manicured lawns evoking times when tigers probably roamed the grounds after dark, provides the most incredible backdrop for a perfect meal. From an ever-changing menu, poultry, special cuts of meats, and fresh seafood are prepared in delicate contemporary Western style. Candlelight, starched linens, silver service, and extremely attentive staff create a magical experience. The wine list is extensive. By Malaysian standards, this is a very expensive meal, but if you compare the quality of the service and cuisine, plus the stellar surroundings, really, you will never find such elegance for this price in Europe or the States. Also, men are asked to kindly wear a shirt with a collar.

Eastern & Oriental Hotel (E&O), 10 Lebuh Farquhar. *(©* **04/222-0000.** Reservations recommended. Main courses RM50–RM100 ($14–$28/£7–£14). AE, DC, MC, V. Daily 7–10:30pm.

Hot Wok Café ★ PERANAKAN   This place is the number-one recommended Peranakan restaurant in the city, and small wonder: The food is great and the atmosphere is fabulous. Filled with local treasures such as wooden lattice work, wooden lanterns, carved Peranakan cabinets, tapestries, and carved wood panels, the decor will make you want to just sit back, relax, and take in sights you'd only ever see in a Peranakan home. Their curry capitan, a famous local dish, is curry chicken stuffed with potatoes, served with a thick, delicious coconut-based gravy. The house specialty is a mean *perut ikan* (fish intestine with roe and vegetable).

125-D Desa Tanjung, Jalan Tanjung. *(©* **04/899-0858.** Reservations recommended for weekends. Main courses RM9–RM15 ($2.50–$4.20/£1.25–£2.10). AE, DC, MC, V. Daily 11am–3pm and 6–11pm.

May Garden Restaurant CANTONESE   This is a top Cantonese restaurant in Georgetown, and while it's noisy and not too big on ambience, it has excellent food. But how many Chinese do you know who go to places for ambience? It's the food that counts! Outstanding dishes include the tofu and broccoli topped with sea snail slices or the fresh steamed live prawns. They also have suckling pig and Peking duck. Don't agree to all the daily specials or you'll be paying a fortune.

70 Jalan Penang. *(©* **04/261-6806.** Reservations recommended. Main courses start at RM8 ($2.20/£1.10). Seafood is priced by weight in kilograms. AE, DC, MC, V. Daily noon–3pm and 6–10:30pm.

Ocean Green ★★ SEAFOOD   I can't rave enough about Ocean Green. If the beautiful sea view and ocean breezes don't make you weep with joy, the food certainly will. A long list of fresh seafood is prepared steamed or fried, with your choice of chili, black-bean, sweet-and-sour, or curry sauces. On the advice of a local food expert, I tried the lobster thermidor, expensive but divine, and the chicken wings stuffed with minced chicken, prawns, and gravy.

48F Jalan Sultan Ahmad Shah. © **04/226-2681.** Reservations recommended. Main courses starting from RM12 ($3.40/£1.70); seafood priced according to market value. AE, MC, V. Daily 9am–11pm.

FOOD STALL DINING

No discussion of Penang dining would be complete without coverage of the local food stall scene, which is famous. Penang hawkers can make any dish you've had in Malaysia, Singapore, or even southern Thailand—only better. Penang may be attractive for many things—history, culture, nature—but it is loved for its food.

Gurney Drive Foodstalls, toward the water just down from the intersection with Jalan Kelawai, is the biggest and most popular hawker center. It has all kinds of food, including local dishes with every influence: Chinese, Malay, Indian. Find *char kway teow* (fried flat noodles with seafood), *char bee hoon* (a fried thin rice noodle), *laksa* (noodles and seafood in a tangy and spicy broth), *murtabak* (mutton, egg, and onion fried inside Indian bread and dipped in dhal), *oh chien* (oyster omelet with chili dip), and *rojak* (a spicy fruit and seafood salad). After you've eaten your way through Gurney Drive, you can try the stalls on Jalan Burmah near the Lai Lai Supermarket.

ATTRACTIONS
IN GEORGETOWN
Cheong Fatt Tze Mansion ★★★ Cheong Fatt Tze (1840–1917), once dubbed "China's Rockefeller" by the *New York Times,* built a vast commercial empire in Southeast Asia, first in Indonesia, then in Singapore. He came to Penang in 1890 and continued his success, giving some of his spoils to build schools throughout the region. His mansion, where he lived with his eight wives, was built between 1896 and 1904.

The mansion is a sight to behold. Mr. Cheong spent lavishly for Chinese detail that reflects the spirit of his heritage and the fashion of the day as well as the rules of traditional feng shui. Every corner is dripping with ambience, outfitted throughout with stained glass, carved moldings, gilded wood-carved doors, ceramic ornaments, lovely courtyard and gardens, plus seven staircases.

In 2000 the mansion won UNESCO's Asia-Pacific Heritage Award for Conservation, so lovingly has this historic treasure been preserved. Guided tours explain the history, personalities, and culture behind the home, plus the details of the conservation efforts. If you're really hooked, the owners host a home-stay program.

Lebuhraya Leith. © **04/262-0006.** Adults RM12 ($3.35/£1.70), Children 6–12 RM6 ($1.70/85p). Daily guided tours at 11am and 3pm.

Fort Cornwallis Fort Cornwallis is built on the site where Capt. Francis Light, founder of Penang, first landed in 1786. The fort was first built in 1793, but this site was an unlikely spot to defend the city from invasion. In 1810 it was rebuilt in an attempt to make up for initial strategic planning errors. In the shape of a star, the only actual buildings still standing are the outer walls, a gunpowder magazine, and a small Christian chapel. The magazine houses an exhibit of old photos and historical accounts of the old fort.

Lebuhraya Leith. No phone. Adults RM3 (80¢/£.40), children RM2 (60¢/30p). Daily 8am–7pm.

Goddess of Mercy Temple Dedicated jointly to Kuan Yin, the goddess of mercy, and Ma Po Cho, the patron saint of sea travelers, this is the oldest Chinese temple in Penang. On the 19th of each second, sixth, and ninth month of the lunar calendar (the months that fall between Feb/Mar, June/July, and Sept/Oct, respectively), Kuan Yin is celebrated with Chinese operas and puppet shows.

Leboh Pitt. Free admission.

Kapitan Keling Mosque   Captain Light donated a large parcel of land on this spot for the settlement's sizable Indian Muslim community to build a mosque and grave-yard. The leader of the community, known as Kapitan Keling (or Kling, which ironi-cally was once a racial slur against Indians in the region), built a brick mosque here. Later, in 1801, he imported builders and materials from India for a new, brilliant mosque. Expansions in the 1900s topped the mosque with stunning domes and tur-rets, adding extensions and new roofs.

Jalan Masjid Kapitan Keling (Leboh Pitt). Free admission.

Khoo Khongsi 👁   The Chinese who migrated to Southeast Asia created clan asso-ciations in their new homes. Based on common heritage, these social groups formed the core of Chinese life in the new homelands. The Khoo clan, who immigrated from Hokkien province in China, acquired this spot in 1851 and set to work building row houses, administrative buildings, and a clan temple around a large square. The tem-ple here now was actually built in 1906 after a fire destroyed its predecessor. It was believed the original was too ornate, provoking the wrath of the gods. One look at the current temple, a Chinese baroque masterpiece, and you'll wonder how that could possibly be. Come here in August for Chinese operas.

Lebuhraya Cannon. 📞 04/261-4609. Free admission. Daily 9am–5pm.

Penang Museum and Art Gallery 👁👁   The historical society has put together this marvelous collection of ethnological and historical findings from Penang, tracing the port's history and diverse cultures through time. It's filled with paintings, photos, costumes, and antiques among much more, all presented with fascinating facts and trivia. Upstairs is an art gallery. Originally the Penang Free School, the building was built in two phases, the first half in 1896 and the second in 1906. Only half of the building remains; the other was bombed to the ground in World War II. It's a favorite stop on a sightseeing itinerary because it's air-conditioned!

Lebuhraya Farquhar. 📞 04/261-3144. Adults RM1 (30¢/15p), children RM.50 (10¢/5p). Sat–Thurs 9am–5pm.

Sri Mariamman Temple   This Hindu temple was built in 1833 by a Chettiar, a group of southern Indian Muslims, and received a major face-lift in 1978 with the help of Madras sculptors. The Hindu Navarithri festival is held here, whereby devo-tees parade Sri Mariamman, a Hindu goddess worshiped for her powers to cure dis-ease, through the streets in a night procession. It is also the starting point of the Thaipusam Festival, which leads to a temple on Jalan Waterfall.

Lebuhraya Queen. Free admission.

St. George's Church   Built by Rev. R. S. Hutchins (who was also responsible for the Free School next door, home of the Penang Museum) and Capt. Robert N. Smith, whose paintings hang in the museum, this church was completed in 1818. Although the outside is almost as it was then, the contents were completely looted during World War II. All that remains are the font and the bishop's chair.

Farquhar St. Free admission.

OUTSIDE GEORGETOWN

Batu Muang Fishing Village   If you'd like to see a local fishing village, here's a good one. This village is special for its shrine to Admiral Cheng Ho, the early Chinese sea adventurer.

Southeast tip of Penang. Free admission. From Georgetown take the Jelutong Expy., then take Teluk Tempoyak into the village.

Botanical Gardens   Covering 30 hectares (70 acres) of landscaped grounds, this botanical garden was established by the British in 1884, with grounds that are perfect for a shady walk and a ton of fun if you love monkeys. They're crawling all over the place and will think nothing of stepping forward for a peanut (which you can buy beneath the DO NOT FEED THE MONKEYS sign). Also in the gardens is a jogging track and kiddie park.

About a 5- or 10-min. drive west of Georgetown. © **04/227-0428**. Free admission. Daily 7am–7pm.

Penang Butterfly Farm   The Penang Butterfly Farm, located toward the north-west corner of the island, is the largest in the world. On its .8-hectare (2-acre) land-scaped grounds there are more than 4,000 flying butterflies from 120 species. At 10am and 3pm there are informative butterfly shows. Don't forget the insect exhibit—there are about 2,000 or so bugs.

Jalan Teluk Bahang. © **04/885-1253**. Admission adults RM15 ($4.20/£2.10), children RM7.50 ($2.10/£1.05); free for children 4 and under. Daily 9am–5pm.

Penang Hill   Covered with jungle growth and 20 nature trails, the hill is great for trekking. Or, you can go to Ayer Hitam, a town in the central part of Penang, and take the Keretapi Bukit Bendera funicular railway to the top. It sends trains up and down the hill every half-hour from 6am to 9pm, weekends from 6am to 11pm, and costs adults RM4 ($1.10/55p) and children RM2 (60¢/30p), round-trip. If you pre-fer to make the trek on foot, go to the "Moon Gate" at the entrance to the Botanical Garden for a 5.5km (3.4-mile), 3-hour hike to the summit.

A 20- to 30-min. drive southwest from Georgetown. The funicular station is on Jalan Stesen Keretapi Bukit.

SHOPPING

The first place anyone here will recommend you to go for shopping is **KOMTAR.** Short for "Kompleks Tun Abdul Razak," it is the largest shopping complex in Penang, a full 65 stories of clothing shops, restaurants, and a couple of large department stores. There's a **duty-free shop** on the 57th floor. On the third floor is a **tourist informa-tion center.**

Good shopping finds in Penang are batik, pewter products, locally produced curios, paintings, antiques, pottery, and jewelry. If you care to walk around in search of finds, there are a few streets in Georgetown that are the hub of shopping activity. In the city center, the area around Jalan Penang, Lebuhrhaya Campbell, Lebuhraya Kapitan Kel-ing, Lebuhraya Chulia, and Lebuhraya Pantai is near the Sri Mariamman Temple, the Penang Museum, the Kapitan Keling Mosque, and other sites of historic interest. Here you'll find everything from local crafts to souvenirs and fashion, and maybe even a bargain or two. Most of these shops are open from 10am to 10pm daily.

Out at Batu Feringgi, the main road turns into a fun **night bazaar** every evening just at dark. During the day, there are also some good shops for batik and souvenirs.

PENANG AFTER DARK

If you're looking for a bar that's a little out of the ordinary, visit **20 Leith Street,** 11-A Lebuh Leith (© **04/261-8873**). Located in an old 1930s house, the place has seating areas fitted with traditional antique furniture in each room of the house. Possibly the most notorious bar in Penang is the **Hong Kong Bar,** 371 Lebuh Chulia (© **04/261-9796**), which opened in 1920 and was a regular hangout for military personnel based in Butterworth. It has an extraordinary archive of photos of the servicemen who have patronized the place throughout the years, plus a collection of medals, plaques, and buoys from ships.

6 Langkawi ★★

Where the beautiful Andaman Sea meets the Strait of Malacca, Langkawi Island positions itself as one of the best emerging island paradise destinations in the region. Since 1990, the Malaysian Tourism Board has dedicated itself to promoting the island and developing it as an ideal travel spot. Now, after a decade and a half of work, the island has proven itself as one of this country's holiday gems.

Its biggest competition comes from Phuket, Thailand's beach-lover fantasy to the north. However, Langkawi was far luckier than Phuket when the tsunami struck the shore in December 2004. Although Phuket suffered massive casualties and collateral damage, Langkawi only reported one casualty, and while most of Langkawi's beach resorts did suffer water damage, it didn't take long for them all to make necessary repairs and get up and running again.

This small island also claims a Hollywood credit, starring in the 1999 film *Anna and the King.* Langkawi played the role of Thailand to Jodie Foster's Anna Leonowens and Chow Yun-Fat's King Mongkut (Rama IV). The Thais wouldn't allow the filmmakers to shoot on location in their kingdom, so Hollywood turned to neighboring Malaysia. The palatial Thai-style buildings constructed for the set have never been torn down, and you can still hear all kinds of local gossip about the film's stars.

Technically, Langkawi is a cluster of islands, the largest of which serves as the main focal point. Ask how many islands actually make up Langkawi and you'll hear either 104 or 99. The official MTB response? "Both are correct. It depends on the tide!" On Langkawi Island itself, the main town, **Kuah,** provides the island's administrative needs, while on the western and northern shores, the beaches have been developed with resorts. The west-coast beaches of **Pantai Cenang** and **Pantai Tengah** are the most developed; however, the concept of "development" here is quite low-key. To the north, **Datai Bay** and **Tanjung Rhu** host the island's finest, and most secluded, resorts.

One final note: Malaysia has declared Langkawi a duty-free zone, so take a peek at some of the shopping in town, and enjoy RM4 ($1.05/50p) beers!

ESSENTIALS

GETTING THERE

BY PLANE Malaysia Airlines (© **1300/883-000;** www.malaysiaairlines.com) and **AirAsia** (© **1300/889-933;** www.airasia.com) make Langkawi very convenient from either mainland Malaysia or Singapore. In addition, **Singapore Airlines** also flies to Langkawi.

The best thing to do is prearrange a shuttle pickup from your resort; otherwise you can grab a taxi out in front of the airport. To Pantai Cenang or Pantai Tengah, the fare

Langkawi

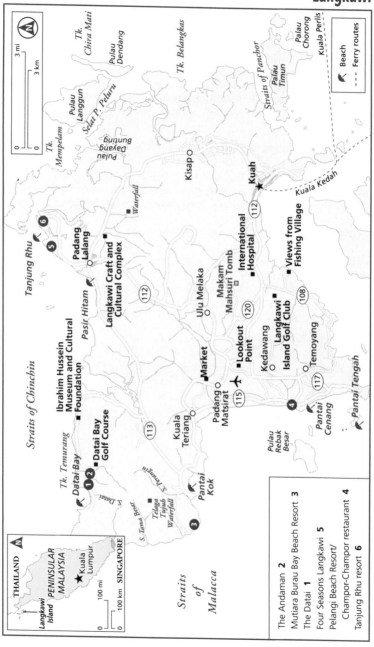

The Andaman 2
Mutiara Burau Bay Beach Resort 3
The Datai 1
Four Seasons Langkawi 5
Pelangi Beach Resort/
Champor-Champor restaurant 4
Tanjung Rhu resort 6

should be about RM20 ($5.60/£2.80), while to the farther resorts at Tanjung Rhu and Datai Bay it will be as high as RM40 and RM50 ($11/£5.60 and $14/£7), respectively.

BY TRAIN   Taking the train can be a bit of a hassle because the nearest stop (in Alor Setar) is quite far from the jetty to the island, requiring a cab transfer. Still, if you prefer rail, hop on the overnight train from KL (the only train), which will put you in to Alor Setar at around 7am. Just outside the train station you can find the taxi stand, with cabs to take you to the Kuala Kedah jetty.

BY BUS   To be honest, I don't really recommend using this route. If you're coming from KL, the bus ride is long and uncomfortable, catching the taxi transfer to the jetty can be problematic, and by the time you reach the island you'll need a vacation from your vacation. Fly or use the train. If you're coming from Penang, the direct ferry is wonderfully convenient.

BY FERRY   From the jetty at Kuala Kedah, there are about five companies that provide ferry service to the island (trip time: about 1 hr. and 45 min.; cost: RM18/$5/£2.50). Ferries let you off at the main ferry terminal in Kuah, where you can hop a taxi to your resort for RM20 to RM50 ($5.60–$14/£2.80–£7).

If you're coming from Penang, the ferry is the way to go. **Bahagia Express** has two early-morning speedboats from Weld Quay in Georgetown for RM45 one-way ($13/£6.30) and RM85 round-trip ($24/£12). Call them in Penang at ✆ **04/263-1943** or visit their office across from the clock tower, just next to the main tourism board office. If you're heading from Langkawi to Penang, you can call Bahagia in Langkawi at ✆ **04/966-0521.**

VISITOR INFORMATION

The MTB office is unfortunately situated in Kuah town on Jalan Persiaran Putra, far from the beach areas. For specific queries, you can call them at ✆ **04/966-7789.** If you're arriving by plane, there's another MTB office at the airport (✆ **04/955-7155**).

GETTING AROUND

BY TAXI   Taxis generally hang around at the airport, the main jetty, the taxi stand in Kuah, and at some major hotels. From anywhere in between, your best bet is to ask your hotel's concierge to call a taxi for you. Keep in mind, if you're going as far as one side of the island to the other, your fare can go as high as RM50 ($14/£7).

CAR & MOTORCYCLE RENTAL   At the airport and from agents in the complex behind the main jetty, car rentals can be arranged starting at RM80 ($22/£11) per day. This is for the standard, no-frills model—actually, mine was more reminiscent of some of the junkers I drove throughout college, but it still got me around. Insurance policies are lax, as are rental regulations. My rental guys seemed more concerned with my passport documents than with my driver's license. If you're out on the beach at Cenang or Tengah, a few places rent jeeps and motorcycles from RM80 ($22/£11) per day and RM30 ($8.40/£4.20) per day, respectively. Pick a good helmet.

BY FOOT   The main beaches at Cenang and Tengah can be walked quite nicely; however, don't expect to be able to walk around to other parts of the island.

FAST FACTS: LANGKAWI

The only major **bank** branches are located far from the beach areas, in Kuah town, mostly around the blocks across the street from the Night Hawker Center (off Jalan Persiaran Putra), or at the airport. Money changers keep long hours out at Pantai

Cenang and Pantai Tengah, but for other resorts you'll have to change your money at the resort itself. Along the Pantai Cenang and Pantai Tengah main road, you'll find at least a half-dozen small **Internet** places.

WHERE TO STAY

The Andaman ✦✦ *Kids*   You will be surprised how large this resort is; its buildings blend so perfectly with the jungle surrounding them. Andaman has far better landscaped garden areas than neighboring Datai (see below), with a sprawl of lush grounds hugging a beautiful white beach, as opposed to Datai which is quite constricted architecturally by its hillside situation. On the other hand, I prefer Datai's mesmerizing tropical Asian simplicity. Sometimes the Andaman uses decorator ideas straight from the West, European-style furnishings and fabrics, which to me detract from the whole spirit of escapism. But one other advantage—The Andaman welcomes families and has special facilities, including a kid's club, and it has a better beach. The entrance and main lobby are overpowering in size but visually quite stunning in open-air local style architecture with vaulted roofs built from polished hardwoods. Guest rooms, in two wings that span out to either side of the main building, are big, with wall-to-wall carpeting and Western-style decor, save a few local textiles for effect. Ground-floor lanai rooms have a private sun deck with umbrella stand. The pool is huge with lots of shady spots, and the spa features traditional Malay herbal beauty and health treatments. Gulai House serves delicious Malay and Indian cuisine in a charming open-air Malay style house by the beach.

Jalan Teluk Datai, P.O. Box 94, 07000 Langkawi, Kedah. © **04/959-1088.** Fax 04/959-1168. www.theandaman.com. RM1,000–RM1,600 ($280–$448/£140–£224) double; RM1,600 ($448/£224) lanai double; from RM2,170 ($608/£304) suite. Prices jump from Dec–Jan. AE, DC, MC, V. **Amenities:** 4 restaurants; 3 lounges; outdoor pools surrounded by gardens; golf course; 2 outdoor lighted tennis courts; fitness center; spa w/Jacuzzi, sauna, steam, and massage; watersports equipment; mountain bike rental; games; concierge; limousine service; 24-hr. room service; babysitting; same-day laundry service; dry cleaning; jungle trekking. *In room:* A/C, TV w/satellite programming and in-house movie, minibar, coffee/tea-making facilities, hair dryer, safe.

The Datai ✦✦✦   Aesthetically speaking, this is one of the most innovative resorts in Southeast Asia. Datai is the epitome of sublime, its tropical resort design incorporating nature at every turn. Beyond the graceful open-air lobby, pass the lily pond courtyard to the Datai's brilliant lounge—a hillside veranda surrounded by lush jungle and suspended above a breathtaking bay. Rooms and villas, also built into the hillside, are expert in their studied Southeast Asian elegance. Minimalist in design, the color schemes stick close to nature, with rosewood tones, deep local tapestries, and regal celadon-colored upholstery. Even lower-priced deluxe rooms have a quaint seating area with a view, plus an oversize bathroom with designer body-care products, separate stall shower, and long bathtub. Guest facilities, which include two pools, a spa, and golf course, show the same meticulous attention to luxury. A top pick.

Jalan Teluk Datai, Langkawi, Kedah. © **800/223-6800** in the U.S. and Canada, 800/181-123 in the U.K., or 04/959-2500. Fax 04/959-2600. www.ghmhotels.com/thedatai. RM1,730 ($484/£242) double; RM2,185 ($612/£306) villa; from RM2,780 ($778/£389) suite. Prices jump from Dec–Jan. AE, DC, MC, V. **Amenities:** 3 restaurants; lounge; 2 outdoor pools surrounded by jungle; golf course; 2 outdoor lighted tennis courts; fitness center w/Jacuzzi, sauna, steam, and massage; spa; watersports equipment; mountain bike rental; concierge; limousine service; limited room service; babysitting; same-day laundry service; dry cleaning; library; jungle trekking. *In room:* A/C, TV w/satellite programming and in-house movie, minibar, coffee/tea-making facilities, hair dryer, safe.

Four Seasons Langkawi ✦✦✦   With this new property, Four Seasons raises the bar for resorts in Malaysia, and possibly in the region. Every detail is perfectly exotic, influenced by contemporary Moorish style, and every view is a picture postcard. Pavilion rooms are surrounded by floor-to-ceiling windows and wraparound verandas. Under soaring ceilings, huge bedrooms have wood floors, ceiling fans, carved wood detailing, and plush soft furnishings. Through double doors, huge bathrooms are majestic, with oversize terrazzo tubs built into arched nooks, separate closets for rain shower and toilet, a huge clothes closet, and a center island with double sinks. Throughout the rooms you'll find touches such as lanterns, hammered bronze work, lovely toiletries on clay pedestals, and cozy throw pillows that add an intimate Middle Eastern flavor. The resort has two infinity pools that look like they're spilling onto the beach, which is a long, wide stretch of perfect sand. Every dining venue is also fronting the beach. At Rhu Bar, Moorish carved latticework arches frame the seaview gorgeously—if you can't stay at Four Seasons I at least recommend a cocktail here amid Turkish water pipes, Indian Moghul hanging swings, glowing lanterns, and snug seating. The spa here is also to die for. The private pavilions are bigger than my whole house (seriously), with tubs for two, space for floor and table massages, private showers, and changing rooms all encased in glass with lovely garden views. This is the most luxurious property in this whole book. Period.

Jalan Tanjung Rhu, 07000 Langkawi, Kedah (*©*) **800/332-3442** in the U.S., 800/268-6282 in Canada, or 04/950-8888. Fax 04/950-8899. www.fourseasons.com. US$495–US$540 pavilion; from US$1,500 villa. Prices jump Dec–Jan. AE, DC, MC, V. **Amenities:** 3 restaurants; 2 bars; 2 outdoor pools; tennis; fitness center; spa w/yoga and juice bar; complimentary nonmotorized watersports; children's center; concierge; limousine service; 24-hr. room service; babysitting; same-day laundry service; dry cleaning; library and tour services; jungle trekking. *In room:* A/C, TV w/satellite programming and in-house movie, minibar, coffee/tea-making facilities, hair dryer, safe.

Mutiara Burau Bay Beach Resort

Burau offers beachside resort accommodations for less money than its upscale neighbors. Not nearly as ritzy, this place feels more like summer camp than a resort. All guest rooms are contained in cabanas, with simple decor that's a bit on the older side. For the price, though, they offer value for money. Burau also organizes golf, massage, jeep treks, jungle treks, mountain biking, tennis, canoeing, catamaran sailing, jet skiing, scuba diving, snorkeling, fishing, water-skiing, windsurfing, and yachting.

Teluk Burau, 07000 Langkawi, Kedah. (*©*) **04/959-1061.** Fax 04/959-1172. www.mutiarahotels.com/mutiara_burau bay. 150 units. RM280 ($78/£39) garden-view chalet; RM310 ($87/£43) sea-view chalet; RM380 ($106/£53) family chalet; RM750 ($210/£105) suite. AE, DC, MC, V. **Amenities:** 3 restaurants; beach bar; outdoor pool; outdoor lighted tennis courts; children's center; game room; concierge; activities desk; car-rental desk; shuttle service; business center; 24-hr. room service; massage; babysitting; same-day laundry service; nonsmoking rooms. *In room:* A/C, TV w/satellite programming and in-house movie, minibar, coffee/tea-making facilities.

Pelangi Beach Resort (★)

For those who prefer a more active vacation or are looking for a resort that's more family-oriented, I recommend Pelangi. A top-quality resort, this place stands out from neighboring five-star resorts for its sheer fun. A long list of organized sports and leisure pastimes make it especially attractive for families, but surprisingly I never found children to be a distraction here. Pelangi's 51 ethnic wooden chalets are huge inside and are divided into either one, two, or four guest rooms. You'll be welcomed by vaulted ceilings, modern bathrooms, and large living spaces. But it's the little things you'll love—I didn't want to get out of bed and leave my squishy down pillows and snuggly bedding! In addition, Pelangi's location, near the central beach strip for island life, means you're not cloistered away from the rest of civilization.

Pantai Cenang, 07000 Langkawi, Kedah. © **04/952-8888.** Fax 04/952-8899. www.pelangibeachresort.com. 350 units. RM756 ($212/£106) double; from RM1,650 ($462/£231) suite. AE, DC, MC, V. **Amenities:** 3 restaurants; 3 bars; 2 large outdoor pools w/swim-up bar; golf nearby; mini-golf course; outdoor lighted tennis courts; squash courts; fitness center w/sauna, steam, and massage; Jacuzzi; concierge; tour desk and watersports center w/equipment rental, boating excursions, and jungle trekking; car-rental desk; limousine service; shuttle service; business center; 24-hr. room service; babysitting; same-day laundry service; dry cleaning. *In room:* A/C, TV w/satellite programming and in-house movie, minibar, coffee/tea-making facilities, hair dryer, safe.

Tanjung Rhu Resort ⋆⋆ The beach at Tanjung Rhu is a wide crescent of dazzlingly pure sand wrapped around a perfect crystal azure bay. Tree-lined karst islets jut up from the sea, dotting the horizon. Just gorgeous. This resort claims 440 hectares (1,100 acres) of jungle in this part of the island, monopolizing the scene for extra privacy, but it has its pros and cons. The pros? Guest rooms are enormous and decorated with sensitivity to the environment, from natural materials to organic recycled-paper-wrapped toiletries. A newly completed second pool and spa facility add value. The cons? Make sure you don't book your vacation during the months of June or December when Malaysia and Singapore celebrate school holidays, because the place draws families like flies. Still, during between-holiday downtime, I love this resort's friendly and casual atmosphere—and, of course, the beach.

Tanjung Rhu, Mukim Ayer Hangat, 07000 Langkawi, Kedah. © **04/959-1033.** Fax 04/959-1899. www.tanjungrhu. com.my. 138 units. RM1,300 ($364/£182) double; RM2,700 ($756/£378) suite. AE, DC, MC, V. **Amenities:** 3 restaurants; bar and library; 2 outdoor pools, 1 saltwater and 1 freshwater; golf nearby; outdoor lighted tennis courts; fitness center and spa w/Jacuzzi, sauna, steam, massage; concierge; activity desk w/watersports (nonmotorized), trekking, and boat tours; limousine service; shuttle service; 24-hr. room service; babysitting; same-day laundry service; dry cleaning. *In room:* A/C, TV w/satellite programming and in-room video w/movie library, compact disc player, minibar, coffee/tea-making facilities, hair dryer, safe.

WHERE TO DINE

If you're out at one of the more secluded resorts, chances are you'll stay there for most of your meals. However, if you're at Pantai Cenang or Pantai Tengah, I strongly recommend taking a stroll down to **Champor-Champor** ⋆, just across the road in the Pelangi Resort (© **04/955-1449**), which serves creative dinners—a local *roti canai* served like a pizza, and local fish doused in sweet sauces. Everything is incredibly fresh, wildly delicious, and amazingly inexpensive. As for decor, the imaginative catchall beach-shack atmosphere really relaxes. After dinner, hang around the bar for the best fun on the island. Because Langkawi is an official duty-free port, one beer costs a wee RM4 ($1.10/50p)! If you're in Kuah town looking for something good to eat, the best local dining experience can be found at the evening **hawker stalls** just along the waterfront near the taxi stand. A long row of hawkers cook up every kind of local favorite, including seafood dishes. You can't get any cheaper or more laid-back. After dinner, from here it's easy to flag down a taxi back to your resort.

ATTRACTIONS

Fifteen years ago, Langkawi was just a backwater island supporting small fishing communities. When the government came in with big money to develop the place for tourism, they thought they needed a catch, so they dug up some old moldy "legends" about the island and have tried to market them as bona fide cultural attractions. Basically, any of these sorts of attractions are more hype than anything else. If you want to experience culture, take a ferry to Penang for an overnight in historic Georgetown. Now *that's* something to see.

In terms of beaches and watersports, most resorts are self-contained units, offering their own equipment rentals and planning their own outings.

Outside of your resort, there's some fairly decent diving to be had. **Asian Overland** (© **04/955-2002;** www.asianoverland.com.my) can arrange day trips with two dives to Payar Marine Park within Langkawi's extensive island network. They charge RM280 ($78/£39). You can also snorkel for the day for RM160 ($45/£22) per person. There's an interesting snorkel attraction off Langkawi—a platform in the middle of the sea that floats above a coral reef. Day trips to the platform include rides in a glass-bottomed boat, snorkeling, and lunch on the platform. It's an all-day affair for RM230 ($64/£32) per person, starting at 8am and getting you back to your resort just before dinnertime.

Asian Overland also plans round-island boat trips to "island-hop" at beaches and into mangrove swamps (interesting) with a stop at the Pregnant Maiden Lake (one of the before-mentioned over-hyped places). See if you can get them to skip the lake and take you to the Batik Art Village instead. They'll cater your tour so you can see anything you want.

Perhaps one of the loveliest additions to Langkawi's attractions is the **Ibrahim Hussein Museum and Cultural Foundation,** Pasir Tengkorak, Jalan Datai (© **04/959-4669**). The artistic devotion of the foundation's namesake fueled the creation of this enchanting modern space designed to showcase Malaysia's contribution to the international fine-arts scene. If you can pull yourself from the beach for any one activity in Langkawi, this is the one I recommend. Mr. Hussein has created a museum worthy of international attention. Truly a gem. It's open Saturday through Thursday from 10am to 6pm; adults pay RM12 ($3.40/£1.70), children visit for free.

SHOPPING

Langkawi's designated Duty Free Port status makes shopping here quite fun and very popular. In Kuah town, two shopping malls, **Langkawi Parade** (Jalan Kelibang; © **04/966-6372**) and **Langkawi Fair** (Persiaran Putra; © **04/969-8100**), both in Kuah town, are filled with duty-free shopping. For local handicrafts, the **Langkawi Craft and Cultural Complex** (Jalan Teluk Yu; © **04/959-1913;** daily 10am–6pm) sells an assortment of batik, baskets, ceramic, silver jewelry, brassware, and more, and also has daily crafts demonstrations and cultural shows.

11

Peninsular Malaysia: The East Coast

Over the past 200 years, while the cities on the western coast of peninsular Malaysia preoccupied themselves with waves of foreign domination, those on the eastern coast developed in relative seclusion. Today, this part of the country remains true to its Malay heritage, from small fishing *kampungs* (villages) in the south to the Islamic strongholds of the north.

The best attractions of the east coast are its islands. Tioman, Redang, and Perhentian attract snorkelers and divers with clear waters, exotic marine life, and comfortable accommodations. In addition, short daily flights from Kuala Lumpur (KL) make Tioman and Redang more accessible than the more renowned (and remote) dive sites of Borneo. The shoreline up the east coast of the peninsula is fringed with long stretches of sandy beaches, home to dozens of holiday resorts. Most accommodations are budget chalets, but a few deluxe resorts stand out from the rest, notably Cherating's Club Med, Terengganu's Tanjong Aru Resort, and the Aryani.

With these few exceptions, tourism is almost entirely neglected in this region. For many, the lack of tourism infrastructure can sound exciting—"authentic" even—but really, although the potential for nature, adventure, and cultural tourism is here, there's just not enough creativity and investment for this area to compete with other destinations in the country. In short, if you come here, don't come for sightseeing. I have, however, found some satisfying shopping, as many of Malaysia's surviving cottage industries are located in this area.

Some notes before you plan your trip: If you're looking for beach fun, the monsoon from mid-October through late February makes the waters very choppy, so avoid the island resorts and take care by the seaside. Also, try not to book during Singapore's holiday seasons, particularly during school holidays from mid-May through June and again in November and December, when resorts are packed to the gills, buffets become battle grounds, and poolsides are less than relaxing.

In the north, with the exception of a few beach resorts and islands, Muslim modesty will probably make you uncomfortable wearing a Western-style bathing suit, especially a bikini, at a public beach (the locals swim fully clothed).

1 Tioman Island

Tioman Island (pronounced *Tee*-oh-mahn), a tiny island off the south of Malaysia's east coast, is a popular destination on Malaysia's east coast, visited mostly by nearby Singaporeans, who can hop a quick ferry ride to the island; backpackers, who have a multitude of cheap chalets to flop in; and scuba enthusiasts, who have a range of coral gardens to explore. The island is only 39km (24 miles) long and 12km (7¼ miles) wide, with sandy beaches that line several small bays, clear water with sea life and coral reefs, and jungle mountain-trekking trails with streams and waterfalls. So idyllic is the setting that Tioman was the location for the 1950s Hollywood film *South Pacific.*

Tioman has been snubbed by scuba enthusiasts because it was developed before its northern island neighbors, Redang and Perhentian. For many, Tioman's accessibility didn't jive with their expectation of "unspoiled" ecology. To be honest, I have many friends who have taken dive trips all over Southeast Asia and claim that Tioman is the same, if not better, than Redang and Perhentian.

Despite the tourist traffic, Tioman has retained much of its tropical island charm, perhaps by virtue of the fact that only one modern resort has been built on it. Activity is spread throughout the kampungs, which spring up in the various bays of the island. In **Tekek,** you'll find the airport, main ferry jetty, and some convenience shops. Other kampungs include **Air Batang,** aka ABC, and **Salang** on the west coast and Juara on the east coast. Each kampung has some sort of accommodations facilities, most of them very, very basic wooden chalets, with some access to canteens or restaurants.

ESSENTIALS

GETTING THERE

BY PLANE   Flights to Tioman originate from KL and Singapore, operated by a private airline, **Berjaya Air,** and coordinated by the folks at the Berjaya Tioman Beach Resort. However, you need not stay at the resort to book passage on these flights. Call their KL office for reservations at ✆ **03/7846-8228.** The airport in Tioman is in Kampung Tekek, just across from the main jetty. If you're staying at Berjaya Tioman, a shuttle will fetch you; however, if you plan to stay elsewhere, you're on your own. See "Getting Around," below.

BY BOAT   Ten speedboats depart from the jetty just next to R&R Plaza in Mersing each day. Book passage from the many agents huddled around the jetty—they're basically all the same, each reserving trips on the same boats. Be warned about the aggressive touts at the jetty here. They are persistent and annoying, trying to lure you to less popular places with substandard facilities. Boats leave Mersing Jetty at intervals that depend on the tide. The trip takes around 1½ hours and can cost between RM20 and RM25 ($5.60–$7/£2.80–£3.50), depending on the power of the boat you hire. Avoid the cheaper ferries that take 4 hours to make the trip (snooze). Boats drop you at either the Berjaya Resort or at the main jetty in Kampung Tekek. The last boat leaves for Tioman between 5 and 6pm every evening. If you miss this boat, you're stuck in Mersing for the night.

BY BUS   **Transnasional** operates six daily buses from KL's Puduraya Bus Terminal on Jalan Pudu (✆ **03/2070-3300**). The 6-hour trip costs RM23 ($6.45/£3.20). From Singapore, Transnasional operates a daily bus from the terminal at Lavendar Street (✆ **65/6294-7034**). The trip takes 3 hours and costs under S$30 (US$19/£10). You'll

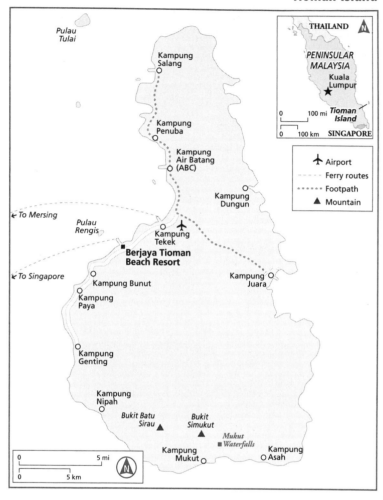

arrive at R&R Plaza, the main bus depot in a town called Mersing. The jetty is located just next door.

GETTING AROUND

There are hiking trails between kampungs along the west coast and another trail overland to the one beach on the east coast. Other than footing it, the most popular mode of transport is **water taxi.** Each village has a jetty; you can pay your fare either at tour offices located near the foot of the pier or pay the captain directly. The taxis stop operating past nightfall, so make sure you get home before 6pm. A few sample fares: from Tekek to ABC is RM12 ($3.40/£1.70) per person, to Salang RM20 ($5.60/£2.80), to Juara RM60 ($17/£8.40). Note that these guys don't like to shuttle around only one person, so if there's only one of you, be prepared to pay double.

Tips Island Travel

If you have not already acquired a good mosquito repellent, do so before heading to any of the islands on Malaysia's east coast. You'll need something with DEET (an active ingredient used in repellents that safely and effectively keeps bugs away from your skin). These mosquitoes are hungry. If you plan to stay in one of the smaller chalet places, you might want to invest in a mosquito net. Also, bring a flashlight to help you get around after sunset.

FAST FACTS

Berjaya Tioman Resort has modern conveniences like postal services, in-room telephones with international direct dial access, money changing, a gift shop, and other services. If you're not staying here, venture into Tekek, where you'll find these services opposite the main jetty.

WHERE TO STAY

Unless you stay at the Best Western Berjaya Tioman Beach Resort, expect to be roughing it. For some travelers, the Berjaya Tioman, with its wonderful modern conveniences, is what it takes to make a tropical island experience relaxing. Your shower is warm, you can order food to your room, and you can arrange any activity through the concierge in the lobby. For others, though, real relaxation comes from an escape from modern distractions. The small chalets in the kampungs have very minimal facilities and few or no conveniences such as hot showers and telephones. Why would you want to stay in them? Because they're simple, quiet, close to the beach, and less touristy than the resort.

Of the budget choices, the most charming is **Bamboo Hill** (© **09/419-1339**) at the northern tip of ABC. These rustic chalets are perched in the forest along a rocky hill overlooking the bay. While the beach here is too rocky, it's just a short walk to the other side of the bay where you can swim, or you can hike over the hill to Kampung Salang to their sandy cove. Bamboo Hill's timber chalets are cozy and quiet, with balconies, refrigerators, teakettles, and mosquito netting. Priced from RM70 to RM120 ($20–$34/£9.80–£17), cash only. You can also opt for air-conditioning. An Internet station and library complete the amenities. Really the only place to eat here is Nazri's Place in the south end of the beach, which serves breakfast, lunch, and fish or chicken barbecue dinner daily.

Berjaya Tioman Beach Resort ★   This is the only true Western-style resort on the island and provides all the conveniences you'd expect from a budget chain hotel. Accommodations are provided in small blocks and private chalets, some with sea views, but most facing gardens. Inside, wood floors, flowery drapes, upholstery, and bedspreads brighten simple rattan furnishings. Each room has a small balcony, but guests are advised against hanging clothes and towels to dry. Attached bathrooms are small, tiled affairs, with combination tub/showers. The beach here is fine, however don't expect much surf because the resort is located on the west coast of the island, protected from the open sea. One benefit is an on-site PADI scuba center, but don't come all this way for Berjaya's ho-hum golf course.

Tioman Island, Pahang Darul Makmur. © **09/419-1000.** Fax 09/419-1718. www.berjayaresorts.com.my. 400 units. RM630–RM680 ($176–$190/£88–£95) chalet; RM1,580 ($442/£221) suite. Nov–Feb rates discounted 50%. AE, DC,

MC, V. **Amenities:** 4 restaurants; beach bar and karaoke lounge; 2 outdoor pools; 18-hole golf course; outdoor lighted tennis courts; tiny fitness center; health and beauty spa services; sauna; game room; activities desk; watersports equipment rentals; PADI scuba center; shuttle service; limited room service; babysitting; same-day laundry service. *In room:* A/C, TV w/satellite programming, minibar, coffee/tea-making facilities, hair dryer.

TIOMAN OUTDOORS

Tioman's beaches can be hit-or-miss. Around Tekek, much of ABC, and spots north of the Berjaya resort, rocks spoil the beach and shallow waters. Salang's beach, a crescent of sand hugging a horseshoe-shaped cove, presents the best beach on the west side of the island. The most ideal beach, however, is on Juara, on the east side of the island. This broad sandy stretch is practically deserted half the time due to its remote location—to get there either hop a water taxi, take the daily ferry, or hike overland. The trek from Tekek to Juara cuts across the center of the island and will take up to 2 hours to complete. Bring water and lots of mosquito repellent, and don't try it unless you are reasonably fit.

Scuba professionals **Dive Asia** (Salang and Tekek ⓒ **09/419-5017;** ABC ⓒ **09/419-1654;** www.diveasia.com.my) have been on Tioman over 30 years. Each day they take divers out for two dives, one at 9:30am and one at 2:30pm (at different places each day) for only RM160 ($45/£22), equipment included. A bargain. Snorkel trips can also be arranged at each beach destination for about RM40 ($11/£5.60), which includes boat transfer to the best snorkeling sites plus equipment rental.

2 Kuantan & Cherating

Pahang, covering about 35,960 sq. km (22,475 sq. miles) of mostly inland forests, is the largest state on peninsular Malaysia. Travelers come to Pahang's east coast resorts for the long sandy beaches, which stretch all the way up the east coast along the South China Sea. Jungle forests promise adventures in trekking, climbing, and river rafting. In fact, much of **Taman Negara,** Malaysia's main peninsular national forest preserve, is in this state, although most people access the forest through Kuala Lumpur (see "Side Trips from Kuala Lumpur," in chapter 10). Kuantan, although it's the capital, doesn't have the feel of a big city; however with the recent construction of a few big shopping malls, there's more choice for entertainment, shopping, and fast food. If you're staying at the beach at Telok Chempedak, 5km (3 miles) north of Kuantan, the atmosphere is even more relaxed.

Here's an interesting piece of trivia: Kuantan has the highest property values in the country, higher than the capital city and cosmopolitan Penang. Why? The discovery of offshore oil reserves means all the big oil companies have operations in this region, and I can assure you, their executives ain't livin' in no wooden bungalows on stilts.

ESSENTIALS
VISITOR INFORMATION

A **Tourist Information Centre** (ⓒ **09/516-1007**) is located on Jalan Penjara in the center of town. The staff is exceptionally helpful and good at answering specific inquiries. The official website for the Pahang tourism board is www.pahangtourism.com.my.

GETTING THERE

The most convenient way to get to Kuantan is by a quick flight from KL. **Malaysia Airlines** (ⓒ **1300/883-000;** www.malaysiaairlines.com) flies daily from KL. Flights arrive at the **Sultan Ahmad Shah Airport** (✆ **09/538-1291**). Just outside the airport is a taxi stand where you can get a cab to Kuantan for RM30 ($8.40/£4.20) or to Cherating for RM60 ($17/£8.40).

Bus routes service Kuantan from all parts of the peninsula, and thanks to the opening in 2004 of a beautiful new highway linking Kuantan to KL, the trip is only 5 hours. Transnasional operates hourly buses for RM17 ($4.75/£2.40) from Puduraya Bus Terminal on Jalan Pudu (✆ **03/2070-3300**). The bus terminal in Kuantan is in Kompleks Makmur. Taxis at the stand just outside the terminal can take you to town for RM10 ($2.80/£1.40).

Outstation taxis from KL (✆ **03/2078-0213**) will cost RM200 ($56/£28) for the 3-hour trip. The outstation taxi stand in Kuantan is at the bus terminal.

GETTING AROUND

The areas in the town's center are nice for walking. Otherwise stick with taxis, which can be waved down on any street. There's also a stand behind the Tourist Information Centre where you'll be sure to find a cab in a pinch. Taxis here are not metered, so you must negotiate the fare before you set out. This is a good deal when you want to hire someone for a few hours to take you around the city. Rates start at about RM15 ($4.20/£2.10) per hour. Use taxis to travel to areas of interest outside the city that are covered in "Attractions Outside Kuantan," below.

FAST FACTS

The **area code** for Kuantan and Cherating is 09. Most major **banks and ATMs** are located appropriately along Jalan Bank, near the State Mosque. **Internet service** is available from a couple of cafes at the Kompleks Makmur; check the shopping mall adjacent to the bus terminal.

WHERE TO STAY

Kuantan is not a very large place, and most of those who vacation here prefer to stay just a little farther north, in **Cherating,** which is more established as a resort destination. If staying close to Kuantan is important to you, the Hyatt Regency, about 5km (3 miles) outside of town on the beach at Telok Chempedak, is the best choice for accommodations.

Hyatt Regency Kuantan ⭐   The Hyatt Regency is part business hotel and part resort. Its two hotel blocks serve business travelers linked to Pahang and Terengganu's oil industry, which is why you'll find executive club services, a business center, and other conveniences for professionals that might seem out of place at a beachside property. On the other hand, Hyatt does front an extensive beachfront, with cool breezes and the relaxing sound of ocean waves, plus a full range of exciting watersports activities. The open-air concept of the hotel, especially the tropical reception area, shows all the efficiency of a Hyatt without the studied professionalism of a city hotel. Inside two large hotel blocks, guest rooms are comfortable with modern conveniences adorned with some local decorator touches but show some signs of wear. Each has a balcony, but not all have sea views, so be sure to inquire when booking.

Telok Chempedak, 25050 Kuantan, Pahang. ✆ **800/233-1234** in the U.S., or 09/566-1234. Fax 09/567-7577. http:// kuantan.regency.hyatt.com. 336 units. RM280–RM345 ($78–$97/£39–£48) double; RM830 ($232/£116) suite. AE, DC, MC, V. **Amenities:** 3 restaurants; 3 bars including a pub w/live entertainment; 2 outdoor pools; 3 outdoor lighted tennis courts; 2 squash courts; fitness center; spa w/sauna, steam, and massage; children's center; concierge; tour desk; limousine service; business center; 24-hr. room service; babysitting; same-day laundry service; dry cleaning; nonsmoking rooms on the top floors; executive-level rooms. *In room:* A/C, TV w/satellite programming and in-house movie, mini-bar, coffee/tea-making facilities, hair dryer, safe.

IN CHERATING

Most people skip Kuantan and head straight for Cherating, some 47km (28 miles) to the north. The anchor resort, Club Med, opened in 1980. Since then a couple dozen smaller resorts have opened up, none of them coming close to Club Med's standard. Resorts here are all mostly self-contained units; to stay here means you'll most likely be dining in-house, participating in beach and watersports activities, and possibly only leaving the resort for tours planned through your resort's activities desk.

Windsurfers take note: Cherating is world famous for excellent conditions and the home of the "Monsoon Madness" international competition, which takes place every January or February, when monsoon conditions make great waves. In addition to windsurfing, resorts can also arrange trips through the mangroves up the Cherating River in a hired bumboat and trips to crafts shops and cultural shows.

Club Med ★★ Kids   Club Med underwent a massive renovation in 2005 that refurbished virtually every nook and cranny of the place. Typical to Club Med style, this "family village" is all about escapism—fun and relaxation. Activities include sailing, kayaking, beach volleyball, plus tennis, wall climbing, and rollerblading. Or try the new bungee-bounce contraption or take flying-trapeze lessons. For relaxation, there are yoga classes and a full-feature Asian spa. Club Med also organizes short trips to villages outside the resort for sightseeing and can arrange golf outside the resort as well. For families, the full menu of children's activities can keep kids occupied every minute of their stay. The property itself fronts a lovely stretch of beachfront on 80 private hectares (200 acres). Malay-style wooden houses are sparsely furnished with clean wooden floors, vibrant fabrics, small balconies, and small bathrooms with standing showers. If you're new to Club Med, their pricing is a bit confusing, depending on the size of your party and the time and duration of your stay. The club works out an overall fee, which is inclusive of all meals and almost all activities, in many cases including international airfare as well. For an idea, a 3-day, 2-night trip, not including transportation to and fro, will set you back RM880 ($246/£123) per night.

Correspondence through KL office only through Vacances, Suite 1.1, 1st Floor Bangunan MAS, Jalan Sultan Ismail, 50250 Kuala Lumpur. © **03/261-4599.** Fax 03/261-7229. www.clubmed.com. 323 units. Refer to text above for pricing information. AE, DC, MC, V. **Amenities:** 2 restaurants; bar; outdoor pool; outdoor lighted tennis courts; squash courts; fitness center; full-service spa; watersports equipment rentals; children's center; game room; tour desk; car-rental desk; shuttle service; babysitting; same-day laundry service. *In room:* A/C, TV, hair dryer, safe.

Swiss Garden Resort & Spa ★   Many choices of accommodations in Cherating offer basic seaside facilities for budget travelers, but you should be warned: Most are plagued by tatty rooms desperate for upgrading, substandard facilities, and apathetic service. Swiss Garden is a better choice, as it's one of the newer properties in this category and is managed by the same people behind Swiss Garden's successful leisure-class hotels in KL. This four-story horseshoe-shaped block surrounds a swimming pool fronting a very pretty beach—if you pay extra for a sea-facing room, make sure you get the top floor for the best view. Swiss Inn's rooms have good space for luggage, sport clean tile floors that make the room feel fresh, small balconies, wood furniture, soft beds, and small TVs. The two best features of the resort are its Balok Beach location, home to Cherating's windsurfing activities, and its Balinese spa, located in a garden courtyard with a long menu of reasonably priced relaxation and beauty treatments.

2656–2657 Mukim Sungai Karang, Balok Beach, 26100 Beserah, Kuantan, Pahang. ⓒ 09/544-7333. Fax 09/544-955. www.swissgarden.com. 303 units. RM331–RM446 ($93–$125/£46–£62) double; from RM550 ($154/£77) suite. AE, DC, MC, V. **Amenities:** 2 restaurants; lounge; outdoor pool; spa; watersports equipment rental; tour desk; car rental; room service; babysitting; same-day laundry service. *In room:* A/C, TV w/satellite programming and in-house movie, coffee/tea-making facilities.

WHERE TO DINE

Most folks staying in the area dine at their resorts, but if you find yourself in town during mealtime, the absolute best place to go is the **outdoor food stalls** by the beach next to the Hyatt Regency. It's a short taxi ride from the center of town, but well worth it. All varieties of very fresh seafood, including whole fish, are cooked to order and are as cheap as RM6 to RM16 ($1.70–$4.50/80p–£2.20) per dish. The flavors and atmosphere are about as local as you can get.

ATTRACTIONS

Kuantan can really be seen in a day. Although there are a few fun crafts shops, the place is not exactly a hotbed of culture. The main attraction in town is the huge **State Mosque,** which is quite beautiful inside and out, with a distinct dome, minarets, and stained glass. Late afternoon is the best time to see it, when the light shines through the glass. You can also have a nice walk down **Jalan Besar,** sampling local delicacies sold on the street and shopping in the smaller craft and souvenir shops.

ATTRACTIONS OUTSIDE KUANTAN

Pahang is home to peninsular Malaysia's oldest rainforests, but to be honest, the best way to experience them is through **Taman Negara,** Malaysia's biggest forest preserve on the peninsula. Overnight trips in decent accommodations with experienced nature guides can be organized very easily from KL (see chapter 10). A few attractions outside Kuantan can make interesting half-day or day trips if you tire of the beach. For these trips, I suggest you book through your hotel or resort—I couldn't find a single independent tour operator with suitable guides, so your resort probably has one or two they work with exclusively.

Gua Charah caves are about 25km (16 miles) outside of Kuantan. Also called Pancing caves (they're located in a town called Pancing), one of the caves in the network is a temple, home to a huge reclining Buddha. It is said that the monk caretaker, who has grown very old, is having difficulty finding another monk who will take over his duties at the caves.

Lake Chini, 12 freshwater lakes 60km (38 miles) southwest of Kuantan, claim local legends a la Loch Ness. They say that there once was an ancient Khmer city at the site of the lakes, but it is now buried deep under the water, protected by monsters. Some have tried to find both city and monsters but have come up with nothing (except litter from tourists—it's a terrible problem). Boats take you across the lake to an *Orang Asli* (indigenous peoples) kampung to see their way of life.

Just south of Kuantan is **Pekan,** which for history and culture buffs is far more interesting than Kuantan. Called "the Royal City," it's where the Sultan of Pahang resides in a beautiful Malay-style *istana,* or palace. The **State Museum** on Jalan Sultan Ahmad has displays depicting the history of Pahang and its royal family, as well as sunken treasures from old Chinese junks.

3 Kuala Terengganu ✦

The capital of the state of Terengganu, Kuala Terengganu has a few more exciting activities to offer a visitor than its southern neighbor, Kuantan, but suffers from the same lack of tourism investment and enthusiasm. In 1999 the state voted into local power the PAS (Pan Malaysian Islamic Party), who immediately trashed tourism plans and instituted very tourist-unfriendly policies, banning Western-style bathing suits and the sale of alcohol in restaurants and pubs. Hotels were even told they'd have to provide separate swimming pools for men and women, among other very strict laws governing "public decency." In reality, very few of these laws were ever enforced, but the bad publicity they generated was enough to drive travelers to more foreigner-friendly destinations in the country.

Thankfully, the national ruling party has been voted back into state power, and one of their first tasks has been to put Terengganu back on the tourism map. It will take some doing, but the highway between Kuantan and Kuala Terengganu is a good start.

Most people come to Terengganu to visit the islands off its coast. Redang and Perhentian islands have excellent opportunities for divers and snorkelers to see an abundance of marine creatures. The mainland's pretty seaside also supports a couple of very atmospheric and serene resorts.

Kuala Terengganu is small and easy to navigate, clustered around a port at the mouth of the Terengganu River. Many livelihoods revolve around the sea, so most of the activity, even today, focuses on the areas closest to the jetties. The region is also home to many of Malaysia's crafts cottage industries, which makes shopping really fun. The local business week is from Saturday to Wednesday, so be prepared for that when you plan your time here—many places close for a half-day on Thursdays and all day on Fridays.

ESSENTIALS

VISITOR INFORMATION

The **Tourism Information Centre** (© 09/622-1553) is on Jalan Sultan Zainal Abidin just next to the post office and across from the central market.

GETTING THERE

Malaysia Airlines (© 1300/883-000; www.malaysiaairlines.com) flies daily from KL to Kuala Terengganu's Sultan Mahmud Airport; for local airport information call © 09/666-4204. From the airport, a taxi to town is about RM20 ($5.60/80p).

Transnasional operates nine daily **buses** from KL's Duta terminal on Jalan Duta (© 03/6201-3463); the trip takes 8 hours and costs RM30 ($8.40/£4.20).

Outstation taxis from Kuantan will cost about RM100 ($28/£14) and can be found at the Makmur Bus terminal in Kuantan.

GETTING AROUND

Although you can stroll around the downtown areas with ease, getting to many of the bigger attractions will require a **taxi.** They're terribly inexpensive, making it well worth your while to hire by the hour or for a half or whole day, so you can go around to places and not worry how you'll get back. Your hotel's concierge can help you book. Rates will be around RM15 ($4.20/£2.10) per hour.

FAST FACTS

Most **banks** are on Jalan Sultan Ismail. The main **post office** is on Jalan Sultan Zainal Abidin (© **09/622-7555**), next to the Tourist Information Centre.

WHERE TO STAY

The Aryani Resort ★★ *Finds*   Raja Dato' Bahrin Shah Raja Ahmad (a most royal name) opened his dream resort here in Terengganu. An internationally celebrated architect, he'd previously designed the State Museum (see below) and wished to translate the beautiful lines of Terengganu aesthetics into a special resort. The resulting Aryani is stunning—organic, stimulating, unique, and best of all, peaceful. In a rural 3.6-hectare (9-acre) spot by the sea, the rooms are private bungalows situated like a village. Inside, each is masterfully decorated to suit both traditional style and modern comfort. The Heritage Suite wins the prize: a 100-year-old timber palace, restored and rebuilt on the site, it's appointed with fine antiques. The design of the outdoor pool is practically an optical illusion, and the spa (for massage and beauty treatments) is in its own Malay house. The resort's rural location has both a plus and a minus: On the plus side it's secluded; on the minus side it's 45 minutes from Kuala Terengganu. The resort can arrange boat trips for snorkeling, tours to town, and golfing.

Jalan Rhu Tapai–Merang, 21010 Setiu, Terengganu, Malaysia. © **09/653-2111**. Fax 09/653-1007. www.thearyani. com. 20 units. RM560–RM656 ($157–$184/£78–£92) double; RM808 ($226/£113) modern suite; RM1,055 ($295/£148) Heritage Suite. AE, DC, MC, V. **Amenities:** 2 restaurants; outdoor infinity pool; spa w/massage; nonmotorized watersports equipment rental; concierge; limousine service; same-day laundry service; library. *In room:* A/C, TV w/satellite programming, minibar, coffee/tea-making facilities.

Primula Parkroyal Kuala Terengganu   A top pick for accommodations in Kuala Terengganu is the Parkroyal. The first resort to open in this area, it commands the best section of beach the city has to offer and still is very close to the downtown area. It has full resort facilities, which include three excellent restaurants and the only bar in the city (perhaps even in the state). Make sure you get a room facing the sea—the view is dreamy. Other facilities include an outdoor pool with grassy lawn, watersports facilities, a lobby shop, and a kid's club.

Jalan Persinggahan, P.O. Box 43, 20904, Kuala Terengganu, Terengganu Darul Iman, Malaysia. © **800/835-7742** in the U.S. and Canada, 800/363-300 in Australia, 0800/801-111 in New Zealand, 09/622-2100, or 09/623-3722. Fax 09/623-3360. www.primulaparkroyal.com 249 units. RM275 ($77/£39) double; RM570 ($160/£80) suite. AE, DC, MC, V. **Amenities:** 3 restaurants; pub; outdoor pool; children's center; concierge; tour desk; limousine service; business center; 24-hr. room service; babysitting; same-day laundry service; dry cleaning. *In room:* A/C, TV w/satellite programming and in-house movie, minibar, coffee/tea-making facilities, hair dryer.

Tanjong Jara Resort ★★★   This is the resort you fantasize about. A small morsel of luxury in a secluded hideaway, Tanjong Jara absorbs the most exotic of Malay traditions to create a resort that truly reflects its host culture. The architectural character of the buildings is designed after 17th-century Malay sultans' palaces, with delicate woodcarvings, hardwood floors and timber accents, thatch roofs, and other natural building materials. Guest rooms come in three varieties. Sermabi rooms, at ground level, are midsize double occupancy rooms with big bathrooms, two vanities, and a huge tub that invites. These rooms also have big private sun decks attached. Just above Serambi rooms are Bumbung rooms, the lowest-priced category; these rooms are exactly like their downstairs neighbors, except they do not have sun decks. My one caveat: upstairs rooms have bird's-eye views of sun decks below. The ultimate accommodations here are the beachfront chalets, called Anjing, with long picture windows

Kuala Terengganu

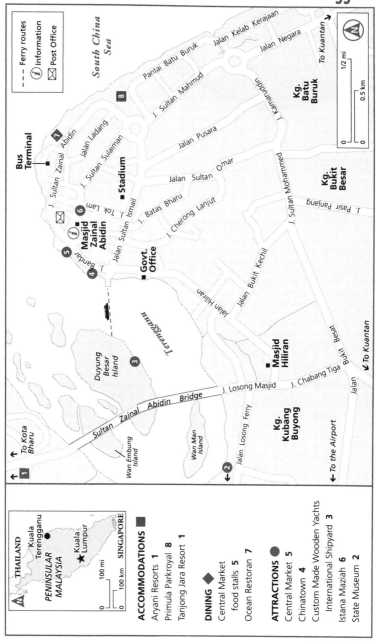

Ferry routes
ⓘ **Information**
⊠ **Post Office**

South China Sea

South China Sea

Pantai Batu Buruk
Jalan Kelab Kerajaan
Jalan Negara
To Kuantan →

Bus Terminal

J. Sultan Zainal Abidin
Jalan Ladang
J. Sultan Sulaiman
J. Sultan Mahmud
J. Kamaruddin

Kg. Batu Buruk

Jalan Pusara

Stadium

Jalan Sultan Omar

Kg. Bukit Besar

J. Batas Bharu
J. Tok Lam
Jalan Sultan Ismail
J. Cherong Lanjut
J. Sultan Mohammed
J. Pasir Panjang

Masjid Zainal Abidin

⊠
ⓘ

J. Bandar

Govt. Office

Jalan Bukit Kechil
Jalan Hiliran
Jalan Bukit Besat
To Kuantan →

Masjid Hiliran

Terengganu

Duyung Besar Island

Wan Embung Island

Sultan Zainal Abidin Bridge

Wan Man Island

J. Losong Masjid
J. Chabang Tiga
J. Losong Ferry

Kg. Kubang Buyong

← To the Airport

← To Kota Bharu

1 ←
←

1/2 mi
0.5 km
0
0

THAILAND
Kuala Terengganu
PENINSULAR MALAYSIA
Kuala Lumpur ★
SINGAPORE

100 mi
100 km

ACCOMMODATIONS ■
Aryani Resorts **1**
Primula Parkroyal **8**
Tanjong Jara Resort **1**

DINING ◆
Central Market food stalls **5**
Ocean Restoran **7**

ATTRACTIONS ●
Central Market **5**
Chinatown **4**
Custom Made Wooden Yachts
International Shipyard **3**
Istana Maziah **6**
State Museum **2**

that open out onto a breezy veranda, big sleeping areas, with separate sofa bed, and huge bathrooms that include outdoor sunken tubs within a private garden. A main attraction here is the Tanjong Club, a peaceful spa in a garden setting featuring traditional Malay health and beauty treatments. The resort's grounds are meticulously maintained, resonating with the sound of wind chimes and Malaysian gamelan music, and the beach is pristine. Watersports, golf, and local tours can be arranged.

Batu 8 off Jalan Dungun, 23000 Dungun, Terengganu © 09/845-1100. Fax 09/845-1200. www.tanjongjararesort. com. 99 units. US$220 Bumbung double; US$260 Serambi double; US$390 Anjing double. AE, DC, MC, V. **Amenities:** 3 restaurants; 2 outdoor pools; 2 outdoor tennis courts; fitness center and spa; concierge; tour desk; limousine; 24-hr. room service; babysitting; same-day laundry service; dry cleaning; library. *In room:* A/C, TV w/satellite programming, minibar, coffee/tea-making facilities, hair dryer.

WHERE TO DINE

Outside of the resorts, you'll be at a loss to find Malay specialties in a nice restaurant setting, because most locals either cook at home or eat at hawker stalls. If you ask for the best dishes, people will point you in all sorts of directions, to roadside places with no signboards or hawkers selling treats from the back of their car even. To sample as many varieties of local Malay cuisine, your best bet is to visit the Central Market food stalls, where you'll find a variety of freshly cooked dishes for cheap. Likewise, Chinese food can be found in food stalls in Chinatown and coffee shops along Jalan Kampong Cina (pronounced *Chee*-na).

If you're in town for mealtime and want a more comfortable dining experience, **Ocean Restoran** is the best pick. Near the waterfront in what looks like a warehouse (Lot 2679 Jalan Sultan Janah Apitin; © **09/623-9154**), Ocean prepares tender prawns, light butterfish, and juicy crab in local and Chinese recipes that are very good. Don't count on much from the alfresco decor.

ATTRACTIONS

Central Market ⊛   Open daily from very early until about 7pm, the central market is a huge maze of shops selling every craft made in the region. There's basket weaving for everything from place mats to beach mats. Batik comes in sarongs (with some very unique patterns), ready-made clothing, and household linens. *Songket,* beautiful fabric woven with gold and silver threads, is sold by the piece or sarong. Brassware pots, candlesticks, and curios are piled high and glistening. Every handicraft item you can think of is here, waiting for you to bargain for and bring home. And when you're done, venture to the back of the market and check out the produce, dried goods, and seafood in the wet market.

Jalan Sultan Zainal Abidin. Free admission. Daily early morning–7pm.

Chinatown   Although Terengganu has only a small Chinese population, its Chinatown is still quite interesting. This street of shophouses close to the water is still alive, only today many of the shops are art galleries and boutiques, showcasing only the finest regional arts. Also along Jalan Bandar you can find travel agents for trips to nearby islands.

Jalan Bandar.

Custom Made Wooden Yachts International Shipyard ⊛   Abdullah bin Muda's family has been building ships by hand for generations. Now Mr. Abdullah is an old-timer, but he gets around, balancing on the planks that surround the dry-docked hulls of his latest masterpieces. He makes fishing boats in western and Asian styles, as well as luxury yachts—all handmade, all from wood. Although Mr. Abdullah doesn't speak any English, he'll let you explore the boats on your own and even tell you how much money he's getting for them. You'll weep when you hear how inexpensive his fine work is. Ask your hotel's concierge to call before you plan to head out, to make sure they're open and that Mr. Abdullah is in.

3592 Duyong Besar. ☎ 09/623-2072. Free admission.

Istana Maziah Probably one of the least ornate *istanas* in Malaysia, this lovely yellow and white royal palace, built in 1897, is today mainly only used for state and royal ceremonies. It is not open to the public, but you can catch glimpses through the gate and over the compound walls. Tucked away down the narrow winding street is its neighbor, the Masjid (mosque) Abidin.

Jalan Masji.

State Museum ★★ The buildings that house the museum's collection were built specifically for this purpose. Designed by a member of the Terengganu royal family, an internationally renowned architect who also built the nearby Aryani resort, it reflects the stunning Terengganu architectural style. Atop stilts (16 of them, the traditional number) with high sloping roofs, the three main buildings are connected by elevated walkways. Inside are fine collections that illustrate the history and cultural traditions of the state.

Bukit Losong. ☎ 09/622-1444. Adults RM5 ($1.40/70p); children RM2 (60¢/30p). Sat–Thurs 9am–5pm.

TERENGGANU'S HANDICRAFTS

Chendering, an industrial town about 40 minutes' drive south of Kuala Terengganu, is where you'll find major handicraft production—factories and showrooms of batiks and other lovely items. All these places are located along one stretch of highway, but all are too far apart to walk. Plan to hire a taxi by the hour to shuttle you between them; they're about a 5-minute hop between each if you're driving. Also, while you're in the area, stop by the **Masjid Tengku Tengah Zahara,** which is only 5km (3 miles) outside of the town. The mosque is more commonly referred to as the "Floating Mosque," as it is built in a lake and appears to be floating on the top.

Noor Arfa Noor Arfa is Malaysia's largest producer of hand-painted batik. This former cottage-industry business now employs 200 workers to create ready-to-wear fashions that are esteemed as designer labels throughout the country. There's also a shop in town at Aked Mara, A3 Jalan Sultan Zainal Abidin (☎ **09/623-5173**).

Lot 1048 K Kawasan Perindustrian Chendering. ☎ **09/617-5700**. Free admission. Sat–Thurs 8am–5pm.

Suteramas Suteramas specializes in batik painting on fine quality silks. At this, their factory showroom, you can buy their latest creations or just watch them being made. Not only do they dye the cloth, they make it from their own worm stock.

Zkawasan Perindustrian Chendering. ☎ **09/617-1355**. Free admission. Sat–Wed 9am–5pm.

Terengganu Craft Cultural Centre Operated by the Malaysian Handicraft Development Corporation, the Craft Cultural Centre, also called Budaya Craft, not only sells handicrafts, but also has blocks of warehouses where artisans create the work. See batik painting, brass casting, basket weaving, and woodcarving as well as other local crafts in progress.

Lot 2195 Kawasan Perindustrian Chendering. ☎ **09/617-1033**. Sat–Wed 8am–5pm; Thurs 8am–12:45pm.

TERENGGANU MARINE PARK

The first marine park in Malaysia, the Terengganu Marine Park is situated around the nine islands of the Redang archipelago, 45km (28 miles) northeast of Kuala Terengganu and 27km (17 miles) out to sea. Sporting the best coral reefs and dive conditions off peninsular Malaysia, the park attracts divers with its many excellent sites. The largest of the islands is Pulau Redang (Redang Island), where most people stay in resorts on overnight diving excursions. Recent completion of an airport on Redang makes it fabulously accessible. **Berjaya Air** (in KL ⊘ **03/2145-2828;** www.berjaya-air.com) flies four times a week from KL. Otherwise, you'll have to make your way from Kuala Terengganu, driving an hour north to the jetty town of Merang, followed by a speedboat trip to any one of the islands for scuba, snorkeling, and sunning on powdery beaches.

The best place to stay on Redang is the **Berjaya Redang Beach Resort** ⊛. It's the best, mainly because they can arrange your entire trip and activities for you—air transfers, accommodations, meals, and activities including scuba. Very no-muss-no-fuss. And while Berjaya commands the best cove on the island, with powdery white-sand beaches, it also happens to be the most comfortable place here, with 152 Malay-style chalets all with en-suite bathroom, air-conditioning, phones, TVs with satellite programs and in-house movies, and minibars. Of their three restaurants, the beach seafood grill is the favorite. In addition to scuba and snorkeling trips to the coral reefs, they'll plan other watersports activities plus treks around the island. Their pool is a gorgeous lagoon-style affair by the beach. Very pretty. Contact Berjaya Redang Beach Resort at ⊘ **09/630-8866;** fax 09/630-8855; or visit online at www.berjayaresorts. com. Rates are RM200 to RM400 ($56–$112/£28–£56) for a double.

PERHENTIAN ISLANDS

The Perhentian Islands (two islands; one big, one small) are part of the same archipelago within the Terengganu Marine Park. Located to the north of Redang, they are not as easy to access as Redang, because there's no easy airport access. It's about an hour's ride to the jetty from Kuala Terengganu, then a speedboat to the island.

There are many bungalow operators on these islands—most of these places are terrible, shoddy huts with poor excuses for beds and scarcely anything else for convenience. One place had a knee-high stinking garbage heap beside the path that leads from the beach to reception. For some reason these small bungalow operators have not learned how to handle waste and rubbish and will eventually spoil the environment that draws people here in the first place.

Perhentian Island Resort is your best option on Perhantian. They have a private beach and are managed properly. Their 106 rooms, housed in cabanas, offer comfortable beds and air-conditioning. Their one restaurant serves buffet meals three times daily. Activities are organized through their PADI dive center, plus there's snorkeling, tennis, trekking, and nonmotorized sea sports. They will arrange your speedboat transfers to and from the jetty.

Note: The resort is closed during the rainy season from December through January. Contact Perhentian Island Resort at ⊘ **09/697-4095;** fax 09/697-8679; or visit online at www.pulauperhentian.com.my. Rates are RM250 to RM350 ($70–$98/£35–£49) double chalet.

4 Kota Bharu

In the northeast corner of peninsular Malaysia, bordering Thailand, is the state of **Kelantan.** Few tourists head this far north up the east coast, but it's a fascinating journey for those interested in seeing Malaysia as it might have been without so many foreign influences. The state is populated mostly by Malays and Bumiputeras, with only tiny factions of Chinese and Indian residents and almost no traces of British colonialism. Not surprisingly, Kelantan is the heart of traditional Islam in modern Malaysia. Although the government in KL constructs social policies based upon a more open and tolerant Islam, religious and government leaders in Kelantan can be counted on for putting forth a strong Muslim ideal where they feel they may have influence.

It is important to note that Kelantan borders Thailand's southern provinces, where since 2004 civil unrest, including bombings in public places, has led to hundreds of deaths of Thai citizens and several international tourists. I advise travelers to use caution in this area and refrain from speaking openly about politics and religion.

Kota Bharu, the state capital, is the heart of the region. The area is rich in Malay cultural heritage, as evidenced in the continuing interest in arts like *silat* (Malay martial arts), *wayang kulit* (puppetry), *gasing* (top spinning), and *wau* (kite flying). For the record, you won't find too much traditional music or dance, as women are forbidden from entertaining in public. Also beware that the state has strict laws controlling the sale of alcoholic beverages, which cannot be purchased in stores, hotels, or most restaurants. You will not find a single bar. Chinese restaurants, however, are permitted to sell beer to their patrons but will probably not allow you to take any away.

If you take a side trip from Terengganu, plan to stay overnight. An outstation taxi from Kuala Terengganu can bring you on the 3-hour drive for around RM100 ($28/£14). Stay at the **Renaissance,** managed by Marriott; it's practically the only hint of the 21st century in all of Kelantan. Rooms are exactly what you would expect from an international business-class hotel chain, but cost a mere RM225 ($63/£32) for double occupancy. Contact the Renaissance at Kota Sri Mutiara, Jalan Yahya Petra (© 09/746-2233; fax 09/746-1122; www.marriott.com). You'll find the **Kelantan Tourist Information Centre** at Jalan Sultan Ibrahim (© 09/748-5534).

Centered around the Padang Merdeka are five of the most significant sights in Kota Bharu, run by the Kelantan State Museum Corporation. They are all open Saturday to Thursday 8:30am to 4:45pm, and closed on Fridays. At the **Istana Jahar** (adults RM2/60¢/30p, children RM1/30¢/15p), Kelantan traditional costumes, antiques, and musical instruments are displayed in context of their usage in royal ceremonies. **Istana Batu** (adults RM2/60¢/30p, children RM1/30¢/15p) takes you through a photographic journey of Kelantan's royal family and offers a peek at their lifestyle through the past 200 years. The **Balai Getam Guri handicraft museum** (adults RM2/60¢/30p, children RM1/30¢/15p) showcases the finest in Kelantanese textiles, basketry, embroidery, batik printing, and silversmithing. You'll also be able to buy crafts in the shops within the compound. The **Islamic Museum (Muzium Islam;** adults RM2/60¢/30p, children RM1/30¢/15p) teaches everything you might want to know about Islam in this state, with a focus on Islamic arts and Kelantan's role in spreading Islam in the region. Finally there is the **War Museum (Bank Kerapu;** adults RM2/60¢/30p, children RM1/30¢/15p), which tells the story of Kelantan during World War II in a 1912 bank building that survived the invasion.

The State Museum (Muzium Negeri) is located on Jalan Hospital (© **09/744-4666;** adults RM2/60¢/30p, children RM1/30¢/15p; Sat–Thurs 8:30am–4:45pm). It's been a long time since this old building served as the colonial land office, but in 1990 major renovations gave it a new life. It now houses the Kelantan Art Gallery, including ceramics, traditional musical instruments, and cultural pastimes exhibits.

For great local handicrafts shopping, visitors to Kelantan need go no farther than **Jalan P.C.B.,** the road that leads to P.C.B. beach from Kota Bharu's Chinatown area. Hire a taxi through your hotel's concierge—it's best to hire by the hour; it should only cost about RM15 ($4.20/£2.10) per hour. Your driver will stop at every roadside factory, showroom, shop, and crafts house (the place crawls with them!) and you'll satisfy every shopping itch that needs scratching. These are all small cottage industries run out of folks' homes, so while some places actually have shops, many are very informal "look sees." You can watch ladies weaving *songket* cloth (fine cotton cloth with interwoven patterns in bright colors and gold or silver threads) on enormous wooden looms, see how kites are made by hand, and learn techniques for painting and dyeing batik cloth, along with many other crafts activities that go on in this area. Your driver can also take you to other shopping places in town for local crafts. The prices are very good—far cheaper than in KL.

12

East Malaysia: Borneo

Borneo for the past 2 centuries has been the epitome of adventure travel. While bustling ports like Penang, Malacca, and Singapore attracted early travelers with dollars in their eyes, Borneo attracted those with adventure in their hearts. Today, the island still draws visitors who seek new and unusual experiences, and few leave disappointed. Rivers meander through dense tropical rainforests, beaches stretch for miles, and caves snake out longer than any in the world. All sorts of creatures you'd never imagine live in the rainforest: deer the size of house cats, owls only 6 inches tall, the odd proboscis monkey, and the endangered orangutan, whose only other natural home is Sumatra. It's also home to the largest flower in the world, the Rafflesia, spanning up to a meter (3 ft.) wide. Small wonder this place has special interest for scientists and researchers the world around.

The people of Borneo can be credited for most of the alluring tales of early travels. The exotically adorned tribes of warring headhunters and pirates of yesteryear, some of whom still live lifestyles little changed (though both headhunting and piracy are now illegal), today share their mysterious cultures and colorful traditions openly with outsiders.

Add to all of this the fabulous tale of the White Raja of Sarawak, Sir James Brooke, whose family ruled the state for just over 100 years, and you have a land filled with allure, mystery, and romance unlike any other.

Malaysia, Brunei Darussalam, and Indonesia have divided the island of Borneo. Indonesia claims Kalimantan to the south and east, and the Malaysian states of **Sarawak** and **Sabah** lie to the north and northwest. The small sultanate of Brunei is nestled between the two Malaysian states on the western coastline.

1 Sarawak ★★★

Tropical rainforest accounts for more than 70% of Sarawak's total landmass, providing homes for not only exotic species of plants and animals, but for the myriad ethnic groups who are indigenous to the area. With more than 10 national parks and 4 wildlife preserves, Malaysia shows its commitment to conserving the delicate balance of life here, while allowing small gateways for travelers to appreciate natural wonders. The national parks located around the state's capital Kuching provide quick access to forest life, while longer, more detailed trips to northern Sarawak lead you deeper into the jungle, to explore remote forests and extensive ancient cave networks. A web of rivers connects the inland areas to the main towns, and a boat trip from Kuching to visit tribal communities and trek into the surrounding forests is the most memorable attraction going.

The indigenous peoples of Sarawak make up more than half the state's population. Early European explorers and settlers referred to all native inhabitants of Borneo with the catchall term Dyaks, which didn't account for the variations between the more than 25 different ethnicities. Of these groups, the Iban are the largest, with more than 30% of the population overall. A nomadic people by tradition, the Ibans were once located all over the region, existing on agriculture, hunting, and fishing. They were also notoriously fierce warriors who would behead enemies—a practice now outlawed but that has retained its cultural significance. The Ibans fought not only with other tribes, but within their own separate tribal units as well.

The next largest group, the Bidayuh, live peacefully in the hills. Their longhouse communities are the most accessible to travelers from Kuching. The Melanu are a coastal people who excel in fishing and boatbuilding. Finally, the Orang Ulu is an association of smaller tribes mostly in the northern parts of the state. Tribes like the Kayah, Kenyah, Kelabit, and Penan, although culturally separate entities, formed an umbrella organization to loosely govern all groups and provide representation. These groups are perhaps the least accessible to outsiders.

The indigenous people who still stay in the forest live in longhouse communities, some of which are open for visitors. Most travelers access these places with the help of local tour operators, who have trips that last from an overnight excursion to a weeklong adventure. While some tours take you to well-trampled villages for the standard "gawk at the funny costumes" trips, many operators can take you to more remote places to meet people in an environment of cultural learning with a sensitivity that is appreciated by all involved. A few adventuresome souls travel solo into these areas, but I recommend that you stick with an operator. I don't care much for visitors who pop in unexpectedly, and I can't imagine why folks in one of these villages wouldn't feel the same way.

Every visitor to Sarawak starts out from **Kuching,** the capital city. With a population of some 400,000 people, it's small but oddly cosmopolitan. In addition to local tribes that gave up forest living, the city has large populations of Malays, Chinese, Indians, and Europeans, most of whom migrated in the last 2 centuries. The city sits at the mouth of the Kuching River, which will be your main artery for trips inland. Before you head off for the river, though, check out the many delights of this mysterious colonial kingdom.

Sarawak was introduced to the Western world by James Brooke, an English adventurer who in 1839 came to Southeast Asia to follow in the footsteps of his idol, Sir Stamford Raffles. Like Raffles's Singapore, there was a region waiting for Brooke to settle and in which to start a bustling community. His wanderings brought him to Borneo, where he was introduced to the sultan of Brunei. The sultan was deeply troubled by warring tribes to the south of his kingdom, who were in constant revolt, sometimes to the point of pirating ships to Brunei's port. Brooke provided the solution, initiating a campaign to befriend some of the warring tribes, uniting them to conquer the others. Soon the tribes were calmed. The sultan, delighted by Brooke, ceded Kuching to him for a small annual fee. In 1841, James Brooke became raja and set about claiming the land that is now Sarawak.

Raja Sir James Brooke became a colonial legend. Known as "The White Raja of Sarawak," he and his family ruled the territory and its people with a firm but compassionate hand. Tribal leaders were appointed to leadership and administrative positions within his government and militia, and as a result, the Brookes were highly respected by the populations they led. However, Brooke was a bit of a renegade, turning his nose up at London's attempts to include Sarawak under the crown. He took no money from the British and closed the doors to British commercial interests in Sarawak.

Instead, he dealt in local trade and trade with Singapore. Still, Kuching was understood to be a British holding, though the city never flourished as did other British ports in Southeast Asia.

After his death in 1868, Raja James Brooke was succeeded by his nephew, Charles Brooke. In 1917, Charles's son, Vyner Brooke, became the last ruling Raja, a position he held until World War II, when the territory was conquered by invading Japanese. After the war Raja Vyner Brooke returned briefly, but soon after, the territory was declared a crown colony. Eventually Malaya was granted independence by Britain, prompting Prime Minister Tunku Abdul Rahman to form Malaysia in 1963, uniting peninsular Malaya with Singapore, Sarawak, and Sabah. Singapore departed from the union 2 years later, but Sarawak and Sabah happily remained.

KUCHING

The perfect introduction to Sarawak begins in its capital. Kuching's museums, cultural exhibits, and historical attractions will help you form an overview of the history, people, and natural wonders of the state. In Kuching your introduction to Sarawak will be comfortable and fun; culture by day and good food and fun by night. Kuching, meaning "cat" in Malay, also has a wonderful sense of humor, featuring monuments and exhibits to its feline mascot on almost every corner.

ESSENTIALS

VISITOR INFORMATION   The **Sarawak Tourism Board's Visitor Information Centre** has literature and staff that can answer any question about activities in the state and city. This is actually the best place to start planning any trips to Sarawak's wonderful national parks, as the main office for the National Parks & Wildlife Centre operates a Visitor Information Centre here as well. Both offices are incredibly informed and are so welcoming, so feel free to take advantage. You'll find them at the Sarawak Tourism Complex in the Old Courthouse opposite the Kuching Waterfront (Sarawak Tourism Board © **082/410-944,** National Parks Centre © **082/248-088;** www.sarawaktourism.com).

GETTING THERE   Almost all travelers to Sarawak enter through Kuching International Airport, just outside the city. **Malaysia Airlines** (© **1300/883-000;** www.malaysiaairlines.com) has international flights from Singapore and Perth, with domestic service from KL, Johor Bahru, and Kota Kinabalu. **AirAsia** (© **1300/889-933;** www.airasia.com) flies between Kuching and KL.

The brand-new airport is a terrific facility with ATMs, money changers, restaurants, and tourist information. Taxis from the airport use coupons that you purchase outside the arrival hall. Priced according to zones, most trips to the central parts of town will be about RM18 ($5.05/£2.50).

GETTING AROUND   Centered around a *padang,* or large ceremonial field, Kuching resembles many other Malaysian cities. Buildings of beautiful colonial style rise on the edges of the field; many of these today house Sarawak's museums. The main sights, as well as the Chinatown area and the riverfront, are easily accessible on foot. Taxis are also available and do not use meters; most rides around town are quoted between RM6 and RM10 ($1.70–$2.80/85p–£1.40). Taxis can be waved down from the side of the road, or if you're in the Chinatown area, the main taxi stand is on Gambier Road near the end of the India Street Pedestrian Mall.

FAST FACTS   Sarawak's area code is 082. Major **banks** have branches on Tunku Abdul Rahman Road near Holiday Inn Kuching or in the downtown area around Khoo Hun Yeang Road. There are a few **Internet** cafes around town; it's best to ask your hotel's concierge for the nearest one before you start wandering around—they're constantly going out of business, then popping up elsewhere.

WHERE TO STAY

Holiday Inn Kuching   Holiday Inn offers Western-style accommodations at a moderate price, and you'll appreciate its location in an excellent part of town. It sits along the bank of the Kuching River, so to get to the main riverside area you need only stroll 10 minutes past some of the city's unique historical and cultural sights, shopping, and good places to dine. Catering to a diverse group of leisure travelers and businesspeople, the hotel has spacious, modern, and comfortable rooms; and although there are few bells and whistles, you won't want for convenience. The outdoor swimming pool and excellent fitness center facility will help you unwind, and the small shopping arcade has one of the best collections of books on Sarawak that can be found in the city.

P.O. Box 2362, Jalan Tunku Abdul Rahman, 93100 Kuching, Sarawak, Malaysia. © **082/423-111.** Fax 082/426-169. www.holidayinn-sarawak.com. 305 units. RM230 ($64/£32) double. AE, DC, MC V. **Amenities:** 3 restaurants; bar; outdoor pool; fitness center w/sauna; concierge; tour desk; limousine service; business center; 24-hr. room service; babysitting; same-day laundry service; dry cleaning; nonsmoking rooms; executive-level rooms. *In room:* A/C, TV w/satellite programming and in-house movie, minibar, coffee/tea-making facilities, hair dryer.

Kuching

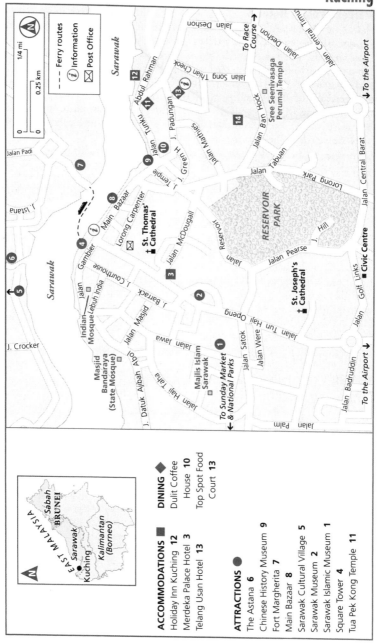

ACCOMMODATIONS ■
Holiday Inn Kuching **12**
Merdeka Palace Hotel **3**
Telang Usan Hotel **13**

DINING ◆
Dulit Coffee
House **10**
Top Spot Food
Court **13**

ATTRACTIONS ●
The Astana **6**
Chinese History Museum **9**
Fort Margherita **7**
Main Bazaar **8**
Sarawak Cultural Village **5**
Sarawak Museum **2**
Sarawak Islamic Museum **1**
Square Tower **4**
Tua Pek Kong Temple **11**

Merdeka Palace Hotel ⚡   Towering over the Padang Merdeka in the center of town is the Merdeka Palace, practically a landmark in its own right (as soon as you see the easily distinguishable tower, you'll always know where you are). This is one of the most fashionable addresses in the city, for guests as well as banquets and functions. From the large marble lobby to the mezzanine shopping arcade stuffed with designer tenants, its reputation for elegance is justified. Large rooms come dressed in European-inspired furnishings and fabrics. Try to get a view of the padang, as the less expensive rooms face the parking lot. The rooftop outdoor swimming pool is small, but the fully equipped fitness center has sauna and steam rooms, plus massage. The pub here is perhaps the most happening one in town.

Jalan Tun Abang Haji Openg, 93000 Kuching, Sarawak, Malaysia. ℂ 082/258-000. Fax 082/425-400. www.merdeka palace.com. 214 units. RM414 ($116/£58) double. AE, DC, MC, V. **Amenities:** 2 restaurants; bar; outdoor pool; fitness center w/Jacuzzi, sauna, steam, and massage; concierge; limousine service; business center; shopping arcade; salon; 24-hr. room service; babysitting; same-day laundry service; dry cleaning; nonsmoking rooms; executive-level rooms. *In room:* A/C, TV w/satellite programming, minibar, coffee/tea-making facilities, safe.

Telang Usan Hotel ⚡⚡ *Value*   While in Kuching I like to stay at the Telang Usan Hotel. It's not as flashy as the higher-priced places, but it's a fantastic bargain for a good room. Most guests here are leisure travelers, and in fact, many are repeat visitors. The small public areas sport murals in local Iban style, revealing the origin of the hotel's owner and operator. While rooms are small and decor is not completely up-to-date, they're spotless. Some rooms have only standing showers, so be sure to specify when making your reservation if a bathtub is important to you. The coffee shop is a fine place to try local food, but they have Western selections as well. There is an excellent tour agency under the same ownership at the hotel.

Ban Hock Rd., P.O. Box 1579, 93732 Kuching, Sarawak, Malaysia. ℂ 082/415-588. Fax 082/245-316. www.telang usan.com. 66 units. RM120 ($34/£17) double. AE, DC, MC, V. **Amenities:** Restaurant; limited room service; same-day laundry service; Internet service. *In room:* A/C, TV, minibar (some rooms).

WHERE TO DINE

Everyone ends up at the **Top Spot Food Court,** a cheap hawker center venue on Jalan Bukit Mata off Jalan Tunku Abdul Rahman just near the Holiday Inn. Various stalls cook Chinese, Malay, and Western food, all sorts of exotic dishes, and local and seafood dishes. Located on the roof of a multistory parking garage, don't expect anything but "local charm" for decor. But the food is good and cheap and you'll bump into plenty of other travelers and locals here to chat with.

A good pick for local specialties is the **Dulit Coffee House** at Telang Usan Hotel (ℂ 082/415-588). Try their local Sarawak version of *laksa*, vermicelli noodles and seafood in a rich and spicy coconut gravy, or the Sarawak black pepper steak, which is a house specialty. Entrees are reasonably priced between RM8 and RM24 ($2.25–$6.75/£1.10–£3.35).

ATTRACTIONS

The Astana and Fort Margherita   At the waterfront by the Square Tower you'll find water taxis to take you across the river to see these two reminders of the White Rajas of Sarawak. The Astana, built in 1870 by Raja Charles Brooke, the second raja of Sarawak, is now the official residence of the governor. It is not open to the public, but visitors may still walk in the gardens. The best view of the Astana, however is from the water.

Raja Charles Brooke's wife, Ranee Margaret, gave her name to Fort Margherita, which was erected in 1870 to protect the city of Kuching. Inside the great castlelike building is a police museum, the most interesting sights of which are the depictions of criminal punishment.

Across the Sarawak River from town. Fort: ℂ **082/244-232**. Free admission. Daily 9am–5pm.

Chinese History Museum

Built in 1912, this old Chinese Chamber of Commerce Building is the perfect venue for a museum that traces the history of Chinese communities in Sarawak. Though small, it's centrally located and a convenient stop while you're in the area.

Corner of Main Bazaar and Jalan Tunku Abdul Rahman. Free admission. Daily 9am–5pm.

Main Bazaar

Main Bazaar, the major thoroughfare along the river, is home to Kuching's antiques and handicraft shops. If you're walking along the river, a little time in these shops is like a walk through a traditional handicrafts art gallery. You'll also find souvenir shops and some nice T-shirt silk screeners.

Along the river. Free admission.

Sarawak Cultural Village ✪

What appears to be a contrived theme park turns out to be a really fun place to learn about Sarawak's indigenous people. Built around a lagoon, the park re-creates the various styles of longhouse dwellings of each of the major tribes. Inside each house are representative members of each tribe displaying cultural artifacts and performing music, teaching dart blowing, and showing off carving talents. Give yourself plenty of time to stick around and talk with the people, who are recruited from villages inland and love to tell stories about their homes and traditions. Performers dance and display costumes at 11:30am and 4:30pm daily. A shuttle bus leaves at regular intervals from the Holiday Inn Kuching on Jalan Tunku Abdul Rahman.

Kampung Budaya Sarawak, Pantai Damai, Santubong. ℂ **082/846-411**. Adults RM45 ($13/£6.30), children RM23 ($6.45/£3.20). Daily 9am–5pm.

Sarawak Islamic Museum

A splendid array of Muslim artifacts at this quiet and serene museum depicts the history of Islam and its spread to Southeast Asia. Local customs and history are also highlighted. Although women are not required to cover their heads, respectable attire that covers the legs and arms is requested.

Jalan P. Ramlee. ℂ **082/244-232**. Free admission. Sat–Thurs 9am–5pm; Fri 9am–12:45pm and 3–5pm.

Sarawak Museum ✪

Two branches, one old and one new, display exhibits of the natural history, indigenous peoples, and culture of Sarawak, plus the state's colonial and modern history. The two branches are connected by an overhead walkway above Jalan Tun Haji Openg. The wildlife exhibit is a bit musty, but the arts and artifacts in the other sections are well-tended. A tiny aquarium sits neglected behind the old branch, but the gardens here are lovely.

Jalan Tun Haji Openg. ℂ **082/244-232**. Free admission. Sat–Thurs 9am–5pm; Fri 9am–12:45pm and 3–5pm.

Square Tower

The tower, built in 1879, served as a prison camp, but today the waterfront real estate is better served by an information center for travel agents. The Square Tower is also a prime starting place for a stroll along the riverside and is where you'll also find out about cultural performances and exhibitions held at the waterfront, or call the number below for performance schedules.

Jalan Gambier near the riverfront. ℂ **082/426-093**. Free admission.

Tua Pek Kong Temple At a main crossroads near the river stands the oldest Chinese temple in Sarawak. Although officially it is dated at 1876, most locals acknowledge the true date of its beginnings as 1843. It's still lively in form and spirit, with colorful dragons tumbling along the walls and incense filling the air.

Junction of Jalan Tunku Abdul Rahman and Jalan Padungan. Free admission.

TOURING LOCAL CULTURE ✸✸✸

One of the highlights of a trip to Sarawak is a visit to a longhouse community. Trips can last from simple overnight stays to 2-week intensive discovery tours. It goes without saying that shorter trips only venture as far as those longhouse villages closest to Kuching. The benefit is that these communities are at ease with foreigners and so are better able to demonstrate their culture. The drawback is that these villages are the ones most trampled by coach-loads of tourists looking to gawk at "primitive tribes." Basically, the more time you have, the deeper you will venture into the interior and the more time you will have to spend with different ethnic groups allowing greater insight into these fascinating cultures.

A typical longhouse trip starts with a van ride from Kuching followed by a longtail boat ride upriver, through gorgeous scenery. If you are only stopping in for the night, you'll be welcomed, fed, and entertained—the food is generally edible and always prepared under sanitary conditions. Fruits are delicious. Your guide, through translations, will help you chat with villagers and ask questions about their lifestyle and customs. At night you will sleep in a longhouse provided especially for guests. It's basic but cool, with mosquito nets (very necessary) provided. The following day includes a very brief jungle trek, plus hunting and fishing demonstrations before your departure back from whence you came. If your trip is for longer, you will probably avoid the closer villages and head straight for more remote communities, depending on how much time (and money) you have.

Your average overnight longhouse tour will set you back up to RM535 ($150/£75) per person. Good tour operators making longhouse tours are **Borneo Adventure,** 55 Main Bazaar (✆ **082/245-175;** fax 082/422-626) and **Telang Usan Travel & Tours,** Ban Hock Road (✆ **082/236-945;** fax 082/236-589). These agencies can also arrange trips into Sarawak's national parks.

TOURING SARAWAK'S NATIONAL PARKS

The Sarawak National Parks & Wildlife Centre has opened access to all of Sarawak's national parks to DIY (do-it-yourself) travelers. From their booking center in Kuching, you can apply for parks permits and book reservations in state-run lodging within each park. They can also advise how to travel to and from each park: Those closer to Kuching will only involve local road and river transportation, while more remote parks will require commercial flights to either Sibu or Miri, plus transfers to ground and river transportation and even chartered flights. If you have the time to plan your travel this way, you will be rewarded with the thrill of "getting there," experiencing local life a little closer to the ground.

Most people do not have the luxury of time, which is why I recommend booking trips that interest you through a tour operator who will arrange all transportation, parks permits, lodging, meals, and guides for you, freeing your time to experience the attractions themselves.

NATIONAL PARKS NOT FAR FROM KUCHING

Borneo Adventure (55 Main Bazaar; © 082/245-175; www.borneoadventure.com) costs a few dollars more than many of the other local operations, but you'll get experienced guides and reliable services, and you do not need to join a huge touristy coach group. Most of these trips are for small groups. Their half-day trips from Kuching take the mystery out of local transportation—they can even be combined for longer itineraries so you can maximize your time. They can also prepare customized itineraries and special theme tours based upon your special interests, for example, crafts, flora, or tribal cultures.

Bako National Park ⨳⨳⨳, established in 1957, is Sarawak's oldest national park. An area of 2,728 hectares (6,820 acres), it combines mangrove forest, lowland jungle, and high plains covered in scrub. Throughout the park you'll see the pitcher plant and other strange carnivorous plants, plus long-tailed macaques, monitor lizards, bearded pigs, and the unique proboscis monkey. Because the park is only 37km (22 miles) from Kuching, half-day trips here are extremely convenient. A day trip for two costs RM278 ($78/£39) per person.

Gunung Gading National Park, about a 2-hour drive west of Kuching, sprawls 4,106 hectares (10,265 acres) over rugged mountains to beautiful beach spots along the coast. Day-trippers and overnighters come to get a glimpse of the Rafflesia, the largest flower in the world. The flowers are short-lived and temperamental, but the national parks office will let you know if any are in bloom. A day tour for two people costs RM278 ($78/£39) per person.

Semenggoh Orang Utan Sanctuary is a rehabilitation center for orangutans and other endangered wildlife species, who are either orphaned or recovering from illness and are being trained for eventual release into the forest. A half-day tour for two people costs RM121 ($34/£17) per person.

NATIONAL PARKS A LITTLE FARTHER OUT

Borneo Adventure (55 Main Bazaar; © 082/245-175; www.borneoadventure.com) also books trips to national parks in other parts of the state. You'll have to fly to Miri or Sibu, as these two towns are the hop-off points for these excursions. Malaysia Airlines and AirAsia both service these two towns from KL and Kuching.

Gunung Mulu National Park provides an amazing adventure with its astounding underground network of caves. The park claims the world's largest cave passage (Deer Cave), the world's largest natural chamber (Sarawak Chamber), and Southeast Asia's longest cave (Clearwater Cave). No fewer than 18 caves offer explorers trips of varying degrees of difficulty, from simple treks with minimal gear to technically difficult caves that require specialized equipment and skills. Aboveground are 544 sq. km (326 sq. miles) of primary rainforest, peat swamps, and mountainous forests teeming with mammals, birds, and unusual insects. Located in the north of Sarawak, Mulu is very close to the Brunei border. Borneo Adventure has a 2-day/1-night package for RM371 ($104/£52) per person (minimum two people). The trip includes accommodations; ground transportation; longboat rides; nature guides to see Deer Cave, Sarawak Chamber, and Clearwater Cave; plus some rainforest trekking (wear a hat in the caves to protect yourself from bat droppings). They can book your flights from Kuching, but you'll have to pay extra.

2 Sabah ⭒⭒⭒

Sabah presents a wonderland of awe-inspiring natural scenery, lush primary rainforest, vibrant coral reefs, and mysterious indigenous cultures. It is, in my opinion, Southeast Asia's hidden treasure. A playground for adventure seekers, extreme sportsters, and bums in search of the ultimate beach, Sabah rewards those who venture here with a holiday in an unspoiled paradise.

Covering 73,711 sq. km (48,480 sq. miles) of the northern part of Borneo, the world's third-largest island, Sabah stretches from the South China Sea in the west to the Sulu Sea in the east, both seas containing an abundance of uninhabited islands, post-card-perfect beaches, and pristine coral reefs bubbling with marine life. In between, more than half of the state is covered in ancient primary rainforest that's protected in national parks and forest reserves. In these forests, some rare species of mammals like the Sumatran rhino and Asian elephant (herds of them) take effort to witness, but other animals, such as the orangutan, proboscis monkey, gibbon, lemur, civet, Malaysian sun bear, and a host of others can be seen on jungle treks if you search them out. Of the hundreds of bird species here, the hornbills and herons steal the show.

Sabah's tallest peak also happens to be the highest mountain between the Himalayas and Irian Jaya. At 4,095m (13,432 ft.), it's the tallest in Southeast Asia, and a challenge to trek or climb. The state's interior has endless opportunities for jungle trekking, river rafting, mountain biking and 4x4 exploration for every level of excitement, from soft adventure to extreme sports.

Not only does this state hold mysterious wildlife and geography, but people as well. Sabahans count among their many ethnic groups some 32 different tribes whose cultures and traditions are vastly different from the Malay majority that makes up the rest of the country. In fact, ethnic Malays are a minority in Sabah.

About one-third of the population are Kadazandusun, a group that inhabits mainly the west coast and in the interior of Sabah. They are one of the first groups travelers come into contact with, especially during the Pesta Kaamatan, or harvest festival, held during May, where the high priest or priestess presides over a ceremony performed to appease the rice spirit. Although it's a Kadazandusun tradition, it has come to be celebrated by all cultures in the state. Although this group produces the majority of Sabah's agricultural products, most members live in towns and hold everyday jobs. The exception is the Runggus, the last group of Kadazandusun to live in traditional longhouse communities, where they produce exquisite basket weaving, fabric weaving, and beadwork in traditional designs.

The Bajau are a group of seafarers who migrated from the Philippines only a couple hundred years ago. The Bajau on the eastern coast of Sabah carry on their traditional connection to the water, living as sea gypsies and coming to shore only for burials. On the west coast, however, many Bajau have settled on dry land as farmers and cattle raisers. Known locally as the "cowboys of the east," Bajau men are very skilled equestrians. During festivals, their brilliant costumes and decorated ponies almost always take center stage.

The third-most prominent indigenous group, the Murut, shares the southwest corner of Sabah with the Bajau, expanding inland along the border with Sarawak and Kalimantan (Indonesia). Skilled hunters, they use spears, blowpipes, poisoned darts, and trained dogs. In past days, these skills were used for headhunting, which thankfully is not practiced today (although many skulls can still be seen during visits to

> ### ⎛Warning⎞ Exercise Caution
>
> In April 2000, 22 people, including 11 foreign tourists, were kidnapped from a dive resort on Sipadan Island off the east coast of Sabah. This would be the first of four incidents of kidnapping, mostly of Malaysian workers, in this area by the *Abu Sayyaf*, a terrorist group in the southern Philippines with known links to Al-Qaeda. While Malaysia responded by placing security forces on 23 islands and six additional strategic locations, the U.S. Department of State still advises Americans to exercise caution when traveling in this area. Despite the warning, foreign visitor arrivals to Sipadan have doubled since the advisory was first issued.

longhouse settlements). One nonlethal Murut tradition involves a trampoline competition. The *lansaran* (the trampoline itself), situated in the community longhouse, is made of split bamboo. During Murut ceremonies, contestants drink rice wine and jump on the trampoline to see who can reach the farthest. A prize is hung above for the winner to grab.

Sabah also has a small community of Chinese families that settled during colonial days.

KOTA KINABALU

The best place to begin exploring Sabah's marine wonders, wildlife and forests, adventure opportunities, and indigenous peoples is from its capital, Kota Kinabalu. A speck of a city on the west coast, it's where you'll find the headquarters for all of Sabah's adventure-tour operators and package-excursion planners. I recommend you spend at least a day here to explore all your options, then set out to the wilds for the adventure of a lifetime.

ESSENTIALS

VISITOR INFORMATION   The **Sabah Tourism Board** (51 Jalan Gaya; ✆ 088/212-121; www.sabahtourism.com) provides the most comprehensive information about the state. It's open daily 9am to 4pm. Although the national MTB has a small office on Jalan Gaya a block down from the Sabah Tourism office, almost all of their information promotes travel in other parts of the country. Still, if you're interested, stop by Ground Floor Uni. Asia Building, no. 1 Jalan Sagunting (✆ 088/248-698).

GETTING THERE   Because of Sabah's remote location, just about everybody will arrive by air through the **Kota Kinabalu International Airport** in the capital city (✆ 088/238-555), about a 20-minute drive south of the central part of the city. A surprising number of direct international flights connect Sabah to the region. Malaysia Airlines flies from Hong Kong, Manila, Osaka, Seoul, Shanghai, Singapore, and Tokyo, among others (✆ 1300/883-000; www.malaysiaairlines.com), and AirAsia flies from Bangkok (✆ 1300/889-933; www.airasia.com).

Malaysia Airlines also has direct domestic flights to Kota Kinabalu from KL, Johor Bahru, Kuching, Sibu, and Miri, with in-state service to Sandakan and other towns. AirAsia has direct domestic flights from KL and Johor Bahru.

The most efficient way to get into town from the airport is by taxi. The cars line up outside the arrival hall and are supposed to use a coupon system—look for the coupon-sales and taxi-booking counter close by. You'll pay about RM12 ($3.40/£1.70) for a trip to town. Ignore the drivers that will try to lure you away from the coupon counter; they will always overcharge you.

GETTING AROUND   In the downtown area, you can get around quite easily on foot between hotels, restaurants, tour operators, markets, and the tourism office. For longer trips, a taxi will be necessary; in town trips cost about RM10 ($2.80/£1.40). Taxis are flagged down on the street or by your hotel's bellhop.

FAST FACTS   The **area code** for Sabah is **088**. Sabah time is 1 hour ahead of peninsular Malaysia. You'll find **banks** with ATMs conveniently located in the downtown area around Jalan Limabelas and along Jalan Gaya and Jalan Pantai. While there are no large **Internet** cafes, per se, you'll find access in small shopfronts around the main parts of town, especially near the shopping malls.

WHERE TO STAY

Hyatt Regency Kinabalu ☆   The only international business-class hotel in town, in some ways the Hyatt seems a little out of place in cozy Kota Kinabalu. Still, it's located close to the waterfront, near all major shopping and travel operators, and has a fantastic assortment of restaurants to choose from. Even if you're staying elsewhere in town, you may appreciate one of their dining options. As modern as you would expect the Hyatt chain to be, rooms here are large and are presented in up-to-date furnishing styles that are not so Western that they take all the charm away from the room. Local tour and car-rental booking in the lobby make the place convenient for leisure travelers. One of the high points is Shenanigan's, the best bar in Kota Kinabalu, with live entertainment. It gets packed, mostly with locals and expatriates out for a sip.

Jalan Datuk Salleh Sulong, 88994 Kota Kinabalu, Sabah. ℂ 800/233-1234 in the U.S. and Canada, 800/131-234 in Australia, 800/441-234 in New Zealand, or 088/221-234. Fax 088/225-972. http://kinabalu.hyatt.com. 288 units. RM270 ($76/£38) double; from RM470 ($132/£66) suite. AE, DC, MC, V. **Amenities:** 3 restaurants; bar; outdoor pool; fitness center; concierge; tour desk; car-rental desk; limousine service; business center; 24-hr. room service; babysitting; same-day laundry service; dry cleaning; nonsmoking rooms; executive-level rooms. In room: A/C, TV w/satellite programming and in-house movie, minibar, coffee/tea-making facilities, hair dryer, safe.

The Jesselton Hotel ☆☆   Listen to me rave about the Jesselton. It's such a nice surprise to find this quaint boutique hotel in the center of Kota Kinabalu, just about the last real reminder in this city of a colonial presence. Even more lovely is the level of personalized service you receive and the comfort of the rooms, which, though completely modern, retain their charm with lovely Audubon-style inks and attractive wallpapers and fabrics—sort of a cross between a cozy guesthouse and a top-class hotel. Due to lack of space in the building, there's no pool, fitness center, or business center, but the staff at the front desk can help you with tour information and transportation. The coffeehouse serves local and Western food, which is quite good. The Gardenia Restaurant looks more upmarket than it really is.

69 Jalan Gaya, 88000 Kota Kinabalu, Sabah. ℂ 088/223-333. Fax 088/240-401. www.jesseltonhotel.com. 32 units. RM280 ($78/£39) double; RM1,000 ($280/£140) suite. AE, DC, MC, V. **Amenities:** Restaurant; bar and lounge; coffee shop; tour desk; limousine service; 24-hr. room service; babysitting; same-day laundry service; complimentary clothes pressing and shoe polishing; nonsmoking rooms; currency exchange. In room: A/C, TV (movies available), minibar, coffee/tea-making facilities, hair dryer, safe.

Shangri-La's Tanjung Aru Resort ☆☆☆ (Kids)   A short ride southwest of Kota Kinabalu and you're at Tanjung Aru, an amazingly gorgeous beach resort area—Sabah's Riviera. The Shangri-La here is located in a most impressive setting, surrounded on

Kota Kinabalu

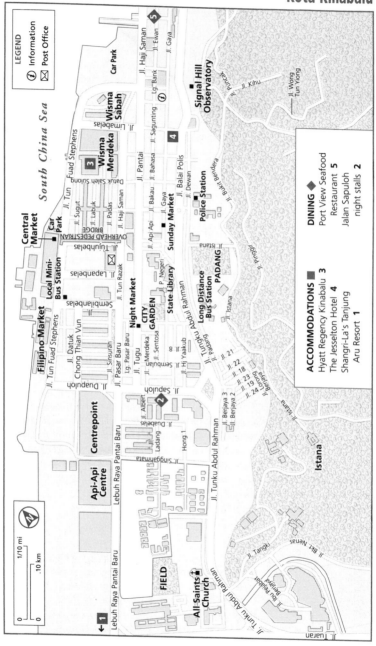

LEGEND
ⓘ Information
⊠ Post Office

South China Sea

Car Park

Wisma Sabah
Wisma Merdeka
Central Market
Car Park
Local Mini-Bus Station
Filipino Market
Centrepoint
Api-Api Centre
Night Market
CITY GARDEN
State Library
Sunday Market
Long Distance Bus Station
Police Station
Signal Hill Observatory
PADANG
Istana
FIELD
All-Saints Church

OVERHEAD PEDESTRIAN BRIDGE

Jl. Haji Saman
Jl. Gaya
Jl. Ewan
Lg. Bank
Jl. Kihu
Jl. Wong Tun Yiong
Jl. Limbelas
Jl. Pantai
Jl. Sagunting
Jl. Bahasa
Jl. Api Api
Jl. Bakau
Jl. Gaya
Jl. Balai Polis
Jl. Dewan
Jl. Bukit Bendera
Jl. Pinggir
Jl. Istana
Datuk Saleh Suong
Jl. Tun Fuad Stephens
Jl. Sugut
Jl. Labuk
Jl. Padas
Jl. Haji Saman
Jl. Tuinubelas
Jl. Lapanbelas
Jl. Tun Razak
Jl. Sembilanbelas
Jl. Tun Fuad Stephens
Jl. Datuk Chong Thian Vun
Jl. Sinsuran
Jl. Pasar Baru
Lg. Pasar Baru
Jl. Tugu
Jl. Merdeka
Jl. Sembulan
Jl. Sentosa
Jl. P. Negeri
Jl. Hj Yaakub
Jl. Tungku Abdul Rahman
Jl. Pasang
Jl. Istana
Jl. Istana
Jl. 21
Jl. 22
Jl. 18
Jl. 23
Jl. 19
Jl. 24
Jl. Lorong
Jl. Berjaya 3
Jl. Berjaya 2
Jl. Istana
Lebuh Raya Pantai Baru
Jl. Albert
Jl. Duabelas
Ladang
Hong 1
Jl. Singgahmata
Jl. Tunku Abdul Rahman
Jl. Sapuloh
Lebuh Raya Pantai Baru
Jl. Tunku Abdul Rahman
Jl. Tangki
Jl. Bkt. Nenas
Jl. Pelabai
Jl. Berjai
Jl. Ibu Pelabai
Istana
Jl. Tuaran
Jl. Tuaran

0 ─── 1/10 mi
0 ─── .10 km

ACCOMMODATIONS ■
Hyatt Regency Kinabalu **3**
The Jesselton Hotel **4**
Shangri-La's Tanjung
Aru Resort **1**

DINING ◆
Port View Seafood
Restaurant **5**
Jalan Sapuloh
night stalls **2**

279

three sides by water. It serves the finest local Sabahan cuisine and freshest seafood you can get in the region. Book a room in the Tanjung Wing, which is nestled amid Shangri-La's signature lush garden setting, as the Kinabalu Wing, while newer, is more like a hotel block. Every room has a stunning view of either the sea or Mount Kinabalu, with a balcony for full appreciation. Tropical touches include rattan furnishings in cool colors and local fabrics with wood details. Their tour desk can arrange everything from scuba to trekking and rafting, and their free shuttle gives you convenient access to town. Special activities for kids make this place a good choice for families.

Locked Bag 174, 88744 Kota Kinabalu, Sabah. © 800/942-5050 in the U.S. and Canada, 800/222-448 in Australia, 800/442-179 in New Zealand, or 088/225-800. Fax 088/217-155. www.shangri-la.com. 499 units. RM700 ($196/£98) double; from RM1,250 ($350/£175) suite. . AE, DC, MC, V. **Amenities:** 3 restaurant; beach bar and lounge; 2 outdoor lagoon-style pools; 4 outdoor lighted tennis courts; fitness center w/Jacuzzi, sauna, steam, and massage; concierge; tour desk; shuttle service; salon; 24-hr. room service; babysitting; same-day laundry service; dry cleaning; nonsmoking rooms. *In room:* A/C, TV w/satellite programming and in-house movie, dataport w/direct Internet access, minibar, coffee/tea-making facilities, hair dryer, safe.

WHERE TO DINE

One of the best local specialties, *hinava,* is a mouthwatering delicacy of raw fish marinated in lime juice, ginger, shallots, herbs, and chilies—I highly recommend trying it!

Kota Kinabalu is known for its fresh seafood, and there are a lot of places to choose from, but the locals and expatriates all agree that **Port View Seafood Restaurant,** Jalan Haji Saman across from the old Customs Wharf, near the downtown area (© 088/252-813), is best. Dishes are prepared primarily in Chinese and Malay styles, are moderately priced (sold by weight) and always succulent.

If you're into the dinner and cultural show thing, head for **Kampung Nelayan** (Taman Tun Fuad, Bukit Padang, Luyang; © 088/231-005). This seafood market-style restaurant is housed in a traditional Malay building floating on a lake in a botanic garden. The nightly show starts at 7:45pm.

ATTRACTIONS

Sabah attracts **scuba** enthusiasts from around the world, who come to dive at Sipadan, an island resort off the east coast of the state. **Sipadan,** ranked as one of the top-10 dive sites in the world, is actually a tall limestone "tower" rising from the bed of the Celebes Sea, supporting vast numbers of marine species, some of which may still be unidentified. As of December 2004, the Malaysian government revoked the licenses of the five dive operators that managed resorts on the tiny island in an effort to prevent environmental degradation—Malaysia is also applying for World Heritage Site recognition for the area. The dive operators will move their base camps to surrounding islands, offering day trips to the area or running live-aboard trips.

Borneo Divers (9th floor, Menara Jubili, 53 Jalan Gaya; © 088/222-226; www.borneodivers.info) was the first full-service dive operator in Borneo and the pioneering operator to Sipadan. They house divers at their resort on Mabul, along a gorgeous sandy beach with easy access to dive sites around the Mabul island and Sipadan. For RM664 ($186/£93) per night per person, you'll get accommodations, meals, airport transfers, and two dives a day. You'll have to pay extra for a round-trip flight into Tawau, which costs about RM390 ($109/£55). Booking can be made through Borneo Divers. Equipment rentals come to RM89 ($25/£12) per day. Sipadan has good diving year-round, but March through October has the best weather.

A newer spot, **Layang Layang,** located off the coast of northwest Borneo in the South China Sea, is also making a splash as an underwater bounty of marine life. **Layang Layang Island Resort** (head office in KL at Blk. A, Ground floor, A-0-3, Megan Ave. II, 12 Jalan Yap Kwan Seng; ✆ **03/2162-2877;** www.layanglayang.com) pioneered this area for divers. Their standard package of 6 days/5 nights runs at RM3,500 ($980/£490) per person, which includes accommodations, meals, and three dives a day. Equipment is extra, as is the chartered helicopter flight to the island, which is expensive at RM714 ($200/£100) round-trip (booked through the dive operator). Layang Layang closes during the monsoon season (early Sept–Feb).

If you want to stay close to Kota Kinabalu, Borneo Divers (see above) makes day trips to **Tunku Abdul Rahman Marine Park.** This group of five islands about 8km (13 miles) off the coast of Kota Kinabalu has been protected since the mid-'70s. Throughout the park, waters are clear and visibility is good. Although not as lauded as Sipadan and Layang Layang, if you're looking for some quick diving excitement but you have time and money constraints, it's highly recommended. A day trip that includes two boat dives and a shore dive costs RM265 ($74/£37), not including equipment rentals. Borneo Divers has a base camp on the smallest island, from which they also conduct complete PADI scuba courses.

Sabah has many other dive sites, including sites such as Pulau Tiga, of *Survivor* TV fame. A couple of sites also offer wreck diving, so if you're interested, inquire when you make your booking.

For other types of watersports, your best bet is to either book these activities through your resort or plan a DIY trip to Tunku Abdul Rahman Park. Catch a ferry at the Jesselton Point Jetty at the Customs House on Jalan Haji Saman opposite Port View Seafood Restaurant (RM24/$6.70/£3.40 round-trip) to take you to the park. It's only 8km (13 miles) from Kota Kinabalu, so you can spend a day trip at one or more of the park's five islands sunning on the beach. **Snorkel** rentals go for around RM10 ($2.80/£1.40), and parasailing charges run RM90 ($25/£13). The latest thrill is **seawalking**—donning an enormous helmet connected to the surface with a tube, which allows you to breathe underwater without tanks. This costs RM200 ($56/£28) a pop. *Tip for snorkelers:* Bring cotton socks to wear under your rental fins to prevent blisters. There are cafes and toilets near the jetties, plus rustic accommodations on two of the islands.

Sabah's rugged terrain makes for terrific hiking, camping, biking, and rafting, for any level, from soft adventure or extreme sports. **TYK Adventure** (Borneo Travel; Lot 48-2F, 2nd floor, Beverly Hill Plaza; ✆ **088/727-825;** www.mega-ecom.come/tham yaukong) was founded by a local Chinese award-winning tour guide Tham Yau Kong, who also happens to hold records for the longest cultural walk (1998) and for leading the first group to circum-cycle Mt. Kinabalu (1999). Mountain biking trips around Papar or Penampang can be arranged for RM310 ($87/£43) per person for the day trip; the rate include hotel transfer, mountain bike and helmet.

Many come to Sabah to climb **Mt. Kinabalu.** It's a terrific trip if you are prepared and if you hit it just right, in terms of weather and timing. It can only be done on an overnight trip, which includes a 4- or 5-hour hike from the park headquarters uphill to a ranger station, where you stay the night. Groups awake at 3am to begin the 3-hour hike to the summit. This is not light trekking, as some parts are steep, altitude sickness can cause headaches and nausea, and remember—you're tooling along in the pitch-darkness, the whole point being to arrive at the summit in time for the spectacular sunrise.

Come prepared with cold weather snugglies, or at the very least a wool sweater or fleece, long pants, windbreaker, rain poncho, and hiking boots. Bring a good, strong flashlight and pack plenty of trail mix and sports drinks for rejuvenation. And finally, there's no guarantee that the weather will cooperate with your itinerary. You might hit rain or find the summit covered in clouds. There's pretty much nothing any tour operator can do to guarantee you'll get a clear view. But I've heard when you hit it right, it's really quite a great adventure with a rewarding view. **TYK Adventure** can also book this tour for you—a 2 day/1 night trip will set you back RM881 ($247/£123). Make sure you book early because they need to make sure there's space available at park accommodations. The price includes transfer, lodging, and your guide to the summit.

TYK also plans regular trips out to Sandakan, on the eastern coast of Sabah, for trips to see the **Sepilok Orang Utan Rehabilitation Center,** the largest orangutan sanctuary in the world with facilities to house and train hundreds of orphaned orangutans for eventual release back into the wilds, with a boat trip to see the **Marine Turtle Conservation Park and Hatchery.**

Monsopiad Cultural Village, a Kadazandusun heritage center with its creepy House of Skulls, is located in Penampang, not far from Kota Kinabalu. During the 3-hour visit to the village you'll tour the place and be treated to a cultural performance. It's about the height of "touristy" Sabah, but can be a fun half-day trip if you want to peep at a bit of local culture. Call them at ℭ **088/774-337** to make a booking; RM95 ($27/£18) includes transportation to and from your hotel, the tour, and show, plus a welcome drink. The tour leaves daily from 9 to 9:30am and again at 2 to 2:30pm.

In 2000, the **North Borneo Railway** (Tanjung Aru Railway; ℭ **088/263-933**) revived the old tradition of steam train travel with the launch of a 1954 fully-renovated British Vulcan steam locomotive pulling six restored carriages. Traversing a 58km (36-mile) route from Tanjung Aru, just outside Kota Kinabalu, to the rural town of Papar, the train passes lovely water and mangrove views, past fishermen and local sea crafts, through a deep mountain tunnel, and out the other side into a vast scenery of paddy fields. Carriages are open-air but comfortable, with soft seats and charming wood and brass accents. A swanky bar car and observation deck round out facilities that also include toilets. The train departs every Wednesday and Saturday at 10am, returning at 2pm; tickets are RM195 ($55/£27).

For another unique view of the countryside, **Sabah Air** (Sabah Air Building, Old Airport Road; ℭ **088/256-733**; www.sabahair.com.my) offers thrilling **helicopter tours,** flying over Kota Kinabalu, tropical wilds, and the jewel-colored sea for 20 minutes. You can also book a 1-hour aerial tour of Mt. Kinabalu. You need a minimum of four people for each trip. The Kota Kinabalu trip is RM257 ($72/£36) per person; the Mt. Kinabalu trip is RM685 ($192/£96) per person.

Appendix: Singapore & Malaysia in Depth

By the 1800s, European powers had already explored much of the world, staking their authority over major trade routes. Southeast Asia's initial attraction was its position between two seasonal monsoons—one-half of the year saw winds that carried sailing vessels from China to Southeast Asia, while the other half of the year favored ships coming from India and Arabia. The English, Dutch, Portuguese, French, and Spanish, recognizing Southeast Asia's advantage, scrambled to set up trading posts to receive valuable tea, opium, silk, spices, and other goods from China.

The British East India Company, in its rivalry with the Dutch East Indies Company, sought to control the Strait of Malacca, the narrow passage between Indonesian Sumatra and the Malay peninsula. They already had a port at Penang, an island in the north of the Strait, but it was proving an economic failure. The company charged one of its officers, Sir Stamford Raffles, with the task of locating a new post. Raffles, who knew the area well, had his heart set on a small island at the tip of the Malay peninsula.

At the time of its "discovery," Singapore was occupied by about 1,000 people, mainly Malay residents, *orang laut* (sea nomads), a handful of Chinese farmers, plus assorted pirates in hiding. The island had little known historical significance. An early settlement on the island, called Temasek, had been visited regularly by Chinese merchants, and later the settlement came under the rule of the far-

reaching Srivijaya Empire (9th–13th c. A.D.), which was based in Palembang in Sumatra. It was the Srivijayas who named the island Singapura, or Lion City, after its leader claimed to have seen a lion on its shores. However, the Srivijayas were eventually overtaken by a neighboring power, the Java-based Majapahits. Sometime around 1390, a young Palembang ruler, Iskander Shah (aka Parameswara), rebelled against the Majapahits and fled to Singapura, where he set up independent rule. The Majapahits were quick to chase him out, and Iskander fled up the Malay peninsula to Malacca, where he founded what would be one of the most successful trading ports in the region at the time.

When Raffles arrived in 1819, Singapura had been asleep for nearly 400 years under the rule of the sultan of Johor, of the southernmost province in Malaya, with local administration handled by a temenggong, or senior minister. It was Temenggong Abdu'r Rahman who, on February 6, 1819, signed a treaty with Raffles to set up a trading post on the island in return for an annual payment to the Sultanate. After this, Raffles didn't stay around for too long, handing over the Residency of the port to his friend and colleague, Colonel William Farquhar.

When Raffles returned 3 years later, Singapore was fast becoming a success story. The ideally situated port was inspired by Raffles's own dream of free trade and Farquhar's skill at orderly administration. The population had grown to more than

11,000—Malays, Chinese, Bugis (from Celebes in Indonesia), Indians, Arabs, Armenians, Europeans, and Eurasians. The haphazard sprawl convinced Raffles to draft the Town Plan of 1822, assigning specific neighborhoods to the many ethnic groups that had settled. These ethnic enclaves remain much the same today—Singapore's Chinatown, the administrative center or Historic District, Kampong Gelam, and other neighborhoods are still the ethnic centers they originally were (of course, with many modern alterations).

This would be the last trip Raffles would make to the island that credits him with its founding. His visit in 1822 was merely a stop on his way back to London to retire. Raffles had big plans for his career with the East India Company but never witnessed any of his ambitions come to fruition. Although Singaporeans celebrate him with statues and street names, the truth is that he eventually succumbed to syphilis in London, dying a failed and penniless man. He remains, however, a hero to modern day Singaporeans.

In 1824, the Dutch finally signed a treaty with Britain acknowledging Singapore as a permanent British possession, and Sultan Hussein of Johor ceded the island to the East India Trading Company in perpetuity. Three years later, Singapore was incorporated, along with Malacca and Penang, to form the Straits Settlements. Penang was acknowledged as the settlements' seat of government, with direction from the Presidency of Bengal in India.

Singapore's first 40 years were filled with all the magic of an Oriental trading port. Chinese coolie laborers came to Singapore in droves to escape economic hardship at home. Most were from one of four major dialect groups: Hokkien, Teochew, Cantonese, and Hakka, all from southern China. Living in crowded bunks in the buildings that sprang up behind the godowns, or warehouses, these immigrants formed secret societies, social and political organizations made up of residents who shared similar ancestry or Chinese hometowns. These clan groups helped new arrivals get settled and find work, and carried money and messages back to workers' families in China. But it was the secret societies' other contribution—to gambling, street crime, and violence—that helped fuel Singapore's image as a lawless boomtown, filled with all the excitement and danger of a frontier town in America's Wild West. Surrounded by boundless opportunity, many Chinese immigrants found great success, building fortunes as businessmen and traders.

Indians were quick to become Singapore's second-largest community. Most were traders or laborers, but many others were troops carried with the Brits. Most

Dateline

- **3rd century A.D.** Singapore mentioned in Chinese records.
- **5th century** Indian and Persian traders arrive in the region.
- **1295** Marco Polo visits Sumatra; has a swell time.
- **1390** Iskander Shah establishes sultanate on Singapura but is soon ousted.

- **1700s** Malay temenggongs rule Singapura.
- **1819** Sir Stamford Raffles lands on Singapura, also has a swell time.
- **1820s** First billiards club, first newspaper, first judicial system, first census (counting 4,727).
- **1824** East India Trading Company buys the island.
- **1827** Straits Settlements is formed, which includes

Malaya and Singapore; first steamship seen in Singapore.
- **1833** East India Trading Company loses its foothold in Southeast Asia; population 20,978.
- **1840** First bank opened; population 33,969.
- **1845** First Masonic Lodge; arrival of first P&O mail boat.
- **1850** Population 52,891.
- **1854** First Singapore postage stamp printed.

came from southern India, from the mainly Tamil-speaking population, including the Chettiars, Muslim money-lenders who financed the building of several places of worship in the early neighborhoods. After 1825, the British turned possession of Bencoolen on Sumatra to the Dutch, transferring the thousands of Indian prisoners incarcerated there to Singapore, where they were put to work constructing the buildings and clearing the land that the fledgling settlement needed. After they'd worked off their sentences, many stayed in Singapore to work their trade as free men.

During this period the Istana Kampong Gelam was built in Raffles's designated Malay enclave, along with the Sultan Mosque. The surrounding streets supported a large but modest Malay settlement of businesses and residences.

Despite early successes, Singapore was almost entirely dependent on entrepôt trade, which was literally at the whim of the winds. Dutch trading power still threatened its economic health, and the opening of Chinese trading ports to Western ships placed Singapore in a precarious position. The soil on the island barely supported a small sago palm industry, and with the lack of natural resources Singapore had to constantly look to trade for survival. True economic stability wouldn't arrive until the 1860s.

Major changes around the globe had an enormous effect on Singapore in the second half of the 19th century. In 1869, the Suez Canal opened, linking the Mediterranean and the Red Sea and putting Singapore in a prime position on the Europe–East Asia route. In addition, steamship travel made the trip to Singapore less dependent on trade winds. The shorter travel time not only saw entrepôt trade leap to new heights but also allowed leisure travelers to consider Singapore a viable stop on their itinerary.

The blossoming Industrial Revolution thirsted for raw materials, namely tin and rubber. Malaya was already being mined for tin, much of which changed hands in Singapore. Rubber didn't enter the scene until 1877, when "Mad" Henry Ridley, director of the Botanic Gardens, smuggled the first rubber seedlings from Brazil to Singapore. After developing a new way to tap latex, he finally convinced planters in Malaya to begin plantations. To this day rubber remains a major industry for Malaysia.

WORLD WAR II Although the British maintained a military base of operations on the island, Singapore was virtually untouched by World War I. Just before the Great Depression, however, Britain bowed to U.S. pressure and broke off relations with Japan due to that country's

---

- **1860** Telegraph opened between Singapore and Batavia; population 81,734.
- **1864** First use of gas street lighting.
- **1867** Singapore is declared a British colony.
- **1869** Suez Canal opens; Singapore leaps to prominence.
- **1871** Singapore's population reaches 94,816; telegraph opened between Singapore and Hong Kong.

- **1877** Experimental rubber seeds smuggled from Brazil, planted at the Botanic Gardens.
- **1877** Chinese Protectorate is formed to curb violence among rival Chinese gangs.
- **1879** First telephone; first official postcards issued.
- **1881** Population 137,722.
- **1886** Steam trams begin operation.

- **1887** Statue of Raffles unveiled.
- **1888** Rubber trees introduced into Malaya as a commercial crop.
- **1891** Singapore Golf Club formed; population 181,602; first concert by Philharmonic Society.
- **1896** First automobile arrives.
- **1901** Population 226,842.

(continued)

increasing military power. Singapore's defense became a primary concern, and the British, thinking any invasion would come by sea, installed heavy artillery along the southern coastline, leaving the north of the island virtually unprotected.

In 1941, on the night of December 7, the Japanese attacked Pearl Harbor, invaded the Philippines and Hong Kong, landed in southern Thailand, and dropped the first bombs on Singapore.

Japanese Lieutenant General Yamashita, emerging from battles in Mongolia, saw a definite advantage in Singapore's unprotected northern flank and stealthily moved three divisions—almost 20,000 troops—down the Malay Peninsula on bicycles. On the evening of February 8, 1942, the army quietly invaded the island. For days, the British tried to hold off their attackers, but lost ground. Within days, the Japanese were firmly entrenched.

The occupation brought terrible conditions to multiethnic Singapore, as the Japanese ruled harshly and punished any word of dissent with prison or worse. Mass executions were commonplace, prisoners of war were tortured and killed, and it was said that the beaches at Changi ran red with blood. Some prisoners that survived were sent to Thailand to work on the railway. Conditions were worst for the island's Chinese, many of whom were arrested indiscriminately simply because

of their ethnicity, rowed out to sea, and dumped overboard. Little information from the outside world reached Singapore's citizens during this time except when the Japanese were victorious.

Mercifully, the Japanese surrender came before Singapore became a battleground once again. On September 5, 1945, British warships arrived, and a week later, the Japanese officially surrendered to Lord Louis Mountbatten, supreme Allied commander in Southeast Asia.

THE POSTWAR YEARS Back under British rule, Singapore spent the following 10 years revitalizing itself, while efforts to become a fully self-governing nation were tantamount. Resentment against the British was still very strong for the way they'd lost the island to the Japanese in 1941.

On the streets, conditions were terrible. The British eventually helped with post-occupation reconstruction to clean up the port and harbor and return them to civilian control, restore public utilities, and overhaul the distrusted police force. Although food was scarce, rice was available at a reasonable price.

THE RISE OF LEE KUAN YEW & SINGAPOREAN INDEPENDENCE In 1949, Lee Kuan Yew, a third-generation Straits Chinese and a law student at Cambridge, formed a discussion group in

- 1903 Singapore-Kranji Railway opens.
- 1905 First frozen foods arrive in Singapore; electric trams introduced.
- 1911 Population 303,321.
- 1914 Outbreak of the Great War in Europe.
- 1915 Singapore Sling invented at the Long Bar in the Raffles Hotel (becomes a smashing success).
- 1919 First airplane arrives in Singapore.
- 1921 Britain severs its defense alliance with Japan; population 418,358.
- 1922 Prince of Wales visits.
- 1929 Direct Singapore-London telegraph link.
- 1931 Population 570,128.
- 1932 Last tiger on island killed.
- 1936 Anti-Japanese riots by Chinese in Singapore; start of wireless broadcasting.
- 1937 Sultan Mosque installs loudspeakers for muezzin's call to prayer; opium sales proceeds providing 25% of Straits Settlements' budget.
- 1939 World War II begins in Europe.
- 1942 Japanese invade Singapore from the north.
- 1945 Japanese surrender; British rule restored.
- 1946 Singapore becomes a Crown Colony.

London aimed at bringing together Malayan overseas students. Upon his return to Singapore, his education completed, Lee made a name for himself as an effective courtroom lawyer. Around this time, Chinese in Malaya were forming the Malaya Communist Party, inspired by mainland China's break from Western hegemonic powers, as a path toward national independence. Although Lee detested their politics, he recognized the strength of their numbers. Backed by local communists, he formed the People's Action Party (PAP).

By 1957, Malaya had gained independence, and Singapore was granted permission to establish its own fully elected, 51-seat Legislative Assembly. In the first elections for this body, in 1959, the popular PAP swept 43 of the seats and Lee Kuan Yew became the city-state's first prime minister. It wasn't until after his election that it became evident that Lee's politics were not in line with communist ideals.

After his election, it was Lee's wish to see Singapore and Malaya unite as one nation, but the Malayan government was fearful of Singapore's dominant Chinese influence and fought to keep the city-state out. In 1963, however, they broke down and admitted Singapore as a member. It was a short-lived marriage. When the PAP began to expand its influence throughout Malaysia, as the new union was renamed, the latter became distrustful and demanded Singapore be expelled. On August 9, 1965, Singapore found itself an entirely independent country. Lee's tearful television broadcast announcing Singapore's expulsion from Malaysia and simultaneous gain of independence is one of the most famous in Singapore's history. In 1971, the last British military forces left the island.

SINGAPORE TODAY

Who would have believed that Singapore would rise to such international fame and become the vaunted "Asian Tiger" it has in recent decades? This small country's political stability and effective government have inspired many other nations to study its methods, and former prime minister (and current minister mentor) Lee Kuan Yew is counted among the most respected political figures in the world. When asked to explain how Singapore's astounding economic, political, and social success was made possible, Lee always takes the credit—and deservedly so—but in the face of international criticism for dictatorial policies, absolutist law enforcement, and human rights violations, he also stands first in line to take the lumps.

THE GOVERNMENT Since Lee's election, and without debate, it has been his unfailing vision of a First World Singapore that's inspired the policies and

- **1948** Communist Party of Malaya attempts to take control of the peninsula; emergency powers instituted to discourage such activities.
- **1955** Constitution allows a freely elected parliament; People's Action Party (PAP) is formed.
- **1958** Singapore granted internal self-government.
- **1959** People's Action Party (PAP) wins general election; Lee Kuan Yew becomes first prime minister.
- **1961** First oil refinery.
- **1963** Singapore is admitted to the Federation of Malaysia; Internal Security Act passed.
- **1965** Singapore expelled from Federation and becomes an independent state; Singapore admitted into the United Nations.
- **1967** Singapore issues its own currency.
- **1981** Changi International Airport opens, named the best service in Southeast Asia.
- **1987** Singapore's policy of limiting families to two children reversed due to declining birth rate; hefty incentives given for third child.

(continued)

plans that created the political and economic miracle we see today. During his tenure he mobilized government, industry, and citizens toward fulfilling his vision, establishing a government almost devoid of corruption, a strong economy built from practically no resources save labor, and a nation of racial and religious harmony from a multiethnic melting pot.

Both critics and admirers refer to Lee Kuan Yew as a strict yet generous "father" to the "children" of Singapore, raising them to a high position on the world stage yet dictating policies that have cost citizens many of their personal freedoms. You'll find that the average Singaporean expresses some duality about this: He or she will be outwardly critical of the government's invasion of privacy and disregard for personal freedoms and of policies that have driven up the cost of housing and healthcare, but will also recognize all that Lee has done to raise Singaporeans' standard of living, expand their opportunities for the future, and ensure tranquility at home—achievements for which many are willing to sacrifice a certain amount of freedom to enjoy. By and large, they wish to see the current government continue its work.

Lee stepped down from the prime minister's chair in 1990, assuming the position of senior minister. He was replaced by Goh Chok Tong, who for 14 years continued the long-term policies driven by Lee and the PAP. Goh was a popular leader, who, in addition to initiating increased citizen participation in the political process, supported local visual and performing arts.

In August 2004, Goh passed the prime minister's baton to Lee Hsien Loong, Lee Kuan Yew's son. The resulting cabinet shift created a new position for Lee Kuan Yew as minister mentor, with Goh filling the senior minister seat. The younger Lee's initial challenges are to connect with the population—he's perceived as a bit stiff—as he continues his father's political legacy.

THE CENSORSHIP QUESTION

One infamous feature of Singapore's government is its control over media, both domestic and international. All national news publications have ties to the government, whose philosophy holds that the role of the media is to promote the government's goals. Articles are censored for any content that might threaten national security, incite riot, or promote disobedience or racism. Offenders face stiff fines.

It doesn't stop at the print media, either. Television is also censored, satellite dishes are banned, and there's only one cable provider, which the government keeps a close eye on for anything resembling pornography.

- **1988** The Mass Rapid Transit System (MRT), an intra-island subway network built to the tune of S$5 billion (US$3.2 billion/£1.65 billion), opens.
- **1990** Singapore celebrates 25 years of independence; Lee Kuan Yew takes a back seat as senior minister, and Goh Chok Tong becomes new prime minister.
- **1992** Chewing gum banned due to vandals plugging up elevator buttons and subway doors.
- **1994** Rogue securities trader Nick Leeson turns fugitive and is eventually captured after the S$2.18 billion (US$1.4 billion/£610 million) collapse of Britain's Barings Bank.
- **1997** Asian Economic Crisis hits; compared with the economic troubles in neighboring Southeast Asian nations, Singapore weathers the storm effectively.
- **1999** S. R. Nathan declared president without election. No other candidates were certified eligible.
- **2003** Lee Kuan Yew becomes minister mentor, Goh Chok Tong becomes senior minister, and Lee Hsien Yew's son, Lee Hsien Loong, becomes prime minister.

The Internet provided Singapore with a tough dilemma. By design, the Net promotes freedom of communication, which is taken advantage of by, among others, every political dissident and pornographer who can get his little hands on a PC. This thought so concerned the Singapore government that it debated long and hard about allowing access to its citizens. However, the possibilities for communications and commerce and their implications for the future of Singapore's economy won.

THE ECONOMY Singapore's economy is a bizarre marriage between free trade and government control. Lee Kuan Yew's vision and resulting policies have created annual national growth rates of 8.9% going on 3 decades. Singapore survived the East Asian Economic Crisis that began in July 1997 because of its firm bank-lending regulations and transparent government and business dealings. Unfortunately, Singapore limped through the economic slump that plagued the globe in the years to follow, and in 2003 suffered from the SARS outbreak. It was slow going to heal its wounded economy, but steady progress has yielded what economists predict to be 7.5% to 8% growth figures for 2006. The biggest moneymakers are the electronics industry, financial and business services, transportation and communications, petroleum refining and shipping, construction, and tourism. Seventy-six percent of Singapore's exports, exclusive of oil exports, go to the United States, Malaysia, the European Union, Hong Kong, and Japan.

Singaporeans enjoy a high standard of living, with average annual incomes reaching S$35,880 (US$23,000/£11,840). The most commonly heard complaint? The rising cost of real estate.

TOURISM The Singapore Tourism Board has far-reaching influence that has helped to turn Singapore into a veritable machine for raising foreign cash. Almost 9 million tourists visited Singapore in 2005, spending over S$10 billion (US$6.4 billion/£3.3 billion) during their stays.

Not content to rest on its laurels, Singapore has big plans to dramatically increase these numbers over the next 10 years with the building of two "integrated resorts." Also called IRs for short, they're basically casinos surrounded by accommodations, dining, shopping, and other diversions. The first IR, adjacent to the downtown financial district, will be geared toward business and convention activities, with massive conference space and hotel facilities suitable for corporate guests. The second, on Sentosa Island, will be supported by a Universal Studios theme park plus countless family-oriented attractions with resort-style accommodations.

- 2004 Underwater quake sends tsunamis throughout South and Southeast Asia. Malaysia suffers 68 casualties from waves that hit Penang, Langkawi, and the northwestern shores of the peninsula. The waters around Singapore are unaffected.
- 2004 Singapore Airlines makes aviation history with the first direct nonstop flight from Singapore to New York. The 18-hour flight covers almost 9,000 nautical miles.
- 2005 Singapore approves controversial plan to legalize gambling in casinos.

A landmark move by the Singapore government, the establishment of legalized gambling marks the end of a conservative era in the history of this notoriously squeaky-clean city-state.

2 The Singaporean People

Many tourists come to Singapore for the shopping or the sights, but I love the people. Most often, when you travel in foreign lands, the people you meet are other international travelers. In Singapore, however, the friends you make are many times Singaporean—perhaps it's because of the common language, perhaps because Singaporeans are very open to western culture.

The median age of the population is around 35, with most Singaporeans struggling to juggle work and family responsibilities the same as any other postindustrialized country. While most Singaporeans of both sexes tend to focus on educational and career goals, most also marry later and have children later, a trend that has left the government worried about a declining birth rate. Yet even with these demands, your average Singaporean never loses sight of "Asian family values" that encourage children to live with and care for their aging parents—many households are quite large.

There's an ever-present image consciousness fuelled by heavy consumerism. Fashion, cars, and social scenes are "in." Money is in. Success is in. Young Singaporeans strive for what they call the 5Cs—career, condo, car, cash, and credit cards—and it sometimes seems they'll stop at nothing to achieve them.

Which leads me to the local term *kiasu*, used to describe a person who is afraid to miss out on anything—so afraid, in fact, that he's willing to make a fool of himself trying to grab anything he can. Mr. Kiasu is a popular cartoon character who epitomizes the kiasu stereotype. He is a local idiot who piles his plate high at buffets to get every last penny's worth of food, wrestles through crowds at sales to get the bargains, and will go to every extent to outdo his neighbors and peers. Unfortunately, he represents a real phenomenon—the Ugly Singaporean, proving that every culture must suffer its own unpleasant side.

As with any modern culture, while the younger generations are busy finding their niche in the world, it is the older generations who keep traditional cultures alive. Singapore's resident population, measured at 3.26 million people in the 2000 census, is a mix of Chinese (76.8%); Malays (13.9%); Indians (7.9%); and others (1.4%), including Eurasians. Though the country is overwhelmingly Chinese the government has embraced all local heritage, recognizing religious holidays and festivals and promoting racial harmony in its policies as part of its plan to foster a single national identity molded from the disparate cultural backgrounds of the Singaporean populace.

Unfortunately, this government social planning may have contributed to one of the common problems that's plaguing Singapore's younger generations today: a lack of identity. No longer immersed in the traditions of their own ethnic groups, growing up with so many cultural influences both from inside Singapore and from outside its borders, and with traditional values being rapidly replaced by commercialism and a whole new set of opportunities, it's not surprising to hear so many young people ask, "Who am I?"

THE CHINESE

When Raffles opened Singapore's port for free trade, junkloads of Chinese immigrated to find their fortunes. Most were poor workers from China's southern regions who brought with them different cultures and dialects from their respective places of origin. Of the mix, the Hokkiens from Fujian Province are the largest percentage of Chinese in Singapore at 42%, followed by the Teochews of Guangdong province, the Cantonese also from Guangdong, the Hakkas from central China, and finally the Hainanese from Hainan island (near Hong Kong) at 6%.

The Chinese are over 50% Buddhist, following the dharma of the Buddha, who taught that all life is suffering and the only way to relieve suffering is to dispel desire. Early immigrants brought Buddhism from China with them, of a sect called Mahayana, or the Greater Vehicle, the branch of Buddhism that also claims Tibetan and Zen Buddhist traditions.

Despite religious affiliation, almost every Chinese is Taoist to some degree. Tao is a philosophy as opposed to religion. Tao, meaning "the way," follows the belief in an energy source, "chi," that permeates all living and nonliving creatures and objects in the universe. This energy force links everything, shifting from place to place, sometimes flowing freely to create positive energy and sometimes stagnating to create bad vibes.

Tao is the philosophy behind feng shui, or Chinese geomancy, laws of nature that dictate how homes and buildings should be situated and the furnishings placed inside, to create either a positive atmosphere that allows chi to flow freely or a negative one wherein chi stagnates and invites bad fortune. Tao is also the reasoning behind Chinese traditional medicine that uses herbs and natural remedies to keep good chi flowing throughout the body. Perhaps the most famous form of traditional Chinese medicine, acupuncture, uses needles inserted at strategic locations throughout the body to either release stagnant chi or invigorate healthy chi.

Chinese tradition is also filled with rich tales of heroes and heroines, gods and goddesses, who watch over the physical world. In Singapore you find statues in temples for Ma Po Cho, the Mother of Heavenly Sages, who protects sailors and other travelers, and Kuan Yin, the Goddess of Mercy—these are only two of a number of gods and goddesses of Chinese legend who still play important roles in the everyday lives of local Singaporeans.

Characteristically, the Chinese are very superstitious with numbers playing a critical role in everyday decisions, preferring auspicious numbers for automobile license plates and choosing dates that contain lucky numbers for business openings. Here's another superstition—don't leave your chopsticks sticking up in your rice bowl, it invites hungry ghosts.

THE MALAYS

When Raffles arrived, Malays had already inhabited the island, fishing the waters and trading with other local seafaring people, and many more were to migrate from the mainland in the decades to follow.

Although Singapore's Malay population is very low in numbers today, the language on the street is Malay, some of the best-loved local dishes are Malay, and even the national anthem is sung in Malay. The shame is that while Malays are recognized as the original inhabitants, they constantly feel marginalized by the dominant Chinese culture and policy. In addition, this group represents an unbalanced percentage of the lower-income classes, with the lowest levels of education and the highest number of criminal offenders. The government prides itself on policies to promote racial harmony, but it is widely accepted that Malays occupy jobs on the low end of the pay scale. Even in the military, while there are many Malays in the enlisted troops, there are almost none in the officer ranks.

On a positive note, it is widely understood that the Malays have the greatest sense of community in Singapore. Families still congregate around the neighborhood mosque, and there's a greater sense of charity and commitment to helping those less fortunate.

Virtually every Malay is Muslim, either practicing or nonpracticing. Most Singaporeans are quite moderate in their beliefs and very open toward those of other faiths. You will, however, notice that quite a few eat only halal food, prepared according to strict Islamic dietary laws. And while some women choose to wear a *tudung,* a scarf to cover their heads, it is purely voluntary here. Actually, Malay women have a great sense of style; their *sarong baju,* long flowing tunics over a matching sarong, often show off lively colors. But don't be surprised if you see younger Malays in the clubs drinking alcohol.

THE PERANAKANS

Until recently you didn't hear much about the Peranakans, also called Straits Chinese, a subculture of the colonial era that grew out of intermarriage between the Chinese and Malays. But recent trends to embrace Singapore's heritage has rekindled interest in this small yet influential group who are unique to Singapore and Malaysia.

In the early days of Singapore, immigration of Chinese women was forbidden, so many Chinese men found wives within the native Malay population. The resultant ethnic group combined characteristics of each culture but found a middle ground in language and religion, which tended to be English and Christianity, respectively. This mixed heritage allowed them to become strong economic and political players, often serving as middlemen between Chinese, Europeans, and other locals. Singapore's early *towkays* (big bosses) were mostly Peranakan, and

in fact Minister Mentor Lee Kuan Yew himself is of this cultural background.

Peranakan literally means Straits-born, so technically speaking, all people born in Singapore and Malaysia can argue they are Peranakan, and in a lot of literature you may see the term used broadly. Today, though with many Singaporeans able to trace their heritage to this ethnic group, a heritage society has developed to support their interests and keep their culture alive.

THE INDIANS

Many Indians were aboard Raffles ship when it first landed on the banks of the Singapore River, making this group some of Singapore's earliest recorded immigrants. In the following decades many more Indians would follow to find work and wealth. Some found positions in the government as clerks, teachers, policemen, and administrators, following the English colonial administration set by the British Raj in India. Others were moneylenders and financiers. Still more were laborers who came to make a buck.

In 1825 hundreds of Indians who had been imprisoned in Bencoolen (in Sumatra) were transferred to Singapore where they worked as laborers. These convicts built many of the government buildings and cathedrals—for instance St. Andrew's Cathedral, Sri Mariamman Temple, and the Istana—and worked on heavy-duty municipal projects. Eventually, they served their sentences and assimilated into society, many remaining in Singapore.

While most Indian immigrants were from the southern regions of India, there is still great diversity within the community. The largest group by far is the Tamils, but you'll also find Malayalis, Punjabis, and Gujaratis. So despite Little India's reputation as an Indian enclave, the Indian population is actually split into groups based on social divisions and settled in pockets all over the city. The

Indians were also divided by religious affiliation, with factions split between Hinduism, which revolved around the holy trinity of Shiva, Vishnu, and Brahma, but includes many, many other deities, and Islam; other groups include Sihks and Christians as well. Interestingly, while the Buddha and Buddhism originally came from India, few Indians follow his teachings in India and around the world.

The Indians tend to be an informal and warm people, adding their own brand of casual ease to Singapore life. But any Singaporean will tell you that one of the most precious contributions the Indians made is their cuisine. Indian restaurants are well patronized by all ethnic groups because the southern Indian vegetarian cooking is the only food that can be enjoyed by all Singaporeans no matter what cultural or religious dietary laws they may have.

Recently Indians have become somewhat discontented with life in Singapore, feeling overwhelmed by a Chinese government they feel promotes Chinese culture. Indians are some of the most open critics of government practices.

3 Malaysian History

If Malaysia can trace its success to one element, it would be geographic location. Placed strategically at a major crossroads between the Eastern and Western worlds, the result of alternating seasonal northeast and southwest monsoons, Malaysia (formerly known as Malaya) was the ideal center for East-West trade activities. The character of the indigenous Malays is credited to their relationship with the sea, while centuries of outside influences shaped their culture.

The earliest inhabitants of the peninsula were the Orang Asli, who are believed to have migrated from China and Tibet as early as 5,000 years ago. The first Malays were established by 1000 B.C., having migrated not only to Malaya, but throughout the entire Indonesian archipelago as well, including Sumatra and Borneo. They brought with them knowledge of agriculture and metalwork, as well as beliefs in a spirit world (attitudes that are still practiced by many groups today).

Malaysia's earliest trading contacts were established by the 1st century B.C., with China and India. India proved most influential, impacting local culture with Buddhist and Hindu beliefs that are evidenced today in the Malay language, literature, and many customs.

Recorded history didn't come around until the Malay Annals of the 17th century, which tell the story of Parameswara, also known as Iskander Shah, ruler of Temasek (Singapore), who was forced to flee to Malacca around A.D. 1400. He set up a trading port and, taking advantage of the favorable geographic location, led it to world-renowned financial glory. Malacca grew in population and prosperity, attracting Chinese, Indian, and Arab traders.

With Arabs and Muslim Indians came Islam, and Iskander Shah's son, who took leadership of Malacca after his father's death, is credited as the first Malay to convert to the new religion. The rule of Malacca was transformed into a sultanate, and the word of Islam won converts not only in Malaya, but throughout Borneo and the Indonesian archipelago. Today the people of this region are very proud to be Muslim by conversion, as opposed to conquest.

Malacca's success was not without admirers, and in 1511 the Portuguese decided they wanted a piece of the action. They conquered the city in 30 days, chased the sultanate south to Johor, built a fortress that forestalled any trouble from the populace, and set up Christian missions. The Portuguese stuck around until 1641, when the Dutch came to town, looking to expand their trading power in the region. For the record, after Malacca's fall to the Portuguese, its success plummeted and was never regained.

The British came sniffing around in the late 1700s, when Francis Light of the British East India Company landed on the island of Penang and cut a deal with the Sultan of Kedah to cede it to the British. By 1805, Penang had become the seat of British authority in Southeast Asia, but the establishment served less as a trading cash cow and more as political leverage in the race to beat out the Dutch for control of the Southeast Asian trade routes. In 1824, the British and Dutch finally signed a treaty dividing Southeast Asia. The British would have Malaya and the Dutch Indonesia. Dutch-ruled Malacca was traded for British-ruled Bencoolen in Sumatra. In 1826, the British East India Company formed the Straits Settlements, uniting Penang, Malacca, and Singapore under Penang's control. In 1867, power over the Straits Settlements shifted from the British East India Company to British colonial rule in London.

The Anglo-Dutch treaty never provided for the island of Borneo. The Dutch sort of took over Kalimantan, but the areas to the northwest were generally held under the rule of the Sultan of Brunei. Sabah was ceded for an annual sum to the British North Borneo Company, ruled by London until the Japanese invaded during World War II. In 1839, Englishman James Brooke arrived in Sarawak. The Sultan of Brunei had been having a hard time with warring factions in this territory and was happy to hand over control of it to Brooke. In 1841, after winning allies and subjugating enemies, Brooke became the Raja of Sarawak, building his capital in Kuching.

Meanwhile, back on the peninsula, Kuala Lumpur sprang to life in 1857 as a settlement at the crook of the Klang and Gombak rivers, about 35km (21 miles) inland from the west coast. Tin miners from India, China, and other parts of Malaya came inland to prospect and set up a trading post, which flourished. In 1896, it became the capital of the British Malayan territory.

In 1941, the Japanese conquered Malaya en route to Singapore. Life for Malayans during the 4-year occupation was a constant and almost unbearable struggle to survive hunger, disease, and separation from the world. After the war, when the British sought to reclaim their colonial sovereignty over Malaya, they found the people thoroughly fed up with foreign rule. The struggle for independence served to unite Malay and non-Malay residents throughout the country. By the time the British agreed to Malayan independence, the states were already united. On August 31, 1957, Malaya was cut loose, and Kuala Lumpur became its official capital. For a brief moment in the early 1960s, the peninsula was united with Singapore and the Borneo states of Sabah and Sarawak. Singapore was ejected from the federation in 1965, and today Malaysia continues on its own path.

MALAYSIA TODAY

The Malaysia of today is a peaceful nation of many races and ethnicities. The 2000 census placed the population at roughly 23.27 million. Of this number, Bumiputeras are the most numerous ethnic group (broadly speaking), and are defined as those with cultural affinities indigenous to the region and to one another. Technically, this group includes people of the aboriginal groups and ethnic Malays. A smaller segment of the population is non-Bumiputera groups such as the Chinese, Indians, Arabs, and Eurasians, most of whom descended from settlers to the region in the past 150 years. It is important to know the difference between the Bumiputera and non-Bumiputera groups to understand Malaysian politics, which favors the first group in every policy. It is equally important to understand that despite ethnic divisions, each group is considered no less Malaysian.

The state religion is Islam. The Muslim way of life is reflected in almost every element of Malaysian life. The strict adherence to Islam will most likely affect your vacation plans in some way. If you're traveling to Malaysia for an extended period of time or are planning to work there, I highly recommend *Malaysian Customs & Etiquette: A Practical Handbook,* by Datin Noor Aini Syed Amir (Times Books, 2003), for its great advice on how to negotiate any situation.

As for the non-Muslim, life goes on under the government's very serious policy to protect freedom of religion. *Note:* Despite its "freedom of religion" policy, Malaysia is very anti-Zionist. Almost daily the local papers report anti-Semitic news, and Israel is the only country in the world to which Malaysian citizens may not travel. If you carry an Israeli passport, you will need to consult your home embassy before considering travel to Malaysia. Jewish people from other countries who still wish to visit are advised to downplay their religion and culture.

THE GOVERNMENT From 1981 to 2003, the government was lead by Dr. Mahathir Mohamad, a popular prime minister who sought to create a competitive economic tiger while maintaining national policies that reflected liberal Islamic values. His outspoken nature created an endless stream of controversies surrounding policies that favored Bumiputeras, protected often shady links between government and industry, and opposed conservative Islamic policies.

In 2003, he stepped down from power so that his successor, Abdullah Badawi, could continue the policies of Mahathir's leading Umno party. Since, Abdullah has established himself as a fair and patient ruler. However, in 2006 the newspapers were filled with controversies surrounding Dr. Mahathir's outspoken criticism of Abdullah's policies, a lot of which were deemed nothing more than hot air.

THE ECONOMY Until the Asian Economic Crisis that began in July 1997, Malaysia was one of the rising stars of the East Asian Miracle, with an economy built upon the manufacturing sector in electronics and rubber products, as well as on agriculture and mining. Though the crisis hit the country hard, the most recent economic reports show that Malaysia's recovery has been one of the strongest in the region.

TOURISM Malaysia has remained cautiously helpful to the U.S. in the war against terrorism. The leading Umno party has denounced extremists who commit crimes in the name of religion. However, the local Islamic Party of Malaysia (PAS) government in Kelantan leans toward strict Islamic-oriented rule to counter Umno's moderate state policies. Malaysia continues to argue a U.S. Department of State travel advisory that warns travelers in the state of Sabah on Borneo. This is in response to the 2000 kidnapping of tourists off an island resort in east Sabah by the Abu-Sayaff, a Philippine based, Al Qaeda–linked terrorist group. Terrorist activities in southern Thailand have stepped up the alert, but Malaysia would like the world to know that terrorist activities have not been carried out by Malaysians in Malaysia and the government has taken every effort to keep the country stable and safe.

Index

See also Accommodations and Restaurant indexes below.

RESTAURANTS

FROMMER'S® COMPLETE TRAVEL GUIDES

FROMMER'S® DAY BY DAY GUIDES

PAULINE FROMMER'S GUIDES! SEE MORE. SPEND LESS.

FROMMER'S® PORTABLE GUIDES

FROMMER'S® CRUISE GUIDES

Alaska Cruises & Ports of Call

Cruises & Ports of Call

European Cruises & Ports of Call

FROMMER'S® NATIONAL PARK GUIDES

Algonquin Provincial Park
Banff & Jasper
Grand Canyon

National Parks of the American West
Rocky Mountain
Yellowstone & Grand Teton

Yosemite and Sequoia & Kings
   Canyon
Zion & Bryce Canyon

FROMMER'S® MEMORABLE WALKS

London
New York

Paris
Rome

San Francisco

FROMMER'S® WITH KIDS GUIDES

Chicago
Hawaii
Las Vegas
London

National Parks
New York City
San Francisco

Toronto
Walt Disney World® & Orlando
Washington, D.C.

SUZY GERSHMAN'S BORN TO SHOP GUIDES

France
Hong Kong, Shanghai & Beijing
Italy

London
New York

Paris
San Francisco

FROMMER'S® IRREVERENT GUIDES

Amsterdam
Boston
Chicago
Las Vegas

London
Los Angeles
Manhattan
Paris

Rome
San Francisco
Walt Disney World®
Washington, D.C.

FROMMER'S® BEST-LOVED DRIVING TOURS

Austria
Britain
California
France

Germany
Ireland
Italy
New England

Northern Italy
Scotland
Spain
Tuscany & Umbria

THE UNOFFICIAL GUIDES®

Adventure Travel in Alaska
Beyond Disney
California with Kids
Central Italy
Chicago
Cruises
Disneyland®
England
Florida
Florida with Kids

Hawaii
Ireland
Las Vegas
London
Maui
Mexico's Best Beach Resorts
Mini Mickey
New Orleans
New York City

Paris
San Francisco
South Florida including Miami &
   the Keys
Walt Disney World®
Walt Disney World® for
   Grown-ups
Walt Disney World® with Kids
Washington, D.C.

SPECIAL-INTEREST TITLES

Athens Past & Present
Best Places to Raise Your Family
Cities Ranked & Rated
500 Places to Take Your Kids Before They Grow Up
Frommer's Best Day Trips from London
Frommer's Best RV & Tent Campgrounds
   in the U.S.A.

Frommer's Exploring America by RV
Frommer's NYC Free & Dirt Cheap
Frommer's Road Atlas Europe
Frommer's Road Atlas Ireland
Great Escapes From NYC Without Wheels
Retirement Places Rated

FROMMER'S® PHRASEFINDER DICTIONARY GUIDES

French

Italian

Spanish

THE NEW TRAVELOCITY GUARANTEE

EVERYTHING YOU BOOK WILL BE RIGHT, OR WE'LL WORK WITH OUR TRAVEL PARTNERS TO MAKE IT RIGHT, RIGHT AWAY.

*To drive home the point,
we're going to use the word "right" in every single sentence.*

Let's get right to it. Right to the meat! Only Travelocity guarantees everything about your booking will be right, or we'll work with our travel partners to make it right, right away. Right on!

Here's a picture taken smack dab right in the middle of Antigua, where the guarantee also covers you.

The guarantee covers all but one of the items pictured to the right.

Now, you may be thinking, "Yeah, right, I'm so sure." That's OK; you have the right to remain skeptical. That is until we mention help is always right around the corner. Call us right off the bat, knowing that our customer service reps are there for you 24/7. Righting wrongs. Left and right.

For example, what if the ocean view you booked actually looks out at a downright ugly parking lot? You'd be right to call – we're there for you. And no one in their right mind would be pleased to learn the rental car place has closed and left them stranded. Call Travelocity and we'll help get you back on the right track.

Now if you're guessing there are some things we can't control, like the weather, well you're right. But we can help you with most things – to get all the details in righting,* visit **travelocity.com/guarantee**.

*Sorry, spelling things right is one of the few things not covered under the guarantee.

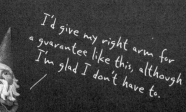

I'd give my right arm for a guarantee like this, although I'm glad I don't have to.

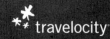
travelocity
You'll never roam alone.™

IF YOU BOOK IT, IT SHOULD BE THERE.

Only Travelocity guarantees it will be, or we'll work
with our travel partners to make it right, right away.
So if you're missing a balcony or anything else you
booked, just call us 24/7. 1-888-TRAVELOCITY.

travelocity
You'll never roam alone.